# CCEA | GCSE
# FURTHER MATHEMATICS

**2nd Edition**

**COLOURPOINT**
EDUCATIONAL

© Neill Hamilton, Sam Stevenson and
Colourpoint Creative Ltd 2019

Second Edition
Third Impression 2020

ISBN: 978-1-78073-191-9

Layout and design: April Sky Design
Printed by: W&G Baird Limited, Antrim

**The Authors**

Neill Hamilton will be well known to Mathematics teachers
in Northern Ireland. Until his retirement in 2012, he was
a teacher of GCSE Mathematics and Additional/Further
Mathematics at a Northern Ireland comprehensive school.
His previous publications include GCSE Maths Revision
Booklets T3 and T4, also published by Colourpoint.

Sam Stevenson has taught Mathematics and Informatics
in grammar schools to a generation. He has a passion for
developing and delivering Further Mathematics at both
GCSE and GCE levels. He will be known to many from the
Northern Ireland Mathematics educational circuit. His
hobbies include family, cycling, keeping tortoises, skiing and
combinatorics, in no particular order.

**COLOURPOINT**
EDUCATIONAL

**Colourpoint Educational**
*An imprint of Colourpoint Creative Ltd*
Colourpoint House
Jubilee Business Park
21 Jubilee Road
Newtownards
County Down
Northern Ireland
BT23 4YH

Tel: 028 9182 6339
E-mail: sales@colourpoint.co.uk
Web site: www.colourpointeducational.com

Note: This book has been written to meet the GCSE
Further Mathematics specification from CCEA. While
the authors and Colourpoint Creative Limited have taken
all reasonable care in the preparation of this book, it is
the responsibility of each candidate to satisfy themselves
that they have covered all necessary material before
sitting an examination or attempting coursework based
on the CCEA specification. The publishers will therefore
accept no legal responsibility or liability for any errors or
omissions from this book or the consequences thereof.

# Contents

# Unit 1: Pure Mathematics

## CHAPTER 1: SIMPLIFYING ALGEBRAIC EXPRESSIONS

### 1.1 Adding And Subtracting Algebraic Expressions

When adding or subtracting you need to find the lowest common denominator. For example:

1. Simplify: $\dfrac{2x + 3}{5} + \dfrac{2x - 3}{6}$

   The lowest common denominator of 5 and 6 is 30. So we change each fraction to a denominator of 30.

   This gives: $\dfrac{12x + 18}{30} + \dfrac{10x - 15}{30}$

   We can then add these fractions to get: $\dfrac{22x + 3}{30}$

2. Simplify: $\dfrac{2x - 5}{6} - \dfrac{4 - 2x}{3}$

   The lowest common denominator of 6 and 3 is 6. So we change the second fraction to a denominator of 6.

   This gives: $\dfrac{2x - 5}{6} - \dfrac{8 - 4x}{6}$

   We can then subtract these fractions to get:

   $\dfrac{6x - 13}{6}$

3. Simplify: $\dfrac{3}{5x - 2} + \dfrac{2}{1 - 2x}$

   The lowest common denominator is $(5x - 2)(1 - 2x)$. So we change each fraction to a denominator of $(5x - 2)(1 - 2x)$.

   This gives: $\dfrac{3 - 6x}{(5x - 2)(1 - 2x)} + \dfrac{10x - 4}{(5x - 2)(1 - 2x)}$

   We can then add these fractions to get:

   $\dfrac{4x - 1}{(5x - 2)(1 - 2x)}$

   You do not need to work out the brackets on the denominator.

**Exercise 1A:** *Simplify the following.*

1. $\dfrac{x + 7}{4} + \dfrac{2x - 1}{3}$

2. $\dfrac{4x - 3}{5} - \dfrac{x + 2}{2}$

3. $\dfrac{3x - 2}{6} + \dfrac{1 - 2x}{4}$

4. $\dfrac{2x - 5}{4} - \dfrac{2 - x}{8}$

5. $\dfrac{3x - 2}{4} - \dfrac{2x - 1}{10}$

6. $\dfrac{4}{3x - 2} - \dfrac{2}{x + 5}$

7. $\dfrac{5}{2 - x} + \dfrac{2}{x + 4}$

8. $\dfrac{4}{3 - 2x} - \dfrac{2}{x - 3}$

9. $\dfrac{5}{2x - 1} + \dfrac{3}{x - 4}$

10. $\dfrac{5}{x - 3} + \dfrac{2}{2x + 1}$

### 1.2 Adding And Subtracting Algebraic Fractions Where Each Denominator Has A Product of Two Terms

For example:

4. Simplify: $\dfrac{6}{(x + 5)(2x - 3)} + \dfrac{2}{x(2x - 3)}$

   The lowest common denominator is $x(x + 5)(2x - 3)$. So we change each fraction to a denominator of $x(x + 5)(2x - 3)$.

   This gives: $\dfrac{6x}{x(x + 5)(2x - 3)} + \dfrac{2x + 10}{x(x + 5)(2x - 3)}$

   We can then add these fractions to get:

   $\dfrac{8x + 10}{x(x + 5)(2x - 3)}$

   You do not need to work out the brackets on the denominator.

5. Simplify: $\dfrac{5}{(x - 6)(3x + 2)} - \dfrac{3}{(x + 4)(x - 6)}$

   The lowest common denominator is $(x + 4)(x - 6)(3x + 2)$. So we change each fraction to a denominator of $(x + 4)(x - 6)(3x + 2)$.

This gives:

$$\frac{5x + 20}{(x + 4)(x - 6)(3x + 2)} - \frac{9x + 6}{(x + 4)(x - 6)(3x + 2)}$$

We can then subtract these fractions to get:

$$\frac{-4x + 14}{(x + 4)(x - 6)(3x + 2)}$$

## Exercise 1B: *Simplify the following.*

1. $\dfrac{7}{(x + 2)(x - 3)} + \dfrac{4}{x(x - 3)}$

2. $\dfrac{5}{2x(x - 3)} + \dfrac{2}{(x + 2)(x - 3)}$

3. $\dfrac{4}{(x + 5)(x + 3)} + \dfrac{3}{(x - 1)(x + 5)}$

4. $\dfrac{5}{(x - 2)(2x + 1)} + \dfrac{1}{(x - 2)(x + 4)}$

5. $\dfrac{3}{x(x - 4)} + \dfrac{2}{x(x + 2)}$

6. $\dfrac{4}{(x - 2)(x + 1)} - \dfrac{3}{(x + 1)(x + 5)}$

7. $\dfrac{5}{2x(x - 3)} - \dfrac{2}{(x + 4)(x - 3)}$

8. $\dfrac{3}{(x - 1)(x + 4)} - \dfrac{4}{(x + 4)(x - 2)}$

9. $\dfrac{2}{(x + 5)(x - 2)} - \dfrac{3}{(x + 5)(x + 2)}$

10. $\dfrac{3}{(x + 2)(2x - 1)} - \dfrac{2}{(x - 4)(2x - 1)}$

## 1.3 Adding And Subtracting Algebraic Fractions With Quadratic Denominators

First, factorise the denominators. Then add or subtract as before. For example:

6. Simplify: $\dfrac{4}{x^2 - 3x} + \dfrac{2}{x^2 - x - 6}$

$x^2 - 3x = x(x - 3)$ by common factors and
$x^2 - x - 6 = (x + 2)(x - 3)$ by quadratic factors.
So we can write the expression as:

$$\frac{4}{x(x - 3)} + \frac{2}{(x + 2)(x - 3)}$$

The lowest common denominator is $x(x + 2)(x - 3)$. So we change each fraction to a denominator of $x(x + 2)(x - 3)$.

This gives: $\dfrac{4x + 8}{x(x + 2)(x - 3)} + \dfrac{2x}{x(x + 2)(x - 3)}$

We can then add these fractions to get:

$$\frac{6x + 8}{x(x + 2)(x - 3)}$$

7. Simplify: $\dfrac{5}{3x^2 + 10x - 8} - \dfrac{2}{x^2 - 16}$

$3x^2 + 10x - 8 = (3x - 2)(x + 4)$ by quadratic factors and $x^2 - 16 = (x - 4)(x + 4)$ by difference of two squares. So we can write the expression as:

$$\frac{5}{(3x - 2)(x + 4)} - \frac{2}{(x - 4)(x + 4)}$$

The lowest common denominator is $(x - 4)(x + 4)(3x - 2)$.

So we change each fraction to a denominator of $(x - 4)(x + 4)(3x - 2)$. This gives:

$$\frac{5x - 20}{(x - 4)(x + 4)(3x - 2)} - \frac{6x - 4}{(x - 4)(x + 4)(3x - 2)}$$

We can then subtract these fractions to get:

$$\frac{-x - 16}{(x - 4)(x + 4)(3x - 2)}$$

## Exercise 1C: *Simplify the following.*

1. $\dfrac{4}{3x^2 + 6x} + \dfrac{3}{x^2 + 3x + 2}$

2. $\dfrac{5}{x^2 + 2x - 8} + \dfrac{2}{x^2 - 4}$

3. $\dfrac{3}{2x^2 + 7x - 4} + \dfrac{5}{x^2 + x - 12}$

4. $\dfrac{3}{2x^2 - 10x} + \dfrac{2}{2x^2 - 11x + 5}$

5. $\dfrac{4}{x^2 + 3x - 10} + \dfrac{3}{x^2 - 7x + 10}$

6. $\dfrac{4}{2x^2 - x} - \dfrac{2}{x^2 + x}$

## Exercise 1C...

7. $\dfrac{3}{x^2 - 2x - 8} - \dfrac{2}{x^2 - 16}$

8. $\dfrac{2}{2x^2 - x - 6} - \dfrac{3}{x^2 - 2x}$

9. $\dfrac{4}{x^2 + x - 12} - \dfrac{5}{2x^2 + 13x + 20}$

10. $\dfrac{3}{4x^2 + 7x - 2} - \dfrac{2}{x^2 - x - 6}$

## 1.4 Multiplying And Dividing Algebraic Expressions

### Multiplying

Cancel as far as possible. Then multiply the numerators and then multiply the denominators. For example:

8. $\dfrac{6x^3}{y^4t^2} \times \dfrac{10y^2}{8tx}$

You can divide 2 into 6 and 8 to get 3 and 4.

You can then divide 2 into 10 and 4 to get 5 and 2.

You can cancel $x^3$ and $x$ by $x$ to get to $x^2$ and 1.

You can cancel $y^2$ and $y^4$ by $y^2$ to get to 1 and $y^2$.

This gives: $\dfrac{3x^2}{y^2t^2} \times \dfrac{5}{2t}$

You can then multiply these to get the answer: $\dfrac{15x^2}{2y^2t^3}$

### Dividing

Dividing by a fraction is the same as multiplying by its reciprocal. So, for example:

9. $\dfrac{10a^3b}{6b^2} \div \dfrac{4c}{5a^2}$

The reciprocal of $\dfrac{4c}{5a^2}$ is $\dfrac{5a^2}{4c}$

So we can multiply: $\dfrac{10a^3b}{6b^2} \times \dfrac{5a^2}{4c}$

You can divide 2 into 10 and 4 to get 5 and 2.

You can cancel b and $b^2$ by b to get to 1 and b.

This gives $\dfrac{5a^3}{6b} \times \dfrac{5a^2}{2c}$

You can then multiply these to get the answer: $\dfrac{25a^5}{12bc}$

## Exercise 1D: *Simplify the following.*

1. $\dfrac{5x^2}{yv} \times \dfrac{2y^2}{vx}$

2. $\dfrac{3vt}{2n^2} \times \dfrac{4n}{6v^2}$

3. $\dfrac{10q}{r^2} \times \dfrac{2qr}{5n}$

4. $\dfrac{4vw}{2t} \times \dfrac{9t^2}{2v^3}$

5. $\dfrac{6qr}{2v^2} \times \dfrac{10vw}{3q^2}$

6. $\dfrac{9a^2}{5b} \div \dfrac{3c}{2ab^3}$

7. $\dfrac{4q^2}{3r} \div \dfrac{5q}{6rn}$

8. $\dfrac{3t^2}{2vw} \div \dfrac{9tn}{4v^2}$

9. $\dfrac{9a}{2b^2} \div \dfrac{7a^2}{4bc}$

10. $\dfrac{4v^2}{3q} \div \dfrac{2r}{5vq^2}$

## 1.5 Dividing Algebraic Fractions With Quadratic Numerators And Denominators

First, factorise each quadratic expression. Then cancel as far as possible. For example:

10. Simplify: $\dfrac{14x^2 - 7x}{4x^2 - 1}$

$14x^2 - 7x = 7x(2x - 1)$ by common factors and

$4x^2 - 1 = (2x - 1)(2x + 1)$ by difference of two squares.

So you can rewrite the fraction as $\dfrac{7x(2x - 1)}{(2x - 1)(2x + 1)}$

You can then cancel out the $(2x - 1)$ to get the final answer:

$\dfrac{7x}{2x + 1}$

11. Simplify: $\dfrac{x^2 + 2x - 15}{3x^2 + 13x - 10}$

$x^2 + 2x - 15 = (x - 3)(x + 5)$ by quadratic factors and

$3x^2 + 13x - 10 = (3x - 2)(x + 5)$ by quadratic factors.

So you can rewrite the fraction as $\dfrac{(x - 3)(x + 5)}{(3x - 2)(x + 5)}$

You can then cancel out the $(x + 5)$ to get the final answer:

$\dfrac{x - 3}{3x - 2}$

## Exercise 1E: *Simplify the following.*

1. $\dfrac{2x^2 + 5x - 3}{x^2 + x - 6}$

2. $\dfrac{3x^2 - 6x}{2x^2 - 5x + 2}$

3. $\dfrac{x^2 - 25}{x^2 - x - 20}$

4. $\dfrac{4x^2 + 5x - 6}{x^2 - x - 6}$

5. $\dfrac{2x^2 + 9x - 5}{2x^2 + 3x - 2}$

6. $\dfrac{4x^2 - 12x}{x^2 - x - 6}$

7. $\dfrac{2x^2 + 7x - 4}{x^2 + 2x - 8}$

8. $\dfrac{3x^2 + 13x - 10}{6x^2 + 5x - 6}$

9. $\dfrac{8x^2 - 4x}{4x^2 - 1}$

10. $\dfrac{5x^2 + 13x - 6}{x^2 - 2x - 15}$

## 1.6 Multiplying And Dividing Quadratic Numerators And Denominators

First, factorise and cancel as far as possible. Then multiply or divide. For example:

12. $\dfrac{2q^2 - 7q + 3}{4} \times \dfrac{6}{q^2 - 9}$

First you need to factorise each quadratic expression:

$2q^2 - 7q + 3 = (q - 3)(2q - 1)$ by quadratic factors and

$q^2 - 9 = (q - 3)(q + 3)$ by difference of two squares.

So you can rewrite the multiplication as:

$\dfrac{(q - 3)(2q - 1)}{4} \times \dfrac{6}{(q - 3)(q + 3)}$

You can divide 6 and 4 by 2 to get 3 and 2. You can then cancel out the $(q - 3)$ to get the final answer:

$\dfrac{3(2q - 1)}{2(q + 3)}$

13. $\dfrac{x^2 + 4x}{5} \div \dfrac{x^2 + 2x - 8}{10}$

The reciprocal of $\dfrac{x^2 + 2x - 8}{10}$ is $\dfrac{10}{x^2 + 2x - 8}$

So we can multiply: $\dfrac{x^2 + 4x}{5} \times \dfrac{10}{x^2 + 2x - 8}$

You need to factorise each quadratic expression.

$x^2 + 4x = x(x + 4)$ by common factors and

$x^2 + 2x - 8 = (x + 4)(x - 2)$ by quadratic factors.

So you can rewrite the multiplication as:

$\dfrac{x(x + 4)}{5} \times \dfrac{10}{(x + 4)(x - 2)}$

You can divide 10 and 5 by 5 to get 2 and 1. You can then cancel out the $(x + 4)$ to get the final answer:

$\dfrac{2x}{x - 2}$

## Exercise 1F: *Work out the following.*

1. $\dfrac{x^2 - 2x}{3} \times \dfrac{6}{x^2 + 2x - 8}$

2. $\dfrac{2x^2 - 5x - 3}{4} \times \dfrac{10}{6x^2 - x - 2}$

3. $\dfrac{x^2 + 2x - 15}{8} \times \dfrac{6}{x^2 - 5x + 6}$

4. $\dfrac{3x^2 + 14x + 8}{6} \times \dfrac{9}{x^2 + 2x - 8}$

5. $\dfrac{4x^2 - 10x}{10} \times \dfrac{8}{3x^2 + 12x}$

6. $\dfrac{4x^2 + 8x}{3} \div \dfrac{3x^2 - x}{6}$

7. $\dfrac{x^2 - 9x + 14}{4} \div \dfrac{x^2 + 3x - 10}{2}$

8. $\dfrac{2x^2 + 9x - 5}{8} \div \dfrac{8x^2 + 2x - 3}{6}$

9. $\dfrac{x^2 + 9x + 18}{9} \div \dfrac{x^2 + x - 6}{12}$

10. $\dfrac{4x^2 + 7x - 2}{4} \div \dfrac{x^2 - 4}{6}$

## 1.7 Expansion Of Three Linear Brackets

To expand three linear brackets you should expand and simplify any two brackets first and then multiply your answer by the third bracket. For example:

14. Expand $(x - 6)(x + 3)(x - 2)$

Expanding two of the brackets, $(x + 3)(x - 2)$, gives:

$x(x - 2) + 3(x - 2) = x^2 - 2x + 3x - 6 = x^2 + x - 6$

Multiplying the answer by the third bracket gives:

$(x - 6)(x^2 + x - 6) = x(x^2 + x - 6) - 6(x^2 + x - 6)$

$\begin{aligned} &= && x^3 &+ && x^2 &- && 6x \\ &+ && && -6x^2 &- && 6x &+ && 36 && \text{(adding)}\\ &= && x^3 &- && 5x^2 &- && 12x &+ && 36 \end{aligned}$

**15.** Find the values of a, b, c and d for which
$(x - 4)(2x + 3)(3x - 2) = ax^3 + bx^2 + cx + d$

Expanding as before gives:

$(2x + 3)(3x - 2) = 2x(3x - 2) + 3(3x - 2)$

$= 6x^2 - 4x + 9x - 6 = 6x^2 + 5x - 6$

Multiplying the answer by the third bracket gives:

$(x - 4)(6x^2 + 5x - 6) = x(6x^2 + 5x - 6) - 4(6x^2 + 5x - 6)$

$= 6x^3 + 5x^2 - 6x$

$$
\begin{aligned}
&= \quad 6x^3 \ + \ 5x^2 \ - \ 6x \\
&+ \underline{\quad\quad -24x^2 \ - \ 20x \ + \ 24} \quad \text{(adding)}\\
&= \quad 6x^3 \ - \ 19x^2 \ - \ 26x \ + \ 36
\end{aligned}
$$

So the answer is: a = 6, b = –19, c = –26, d = 24

**16.** Expand $(x + y)^3$

$(x + y)^3 = (x + y)(x + y)(x + y)$

$(x + y)(x + y) = x(x + y) + y(x + y) = x^2 + xy + xy + y^2$
$= x^2 + 2xy + y^2$

Multiplying the answer by the third bracket gives:

$(x + y)(x^2 + 2xy + y^2)$

$= x(x^2 + 2xy + y^2) + y(x^2 + 2xy + y^2)$

$$
\begin{aligned}
&= \quad x^3 \ + \ 2x^2y \ + \ xy^2 \\
&+ \underline{\quad\quad x^2y \ + \ 2xy^2 \ + y^3} \quad \text{(adding)}\\
&= \quad x^3 \ + \ 3x^2y \ + \ 3xy^2 \ + \ y^3
\end{aligned}
$$

## Exercise 1G: *Expand the brackets in questions 1 to 12*

1. $(x + 1)(x + 2)(x + 5)$

2. $(x - 3)(x + 2)(x + 4)$

3. $(x - 1)(x + 4)(x + 5)$

4. $(x - 4)(x + 2)(x - 3)$

5. $(x + 1)(3x - 2)(x + 4)$

6. $(2x - 1)(3x - 2)(x + 5)$

7. $(4x + 3)(2x + 1)(3x - 4)$

8. $(x + 4)^3$

9. $(x - 3)^3$

10. $(2x + 5)^3$

11. $(x + 2y)^3$

12. $(x - 3y)(x + y)(x + 5y)$

13. Find the values of a, b, c and d for which
$(x - 6)(2x + 1)(5x - 2) = ax^3 + bx^2 + cx + d$

## Exercise 1G...

14. Find the values of a, b, c and d for which
$(3x - 4)(x + 3)(x - 2) = ax^3 + bx^2 + cx + d$

15. Find the values of a, b, c and d for which
$(7x - 4)(2x + 1)(3x - 8) = ax^3 + bx^2 + cx + d$

## 1.8  Applied Questions

Sometimes questions require you to simplify an expression to solve a problem. For example:

17. The sides of a cube are $(4x - 7)$ cm long. Find an expression, in its simplest form, for the volume of the cube.

Volume $= (4x - 7)^3 = (4x - 7)(4x - 7)(4x - 7)$

$(4x - 7)(4x - 7) = 4x(4x - 7) - 7(4x - 7)$

$= 16x^2 - 28x - 28x + 49 = 16x^2 - 56x + 49$

Multiplying the answer by the third bracket gives:

$(4x - 7)(16x^2 - 56x + 49)$

$= 4x(16x^2 - 56x + 49) - 7(16x^2 - 56x + 49)$

$$
\begin{aligned}
&= \quad 64x^3 \ - \ 224x^2 \ + \ 196x \\
&+ \underline{\quad\quad -112x^2 \ + \ 392x \ - \ 343} \quad \text{(adding)}\\
&= \quad (64x^3 \ - \ 336x^2 \ + \ 588x \ - \ 343) \ \text{cm}^3
\end{aligned}
$$

18. A car travels at a constant speed of $(x + 3)(2x - 5)$ m s$^{-1}$ for $(3x + 2)$ seconds. Find an expression, in its simplest form, for the distance travelled, in terms of $x$.

Distance = speed × time $= (x + 3)(2x - 5)(3x + 2)$

$(2x - 5)(3x + 2) = 2x(3x + 2) - 5(3x + 2)$

$= 6x^2 + 4x - 15x - 10 = 6x^2 - 11x - 10$

Multiplying the answer by the third bracket gives:

$(x + 3)(6x^2 - 11x - 10)$

$= x(6x^2 - 11x - 10) + 3(6x^2 - 11x - 10)$

$$
\begin{aligned}
&= \quad 6x^3 \ - \ 11x^2 \ - \ 10x \\
&+ \underline{\quad\quad 18x^2 \ - \ 33x \ - \ 30} \quad \text{(adding)}\\
&= \quad (6x^3 \ + \ 7x^2 \ - \ 43x \ - \ 30) \ \text{m}
\end{aligned}
$$

## Exercise 1H

1. The length, breadth and height of a cuboid are $(x + 5)$ cm, $(x - 2)$ cm and $(3x + 4)$ cm. Find an expression, in its simplest form, for the volume of the cuboid.

2. The sides of a cube are $(2x - 1)$ cm long. Find an expression, in its simplest form, for the volume of the cube.

3. A cylinder has base radius $(x - 4)$ cm and perpendicular height $(x + 3)$ cm. Find an expression, in its simplest form, for its volume, in terms of $\pi$.

4. The cost of a rectangular plastic sheet is £$(2x - 1)$ per m². Its length and breadth are $(x + 4)$ m and $(x - 2)$ m. Find the total cost.

5. The length, breadth and height of a cuboid are $(2x + 3)$ cm, $(x - 5)$ cm and $(x + 2)$ cm. Find an expression, in its simplest form, for the volume of the cuboid.

## 1.9 More Complex Questions

Some questions require you to simplify an expression which is itself a numerator or denominator. For example:

19. Simplify $\dfrac{(x - 2)(3x + 2)(x - 4) - 3(x^3 - 5x^2 + 4x)}{x^2 + 4x}$

We need to simplify the numerator by expanding the brackets and collecting like terms.

Firstly, expand $(x - 2)(3x + 2)(x - 4)$:

$(3x + 2)(x - 4) = 3x(x - 4) + 2(x - 4) = 3x^2 - 12x - 8x$

$= 3x^2 - 10x - 8$

and then multiply the answer by the third bracket:

$(x - 2)(3x^2 - 10x - 8)$

$= x(3x^2 - 10x - 8) - 2(3x^2 - 10x - 8)$

$= 3x^2 - 10x^2 - 8x$

$= \quad 3x^3 - 10x^2 - 8x$

$+ \quad\underline{\quad - 6x^2 + 20x + 16}$ (adding)

$= \quad 3x^3 - 16x^2 + 12x + 16$

Next, expanding $3(x^3 - 5x^2 + 4x)$ gives:

$3x^3 - 15x^2 + 12x$

Then, combine the two parts of the numerator:

$(3x^3 - 16x^2 + 12x + 16) - (3x^3 - 15x^2 + 12x)$ giving:

$3x^3 - 16x^2 + 12x + 16 - 3x^3 + 15x^2 - 12x = -x^2 + 16$

We can then rewrite the expression as:

$\dfrac{16 - x^2}{x^2 + 4x}$

We can then factorise both numerator and denominator to simplify this fully giving:

$\dfrac{(4 - x)(4 + x)}{x(x + 4)}$

We can then cancel out the $(x + 4)$ to get the final simplified answer of:

$\dfrac{4 - x}{x}$

## Exercise 1J: *Simplify the following.*

1. $\dfrac{(2x + 1)(x - 2)(x + 3) - 2x(x^2 - 1) + 6x}{3x - 6}$

2. $\dfrac{(x - 4)(x + 2)^2 - x(x^2 - 4)}{x^2 - 2x - 8}$

3. $\dfrac{(2x + 3)^3 - 2x(4x^2 + 15x + 12) - 3}{3x + 3}$

4. $\dfrac{(x - 1)(x + 2)(2x + 1) - 2x^2(x + 1) + 2}{x^2 - 9}$

# CHAPTER 2: EQUATIONS

## 2.1 Quadratic Equations

A quadratic equation is an equation where the highest power of the variable is 2. You can solve quadratic equations by factorising **but only when it can be factorised.** You can also solve quadratic equations by using the quadratic formula. Solving quadratics by factorising or the formula method will not be asked specifically in the examination but is required in answering questions set on other topics.

### Factorising

For example, solve the following:

1.  $4x^2 - 25 = 0$

    You can factorise $4x^2 - 25$ by the difference of two squares to get: $(2x - 5)(2x + 5) = 0$

    So either:     $2x - 5 = 0$
    in which case:    $2x = 5$, giving $x = 2½$ or 2.5
    or            $2x + 5 = 0$
    in which case:    $2x = -5$, giving $x = -2½$ or $-2.5$

2.  $4x^2 - 7x = 0$

    You can factorise $4x^2 - 7x$ by common factors to get: $x(4x - 7) = 0$

    So either:         $x = 0$
    or            $4x - 7 = 0$
    in which case:    $4x = 7$, giving $x = 1¾$ or 1.75

3.  $2x^2 + 9x - 5 = 0$

    You can factorise $2x^2 + 9x - 5$ by quadratic factors to get: $(2x - 1)(x + 5) = 0$

    So either:     $2x - 1 = 0$
    in which case:    $2x = 1$, giving $x = ½$ or 0.5
    or            $x + 5 = 0$, giving $x = -5$

### Using The Quadratic Formula

The solutions to $ax^2 + bx + c = 0$ are found from substituting the values of $a$, $b$ and $c$ into the formula

$$\frac{-b \pm \sqrt{b^2 - 4ac}}{2a}$$

For example, solve the following, giving your answers correct to 2 decimal places:

4.  $2x^2 + x - 11 = 0$

    In this case: a = 2, b = 1 and c = −11.

    So       $x = \dfrac{-1 \pm \sqrt{1^2 - 4 \times 2 \times (-11)}}{2 \times 2}$

                $x = \dfrac{-1 \pm \sqrt{89}}{4}$

                $x = \dfrac{-1 + \sqrt{89}}{4}$ or $\dfrac{-1 - \sqrt{89}}{4}$

                $x = 2.108$ or $-2.608$

    So $x = 2.11$ or $-2.61$, to 2 decimal places.

5.  $3x^2 - 6x + 1 = 0$

    In this case: a = 3, b = −6 and c = 1.

    So       $x = \dfrac{6 \pm \sqrt{36 - 4 \times 3 \times 1}}{2 \times 3}$

                $x = \dfrac{6 \pm \sqrt{36 - 12}}{6}$

                $x = \dfrac{6 \pm \sqrt{24}}{6}$

                $x = \dfrac{6 + \sqrt{24}}{6}$ or $\dfrac{6 - \sqrt{24}}{6}$

                $x = 1.816$ or 0.184

    So $x = 1.82$ or 0.18, to 2 decimal places.

### Exercise 2A: *Solve the following by factorising.*

1.  $9x^2 - 16 = 0$
2.  $3x^2 - x - 2 = 0$
3.  $12x^2 + 42x = 0$
4.  $2x^2 - 7x - 15 = 0$
5.  $6x^2 - x - 2 = 0$
6.  $3x^2 - 10x - 8 = 0$
7.  $4x^2 + 17x - 15 = 0$
8.  $6x^2 - 14x = 0$
9.  $6x^2 + 23x - 18 = 0$
10. $2x^2 - 17x + 21 = 0$
11. $6x^2 + 7x + 2 = 0$
12. $25x^2 - 4 = 0$

### Exercise 2B: *Solve the following, giving your answers correct to 2 decimal places.*

1.  $x^2 - 6x + 3 = 0$
2.  $2x^2 + x - 7 = 0$
3.  $3x^2 - 2x - 9 = 0$
4.  $x^2 + 9x + 2 = 0$
5.  $2x^2 - x - 7 = 0$
6.  $3x^2 + 2x - 2 = 0$
7.  $5x^2 - x - 8 = 0$
8.  $2x^2 + 8x + 2 = 0$
9.  $4x^2 + 5x - 3 = 0$
10. $x^2 - 2x - 9 = 0$

## 2.2 Setting Up And Solving Quadratic Equations

Sometimes a problem requires us to set up and then solve a quadratic equation. For example:

6.  The area of a rectangle is 60 cm². The perimeter is 34 cm. Form an equation and solve it to find the lengths of the two sides.

    Call the two sides $x$ and $y$. Then we have:
    $$xy = 60 \text{ (area of rectangle), and}$$
    $$2x + 2y = 34 \text{ (perimeter of rectangle)}$$

    We can rewrite the perimeter equation in terms of $y$ and then substitute this into the area equation:
    $$2y = 34 - 2x$$
    $$y = 17 - x \text{ (dividing by 2) giving:}$$
    $$x(17 - x) = 60$$
    $$17x - x^2 = 60 \text{ which rearranges to give:}$$
    $$0 = x^2 - 17x + 60$$

    We can then factorise this or use the formula to find $x$:
    $$(x - 5)(x - 12) = 0$$
    So: $\qquad\qquad x = 5 \text{ or } 12$

    Substituting for $y$ gives:
    $$y = 17 - x$$
    so either $y = 17 - 5 = 12$
    or $\qquad y = 17 - 12 = 5$
    So the lengths of the two sides are 5 cm and 12 cm.

### Exercise 2C

1.  ABC is a right angled triangle with AC = 15 cm. AB is 3 cm less than BC. Form an equation and solve it to find the lengths of AB and BC.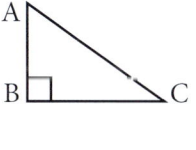

2.  The area of a rectangle is 48 cm². The perimeter is 28 cm. Form an equation and solve it to find the lengths of the two sides.

3.  Aoife buys $x$ books costing $y$ pence each for £2.80. The cost of the books are then increased by 5p each. She can now buy 2 fewer books for £2.40. Form an equation and solve it to find the initial cost of each book.

4.  The width of a rectangle is 5 cm less than its length. The diagonal is 25 cm long. Form an equation and solve it to find the length and width.

## 2.3 Fractional Equations

For example, solve:

7.  $\dfrac{6}{x - 3} + \dfrac{2}{x - 4} = 5$

    You need to add the fractions by using the lowest common denominator, which is $(x - 3)(x - 4)$

    So we get: $\dfrac{6(x - 4) + 2(x - 3)}{(x - 3)(x - 4)} = 5$

    You now need to work out and simplify the numerator:
    $$6(x - 4) + 2(x - 3) = 6x - 24 + 2x - 6 = 8x - 30$$

    This gives: $\dfrac{8x - 30}{(x - 3)(x - 4)} = 5$

    You now need to work out and simplify the denominator:
    $$(x - 3)(x - 4) = x^2 - 7x + 12$$

    This gives: $\dfrac{8x - 30}{x^2 - 7x + 12} = 5$

    You can now cross multiply to get:
    $$8x - 30 = 5(x^2 - 7x + 12)$$

    You can now work out the brackets and then put all the terms on one side (with the $x^2$ term first and positive because it is a quadratic equation):
    $$8x - 30 = 5x^2 - 35x + 60$$
    $$0 = 5x^2 - 35x - 8x + 60 + 30$$
    So: $\quad 5x^2 - 43x + 90 = 0$

    You can now solve this equation, either by factorising or using the quadratic formula, to get:
    $$(x - 5)(5x - 18) = 0$$
    So either $\qquad x - 5 = 0$, giving $x = 5$
    or $\qquad\qquad 5x - 18 = 0, 5x = 18$ giving $x = \dfrac{18}{5}$

8.  $\dfrac{4}{x - 1} - \dfrac{2}{1 - x} = 3$ where $x$ cannot equal 1

    You need to add the fractions by using the lowest common denominator which is $(x - 1)(1 - x)$.

    So we get: $\dfrac{4(1 - x) - 2(x - 1)}{(x - 1)(1 - x)} = 3$

    You now need to work out and simplify the numerator:

$4(1 - x) - 2(x - 1) = 4 - 4x - 2x + 2 = -6x + 6$

This gives: $\dfrac{-6x + 6}{(x - 1)(1 - x)} = 3$

You now need to work out and simplify the denominator:

$(x - 1)(1 - x) = -x^2 + 2x - 1$

This gives: $\dfrac{-6x + 6}{-x^2 + 2x - 1} = 3$

You can now cross multiply to get:
$-6x + 6 = 3(-x^2 + 2x - 1)$

You can now work out the brackets and then put all the terms on one side (with the $x^2$ term first and positive because it is a quadratic equation):
$$-6x + 6 = -3x^2 + 6x - 3$$
$$3x^2 - 12x + 9 = 0$$

You can divide all these terms by 3 to get:

$$x^2 - 4x + 3 = 0$$

You can now solve this equation, by factorising or using the quadratic formula, to get:

$$(x - 3)(x - 1) = 0$$
So either $\quad\quad x - 3 = 0$, giving $x = 3$
or $\quad\quad\quad\quad x - 1 = 0$, giving $x = 1$

Since we are told in the question that $x$ cannot equal 1 the only solution is $x = 3$.

**Exercise 2D**: *Solve the following.*

1. $\dfrac{4}{x - 2} + \dfrac{3}{2x - 5} = 3$

2. $\dfrac{6}{2x - 1} - \dfrac{4}{1 - x} = 6$

3. $\dfrac{4}{3x - 2} - \dfrac{6}{x + 1} = 1$

4. $\dfrac{2}{x - 2} + \dfrac{3}{2x - 3} = 3$

5. $\dfrac{3}{x + 1} - \dfrac{6}{1 - 2x} = 3$

6. $\dfrac{4}{x - 3} - \dfrac{4}{1 - x} = 3$

7. $\dfrac{6}{x - 1} - \dfrac{5}{1 - 2x} = 4$

8. $\dfrac{3}{x + 1} + \dfrac{6}{2x - 1} = 3$

9. $\dfrac{4}{x - 1} - \dfrac{2}{2 - x} = 4$

10. $\dfrac{3}{x - 2} - \dfrac{2}{3 - x} = 2$

## 2.4 Fractional Equations With Both Numerator And Denominator Expressions Involving $x$

For example, solve:

9. $\dfrac{x + 1}{x - 1} + \dfrac{3x - 1}{2x + 1} = 4$

You need to add the fractions by using the lowest common denominator which is $(x - 1)(2x + 1)$.

So we get: $\dfrac{(x + 1)(2x + 1) + (3x - 1)(x - 1)}{(x - 1)(2x + 1)} = 4$

You now need to work out and simplify the numerator:

$(x + 1)(2x + 1) = 2x^2 + 3x + 1$ and

$(3x - 1)(x - 1) = 3x^2 - 4x + 1$

So the numerator is:

$2x^2 + 3x + 1 + 3x^2 - 4x + 1 = 5x^2 - x + 2$

This gives: $\dfrac{5x^2 - x + 2}{(x - 1)(2x + 1)} = 4$

You now need to work out and simplify the denominator:

$(x - 1)(2x + 1) = 2x^2 - x - 1$

This gives: $\dfrac{5x^2 - x + 2}{2x^2 - x - 1} = 4$

You can now cross multiply to get:

$5x^2 - x + 2 = 4(2x^2 - x - 1)$

You can now work out the brackets and then put all the terms on one side (with the $x^2$ term first and positive, as it is a quadratic equation):

$$5x^2 - x + 2 = 8x^2 - 4x - 4$$
$$0 = 8x^2 - 5x^2 - 4x + x - 4 - 2$$

So: $\quad\quad 3x^2 - 3x - 6 = 0$

You can divide all these terms by 3 to get:

$$x^2 - x - 2 = 0$$

You can now solve this equation, by factorising or using the quadratic formula, to get:

$$(x - 2)(x + 1) = 0$$

So either $\quad\quad x - 2 = 0$, giving $x = 2$

or $\quad\quad\quad\quad x + 1 = 0$, giving $x = -1$

**10.** $\dfrac{x+3}{x-1} - \dfrac{x-2}{1-2x} = 5$

You need to add the fractions by using the lowest common denominator which is $(x-1)(1-2x)$.

So we get: $\dfrac{(x+3)(1-2x) - (x-2)(x-1)}{(x-1)(1-2x)} = 5$

You now need to work out and simplify the numerator:

$(x+3)(1-2x) = -2x^2 - 5x + 3$ and

$(x-2)(x-1) = x^2 - 3x + 2$

So the numerator is:

$-2x^2 - 5x + 3 - (x^2 - 3x + 2)$

$= -2x^2 - 5x + 3 - x^2 + 3x - 2$

$= -3x^2 - 2x + 1$

This gives: $\dfrac{-3x^2 - 2x + 1}{(x-1)(1-2x)} = 5$

You now need to work out and simplify the denominator:

$(x-1)(1-2x) = -2x^2 + 3x - 1$

This gives $\dfrac{-3x^2 - 2x + 1}{-2x^2 + 3x - 1} = 5$

You can now cross multiply to get:

$-3x^2 - 2x + 1 = 5(-2x^2 + 3x - 1)$

You can now work out the brackets and then put all the terms on one side (with the $x^2$ term first and positive, as it is a quadratic equation):

$$-3x^2 - 2x + 1 = -10x^2 + 15x - 5$$

$$10x^2 - 3x^2 - 2x - 15x + 1 + 5 = 0$$

So: $\qquad 7x^2 - 17x + 6 = 0$

You can now solve this equation, by factorising or using the quadratic formula, to get:

$$(x-2)(7x-3) = 0$$

So either $\qquad\qquad x - 2 = 0$, giving $x = 2$

or $\qquad\qquad 7x - 3 = 0$

$$7x = 3, \text{ giving } x = \dfrac{3}{7}$$

---

**Exercise 2E**: Solve the following.

**1.** $\dfrac{x+1}{x-2} + \dfrac{3x-1}{x+1} = 6$ 　　**6.** $\dfrac{x+1}{3x-1} + \dfrac{4x-2}{x+1} = 3$

**2.** $\dfrac{x+7}{1-x} + \dfrac{2}{x+2} = -1$ 　　**7.** $\dfrac{x+1}{x+3} - \dfrac{3x+2}{1-x} = 5$

**3.** $\dfrac{x+3}{3-x} - \dfrac{1-2x}{x-2} = -1$ 　　**8.** $\dfrac{2x}{x-2} + \dfrac{1-3x}{x-1} = 2$

**4.** $\dfrac{x+4}{x-2} - \dfrac{2x-5}{x-1} = 3$ 　　**9.** $\dfrac{x+3}{x-3} - \dfrac{x+4}{4-x} = 8$

**5.** $\dfrac{4-x}{x+4} + \dfrac{x+2}{x+1} = 3$

## 2.5　Completing The Square

Another way to solve a quadratic equation is to complete the square for the variable. When completing the square the coefficient of $x^2$ will always be 1. For example, solve the following by completing the square:

---

**11.** $x^2 + 8x - 5 = 0$

To complete the square we must take half of the coefficient of the $x$ term and then expand as follows:

½ of 8 = 4, so we expand $(x+4)^2$

Now $(x+4)^2 = x^2 + 4x + 4x + 16 = x^2 + 8x + 16$

So we can replace $x^2 + 8x$ with $(x+4)^2 - 16$

This gives:

$$(x+4)^2 - 16 - 5 = 0$$

$$(x+4)^2 = 16 + 5 = 21$$

So $\qquad\qquad x + 4 = \pm\sqrt{21}$

$$x = -4 \pm\sqrt{21}$$

---

This example shows us that the general rule for solving $x^2 + bx + c = 0$ by completing the square is:

**a.** Work out ½b

**b.** Rewrite $x^2 + bx + c = 0$ as $(x + ½b)^2 - (½b)^2 + c = 0$

For example, solve the following by completing the square:

---

12. $x^2 - 9x + 2 = 0$

To complete the square we must take half of the coefficient of the $x$ term and then expand as follows:

½ of $-9 = \dfrac{-9}{2}$, so we expand $(x - \dfrac{9}{2})^2$

Now $\quad (x - \dfrac{9}{2})^2 = x^2 - \dfrac{9}{2}x - \dfrac{9}{2}x + (\dfrac{9}{2})^2$

$$= x^2 - 9x + \dfrac{81}{4}$$

So we can replace $x^2 - 9x$ with $(x - \dfrac{9}{2})^2 - \dfrac{81}{4}$

This gives:

$$(x - \dfrac{9}{2})^2 - \dfrac{81}{4} + 2 = 0$$

$$(x - \dfrac{9}{2})^2 = \dfrac{81}{4} - 2 = \dfrac{81}{4} - \dfrac{8}{4} = \dfrac{73}{4}$$

So $\quad x - \dfrac{9}{2} = \pm\sqrt{\dfrac{73}{4}} = \dfrac{\pm\sqrt{73}}{2}$

$$x = \dfrac{9}{2} \pm \dfrac{\sqrt{73}}{2}$$

So $\quad x = \dfrac{9 \pm \sqrt{73}}{2}$

---

**Exercise 2F**: *Solve the following by completing the square.*

1. $x^2 + 6x - 3 = 0$
2. $x^2 - 2x - 5 = 0$
3. $x^2 + x - 4 = 0$
4. $x^2 - 3x - 5 = 0$
5. $x^2 + 8x + 5 = 0$
6. $x^2 - 10x - 2 = 0$
7. $x^2 + 5x - 4 = 0$
8. $x^2 - 7x - 5 = 0$
9. $x^2 + 4x - 9 = 0$
10. $x^2 - 10x - 3 = 0$

11. A square has sides $x$ cm. If one side is doubled in length and the other reduced by 2 cm to form a rectangle, then the rectangle formed has an area 10 m² greater than the square.
    (a) Form a quadratic equation.
    (b) Hence find $x$ by completing the square.

## 2.6 Finding Minimum Points By Completing The Square

You can find minimum turning points and the value of $x$ for which they occur by completing the square. For example:

13. Find:
    (a) the minimum value of $y = x^2 - 8x - 5$ by completing the square, and
    (b) the value of $x$ at this minimum value.

    (a) $\qquad\qquad y = x^2 - 8x - 5$
    So: $\qquad\quad y = (x - 4)^2 - 16 - 5$
    Giving: $\qquad y = (x - 4)^2 - 21$

    The smallest possible value of $(x - 4)^2$ is 0 (as all square numbers are positive except 0). So the minimum value of $y = x^2 - 8x - 5$ is $0 - 21 = -21$

    (b) $(x - 4)^2 = 0$ when $x - 4 = 0$
    i.e. when $x = 4$

---

### Exercise 2G

Find (a) the minimum value of the following expressions by completing the square, and (b) the value of $x$ at each minimum value.

1. $y = x^2 + 6x - 3$
2. $y = x^2 - 4x + 1$
3. $y = x^2 + 8x + 5$
4. $y = x^2 - 2x - 8$
5. $y = x^2 - x - 3$
6. $y = x^2 + 3x + 8$
7. $y = x^2 - 6x + 11$
8. $y = x^2 + 10x + 35$

# CHAPTER 3: SIMULTANEOUS EQUATIONS

## 3.1 Simultaneous Equations With Three Unknowns

These can be solved by using these rules:
a. Eliminate one unknown from 2 of these equations.
b. Eliminate the same unknown from another 2 of these equations.
c. This leaves you with 2 equations with 2 unknowns.

For example, solve the following simultaneous equations:

1.
$$3x + 2y - z = 64 \quad (1)$$
$$2x + y + 3z = 84 \quad (2)$$
$$4x - 3y + 2z = 80 \quad (3)$$

Let us get rid of $z$. You can multiply equation (1) by 3 and then add this to equation (2):

$$
\begin{array}{l}
9x + 6y - 3z = 192 \quad (4) \\
+ \ 2x + y + 3z = \ \ 84 \quad (2) \\
\hline
11x + 7y \quad\quad = 276 \quad (5)
\end{array}
$$

You can multiply equation (1) by 2 and then add this to equation (3):

$$
\begin{array}{l}
6x + 4y - 2z = 128 \quad (6) \\
+ \ 4x - 3y + 2z = \ \ 80 \quad (3) \\
\hline
10x + y \quad\quad\quad = 208 \quad (7)
\end{array}
$$

You now have to solve the following equations:

$$11x + 7y = 276 \quad (5)$$
$$10x + y = 208 \quad (7)$$

You can multiply equation (7) by 7 and then subtract equation (5):

$$
\begin{array}{l}
70x + 7y = 1456 \ (8) \\
- \ 11x + 7y = \ \ 276 \ (5) \\
\hline
59x \quad\quad = 1180
\end{array}
$$

So
$$x = \frac{1180}{59} = 20$$

Substituting $x = 20$ into (7) gives:

$$10x + y = 208$$
$$200 + y = 208$$
$$y = 208 - 200$$
$$y = 8$$

Substituting $x = 20$ and $y = 8$ into (2) gives

$$2x + y + 3z = 84$$
$$40 + 8 + 3z = 84$$
$$3z = 84 - 40 - 8$$
$$3z = 36$$
$$z = \frac{36}{3} = 12$$

You can check your answers by substituting $x = 20$, $y = 8$ and $z = 12$ into (1):

$$3x + 2y - z = 64$$
$$60 + 16 - 12 = 64$$

2.
$$4x + 2y + 3z = 58 \quad (1)$$
$$3x + 4y + 5z = 70 \quad (2)$$
$$2x - y + 4z = 36 \quad (3)$$

Let us get rid of $y$. You can multiply equation (3) by 2 and then add this to equation (1):

$$
\begin{array}{l}
4x - 2y + 8z = \ \ 72 \ (4) \\
+ \ 4x + 2y + 3z = \ \ 58 \ (1) \\
\hline
8x + \quad\quad 11z = 130 \ (5)
\end{array}
$$

You can multiply equation (1) by 2 and then subtract equation (2):

$$
\begin{array}{l}
8x + 4y + 6z = 116 \quad (6) \\
- \ 3x + 4y + 5z = \ \ 70 \quad (2) \\
\hline
5x + \quad\quad z = \ \ 46 \quad (7)
\end{array}
$$

You now have to solve the following equations:

$$8x + 11z = 130 \quad (5)$$
$$5x + z = 46 \quad (7)$$

You can multiply equation (7) by 11 and then subtract equation (5):

$$
\begin{array}{l}
55x + 11z = 506 \quad (8) \\
- \ 8x + 11z = 130 \quad (5) \\
\hline
47x \quad\quad = 376
\end{array}
$$

So
$$x - \frac{376}{47} = 8$$

Substituting $x = 8$ into (7) gives:

$$5x + z = 46$$
$$40 + z = 46$$
$$z = 46 - 40$$
$$z = 6$$

Substituting $x = 8$ and $z = 6$ into (1) gives:

$$4x + 2y + 3z = 58$$
$$32 + 2y + 18 = 58$$
$$2y = 58 - 32 - 18$$
$$2y = 8$$

So
$$y = \frac{8}{2} = 4$$

You can check your answers by substituting $x = 8$, $y = 4$ and $z = 6$ into (2):

$$3x + 4y + 5z = 70$$
$$24 + 16 + 30 = 70$$

## Exercise 3A: *Solve the following.*

1. $3x + 2y + 4z = 33$
$x - 3y + 2z = 10$
$2x + y - 3z = -1$

2. $3x + y - 4z = -9$
$x - 2y + z = 4$
$2x + 3y - 2z = 2$

3. $4x - y + 2z = 20$
$2x - 3y - z = -1$
$x + 2y - 3z = -1$

4. $3x + y - 2z = -5$
$x - 2y - 5z = -3$
$2x + 3y + z = -8$

5. $2x - 3y + z = 9$
$x + y - 2z = 7$
$3x - 2y + 4z = 6$

6. $2x - y + 3z = 5$
$3x + 2y - z = -4$
$x - 3y - 2z = -19$

7. $2x - 3y + z = 8$
$3x + y - 2z = 9$
$x + 2y - 5z = -11$

8. $4x + 3y - z = 14$
$x + 2y + 3z = 16$
$2x - y + z = 22$

9. $x - 3y + z = -15$
$2x + y - 3z = 23$
$3x - 2y - z = 3$

10. $x + 2y - 3z = -7$
$2x - y + z = 13$
$3x + 4y - 2z = 15$

## 3.2 Problems Involving Simultaneous Equations

Many real life problems can be solved using simultaneous equations. For example:

3. Four people are training for the triathlon. They use three different circuits. The swimming circuit is $x$ km long. The cycling circuit is $y$ km long. The running circuit is $z$ km long.

   (a) Lennon does 3 swimming, 6 cycling and 12 running circuits in a week. He covers 90 km altogether. Show that $x + 2y + 4z = 30$.

   (b) Siobhan does 16 swimming, 12 cycling and 4 running circuits in a week. She covers 120 km altogether. Show that $4x + 3y + z = 30$.

   (c) Martin swims an extra 2 km each time he does a swimming circuit. Martin cycles 1 km less each time he does a cycling circuit. Martin runs the normal running circuit. Martin does 4 swimming, 10 cycling and 12 running circuits in a week. He covers 104 km altogether. Show that $2x + 5y + 6z = 53$.

   (d) Hence find the value of $x$, $y$ and $z$.

   (e) Nuala wants to cover 77 km in a week. She does 7 running circuits and an equal number of swimming and cycling circuits. How many circuits does she do altogether?

(a) $3x + 6y + 12z = 90$
You can divide all these terms by 3 to get:
$x + 2y + 4z = 30$   (1)

(b) $16x + 12y + 4z = 120$
You can divide all these terms by 4 to get:
$4x + 3y + z = 30$   (2)

(c) Each swimming circuit $= x + 2$
Each cycling circuit $= y - 1$
Each running circuit $= z$

So: $4(x + 2) + 10(y - 1) + 12z = 104$
$4x + 8 + 10y - 10 + 12z = 104$
$4x + 10y + 12z - 2 = 104$
$4x + 10y + 12z = 104 + 2$
$4x + 10y + 12z = 106$
You can divide all these terms by 2 to get:
$2x + 5y + 6z = 53$   (3)

(d) Multiplying (1) by 4 and subtracting (2) gives:

$$4x + 8y + 16z = 120$$
$$- \ 4x + 3y + \ \ \ z = 30$$
$$5y + 15z = 90 \quad (4)$$

Multiplying (1) by 2 and subtracting (3) gives:

$$2x + 4y + 8z = 60$$
$$- \ \ 2x + 5y + 6z = 53$$
$$-y + 2z = 7 \quad (5)$$

Multiplying (5) by 5 and adding (4) gives:

$$-5y + 10z = 35$$
$$+ \ \ 5y + 15z = 90$$
$$25z = 125$$
$$z = 5$$

Substituting $z = 5$ into (4) gives:

$$5y + 15z = 90$$
$$5y + 75 = 90$$
$$5y = 90 - 75 = 15$$
$$y = 3$$

Substituting $z = 5$ and $y = 3$ into (1) gives:

$$x + 2y + 4z = 30$$
$$x + 6 + 20 = 30$$
$$x = 30 - 6 - 20$$
$$x = 4$$

You can check your answers by substituting $x = 4$, $y = 3$ and $z = 5$ into (2):

$$4x + 3y + z = 30$$
$$16 + 9 + 5 = 30$$

(e) Swimming circuit = 4 km
Cycling circuit = 3 km
Running circuit = 5 km

7 running circuits = $7 \times 5 = 35$ km.
So there are $77 - 35 = 42$ km left to cover.
1 swimming + 1 cycling = $4 + 3 = 7$ km.
So there must be $42 \div 7 = 6$ swimming and 6 cycling circuits.
Total number altogether: $6 + 6 + 7 = 19$ circuits.

## Exercise 3B

1. A shop sells rulers at $x$ pence each, pens at $y$ pence each and pencils at $z$ pence each.
   (a) Cadence buys 12 rulers, 8 pens and 20 pencils for £14. Show that $3x + 2y + 5z = 350$.
   (b) Lily buys 35 rulers, 15 pens and 30 pencils for £32.25. Show that $7x + 3y + 6z = 645$.
   (c) David buys 15 rulers, 12 pens and 24 pencils for £18. Show that $5x + 4y + 8z = 600$.
   (d) Hence find the values of $x$, $y$ and $z$.
   (e) Carly buys 40 of each item and gets 15% discount. How much does she pay altogether?

2. In a computer game you get awarded gold, silver or bronze medals. A gold medal earns $x$ points. A silver medal earns $y$ points. A bronze medal earns $z$ points.
   (a) Leslie gets 20 gold, 10 silver and 15 bronze medals. He scores 255 points. Show that $4x + 2y + 3z = 51$.
   (b) Aoife gets 12 gold, 16 silver and 8 bronze medals. She scores 200 points. Show that $3x + 4y + 2z = 50$.
   (c) Dylan gets 15 gold, 5 silver and 20 bronze medals. He scores 205 points. Show that $3x + y + 4z = 41$.
   (d) Hence find the values of $x$, $y$ and $z$.
   (e) Siobhain gets twice as many gold medals as silver and the same number of silver and bronze medals. She gets 672 points altogether. How many medals did she get altogether?

3. There are 3 types of room in a hotel. Family rooms cost £$x$ per night. Double rooms cost £$y$ per night. Single rooms cost £$z$ per night.
   (a) On one Wednesday, 12 family, 6 double and 18 single rooms were occupied.

The total cost was £4170. Show that $2x + y + 3z = 695$.
   (b) On one Thursday, 30 family, 10 double and 25 single rooms were occupied. The total cost was £8125. Show that $6x + 2y + 5z = 1625$.
   (c) On Fridays the cost of a family room is increased by £20 and the cost of a double room is increased by £15. The cost of a single room is unchanged. On one Friday, 16 family, 12 double and 24 single rooms were occupied. The total cost was £6540. Show that $4x + 3y + 6z = 1510$.
   (d) Hence find the values of $x$, $y$ and $z$.
   (e) A tourist company needs 4 family, 6 double and 3 single rooms. How much would they save by booking a Thursday rather than a Friday?

4. A shop sells shirts at £$x$ each. It sells trousers at £$y$ each. It sells jackets at £$z$ each.
   (a) In a sale, Eric bought a shirt at 20% discount, a pair of trousers at 10% discount and a jacket at 40% discount. These cost £97 altogether. Show that $8x + 9y + 6z = 970$.
   (b) In a different sale Padraig bought a shirt at 40% discount, a pair of trousers at 20% discount and a jacket at 20% discount. These cost £108 altogether. Show that $3x + 4y + 4z = 540$.
   (c) In a different sale Trevor bought a shirt at 10% discount, a pair of trousers at 15% discount and a jacket at 25% discount. These cost £111 altogether. Show that $18x + 17y + 15z = 2220$.
   (d) Hence find the values of $x$, $y$ and $z$
   (e) When Kevin went to the shop, shirts and trousers were on sale at half price. He bought a shirt, a pair of trousers and a jacket for £83.50. How much percentage discount did he get for the jacket?

5. A shop sells Blu-Ray discs at £$x$ each, DVDs at £$y$ each and Box Sets at £$z$ each.
   (a) Eleanor bought 8 Blu-Ray discs, 4 DVDs and 12 Box Sets for £137. Show that $200x + 100y + 300z = 3425$.
   (b) Leah bought 15 Blu-Ray discs, 20 DVDs and 10 Box Sets for £247.50. Show that $30x + 40y + 20z = 495$.

## Exercise 3B...

(c) In a sale the Blu-Ray discs were sold at 50p off each disc and the Box Sets were sold at a 10% reduction. Sarah bought 4 Blu-Ray discs, 2 DVDs and 3 Box Sets in the sale for £48.35. Show that $80x + 40y + 54z = 1007$.

(d) Hence find the values of $x$, $y$ and $z$.

(e) Claire bought a number of Blu-Ray discs, DVDs and Box Sets in the ratio 3:2:4 in the sale for £141.90. How many Box Sets did she buy?

6. Four children collect model cars, trains and buses. Each model car weighs $x$ grams. Each model train weighs $y$ grams. Each model bus weighs $z$ grams.

(a) Quinn has 6 cars, 8 trains and 20 buses. Their total weight is 28.6 kg. Show that $3x + 4y + 10z = 14300$.

(b) Arthur has 10 cars, 5 trains and 10 buses. Their total weight is 19.45 kg. Show that $2x + y + 2z = 3890$.

(c) Martin has 12 cars, 15 trains and 3 buses. Their total weight is 24.06 kg. Show that $4x + 5y + z = 8020$.

(d) Hence find the values of $x$, $y$ and $z$.

(e) Nicola has a number of cars, trains and buses in the ratio 7:8:5. Their total weight is 48.45 kg. How many of each vehicle does she have?

7. Teams play hockey matches in a tournament. Each team scores $x$ points for every game won. Each team scores $y$ points for every game drawn. Each team loses $z$ points for every game lost. The table below shows the results and points for four of the teams. Use it to work out the total number of points Dungiven scored.

| Team | Win | Draw | Lose | Total Points |
|------|-----|------|------|--------------|
| Portstewart | 9 | 6 | 3 | 75 |
| Ardglass | 4 | 10 | 6 | 46 |
| Coagh | 4 | 12 | 8 | 48 |
| Dungiven | 7 | 9 | 5 | |

8. The equation of a curve is $y = ax^3 + bx^2 + cx + 4$. The curve passes through $(-2, -14)$, $(2, -2)$ and $(6, 298)$. Prove that $(-5, -296)$ lies on this curve.

## 4.1 Trigonometric Graphs

It is important to be able to draw graphs of the functions sine (sin), cosine (cos) and tangent (tan).

### Sine

The table below gives values of $y = \sin x$ for the range $-360° \leq x \leq 360°$.

| $x$ | $-360°$ | $-270°$ | $-180°$ | $-90°$ | $0°$ | $90°$ | $180°$ | $270°$ | $360°$ |
|---|---|---|---|---|---|---|---|---|---|
| $y$ | 0 | 1 | 0 | $-1$ | 0 | 1 | 0 | $-1$ | 0 |

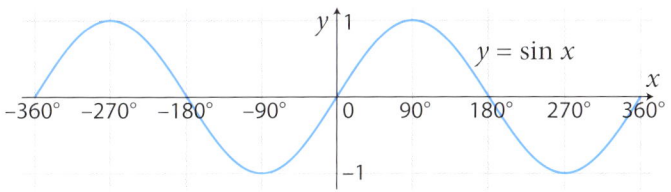

### Cosine

The table below gives values of $y = \cos x$ for the range $-360° \leq x \leq 360°$.

| $x$ | $-360°$ | $-270°$ | $-180°$ | $-90°$ | $0°$ | $90°$ | $180°$ | $270°$ | $360°$ |
|---|---|---|---|---|---|---|---|---|---|
| $y$ | 1 | 0 | $-1$ | 0 | 1 | 0 | $-1$ | 0 | 1 |

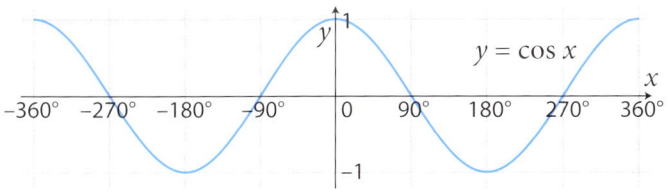

### Tangent

The table below gives values of $y = \tan x$ for the range $-360° \leq x \leq 360°$. Note that the tan function is undefined for the values $-270°$, $-90°$, $90°$ and $270°$. This means that we can only draw it in discontinuous sections, as shown in the graph.

| $x$ | $-360°$ | $-180°$ | $0°$ | $180°$ | $360°$ |
|---|---|---|---|---|---|
| $y$ | 0 | 0 | 0 | 0 | 0 |

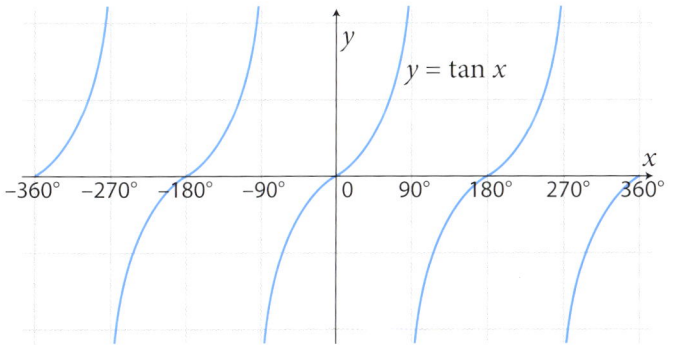

### Exercise 4A: *Sketch the graphs of the following.*

1. $y = \sin x$ for $0° \leq x \leq 360°$
2. $y = \cos x$ for $-90° \leq x \leq 360°$
3. $y = \tan x$ for $-180° \leq x \leq 360°$
4. $y = \sin x$ for $-180° \leq x \leq 360°$
5. $y = \cos x$ for $-90° \leq x \leq 270°$
6. $y = \tan x$ for $0° \leq x \leq 180°$

### Trigonometric Ratios

When turning through an angle, we always start with the positive horizontal axis. Therefore the angle at this line is always taken as $0°$. As we turn from the positive horizontal axis in an anti-clockwise direction the angles change from $0°$ to $360°$.

**Consider these angles from $0°$ to $360°$:**

- All the sines, cosines and tangents of all the angles between $0°$ and $90°$ are positive, eg:
$$\sin 30° = 0.5$$
$$\cos 45° = 0.707$$
$$\tan 60° = 1.732$$

- However between $90°$ and $180°$ only the sines are positive, eg:
$$\sin 100° = 0.985$$
$$\cos 145° = -0.819$$
$$\tan 160° = -0.364$$

- Between $180°$ and $270°$ only the tangents are positive, eg:
$$\sin 200° = -0.342$$
$$\cos 245° = -0.423$$
$$\tan 260° = 5.671$$

- Between $270°$ and $360°$ only the cosines are positive, eg:
$$\sin 300° = -0.866$$
$$\cos 345° = 0.966$$
$$\tan 350° = -0.176$$

We can summarise these ideas in the sketch below (where 'A' means that all three are positive in that quadrant):

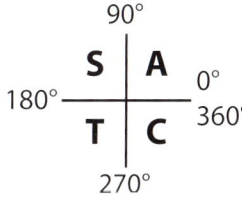

As we turn from the positive horizontal axis in a clockwise direction the angles change from 0° to –360°.

**Now, consider the angles from –180° to 180°:**

Similarly, we can summarise the sines, cosines and tangents of all these angles in the sketch below:

$$
\begin{array}{c|c}
 & 90° \\
\text{S} & \text{A} \\
\hline
\text{T} & \text{C} \\
 & -90°
\end{array}
$$

180°
–180° ————— 0°

## 4.2 Solving Trigonometric Equations Between 0° and 360°

We can use the ideas discussed in section 4.1 to help us solve trigonometric equations between 0° and 360°. For example:

1. Solve sin $x$ = 0.7 for 0° ≤ $x$ ≤ 360°

   There are two quadrants in which the sin is positive as shown below:

$$
\begin{array}{c|c}
 & 90° \\
\text{S} & \text{A} \\
\hline
\text{T} & \text{C} \\
 & 270°
\end{array}
$$

180° ————— 0°
360°

   You can find one of the solutions using the inverse sine button on your calculator, i.e. sin⁻¹ 0.7 = 44.43°.

   We know that the other angle must be in the quadrant between 90° and 180°. So you find it by subtracting 44.43 from 180 as shown below:

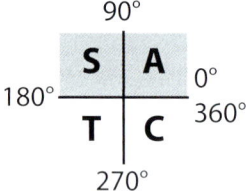

44.43°        180 – 44.43 = 135.57°

   So the answer is 44.43° or 135.57°

2. Solve cos $x$ = –0.345 for 0° ≤ $x$ ≤ 360°

   There are two quadrants in which the cos is negative as shown below:

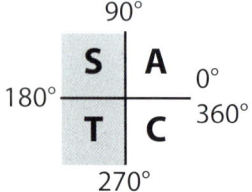

First using the inverse cos button on your calculator find the value of $x$ when cos $x$ = 0.345, i.e.:

cos⁻¹ 0.345 = 69.82°

Then use your answer to find the two solutions, given that the value of cos $x$ is negative. You can find the angle in the quadrant between 90° and 180° by subtracting 69.82 from 180 as shown below:

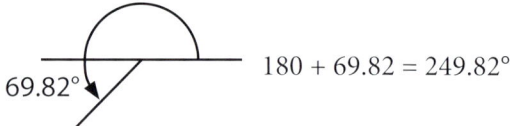

69.82°        180 – 69.82 = 110.18°

You can find the angle in the quadrant between 180° and 270° by adding 69.82 to 180 as shown below:

69.82°        180 + 69.82 = 249.82°

So the answer is 110.18° or 249.82°.

3. Solve tan $x$ = –4 for 0° ≤ $x$ ≤ 360°

   There are two quadrants in which the tan is negative as shown below:

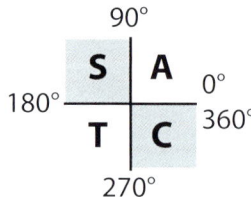

First using the inverse tan button on your calculator find the value of $x$ when tan $x$ = 4, i.e.:

tan⁻¹ 4 = 75.96°.

Then use your answer to find the two solutions, given that the value of tan $x$ is negative. You can find the angle in the quadrant between 90° and 180° by subtracting 75.96 from 180 as shown below:

75.96°        180 – 75.96 = 104.04°

You can find the angle in the quadrant between 270° and 360° by subtracting 75.96 from 360 as shown below:

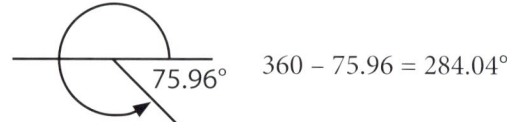

75.96°        360 – 75.96 = 284.04°

So the answer is 104.04° or 284.04°.

1. $\cos x = 0.462$
2. $\sin x = -0.762$
3. $\tan x = 3$
4. $\sin x = 0.2$
5. $\cos x = -0.75$
6. $\tan x = -0.6$

## 4.3 Solving Trigonometric Equations Between $-180°$ And $180°$

The same approach can be used when the angle is between $180°$ and $180°$. For example:

4. Solve $\sin x = -0.43$ for $-180° \leq x \leq 180°$

There are two quadrants in which the sin is negative as shown below:

90°
180° S | A
-180° ——— 0°
T | C
-90°

First using the inverse sin button on your calculator find the value of $x$ when $\sin x = 0.43$, i.e.:

$\sin^{-1} 0.43 = 25.47°$

Then use your answer to find the two solutions, given that the value of $\sin x$ is negative. You can find the angle in the quadrant between $0°$ and $-90°$ by changing the sign to negative as shown below:

25.47°        −25.47°

You can find the angle in the quadrant between $-90°$ and $-180°$ by subtracting 25.5 from 180 and changing the sign to a negative as shown below:

25.47°        $180 - 25.47 = 154.53°$

So the answer is $-25.47°$ or $-154.53°$

5. $\cos x = 0.845$ for $-180° \leq x \leq 180°$

There are two quadrants in which the cos is positive as shown below:

90°
180° S | A
-180° ——— 0°
T | C
-90°

You can find one of the solutions using the inverse cos button on your calculator, i.e. $\cos^{-1} 0.845 = 32.33°$.

The other angle is in the quadrant between $0°$ and $-90°$ and so it will just be $-32.33$:

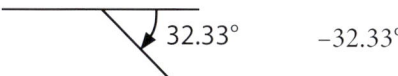

32.33°        −32.33°

So the answer is $32.33°$ or $-32.33°$.

6. $\tan x = 0.2$ for $-180° \leq x \leq 180°$

There are two quadrants in which the tan is positive as shown below:

90°
180° S | A
-180° ——— 0°
T | C
-90°

You can find one of the solutions using the inverse tan button on your calculator, i.e. $\tan^{-1} 0.2 = 11.31°$.

The other angle is in the quadrant between $-90°$ and $-180°$. You can find this angle by subtracting 11.31 from 180 and changing the sign to a negative as shown below:

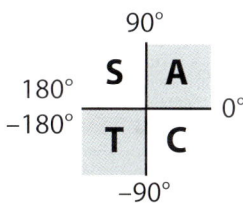

11.31°        $180 - 11.31 = 168.69°$

So the answer is $11.31°$ or $-168.69°$.

1. $\cos x = 0.6$
2. $\sin x = -0.34$
3. $\tan x = -2$
4. $\sin x = 0.739$
5. $\cos x = -0.349$
6. $\tan x = -1.5$

## 4.4 More Complex Trigonometry Equations

Some questions are less straightforward. For example:

7. Solve $\cos 5x = 0.482$ where $0° \leq x \leq 72°$

    It is easier to let $y = 5x$ and solve $\cos y = 0.482$ as before. Then you can set up an algebraic equation for $x$ and solve.

    So first solve $\cos y = 0.482$. There are two quadrants in which the cos is positive from 0° to 360° as shown:

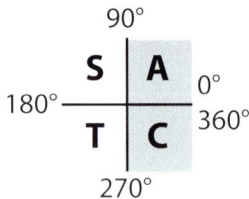

    You can find one of the solutions using the inverse cos button on your calculator, i.e. $\cos^{-1} 0.482 = 61.184°$.

    The other angle is in the quadrant between 270° and 360°. You can find it by subtracting 61.184 from 360 as shown below:

    61.184°   360 – 61.184 = 298.816°

    So $y = 61.184°$ or $298.816°$

    You can now set up equations for $x$ by substituting $5x = y$, i.e.:

    $5x = 61.184°$, giving $x = 12.24°$

    or    $5x = 298.816°$ giving $x = 59.76°$

    These angles are both between 0° and 72° (since 360 ÷ 5 = 72).

8. Solve $\tan(3x - 10) = -3$ where $-60° \leq x \leq 60°$

    It is easier to let $y = 3x - 10$ and solve $\tan y = -3$ as before. Then you can set up an algebraic equation for $y$ and solve:

    So first solve $\tan y = -3$. There are two quadrants in which the tan is negative from –180° to 180° as shown below:

    90°

    180°  S | A
    –180°  ――――  0°
          T | C

    –90°

First using the inverse tan button on your calculator find the value of $x$ when $\tan x = 3$, i.e.:

$\tan^{-1} 3 = 71.565°$

Then use your answer to find the two solutions, given that the value of tan $x$ is negative. One angle is in the quadrant between 0° and –90° as shown below:

71.565°    –71.565°

The other angle is in the quadrant between 90° and 180°. You can find it by subtracting 71.565 from 180 as shown below:

71.565°    180 – 71.565 = 108.435°

So $y = -71.565°$ or $108.435°$.

You can now set up equations for $x$ by substituting $3x - 10 = y$, i.e.:

$$3x - 10 = -71.565°$$
$$3x = -71.565° + 10$$
$$3x = -61.665°$$
$$x = -20.52°$$

or    $3x - 10 = 108.435°$
$$3x = 108.435° + 10$$
$$3x = 118.435°$$
$$x = 39.48°$$

These angles are both between –60° and 60° (since ±180 ÷ 3 = ±60).

## Exercise 4D: *Solve the following.*

1.  $\sin 3x = 0.467$ where $0° \leq x \leq 120°$

2.  $\cos 2x = -0.16$ where $0° \leq x \leq 180°$

3.  $\tan 4x = 1.3$ where $0° \leq x \leq 90°$

4.  $\sin(x + 40) = -0.96$ where $0° \leq x \leq 360°$

5.  $\cos(x - 25) = 0.12$ where $0° \leq x \leq 360°$

6.  $\tan(x - 10) = -0.5$ where $-180° \leq x \leq 180°$

7.  $\cos(\frac{1}{3}x - 47) = 0.12$ where $-540° \leq x \leq 540°$

8.  $\tan(x - 25) = 2$ where $-180° \leq x \leq 180°$

9.  $\tan(5x + 22) = -0.34$ where $-36° \leq x \leq 36°$

10. $\sin(\frac{1}{2}x + 15) = -0.174$ where $0° \leq x \leq 720°$

# CHAPTER 5: QUADRATIC INEQUALITIES

## 5.1 Quadratic Expressions And Curves

All quadratic expressions will be of the form $x^2 \pm bx \pm c$. When trying to solve a quadratic inequality you must first be able to factorise quadratic equations.

You also need to know the shape of the quadratic function $x^2 \pm bx \pm c$, which is a U-shape as shown in the example graph below.

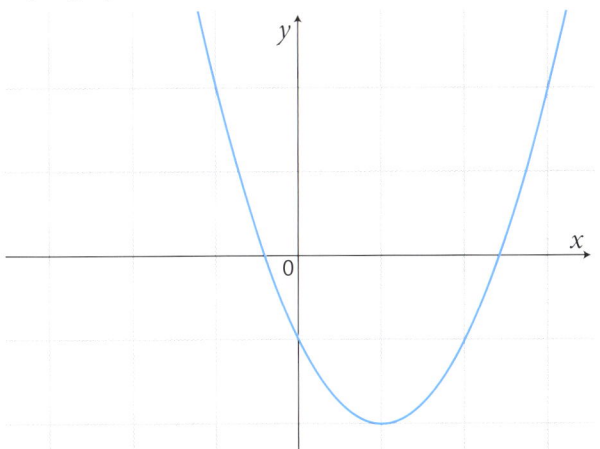

## 5.2 Solving Quadratic Inequalities

Quadratic inequalities can be solved by using these rules:
a. Solve the corresponding quadratic equation.
b. Sketch the graph of this quadratic expression.
c. Choose the correct region or regions from the graph that make the inequality correct.

For example:

1. Solve $x^2 + 7x + 10 \leq 0$

   First solve the quadratic equation
   $x^2 + 7x + 10 = 0$

   This factorises to give: $(x + 2)(x + 5) = 0$

   So either    $x + 2 = 0$, giving $x = -2$
   or          $x + 5 = 0$, giving $x = -5$

   Then sketch the graph of $f(x) = x^2 + 7x + 10$. This is a U-shaped graph. Mark the points where the graph crosses the $x$-axis, i.e. $x = -5$ and $-2$.

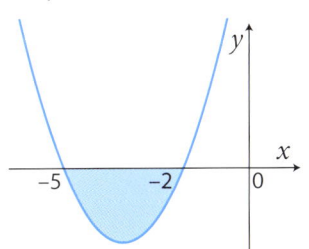

The correct region where $x^2 + 7x + 10 \leq 0$ is the region below the $x$-axis, i.e. the region between $x = -5$ and $-2$ (shaded on the graph).

This is written algebraically as $-5 \leq x \leq -2$.

---

2. Solve $x^2 + 7x > 0$

   First solve the quadratic equation $x^2 + 7x = 0$

   This factorises to give: $x(x + 7) = 0$

   So either    $x = 0$
   or          $x + 7 = 0$, giving $x = -7$

   Then sketch the graph of $f(x) = x^2 + 7x$. This is a U-shaped graph. Mark the points where the graph crosses the $x$-axis, i.e. $x = -7$ and 0.

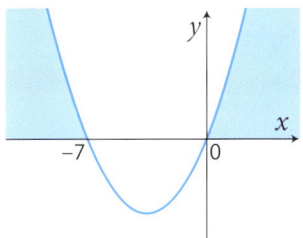

The correct region where $x^2 + 7x > 0$ is the region above the $x$-axis, i.e. the region before $x = -7$ and after $x = 0$ (shaded on the graph).

This is written algebraically as $x < -7$ or $x > 0$.

---

3. Solve $2x^2 + 5x - 3 < 0$

   You first need to solve the quadratic equation
   $2x^2 + 5x - 3 = 0$

   This factorises to give: $(2x - 1)(x + 3) = 0$

   So either    $2x - 1 = 0$, giving $x = \frac{1}{2}$
   or          $x + 3 = 0$, giving $x = -3$

   Then sketch the graph of $f(x) = 2x^2 + 5x - 3 < 0$. This is a U-shaped graph. Mark the points where the graph crosses the $x$-axis, i.e. $x = -3$ and $\frac{1}{2}$.

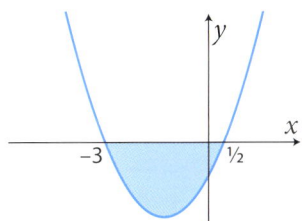

The correct region where $2x^2 + 5x - 3 < 0$ is the

region below the $x$-axis, i.e. the region between $x = -3$ and ½.

This is written algebraically as $-3 < x < $ ½.

## Exercise 5A: *Solve the following quadratic inequalities.*

1. $x^2 + 8x + 15 \leq 0$
2. $x^2 - 2x > 0$
3. $x^2 - 16 < 0$
4. $x^2 + 7x + 10 \geq 0$
5. $x^2 - 9x + 20 < 0$
6. $x^2 - 8x \geq 0$
7. $x^2 + x - 6 \leq 0$
8. $x^2 - 4 > 0$
9. $x^2 + 9x + 14 < 0$
10. $x^2 + x \geq 0$
11. $x^2 - 5x - 14 \leq 0$
12. $x^2 - 81 \geq 0$
13. $x^2 - 6x + 8 \geq 0$
14. $x^2 + 3x - 18 < 0$
15. $x^2 - 9x > 0$
16. $x^2 - 36 \leq 0$
17. $3x^2 - 14x + 8 < 0$
18. $2x^2 + 7x + 3 > 0$
19. $16x^2 - 1 \leq 0$
20. $6x^2 - 5x - 6 \geq 0$
21. $4x^2 - 5x - 6 < 0$
22. $25x^2 - 9 > 0$
23. $3x^2 - 13x + 4 < 0$
24. $5x^2 + 9x - 2 \geq 0$

## 5.3 Solving Quadratic Inequalities In Context

These are solved in exactly the same way as before. However you need to check the answers to work out how much of the identified region is appropriate for the context. For example:

4. Quinn's weekly pocket money, £P, satisfies the inequality $P^2 - 8P - 20 < 0$. Work out the range of Quinn's weekly pocket money.

   You solve the inequality as before. First solve the quadratic equation $P^2 - 8P - 20 = 0$.

   This factorises to give: $(P - 10)(P + 2) = 0$

   So either    $P - 10 = 0$, giving $P = 10$
   or             $P + 2 = 0$, giving $P = -2$

   Then sketch the graph of $f(P) = P^2 - 8P - 20$. This is a U-shaped graph. Mark the points where the graph crosses the horizontal axis i.e. $P = -2$ and 10.

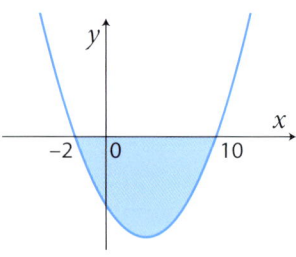

The solution of the inequality is then $-2 < P < 10$.

However, you must now check to see how much of the identified region is appropriate for the context.

Since the amount of pocket money cannot be negative the final answer can only be $0 < P < 10$.

5. The ages, A years, of people at an Under-21s summer camp satisfy the inequality $A^2 - 12A > 0$. Work out the range of the ages.

   You solve the inequality as before. First solve the quadratic equation $A^2 - 12A = 0$.

   This factorises to give: $A(A - 12) = 0$

   So either    $A = 0$
   or             $A - 12 = 0$, giving $A = 12$

   Then sketch the graph of $f(A) = A^2 - 12A$. This is a U-shaped graph. Mark the points where the graph crosses the horizontal axis, i.e. $A = 0$ and 12.

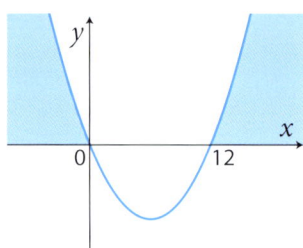

The solution of the inequality is then $A < 0$ and $A > 12$.

You must now check to see how much of the identified region is appropriate for the context.

Since an age cannot be negative we must omit $A < 0$.

Since the people are all under 21 we must amend the other region to $12 < A < 21$.

## Exercise 5B

1.  The amount of money, X, in thousands of pounds, that Claire deposits in an investment fund satisfies the inequality. $X^2 - 6X - 27 \geq 0$. Work out the least amount of money that could be invested.

2.  The length, $x$ cm, of a rectangle, satisfies the inequality $x^2 + 3x - 40 \leq 0$. Work out the range of possible lengths.

3.  The temperatures, T°C, recorded one day satisfy the inequality $T^2 - 49 \geq 0$. Work out the range of possible temperatures.

4.  The acceleration, $a$ m s$^{-2}$, of an object satisfies the inequality $a^2 - 2a > 0$. Work out the range of possible accelerations.

5.  Ruari's score in a test, $x$, satisfies the inequality $x^2 - 14x + 33 \leq 0$. Work out the greatest score Ruari could have.

6.  The ages, A years, of people at a summer camp satisfy the inequality. $A^2 - 2A - 120 < 0$. Work out the range of the ages.

7.  A rectangle 6 cm long and $x$ cm wide has a perimeter less than 26 cm. $x$ satisfies the inequality $x^2 - 11x + 18 < 0$. Work out the range of possible values of $x$.

8.  The heights, $h$ m, of buildings on a street in Ballymena satisfy the inequality $h^2 - 5h \geq 0$. The highest building is 40 m high. Work out the range of possible heights.

# CHAPTER 6: DIFFERENTIATION

## 6.1 Rules of Differentiation

You can differentiate any algebraic function using the following rules:

### Powers of $x$ other than 1:
a. Multiply by the power.
b. Take 1 off the power.

$y = kx^n$ (where $k$ is any constant)

$$\frac{dy}{dx} = nkx^{n-1}$$

### $y = kx$ (where $k$ is any constant)

$$\frac{dy}{dx} = k$$

### $y = k$ (where $k$ is any constant)

$$\frac{dy}{dx} = 0$$

For example, differentiate the following with respect to $x$:

1. $y = 4x^3 + 6x^2 - 7x - 5$

   By the above rules, $\frac{dy}{dx} = 12x^2 + 12x - 7$

2. $y = 2x^3 + mx^2 - nx + 3$

   Treat m and n as constants. So:

   $$\frac{dy}{dx} = 6x^2 + 2mx - n$$

### Exercise 6A: Differentiate the following with respect to x.

1. $y = 6x + 2$
2. $y = 2x^2 - 3x + 4$
3. $y = 3x^2 + x - 5$
4. $y = 2x^3 + 3x^2 - 5x + 2$
5. $y = 4x^3 - 6x^2 + x - 7$
6. $y = 2 + 3x - x^2 + 7x^3$
7. $y = 8 - 3x + 2x^2 - x^3$
8. $y = x^4 - 2x^2 + 7$
9. $y = 6x^3 - 3x + 5$
10. $y = 4x^2 - x^3 + 2x^4$
11. $y = 2x^5 - 3x^4 + 2x^3 - 6x^2 + x$

### Exercise 6A...

12. $y = 4x^3 - 7x^2 + 2$
13. $y = 6x^4 - 2x^2 + x$
14. $y = 4 + 3x - x^3$
15. $y = 2x^3 - 4x^2 - 7x$
16. $y = 6 - 2x + 3x^2 - x^3$
17. $y = 2x^3 - x^2 + 4x - 3$
18. $y = 4x^2 - 5x + 3$
19. $y = ax^2 + bx$
20. $y = 8x^3 - vx$
21. $y = 9x^2 + tx - w$

## 6.2 Differentiation With Fractional Coefficients

If there are fractional coefficients, you follow the same rules. But remember that when you multiply a fraction by a whole number you only multiply the **numerator** of the fraction by the whole number, i.e.:

$$\frac{2}{5} \times 6 = \frac{12}{5}$$

For example, differentiate the following with respect to $x$:

3. $y = \frac{1}{8}x^4 - \frac{3}{5}x^2 + 7x$

   So: $\frac{dy}{dx} = \frac{4}{8}x^3 - \frac{6}{5}x + 7$

   You should cancel the fraction if possible, so the final answer is:

   $$\frac{dy}{dx} = \frac{1}{2}x^3 - \frac{6}{5}x + 7$$

4. $y = 8 + x - \frac{2}{9}x^3 + \frac{3}{4}x^8$

   So: $\frac{dy}{dx} = 1 - \frac{6}{9}x^2 + \frac{24}{4}x^7$

   You should then cancel the fraction, so the final answer is:

   $$\frac{dy}{dx} = 1 - \frac{2}{3}x^2 + 6x^7$$

1. $y = \frac{1}{4}x^3 - \frac{2}{5}x^2 + x$

2. $y = 2x^3 - \frac{1}{5}x^2 + \frac{3}{4}x$

3. $y = 4x^3 - \frac{2}{7}x^2 + \frac{1}{3}x$

4. $y = \frac{1}{5}x^3 - \frac{3}{2}x^2 + 4x$

5. $y = \frac{2}{9}x^3 + \frac{1}{4}x^2 - 3$

6. $y = \frac{3}{4}x^2 + \frac{1}{5}x - 6$

7. $y = 3x^3 - \frac{3}{4}x^2 + x$

8. $y = 4 - \frac{1}{5}x + \frac{5}{2}x^2$

9. $y = \frac{7}{3}x^3 - \frac{2}{5}x^2 + \frac{1}{4}x$

10. $y = 3 + \frac{1}{2}x - \frac{5}{6}x^2 + \frac{7}{3}x^3$

## 6.3 Differentiation With The $x$ Term On The Denominator

In this case, you must rewrite the $x$ term using the rule

$\frac{1}{x^n} = x^{-n}$

For example, differentiate the following with respect to $x$:

5. $y = \frac{8}{x^3}$

Rewriting gives: $y = 8x^{-3}$

So: $\frac{dy}{dx} = -24x^{-4}$

You should then rewrite the answer with a positive index. So the final answer is:

$\frac{dy}{dx} = \frac{-24}{x^4}$

6. $y = \frac{9}{8x^2}$

Rewriting gives: $y = \frac{9}{8}x^{-2}$

So: $\frac{dy}{dx} = \frac{-18}{8}x^{-3}$

You should then cancel the fraction.

So: $\frac{dy}{dx} = \frac{-9}{4}x^{-3}$

Then rewrite the answer with a positive index. So the final answer is:

$\frac{dy}{dx} = \frac{-9}{4x^3}$

7. $y = \frac{1}{3x^6}$

Rewriting gives: $y = \frac{1}{3}x^{-6}$

Then $\frac{dy}{dx} = \frac{-6}{3}x^{-7}$

You should then cancel the fraction.

So: $\frac{dy}{dx} = -2x^{-7}$

Then rewrite the answer with a positive index. So the final answer is:

$\frac{dy}{dx} = \frac{-2}{x^7}$

1. $y = \frac{6}{x^2}$

2. $y = \frac{4}{x^3}$

3. $y = \frac{5}{x^4}$

4. $y = \frac{3}{2x^7}$

5. $y = \frac{5}{4x^2}$

6. $y = \frac{2}{7x^3}$

7. $y = \frac{4}{x^3}$

8. $y = \frac{3}{x^5}$

9. $y = \frac{1}{2x^3}$

10. $y = \frac{2}{4x^2}$

## 6.4 Further Differentiation

Some questions contain both fractional coefficients and the $x$ term on the denominator. For example, differentiate the following with respect to $x$:

8. $y = \dfrac{2}{9}x^3 + \dfrac{1}{4}x^2 - \dfrac{8}{x^3}$

Rewriting gives: $y = \dfrac{2}{9}x^3 + \dfrac{1}{4}x^2 - 8x^{-3}$

So: $\dfrac{dy}{dx} = \dfrac{6}{9}x^2 + \dfrac{2}{4}x + 24x^{-4}$

You should then cancel the fractions to get:

$\dfrac{dy}{dx} = \dfrac{2}{3}x^2 + \dfrac{1}{2}x + 24x^{-4}$

You should then rewrite the answer with a positive index. So the final answer is:

$\dfrac{dy}{dx} = \dfrac{2}{3}x^2 + \dfrac{1}{2}x + \dfrac{24}{x^4}$

## Exercise 6D: Differentiate the following with respect to x.

1. $y = 6x^3 + \dfrac{2}{x^4}$

2. $y = 2x + \dfrac{3}{x^5}$

3. $y = 2x^5 + 3x - \dfrac{4}{x^2}$

4. $y = \dfrac{2}{3}x^6 - 4 + \dfrac{2}{3}x^2$

5. $y = \dfrac{3}{4}x^4 + x - \dfrac{3}{4x^3}$

6. $y = \dfrac{7}{2}x^2 - \dfrac{2}{7x^2}$

7. $y = 4x^3 + x^2 - \dfrac{1}{x^4}$

8. $y = 2x^2 + 6 + \dfrac{1}{3x^2}$

9. $y = 4x^2 - 7x + \dfrac{2}{x^2}$

10. $y = 5x + \dfrac{2}{3x^4}$

11. $y = 7x^2 - 8 + \dfrac{2}{x^6}$

12. $y = 3x^4 + \dfrac{2}{x^5} - 3x$

13. $y = \dfrac{4}{3}x^6 - \dfrac{3}{4x^6}$

14. $y = 2x^4 + 5x - \dfrac{2}{3x^5}$

15. $y = 3x^5 + \dfrac{2}{3}x^3 - \dfrac{3}{2x^2}$

## 6.5 Differentiation of $\dfrac{dy}{dx}$

You can differentiate $\dfrac{dy}{dx}$ to get $\dfrac{d^2y}{dx^2}$.

You use the same rules as before. For example:

9. $y = 2x^3 + 3x^2 - 5x + 2$   Find $\dfrac{dy}{dx}$ and $\dfrac{d^2y}{dx^2}$.

$\dfrac{dy}{dx} = 6x^2 + 6x - 5$

$\dfrac{d^2y}{dx^2} = 12x + 6$

10. $y = 3x^4 + \dfrac{2}{x^5} - 3x$   Find $\dfrac{dy}{dx}$ and $\dfrac{d^2y}{dx^2}$.

$y = 3x^4 + 2x^{-5} - 3x$

$\dfrac{dy}{dx} = 12x^3 - 10x^{-6} - 3$

In this case, you should leave the index as a negative power to make it easier to differentiate again. So:

$\dfrac{d^2y}{dx^2} = 36x^2 + \dfrac{60}{x^7} = 36x^2 + 60x^{-7}$

## Exercise 6E: Find $\dfrac{dy}{dx}$ and $\dfrac{d^2y}{dx^2}$ in the following.

1. $y = 3x^4 - 7x^3 + 2x^2$

2. $y = 6x + 2x^2 - 7$

3. $y = 2x^3 + 7x^2 - 5x + 4$

4. $y = 3x + \dfrac{2}{x^2}$

5. $y = 2 - x - x^2$

6. $y = 4x - 2x^2 + 1$

7. $y = 6x^2 + \dfrac{1}{x^2}$

8. $y = \dfrac{2}{3}x^3 - 4x - 2$

9. $y = \dfrac{3}{5}x^{10} + \dfrac{1}{5x^2}$

10. $y = \dfrac{3}{2}x^2 + \dfrac{2}{3x^2}$

11. $y = 4x^3 - 4 - \dfrac{2}{x^3}$

12. $y = 6x^2 - \dfrac{1}{6x^3}$

13. $y = 3x^2 - x - \dfrac{1}{x^2}$

14. $y = 2x + 3x^2 - \dfrac{4}{x^3}$

15. $y = 6x + \dfrac{2}{5x^4}$

# CHAPTER 7: TANGENTS AND NORMALS

## 7.1 Gradient

You can find the gradient of the tangent to any curve $y = f(x)$ at any point by:

a. Differentiating $y$ to get $\dfrac{dy}{dx}$.

b. Substituting the $x$-coordinate of the point into $\dfrac{dy}{dx}$

For example:

---

1. Find the gradient of the tangent to the curve $y = 4x^3 + 2x^2 - 6x + 4$ at the point where $x = 2$.

$$\dfrac{dy}{dx} = 12x^2 + 4x - 6$$

Substituting $x = 2$ gives:

$48 + 8 - 6 = 50$

Answer: Gradient = 50

---

2. Find the gradient of the tangent to the curve $y = \dfrac{2}{3}x^2 + 7x + \dfrac{3}{x^2}$ at the point $(-1, -3\dfrac{1}{3})$.

$$\dfrac{dy}{dx} = \dfrac{4}{3}x + 7 - \dfrac{6}{x^3}$$

Substituting $x = -1$ gives:

$\dfrac{-4}{3} + 7 + 6 = 11\dfrac{2}{3}$

Answer: Gradient = $11\dfrac{2}{3}$

---

**Exercise 7A**: *Find the gradient of the tangent to the following curves at the following points:*

1. $y = 2x^2 - 7x + 3$ at the point where $x = 2$

2. $y = 3x + 4x^2 - 1$ at the point where $x = 3$

3. $y = 6 - x + x^2$ at the point where $x = -2$

4. $y = 2x^3 + 4x - 5$ at the point where $x = -1$

5. $y = \dfrac{2}{5}x^2 + \dfrac{1}{3}x + 2$ at the point where $x = 4$

6. $y = \dfrac{3}{4}x^2 - x - 4$ at the point where $x = 2$

7. $y = \dfrac{2}{3}x^3 + \dfrac{1}{2}x^2 + x$ at the point where $x = -3$

8. $y = \dfrac{4}{x^2}$ at $(2, 1)$

---

**Exercise 7A...**

9. $y = \dfrac{1}{x^3}$ at $(2, \dfrac{1}{8})$

10. $y = 6x + \dfrac{1}{x^2}$ at $(-2, -11\dfrac{3}{4})$

11. $y = \dfrac{10}{x^4}$ at the point where $x = 2$

12. $y = (x + 2)(3x - 1)$ at $(2, 20)$

13. $y = (2x - 1)^2$ at $(-2, 25)$

14. $y = 3x^2 + x - \dfrac{1}{x^2}$ at the point where $x = 4$

15. $y = 4 - \dfrac{2}{x^3}$ at the point where $x = -2$

You can also find $x$ and $y$ when the gradient is known. The rules are as follows:

a. Differentiate $y$ to get $\dfrac{dy}{dx}$.

b. Put $\dfrac{dy}{dx}$ equal to the gradient.

c. Solve your equation to find $x$.

d. Substitute $x$ into $y$ to find $y$.

For example:

---

3. Find where the gradient of the tangent to the curve $y = 2x^2 - 7x + 8$ is 5.

$$\dfrac{dy}{dx} = 4x - 7$$

Solve for $x$:  $4x - 7 = 5$

$4x = 12$

$x = 3$

Then find $y$:  $y = 2x^2 - 7x + 8$

$y = 2(3)^2 - 7(3) + 8$

$y = 18 - 21 + 8$

$y = 5$

Answer $(3, 5)$

---

## Exercise 7B

1. Find where the gradient of the tangent to the curve $y = 2x^2 - 5x + 3$ is 7.

2. Find where the gradient of the tangent to the curve $y = 8 + x - 2x^2$ is 9.

3. Find where the gradient of the tangent to the curve $y = 4x^2 - 5x + 3$ is 27.

4. Find where the gradient of the tangent to the curve $y = 10 - 2x + x^2$ is $-4$.

5. Find where the gradient of the tangent to the curve $y = \frac{3}{2}x^2 - 4x + 3$ is 2.

6. Find where the gradient of the tangent to the curve $y = 6 - 2x - 3x^2$ is 10.

7. Find where the gradient of the tangent to the curve $y = (x + 4)(2x - 1)$ is $-5$.

8. Find where the gradient of the tangent to the curve $y = (3x - 5)^2$ is 24.

9. Find where the gradient of the tangent to the curve $y = x^2 - 10x + 8$ is $-18$.

10. Find where the gradient of the tangent to the curve $y = 4 + 5x - 2x^2$ is $-3$.

11. Find where the gradient of the tangent to the curve $y = 4x^2 - 5x + 7$ is parallel to the $x$-axis.

12. Find where the gradient of the tangent to the curve $y = \frac{5}{2}x^2 + 2x - 1$ is horizontal.

13. Find where the gradient of the tangent to the curve $y = 7 - 2x - 3x^2$ is horizontal.

In some cases the equation of the gradient is itself a quadratic equation which needs to be solved. For example:

4. Find the coordinates of the points where the gradient of the tangent to the curve $y = 2x^3 - 9x^2 + 10x - 2$ is 34.

$$\frac{dy}{dx} = 6x^2 - 18x + 10$$
$$6x^2 - 18x + 10 = 34$$
$$6x^2 - 18x - 24 = 0$$

Dividing through by 6 gives:
$$x^2 - 3x - 4 = 0$$

This is a quadratic equation and you can solve it by factorising to get:
$$(x - 4)(x + 1) = 0$$

So:     $x = 4 \text{ or } -1$

Now we find $y$ by substituting into the original equation:

$$y = 2x^3 - 9x^2 + 10x - 2$$

$x = 4$ gives:
$$y = 2(4)^3 - 9(4)^2 + 10(4) - 2$$
$$y = 128 - 144 + 40 - 2$$
$$y = 22$$

$x = -1$ gives:
$$y = 2(-1)^3 - 9(-1)^2 + 10(-1) - 2$$
$$y = -2 - 9 - 10 - 2$$
$$y = -23$$

Answers:  (4, 22) and ($-1$, $-23$)

## Exercise 7C: *Find the coordinates of the points where the gradient of the tangent to the curve:*

1. $y = 2x^3 - 3x^2 + 4x - 2$ is 4.

2. $y = 5 + 2x - x^2 + 4x^3$ is 46.

3. $y = 4x - 2x^2 + 3x^3$ is 17.

4. $y = 3 + 2x - x^2 - 2x^3$ is $-18$.

5. $y = x^3 - 2x^2 + 5x - 2$ is 9.

6. $y = \frac{1}{3}x^3 + \frac{3}{2}x^2 - 3x + 1$ is 1.

7. $y = x^3 - x^2 + 4x - 3$ is 9.

8. $y = \frac{2}{3}x^3 - \frac{3}{2}x^2 + x - 4$ is 3.

9. $y = 4x^3 - 2x^2 + 5x + 1$ is 21.

10. $y = 7 - 2x + 3x^2 - x^3$ is $-2$.

11. $y = 4x^3 + 15x^2 - 18x + 2$ is parallel to the $x$-axis.

12. $y = x^3 - 5x^2 - 8x - 3$ is horizontal.

13. $y = x^3 - 3x^2 - 24x + 5$ is horizontal.

## 7.2  Equation Of A Tangent

To find the equation of a tangent to a curve at any point you should:

a. Find the gradient as before.

b. Substitute the gradient and coordinates of the point into $y = mx + c$.

For example:

5. Find the equation of the tangent to the curve $y = 4x^3 + 15x^2 - 9x - 6$ at the point where $x = -3$.

You must first find the $y$–coordinate of the point by substituting $x = -3$ into $y$ to get:

$y = 4(-3)^3 + 15(-3)^2 - 9(-3) - 6$

$y = -108 + 135 + 27 - 6$

$y = 48$

Then differentiate the equation of the curve:

$$\frac{dy}{dx} = 12x^2 + 30x - 9$$

Substituting $x = -3$ gives:

$$\frac{dy}{dx} = 108 - 90 - 9$$

So:   m = 9

Substituting $x = -3$, $y = 48$ and m = 9 into $y = mx + c$ gives:

$y = 9x + c$

$48 = 9(-3) + c$

$48 = -27 + c$

$75 = c$

Answer: $y = 9x + 75$

### Exercise 7D: *Find the equation of the tangent to the curve:*

1.  $y = 2x^3 - 5x^2 + 3x - 2$ at the point where $x = 2$.

2.  $y = 4x^3 + x^2 - 2x + 1$ at (1, 4).

3.  $y = 4 - 2x + 3x^2 - x^3$ at the point where $x = 3$.

4.  $y = 6 + 3x - 2x^2 + x^3$ at (-2, -16).

5.  $y = 3x^3 - 4x^2 + 2x - 1$ at (-1, -10).

6.  $y = x^3 - 2x^2 + 5x - 4$ at the point where $x = -2$.

7.  $y = \frac{2}{x^2}$ at (-1, 2).

8.  $y = \frac{1}{3}x^3 - \frac{3}{2}x^2 + 4x - 1$ at the point where $x = 3$.

9.  $y = \frac{4}{x}$ where $x = 4$.

10. $y = 2x + \frac{1}{2x}$ where $x = 1$.

## 7.3  Equation of a Normal

A normal is a line which is perpendicular to a tangent at a point. Remember that the product of two perpendicular gradients is –1. To find the equation of a normal to a curve at any point you should:

a.  Find the gradient of the tangent as before.

b.  Find the gradient of the normal.

c.  Substitute this gradient and coordinates of the point into $y = mx + c$.

For example:
-----

6.  Find the equation of the normal to the curve $y = x^3 - x^2 - 5x$ at (2, –6).

$$\frac{dy}{dx} = 3x^2 - 2x - 5$$

Substituting $x = 2$ gives:

$12 - 4 - 5 = 3$

So the gradient of the tangent = 3.

So the gradient of the normal will be $\frac{-1}{3}$.

Substituting $x = 2$, $y = -6$ and m = $\frac{-1}{3}$ into $y = mx + c$ gives:

$$y = \frac{-1}{3}x + c$$

$$-6 = \frac{-1}{3}(2) + c$$

$$-6 = \frac{-2}{3} + c$$

$$-6 + \frac{2}{3} = c$$

$$-5\frac{1}{3} = c$$

Answer: $y = \frac{-1}{3}x - 5\frac{1}{3}$

### Exercise 7E: *Find the equation of the normal to the curve:*

1.  $y = 2x^3 - 3x^2 + 5x$ at (2, 14).

2.  $y = 3x^2 + x - 4$ where $x = 1$.

3.  $y = x^3 - 2x^2 + x - 5$ at (– 2, –23).

4.  $y = 4x^3 - x^2 + 5x - 1$ where $x = -1$.

5.  $y = 7 - 2x + 3x^2 - x^3$ at the point where $x = 2$.

6.  $y = 10 + 3x - x^2 - 4x^3$ at (1, 8).

7.  $y = \frac{3}{x^2}$ where $x = 2$.

8.  $y = \frac{4}{3}x^3 - \frac{1}{2}x^2 + x - 2$ at $(-1, \frac{-29}{6})$.

9.  $y = \frac{2}{x}$ where $x = -2$.

10. $y = 4x^2 - \frac{1}{4x}$ where $x = -1$.

Further examples:

7. (a) Find the equation of the tangent to the curve $y = 2x^2 - 4x - 15$ at $(-1, -9)$.
   (b) Find where the tangent crosses the (i) $y$-axis (ii) $x$-axis.

(a)
$$\frac{dy}{dx} = 4x - 4$$
Substituting $x = -1$ gives:
$$\frac{dy}{dx} = -4 - 4$$
$$= -8$$
So:  m = -8

Substituting $x = -1$, $y = -9$ and m = -8 into $y = mx + c$ gives:
$$y = -8x + c$$
$$-9 = -8(-1) + c$$
$$-9 = 8 + c$$
$$-17 = c$$
Answer:  $y = -8x - 17$

(b) (i) The tangent will cross the $y$-axis when $x = 0$. So, substituting $x = 0$ into $y = -8x - 17$ gives:
$$y = -17$$
Answer: $(0, -17)$

(ii) The tangent will cross the $x$-axis when $y = 0$. So, substituting $y = 0$ into $y = -8x - 17$ gives:
$$0 = -8x - 17$$
$$8x = -17$$
$$x = \frac{-17}{8}$$
Answer: $(\frac{-17}{8}, 0)$

8. (a) Find the equation of the normal to the curve $y = 7 - 4x - x^2$ at $(2, -5)$.
   (b) Find where the normal meets the straight line $8y + 3x = 2$.

(a)
$$\frac{dy}{dx} = -4 - 2x$$
Substituting $x = 2$ gives:
$$\frac{dy}{dx} = -4 - 4$$
$$= -8$$
So the gradient of the tangent = -8.

Therefore the gradient of the normal will be $\frac{1}{8}$.

Substituting $x = 2$, $y = -5$ and m = $\frac{1}{8}$ into $y = mx + c$ gives:

$$y = \frac{1}{8}x + c$$
$$-5 = \frac{1}{8}(2) + c$$
$$-5 - \frac{1}{4} = c$$
$$-5\frac{1}{4} = c$$
Answer:  $y = \frac{1}{8}x - 5\frac{1}{4}$

(b) You can find where the normal
$y = \frac{1}{8}x - 5\frac{1}{4}$ meets the line $8y + 3x = 2$ by solving these simultaneous equations.

$$\left[ y = \frac{1}{8}x - 5\frac{1}{4} \right] \times 8 \text{ gives:}$$
$$8y = x - 42$$

You can rewrite this as $8y - x = -42$ and then solve by subtraction:
$$\begin{array}{r} 8y - \phantom{3}x = -42 \\ -\phantom{(}8y + 3x = \phantom{-}2 \\ \hline -4x = -44 \\ x = 11 \end{array}$$

You can substitute $x = 11$ into either equation to get $y$:

$$y = \frac{1}{8}x - 5\frac{1}{4}$$
$$y = \frac{1}{8}(11) - 5\frac{1}{4}$$
$$y = 1\frac{3}{8} - 5\frac{1}{4}$$
$$y = -3\frac{7}{8}$$
Answer: $(11, -3\frac{7}{8})$

## Exercise 7F

1. (a) Find the equation of the tangent to the curve $y = 4x^2 - 3x + 5$ at $(2, 15)$.
   (b) Find where the tangent crosses the (i) $y$-axis (ii) $x$-axis.

2. (a) Find the equation of the normal to the curve $y = 4 + 3x + 2x^2$ at $(-3, 13)$.
   (b) Find where the normal crosses the (i) $y$-axis (ii) $x$-axis.

3. (a) Find the equation of the tangent to the curve $y = x^3 + 2x^2 - 5x + 3$ at $(-1, 9)$.
   (b) Find where the tangent meets the straight line $y + 4x = 9$.

## Exercise 7F...

4.  (a)  Find the equation of the normal to the curve $y = 7 - x + x^2 - x^3$ at (2, 1).
    (b)  Find where the normal meets the straight line $3y + x = 9$.

5.  (a)  Find the equation of the tangent to the curve $y = \frac{2}{3}x^3 - \frac{1}{2}x^2 + x$ where $x = -1$.
    (b)  Find where the tangent crosses the $y$-axis.

6.  (a)  Find the equation of the normal to the curve $y = (3x + 2)^2$ at (−1, 1).
    (b)  Find where the normal (i) crosses the $x$-axis (ii) meets the straight line $4y + x = 8$.

7.  (a)  Find the equation of the tangent to the curve $y = 2x^3 + 3x^2 - x + 5$ at (−2, 3).
    (b)  Find where the tangent (i) crosses the $x$-axis (ii) meets the straight line $y = 3x + 1$.

8.  (a)  Find the equation of the normal to the curve $y = 5x - x^2 + 4$ at (−1, −2).
    (b)  Find where the normal (i) crosses the $y$-axis (ii) meets the straight line $y = x - 9$.

9.  (a)  Find the equation of the tangent to the curve $y = (x - 4)(2x - 1)$ at (2, −6).
    (b)  Find where the tangent (i) crosses the $y$-axis (ii) meets the straight line $y + 2x = 1$.

10. (a)  Find the equation of the normal to the curve $y = \frac{5}{2x^2}$ where $x = -1$
    (b)  Find where the normal (i) crosses the $x$-axis (ii) meets the straight line $2y + x = 7$.

You can use a similar technique to find where a tangent is parallel to a straight line. The rules are as follows:

a.  Find the gradient of the tangent (by differentiating).

b.  Find the gradient of the straight line (rearranging equation into $y = mx + c$).

c.  Put the two expressions equal to each other, and solve for $x$.

d.  Substitute the value for $x$ into the equation of the curve to find the $y$ coordinate.

For example:

9.  Find where the tangent to the curve $y = 5x^2 - 6x + 1$ is parallel to the straight line $x + y = 4$.

The gradient of the tangent is:
$$\frac{dy}{dx} = 10x - 6$$
Rearranging the equation of the straight line gives:
$$x + y = 4$$
$$y = -x + 4$$
So the gradient of the straight line is −1. The gradients are equal, so:
$$10x - 6 = -1$$
$$10x = -1 + 6$$
$$10x = 5$$
$$x = \frac{5}{10} = \frac{1}{2}$$
Substituting the value for $x$ into the equation of the curve gives:
$$y = 5x^2 - 6x + 1$$
$$y = 5(\frac{1}{2})^2 - 6(\frac{1}{2}) + 1$$
$$y = \frac{5}{4} - 3 + 1$$
$$y = \frac{-3}{4}$$
Answer  $(\frac{1}{2}, \frac{-3}{4})$.

10. Find where the tangent to the curve $y = 5x - x^2 + 4$ is perpendicular to the straight line joining the points (−2, 3) and (3, 2).

In this case, we need to:
• Find the gradient of the tangent (by differentiating).
• Find the gradient of the straight line (using the coordinate formula).
• Find the gradient of the perpendicular to the straight line.

The gradient of the tangent is:
$$\frac{dy}{dx} = 5 - 2x$$

The gradient of a straight line is given by $\frac{y_2 - y_1}{x_2 - x_1}$.

Gradient $= \frac{2 - 3}{3 - (-2)} = \frac{-1}{5}$

So the gradient of the perpendicular = 5.

Putting these equal gives:
$$5 - 2x = 5$$
$$-2x = 0$$
$$x = 0$$

Substituting the value for $x$ into the equation of the curve gives:

$$y = 5x - x^2 + 4$$
$$y = 5(0) - (0)^2 + 4$$
$$y = 4$$

Answer $= (0, 4)$

-------------------------------------------------

11. Find the coordinates of the points where the tangent to the curve $y = 4x^3 - 15x^2 - 60x + 2$ is parallel to the straight line $y = 4 + 12x$.

The gradient of the tangent is:

$$\frac{dy}{dx} = 12x^2 - 30x - 60$$

Rearranging the equation of the straight line

$$y = 4 + 12x$$

gives:

$$y = 12x + 4$$

So the gradient of the straight line is 12. Putting these equal gives:

$$12x^2 - 30x - 60 = 12$$
$$12x^2 - 30x - 72 = 0$$

Dividing by 6 gives:

$$2x^2 - 5x - 12 = 0$$
$$(2x + 3)(x - 4) = 0$$

So:

$$x = \frac{-3}{2} \text{ or } 4$$

Substituting into the equation of the curve

where $x = \frac{-3}{2}$:

$$y = 4x^3 - 15x^2 - 60x + 2$$

$$y = 4(\frac{-3}{2})^3 - 15(\frac{-3}{2})^2 - 60(\frac{-3}{2}) + 2$$

$$y = -13\frac{1}{2} - 33\frac{3}{4} + 90 + 2$$

$$y = 44\frac{3}{4}$$

where $x = 4$:

$$y = 4x^3 - 15x^2 - 60x + 2$$
$$y = 4(4)^3 - 15(4)^2 - 60(4) + 2$$
$$y = -222$$

Answer: $(\frac{-3}{2}, 44\frac{3}{4})$ and $(4, -222)$

-------------------------------------------------

1. Find where the tangent to the curve $y = 2x^2 - 3x + 2$ is parallel to the straight line $y = 5x - 1$.

2. Find where the tangent to the curve $y = 7 + 2x - 3x^2$ is perpendicular to the straight line $4y - x = 5$.

3. Find where the tangent to the curve $y = x^3 - 2x^2 + x - 4$ is parallel to the $x$-axis.

4. Find where the tangent to the curve $y = 7 - 2x + 2\frac{1}{2}x^2 - 2x^3$ is parallel to the straight line $y + 3x = 4$.

5. Find where the tangent to the curve $y = \frac{4}{x}$ is perpendicular to the straight line $9y = 6 + 4x$.

6. Find where the tangent to the curve $y = 4 - 6x + x^2$ is perpendicular to the straight line $2y + x = 5$.

7. Find where the tangent to the curve $y = (x - 3)(3x + 1)$ is parallel to the straight line $y = 5 + x$.

8. Find where the tangent to the curve $y = 4x + \frac{4}{x}$ is perpendicular to the straight line $5y = x - 2$.

9. Find where the tangent to the curve $y = x^3 - 4x^2 + 2x - 1$ is parallel to the straight line $y + 2x = 1$.

10. Find where the tangent to the curve $y = \frac{2}{3}x^3 - \frac{9}{2}x^2 - 3x + 1$ is perpendicular to the straight line $4y + 2x = 7$.

## 8.1 Turning Points

A curve can have two types of turning point, a point where the gradient of a curve changes from either:

**(a)** positive to 0 to negative, as shown below.

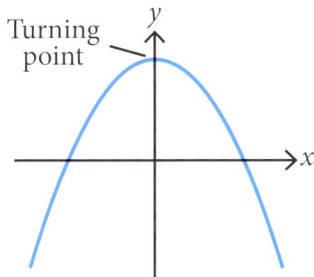

This is called a **maximum** turning point.

**(b)** negative to 0 to positive, as shown below.

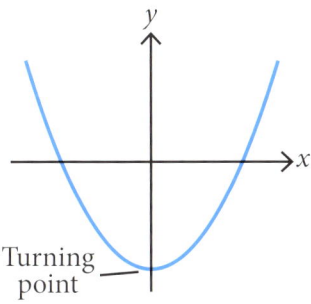

This is called a **minimum** turning point.

The **gradient of the curve is 0** at both types of turning point. You can therefore find the turning point(s) of a curve by following these rules:

a. Differentiate to find $\frac{dy}{dx}$.

b. Put $\frac{dy}{dx} = 0$ and solve to find $x$.

c. Substitute $x$ into $y$ to find the $y$ coordinate, if necessary.

You also need to be able to distinguish between maximum and minimum turning points. You can do this either by finding the gradients before and after the turning point, or by differentiating $\frac{dy}{dx}$ again to get $\frac{d^2y}{dx^2}$.

$\frac{d^2y}{dx^2}$ measures the **rate of change** of the gradient $\frac{dy}{dx}$ as $x$ changes.

For a maximum turning point the gradient changes from positive to 0 to negative, i.e. it is getting smaller.

So if $\frac{d^2y}{dx^2}$ is **negative** the turning point will be a **maximum**.

For a minimum turning point the gradient changes from negative to 0 to positive, i.e. it is getting bigger.

So if $\frac{d^2y}{dx^2}$ is **positive** the turning point will be a **minimum**.

When you are asked to say what type of turning point there is, you must justify your answer by using either of the above methods.

## 8.2 Quadratic Curves

We can now apply this theory to quadratic curves. For example, find the turning points of the following curves and say what type each turning point is.

1.  $y = 2x^2 - 7x + 3$

    First, differentiate: $\frac{dy}{dx} = 4x - 7$

    Now set this equal to 0 to find the $x$-coordinate of the turning point:
    $$4x - 7 = 0$$
    $$4x = 7$$
    $$x = 1.75$$

    Substitute this back into the original equation to find the $y$-coordinate:
    $$y = 2(1.75)^2 - 7(1.75) + 3$$
    $$y = -3.125$$

    So the turning point is at $(1.75, -3.125)$. You must now say what type it is and justify this. Either:

    (a)  Substitute $x = 1$ into $\frac{dy}{dx}$ to get $4 - 7 = -3$
        and $x = 2$ into $\frac{dy}{dx}$ to get $8 - 7 = 1$
        The gradient is getting bigger, so it must be a minimum turning point.

    (b)  Or find $\frac{d^2y}{dx^2} = 4$
        It must be a minimum because $\frac{d^2y}{dx^2}$ is positive.

2.  $y = 7 - 8x - x^2$

    First, differentiate: $\frac{dy}{dx} = -8 - 2x$

    Now set this equal to 0 to find the $x$-coordinate of the turning point:
    $$-8 - 2x = 0$$
    $$-2x = 8$$
    $$x = -4$$

Substitute this back into the original equation to find the $y$-coordinate:

$$y = 7 - 8(-4) - (-4)^2$$
$$y = 23$$

So the turning point is at $(-4, 23)$. You must now say what type it is and justify this. Either:

(a)  Substitute $x = -5$ into $\dfrac{dy}{dx}$ to get $-8 + 10 = 2$

And $x = 0$ into $\dfrac{dy}{dx}$ to get $-8 - 0 = -8$

The gradient is getting smaller, so it must be a maximum turning point.

(b)  Or find $\dfrac{d^2y}{dx^2} = -2$

It must be a maximum because $\dfrac{d^2y}{dx^2}$ is negative.

3.  $y = (x + 4)(2x - 1)$

You must first work out the brackets to get:

$$y = x(2x - 1) + 4(2x - 1)$$
$$y = 2x^2 - 1x + 8x - 4$$
$$y = 2x^2 + 7x - 4$$

Then differentiate: $\dfrac{dy}{dx} = 4x + 7$

Now set this equal to 0 to find the $x$-coordinate of the turning point:

$$4x + 7 = 0$$
$$4x = -7$$
$$x = -1.75$$

Substitute this back into the original equation to find the $y$-coordinate:

$$y = 2(-1.75)^2 + 7(-1.75) - 4$$
$$y = -10.125$$

So the turning point is at $(-1.75, -10.125)$. You must now say what type it is and justify this. Either:

(a)  Substitute $x = -2$ into $\dfrac{dy}{dx}$ to get $-8 + 7 = -1$

And $x = 0$ into $\dfrac{dy}{dx}$ to get $0 + 7 = 7$

The gradient is getting bigger, so it must be a minimum turning point.

(b)  Or find $\dfrac{d^2y}{dx^2} = 4$.

It must be a minimum because $\dfrac{d^2y}{dx^2}$ is positive.

*Find the turning points of the following curves and say what type each is.*

1.  $y = 3x^2 - 12x + 1$

2.  $y = x^2 + 4x - 7$

3.  $y = 9 + 6x - x^2$

4.  $y = x^2 - 5x - 3$

5.  $y = 3 - 8x - 2x^2$

6.  $y = 1 + 7x - x^2$

7.  $y = 4x^2 + 2x - 5$

8.  $y = 5 - x - x^2$

9.  $y = x^2 - 6x - 7$

10. $y = 8 - 4x - x^2$

## 8.3  Cubic Curves

A cubic curve has **two** turning points: a maximum and a minimum. You can find the turning points of a cubic curve by a similar method. For example, find the turning points of the following curves, and say what type each turning point is:

4.  $y = 4x^3 + 2x^2 - 6x + 4$

First differentiate: $\dfrac{dy}{dx} = 12x^2 + 4x - 6$

Now set this equal to 0 to find the $x$-coordinates of the turning points:

$12x^2 + 4x - 6 = 0$

Solve using the quadratic formula $\dfrac{-b \pm \sqrt{b^2 - 4ac}}{2a}$:

where  $a = 12, b = 4, c = -6$

So:  $x = \dfrac{-4 \pm \sqrt{4^2 - (4 \times 12 \times -6)}}{2 \times 12}$

$x = \dfrac{-4 \pm \sqrt{304}}{24}$

$x = \dfrac{-4 + \sqrt{304}}{24}$ or $\dfrac{-4 - \sqrt{304}}{24}$

So  $x = 0.560$ or $-0.893$ to 3 decimal places.

Substitute these back into the original equation to find the $y$-coordinates:

$x = 0.560$   $y = 4(0.560)^3 + 2(0.560)^2 - 6(0.560) + 4$
$\qquad\qquad y = 1.970$

$x = -0.893$   $y = 4(-0.893)^3 + 2(-0.893)^2 - 6(-0.893) + 4$
$\qquad\qquad y = 8.104$

So the turning points are at $(0.560, 1.970)$ and $(-0.893, 8.104)$. Now show what type each turning point is by getting $\dfrac{d^2y}{dx^2}$.

Since:  $\dfrac{dy}{dx} = 12x^2 + 4x - 6$

So:  $\dfrac{d^2y}{dx^2} = 24x + 4$

When $x = 0.560$, $\frac{d^2y}{dx^2} = 24(0.560) + 4 = 17.44$.

This is positive, and so it is a minimum.

When $x = -0.893$, $\frac{d^2y}{dx^2} = 24(-0.893) + 4 = -17.432$.

This is negative, so it is a maximum.

5. $y = 3 + 2x - x^2 - 2x^3$

Rearrange: $\quad\quad y = -2x^3 - x^2 + 2x + 3$

Differentiate: $\quad\quad \frac{dy}{dx} = -6x^2 - 2x + 2$

Now set this equal to 0 to find the $x$-coordinates of the turning points:

$-6x^2 - 2x + 2 = 0$

Solve using the quadratic formula $\frac{-b \pm \sqrt{b^2 - 4ac}}{2a}$:

where $\quad$ a = $-6$, b = $-2$, c = 2

So: $\quad x = \frac{2 \pm \sqrt{(-2)^2 - (4 \times -6 \times 2)}}{2 \times -6}$

$\quad\quad x = \frac{2 \pm \sqrt{52}}{-12}$

$\quad\quad x = \frac{2 + \sqrt{52}}{-12}$ $\quad$ or $\quad \frac{2 - \sqrt{52}}{-12}$

So: $\quad x = -0.768$ or $0.434$ to 3 decimal places.

Substitute these back into the original equation to find the $y$-coordinates:

$x = -0.768$ $\quad y = 3 + 2x - x^2 - 2x^3$

$\quad\quad\quad\quad\quad y = 3 + 2(-0.768) - (-0.768)^2 - 2(-0.768)^3$

$\quad\quad\quad\quad\quad y = 1.780$

$x = 0.434$ $\quad y = 3 + 2(0.434) - (0.434)^2 - 2(0.434)^3$

$\quad\quad\quad\quad\quad y = 3.516$

So the turning points are at $(-0.768, 1.780)$ and $(0.434, 3.516)$. Now show what type each turning point is by getting $\frac{d^2y}{dx^2}$.

Since: $\quad \frac{dy}{dx} = -6x^2 - 2x + 2$

So: $\quad \frac{d^2y}{dx^2} = -12x - 2$

When $x = -0.768$, $\frac{d^2y}{dx^2} = -12(-0.768) - 2 = 7.216$.

This is positive, so it is a minimum.

When $x = 0.434$ $\frac{d^2y}{dx^2} = -12(0.434) - 2 = -7.208$.

This is negative, so it is a maximum.

6. $y = x(x + 4)(2x - 1)$

First expand the brackets to get:

$y = 2x^3 + 7x^2 - 4x$

Differentiate: $\frac{dy}{dx} = 6x^2 + 14x - 4$

Now set this equal to 0 to find the $x$-coordinates of the turning points:

$6x^2 + 14x - 4 = 0$

Solve using the quadratic formula $\frac{-b \pm \sqrt{b^2 - 4ac}}{2a}$:

where $\quad$ a = 6, b = 14, c = $-4$

So: $\quad x = \frac{-14 \pm \sqrt{(14)^2 - (4 \times 6 \times -4)}}{2 \times 6}$

$\quad\quad x = \frac{-14 \pm \sqrt{292}}{12}$

$\quad\quad x = \frac{-14 + \sqrt{292}}{12}$ $\quad$ or $\quad \frac{-14 - \sqrt{292}}{12}$

So: $\quad x = 0.257$ or $-2.591$ to 3 decimal places.

Substitute these back into the original equation to find the $y$-coordinates:

$x = 0.257$ $\quad y = x(x + 4)(2x - 1)$

$\quad\quad\quad\quad\quad y = 0.257(0.257 + 4)(2 \times 0.257 - 1)$

$\quad\quad\quad\quad\quad y = -0.532$

$x = -2.591$ $\quad y = -2.591(-2.591 + 4)(2 \times -2.591 - 1)$

$\quad\quad\quad\quad\quad y = 22.569$

So the turning points are at $(0.257, -0.532)$ and $(-2.591, 22.569)$. Now show what type each turning point is by getting $\frac{d^2y}{dx^2}$.

Since: $\quad \frac{dy}{dx} = 6x^2 + 14x - 4$

So: $\quad \frac{d^2y}{dx^2} = 12x + 14$

When $x = 0.257$ $\frac{d^2y}{dx^2} = 12(0.257) + 14 = 17.084$.

This is positive, so it is a minimum.

When $x = -2.591$ $\frac{d^2y}{dx^2} = 12(-2.591) + 14 = -17.092$.

This is negative, so it is a maximum.

**Exercise 8B:** *Find the turning points of the following curves and say what type each is.*

1. $y = 2x^3 + 3x^2 - 36x + 4$

2. $y = 2x^3 - 9x^2 - 24x + 3$

3. $y = x^3 - 9x^2 + 24x - 7$

## Exercise 8B...

4. $y = x^3 + 4x^2 - 3x - 2$

5. $y = 4x^3 - 3x + 2$

6. $y = x^3 - 5x^2 + 8x + 2$

7. $y = 4x^3 - 23x^2 + 30x - 5$

8. $y = x^3 + 5x^2 - 8x$

9. $y = 4x^3 - x^2 - 30x + 3$

10. $y = x^3 + 3x^2 - 72x - 8$

11. $y = 5 + 45x - 3x^2 - x^3$

12. $y = 3 - 12x - 9x^2 - 2x^3$

13. $y = 24 - 12x + 15x^2 - 4x^3$

## 8.4  Curve Sketching – Quadratic Curves

To sketch a quadratic curve, you need to find three points:

a.  Find where the curve crosses the $y$-axis by putting $x = 0$;

b.  Find where the curve crosses the $x$-axis by putting $y = 0$;

c.  Find the turning point.

Then mark these points on a grid, and draw a smooth curve through these points. For example, sketch the following:

.....................................................................................

7.  $y = 3x^2 + 22x - 16$

The curve crosses the $y$-axis when $x = 0$.
So:     $y = 0 + 0 - 16$
          $= -16$

The curve crosses the $x$-axis when $y = 0$.
So:    $3x^2 + 22x - 16 = 0$
        $(3x - 2)(x + 8) = 0$
So either:      $3x - 2 = 0$
                    $3x = 2$
                    $x = \dfrac{2}{3}$
or:           $x + 8 = 0$
                  $x = -8$

The turning point is when $\dfrac{dy}{dx} = 0$.
So:                 $y = 3x^2 + 22x - 16$

Hence:          $\dfrac{dy}{dx} = 6x + 22 = 0$
                      $6x = -22$
                      $x = \dfrac{-22}{6} = \dfrac{-11}{3}$ (or $-3\tfrac{2}{3}$)

You should work with fractions or mixed numbers rather than decimals.

You now find the $y$-coordinate of the turning point by substituting $x = \dfrac{-11}{3}$ into the equation for $y$:

$$y = 3x^2 + 22x - 16$$

$$y = 3(\tfrac{-11}{3})^2 + 22(\tfrac{-11}{3}) - 16$$

$$y = \frac{121}{3} - \frac{242}{3} - 16 = -56\tfrac{1}{3}$$

So the turning point is at $(-3\tfrac{2}{3}, -56\tfrac{1}{3})$.

Now work out what type of turning point it is by getting $\dfrac{d^2y}{dx^2}$.

Since:   $\dfrac{dy}{dx} = 6x + 22$

So:     $\dfrac{d^2y}{dx^2} = 6$

This is positive, so it is a minimum.

You can now sketch the curve:

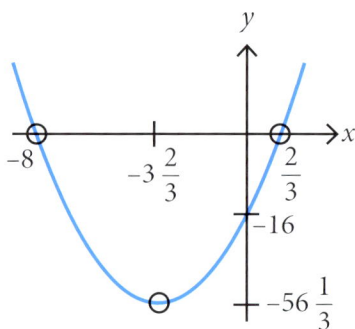

.....................................................................................

8.  $y = 9 - 4x^2$

The curve crosses the $y$-axis when $x = 0$.
So:       $y = 9 - 0$
            $= 9$

The curve crosses the $x$-axis when $y = 0$.
So:           $9 - 4x^2 = 0$
        $(3 - 2x)(3 + 2x) = 0$
So either:     $3 - 2x = 0$
                  $-2x = -3$
                  $x = \dfrac{3}{2}$
or:          $3 + 2x = 0$
                 $2x = -3$
                 $x = -\dfrac{3}{2}$

The turning point is when $\dfrac{dy}{dx} = 0$.

So:  $y = 9 - 4x^2$

Hence: $\frac{dy}{dx} = -8x = 0$

$x = 0$

You already know the value of $y$ when $x = 0$ (i.e. 9). So the turning point is at (0, 9). Now work out what type of turning point it is by getting $\frac{d^2y}{dx^2}$.

$\frac{dy}{dx} = -8x$

$\frac{d^2y}{dx^2} = -8$

This is negative, so it is a maximum.

You can now sketch the curve:

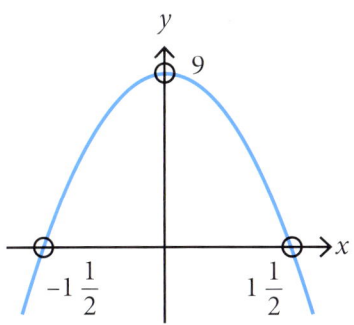

**Exercise 8C**: *Sketch the following curves.*

1. $y = x^2 - 6x + 8$
2. $y = 5 - 4x - x^2$
3. $y = 2x^2 + 5x - 3$
4. $y = 3x^2 - 10x - 8$
5. $y = 1 - 16x^2$
6. $y = 3x^2 - 12x$
7. $y = 2 - x - 6x^2$
8. $y = x^2 + 9x + 18$
9. $y = 8x - 12x^2$
10. $y = 10 - 13x - 3x^2$

## 8.5  Curve Sketching – Cubic Curves

The rules for sketching cubic curves are as follows:

a.  Find where the curve crosses the $x$-axis by putting $y = 0$. Note that $x$ may be a common factor, or the factors may be given.

b.  Find the turning points.

c.  Distinguish between the turning points, clearly showing your method.

d.  Mark these points on a grid.

e.  Draw a smooth curve through these points.

For example:

9.  Sketch the curve $y = 4x^3 + 7x^2 - 10x$ giving the coordinates of the points where it crosses the $x$-axis correct to 2 decimal places where appropriate.

The curve crosses the $x$-axis when $y = 0$.

So:  $4x^3 + 7x^2 - 10x = 0$

$x(4x^2 + 7x - 10) = 0$

So either $x = 0$ or $4x^2 + 7x - 10 = 0$.

You need to use the quadratic formula $\dfrac{-b \pm \sqrt{b^2 - 4ac}}{2a}$ to solve $4x^2 + 7x - 10 = 0$.

where   $a = 4$, $b = 7$, $c = -10$

So:  $x = \dfrac{-7 \pm \sqrt{(7)^2 - (4 \times 4 \times -10)}}{2 \times 4}$

$x = \dfrac{-7 \pm \sqrt{209}}{8}$

$x = \dfrac{-7 + \sqrt{209}}{8}$ or $\dfrac{-7 - \sqrt{209}}{8}$

So:  $x = 0.93$ or $-2.68$, to 2 decimal places.

Hence the curve crosses the $x$-axis at (0, 0) (0.93, 0) and (−2.68, 0).

The turning points are when $\frac{dy}{dx} = 0$.

$y = 4x^3 + 7x^2 - 10x$

$\frac{dy}{dx} = 12x^2 + 14x - 10 = 0$

Dividing through by 2 gives:

$6x^2 + 7x - 5 = 0$

$(2x - 1)(3x + 5) = 0$

So either:   $2x - 1 = 0$

$2x = 1$

$x = \dfrac{1}{2}$

or:   $3x + 5 = 0$

$3x = -5$

$x = \dfrac{-5}{3}$

You now find $y$ by substituting $x = \dfrac{1}{2}$ or $\dfrac{-5}{3}$ into the equation for $y$.

$y = 4x^3 + 7x^2 - 10x$

$y = 4(\tfrac{1}{2})^3 + 7(\tfrac{1}{2})^2 - 10(\tfrac{1}{2})$

$y = \dfrac{1}{2} + \dfrac{7}{4} - 5 = -2\dfrac{3}{4}$

This turning point is at $(\tfrac{1}{2}, -2\tfrac{3}{4})$.

$$y = 4x^3 + 7x^2 - 10x$$

$$y = 4(\tfrac{-5}{3})^3 + 7(\tfrac{-5}{3})^2 - 10(\tfrac{-5}{3})$$

$$y = \frac{-500}{27} + \frac{175}{9} + \frac{50}{3} = 17\frac{16}{27}$$

This turning point is at $(\tfrac{-5}{3}, 17\tfrac{16}{27})$. Now show what type each turning point is by getting $\frac{d^2y}{dx^2}$.

Since: $\frac{dy}{dx} = 12x^2 + 14x - 10$

So: $\frac{d^2y}{dx^2} = 24x + 14$

When $x = \frac{1}{2}$: $\frac{d^2y}{dx^2} = 12 + 14 = 26$. This is positive, so it is a minimum.

When $x = \frac{-5}{3}$: $\frac{d^2y}{dx^2} = -40 + 14 = -26$. This is negative, so it is a maximum.

You can now sketch the curve:

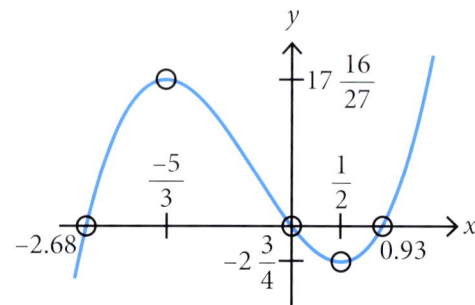

10. Sketch the curve $y = x^3 - 9x^2 + 24x$

The curve crosses the $x$-axis when $y = 0$.
So: $x^3 - 9x^2 + 24x = 0$
$x(x^2 - 9x + 24) = 0$
So either $x = 0$ or $x^2 - 9x + 24 = 0$.

You need to use the quadratic formula $\dfrac{-b \pm \sqrt{b^2 - 4ac}}{2a}$ to solve $x^2 - 9x + 24 = 0$.

where: $a = 1, b = -9, c = 24$

So: $x = \dfrac{9 \pm \sqrt{(-9)^2 - (4 \times 1 \times 24)}}{2 \times 1}$

$x = \dfrac{9 \pm \sqrt{-15}}{2}$

However, $\sqrt{-15}$ does not exist. Therefore this curve only crosses the $x$-axis at $(0, 0)$.

The turning points are when $\frac{dy}{dx} = 0$.

$y = x^3 - 9x^2 + 24x$

$\frac{dy}{dx} = 3x^2 - 18x + 24 = 0$

Dividing through by 3 gives:
$$x^2 - 6x + 8 = 0$$
$$(x - 2)(x - 4) = 0$$
So either: $x - 2 = 0$
$x = 2$
or: $x - 4 = 0$
$x = 4$

You now find $y$ by substituting $x = 2$ or $4$ into the equation for $y$.
$$y = x^3 - 9x^2 + 24x$$
$$y = (2)^3 - 9(2)^2 + 24(2)$$
$$y = 8 - 36 + 48 = 20$$

This turning point is at $(2, 20)$.
$$y = x^3 - 9x^2 + 24x$$
$$y = (4)^3 - 9(4)^2 + 24(4)$$
$$y = 64 - 144 + 96 = 16$$

This turning point is at $(4, 16)$.

Now work out what type each turning point is by getting $\frac{d^2y}{dx^2}$.

Since: $\frac{dy}{dx} = 3x^2 - 18x + 24$

So: $\frac{d^2y}{dx^2} = 6x - 18$

When $x = 2$: $\frac{d^2y}{dx^2} = 12 - 18 = -6$. This is negative, so it is a maximum.

When $x = 4$: $\frac{d^2y}{dx^2} = 24 - 18 = 6$. This is positive, so it is a minimum.

You can now sketch the curve:

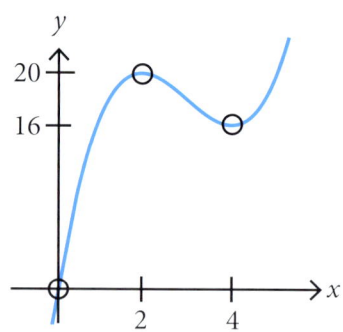

11. Sketch the curve $y = (x - 1)(x + 2)(x + 3)$

The curve crosses the $y$-axis when $x = 0$.
ie $y = (0 - 1)(0 + 2)(0 + 3) = -6$

The curve crosses the $x$-axis when $y = 0$.
So: $(x - 1)(x + 2)(x + 3) = 0$
So $x = 1$ or $-2$ or $-3$.

To find the turning points we need to expand the brackets first:

First expand $(x + 2)(x + 3) = x^2 + 5x + 6$

Then expand $(x - 1)(x^2 + 5x + 6) = x^3 + 4x^2 + x - 6$

So: $\qquad y = x^3 + 4x^2 + x - 6$

And: $\quad \dfrac{dy}{dx} = 3x^2 + 8x + 1$

Since $\dfrac{dy}{dx} = 0$ at a turning point, we can solve this using the quadratic formula to get $x = \dfrac{-8 \pm \sqrt{52}}{6}$ giving $x = -0.13$ or $-2.54$.

Substituting into $y$ gives $y = -6.06$ or $0.88$.

So the turning points are $(-0.13, -6.06)$ and $(-2.54, 0.88)$.

Now work out what type each turning point is by getting $\dfrac{d^2y}{dx^2}$.

$$\dfrac{d^2y}{dx^2} = 6x + 8$$

When $x = -0.13$: $\quad \dfrac{d^2y}{dx^2} = 7.22$. This is positive, so it is a minimum.

When $x = -2.54$: $\quad \dfrac{d^2y}{dx^2} = -7.24$. This is negative, so it is a maximum.

You can now sketch the curve:

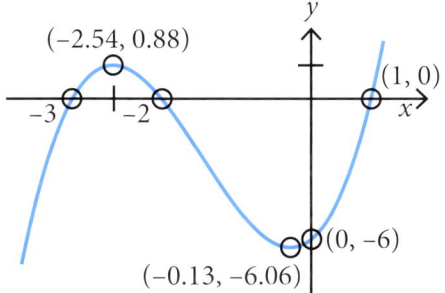

### Exercise 8D: *Sketch the following curves, giving the coordinates of the point(s) where each crosses the x-axis, correct to 2 decimal places where appropriate.*

1. $y = x^3 - 3x^2 - 24x$

2. $y = 4x^3 - 21x^2 - 24x$

3. $y = 3x^3 - x$

4. $y = 2x^3 - 3x^2 - 120x$

5. $y = x^3 + 6x^2 - 36x$

6. $y = x^3 - 2x^2$

7. $y = 2x^3 - 21x^2 + 60x$

8. $y = x(x - 3)(x + 8)$

9. $y = 2x(2x - 1)(x + 3)$

10. $y = 3x(x - 2)(2x + 5)$

11. $y = (x - 4)(x - 1)(x + 2)$

12. $y = (x + 3)(x + 1)(2x - 5)$

## 8.6 Optimising Problems

You can use differentiation to solve optimising problems. For example:

12. The sum of two numbers is 12. Find the minimum value of the sum of their squares.

Call the numbers $x$ and $y$. So:
$$x + y = 12$$

The sum of their squares, S, is given by:
$$S = x^2 + y^2$$

Then replace one of the variables in terms of the other. $\qquad y = 12 - x$

This gives: $\qquad S = x^2 + (12 - x)^2$
$$= x^2 + x^2 - 24x + 144$$
$$= 2x^2 - 24x + 144$$

Then find the minimum value by first differentiating S with respect to $x$:
$$S = 2x^2 - 24x + 144$$
$$\dfrac{dS}{dx} = 4x - 24$$

Then equate this to 0:
$$4x - 24 = 0$$
$$4x = 24$$
$$x = 6$$

You should prove that this gives a minimum value by finding $\dfrac{d^2S}{dx^2}$:
$$\dfrac{d^2S}{dx^2} = 4 \text{ and so it is a minimum}$$

You can now find the value of $y$:
$$y = 12 - x$$
So $\qquad y = 12 - 6$
$$y = 6$$

You can now find the minimum value of the sum of their squares:
$$S = x^2 + y^2$$
$$S = 6^2 + 6^2$$
$$S = 36 + 36$$
$$S = 72$$

## Exercise 8E

1. The difference of two numbers $x$ and $y$ is 8 where $x$ is greater than $y$. Find the minimum value of $4x^2 - 3y^2$ proving that it is a minimum.

2. A farmer wants to enclose a rectangular area using a hedge hedge as one side and fencing for the other three sides, as shown below. The total length of the fencing is 60 m. Find:

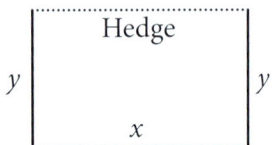

The perimeter has to be 60 m. Find:
   (a) the values of $x$ and $y$ that give a maximum area, proving that it is a maximum.
   (b) the maximum possible area.

3. The number of monthly visitors, N, to a leisure complex is modelled by $N = 3140 + 160x - 25x^2$ where $x$ km is the distance of the centre from the nearest town. The manager wants to reposition the centre so that the total number of visitors is a maximum. Find how far from the town the centre should now be positioned, proving that this gives the maximum number.

4. $x$ pencils cost $y$ p each. $y$ pens cost $2x$ p each. The total number of pencils and pens must be 20. Find:
   (a) the values of $x$ and $y$ for which the total cost will be a maximum, proving that it is a maximum.
   (b) the maximum possible cost.

5. A farmer wants to enclose an area in the shape of a trapezium using a hedge as one side and fencing for the other three sides, as shown below.

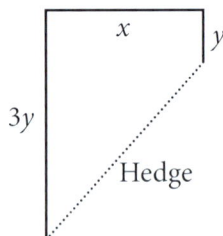

The area has to be 288 m². Find:
   (a) the values of $x$ and $y$ that give a minimum length of fencing, proving that it is a minimum.
   (b) the minimum possible length of fencing.

## Exercise 8E...

6. A farmer wants to enclose a rectangular area using a hedge as one side and fencing for the other three sides, as shown below.

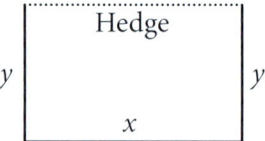

The area has to be 338 m². Find:
   (a) the values of $x$ and $y$ that give a minimum length of fencing, proving that it is a minimum.
   (b) the minimum possible length of fencing.

7. The perimeter of the L-shape below has to be 48 cm.

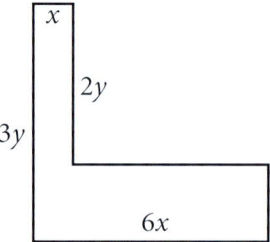

Find:
   (a) the values of $x$ and $y$ that give a maximum area, proving that it is a maximum.
   (b) the maximum possible area.

8. The share price, £P, of a company since 2010 can be modelled by $P = 9 + 15t - 3t^2$ where $t$ is the time in years since 2010. Work out the maximum share price since 2010, proving this is the maximum.

9. The area of tarmac needed, A m², to surround a square pool of length $x$ metres can be modelled by $A = 3x + \dfrac{432}{x} + 6$. Work out the value of $x$ which will minimise the area, proving it is the minimum.

10. Fred invests £1000 and keeps it for 5 years. The value of his investment, £V, can be modelled by $V = 2x^3 - 30x^2 + 126x + 1000$ where $x$ is the number of years since the investment was set up. After how many years should he have sold his investment to get maximum profit?

# CHAPTER 9: INTEGRATION

## 9.1 Integration

Consider: $\quad y = 4x^3 + 6x^2$

Then: $\qquad \dfrac{dy}{dx} = 12x^2 + 12x$

Suppose you started with the answer for $\dfrac{dy}{dx}$ and wanted to find the function $y$.

You would have to do the exact opposite each time, i.e.:
- add 1 on to the power;
- divide by the new power.

Thus for $12x^2$ you would:
- add 1 on to the power to get 3;
- divide 12 by 3 to get 4.

Similarly for $12x$ you would:
- add 1 on to the power to get 2;
- divide 12 by 2 to get 6.

This process is called **integration**. You write this as:

$\int (12x^2 + 12x)\, dx$

The '$dx$' shows that you are integrating with respect to $x$.

Now consider: $\ y = 4x + 6$

Then: $\qquad \dfrac{dy}{dx} = 4$

Again, suppose you started with the answer for $\dfrac{dy}{dx}$ and wanted to find the function $y$.

You would again have to do the exact opposite, i.e.:
- add 1 on to the power;
- divide by the new power.

The power of $x$ in the number 4 is 0, so you would add 1 on to 0 to get 1. You would then divide 4 by 1 to get 4.

You write this as: $\int 4\, dx$

### The Constant Of Integration
In the second example, you may have noticed that we did not arrive back at the original equation by integrating.

Consider: $\qquad\quad y = 4x + 7$

Then: $\qquad\quad \dfrac{dy}{dx} = 4$

Now consider: $\qquad y = 4x - 60$

Then: $\qquad\quad \dfrac{dy}{dx} = 4$

And consider: $\qquad y = 4x$

Then: $\qquad\quad \dfrac{dy}{dx} = 4$

In each example you get 4 as the answer, even though the

equations are different. This is because you get 0 when you differentiate a constant number. This means that when you integrate **any** function you must always include the **constant of integration**, written as **C**. C can take any value. Thus the complete answers to the two integrations above are:

1. $\int (12x^2 + 12x)\, dx = 4x^3 + 6x^2 + C$

2. $\int 4\, dx = 4x + C$

Integration is the exact **opposite** of differentiation.

## 9.2 Rules For Integration

Therefore the rules for integrating are:

a. add 1 on to the power;

b. divide by the new power;

c. add on the constant of integration.

For example, integrate the following:

1. $\int (7x - 2)\, dx$

   Answer $= \dfrac{7}{2}x^2 - 2x + C$

2. $\int (x^3 - 5x^2)\, dx$

   Answer $= \dfrac{1}{4}x^4 - \dfrac{5}{3}x^3 + C$

3. $\int \left(6x - 6x^2 - \dfrac{2}{3}x^3\right) dx$

   Answer $= 3x^2 - 2x^3 - \dfrac{1}{6}x^4 + C$

### Exercise 9A: *Integrate the following.*

1. $\int (6x + 3)\, dx$

2. $\int (12x^2 + 4x - 2)\, dx$

3. $\int (16x^3 - 9x^2 - 6x + 3)\, dx$

4. $\int (7 - 2x)\, dx$

5. $\int (4x + 3x^2)\, dx$

6. $\int (6x^3 - 4x - 1)\, dx$

7. $\int (3x^4 - 2x^3 + 7x^2)\, dx$

8. $\int \left(\dfrac{2}{5}x^4 + 6x\right) dx$

9. $\int \left(\dfrac{3}{7}x^2 - 2x\right) dx$

10. $\int \left(\dfrac{5}{8}x^3 + \dfrac{1}{4}x^2 + x\right) dx$

11. $\int (6x - 4x^2 + 7)\, dx$

12. $\int (9 - 2x - 6x^2)\, dx$

13. $\int (10x + x^2 - 3)\, dx$

14. $\int \left(\dfrac{2}{3}x^3 + \dfrac{6}{5}x^2 - 1\right) dx$

## Exercise 9A...

**15.** $\int (4x - \frac{2}{5}x^4 + 5)\, dx$

**16.** $\int (4x - 7)\, dx$

**17.** $\int (4x^3 - 7x^2 + 5x - 2)\, dx$

**18.** $\int (6x - \frac{2}{3}x^5)\, dx$

## 9.3 Integrating Expressions Where The $x$ Term Is On The Denominator

In this case, you must bring the $x$ term to the numerator before integrating, using the same index rules you used for differentiating. For example, integrate the following:

**4.** $\int \frac{6}{x^2}\, dx$

Reorganise: $\quad \frac{6}{x^2} = 6x^{-2}$

So: $\qquad \int 6x^{-2} = -6x^{-1} + C$

$\qquad\qquad\quad = \frac{-6}{x} + C$

**5.** $\int (\frac{2}{5x^3} + 5x^3)\, dx$

Reorganise: $\quad \frac{2}{5x^3} = \frac{2}{5}x^{-3}$

So: $\int (\frac{2}{5}x^{-3} + 5x^3)\, dx = \frac{-1}{5}x^{-2} + \frac{5}{4}x^4 + C$

$\qquad\qquad\qquad = \frac{-1}{5x^2} + \frac{5x^4}{4} + C$

## Exercise 9B: *Integrate the following.*

**1.** $\int \frac{4}{x^2}\, dx$

**2.** $\int \frac{8}{x^3}\, dx$

**3.** $\int \frac{2}{x^5}\, dx$

**4.** $\int \frac{3}{5x^2}\, dx$

**5.** $\int \frac{2}{7x^3}\, dx$

**6.** $\int \frac{3}{5x^4}\, dx$

**7.** $\int (4x - \frac{4}{x^2})\, dx$

**8.** $\int (x^2 + 3 - \frac{2}{x^3})\, dx$

**9.** $\int (\frac{3x^2}{2} - \frac{2}{3x^2})\, dx$

**10.** $\int (6 + \frac{2}{4x^2})\, dx$

**11.** $\int (4x - \frac{1}{2x^5})\, dx$

**12.** $\int (\frac{5}{3x^2} + x^2)\, dx$

**13.** $\int (2x^3 - \frac{1}{2x^3})\, dx$

**14.** $\int (6x + 2 - \frac{4}{x^2})\, dx$

**15.** $\int (3x^2 - 5 + \frac{2}{5x^2})\, dx$

## 9.4 Definite Integration

Integrals such as those you have worked out so far are called **indefinite** integrals because of the unknown constant of integration, C. **Definite** integration is when you are given two numbers to substitute into your answer. You then subtract the totals, and in so doing the constant C cancels out leaving a **definite** integration. Definite integration is written as follows:

$\int_a^b f(x)\, dx \qquad$ where $f(x)$ is a function of $x$, and $a$ and $b$ are two numbers you are given.

The rules for definite integration are:

a.  Integrate $f(x)$;

b.  Substitute $x = b$ into the answer;

c.  Substitute $x = a$ into the answer;

d.  Subtract the two results.

For example, work out:

**6.** $\int_1^4 (12x^2 + 4x - 2)\, dx$

$= [4x^3 + 2x^2 - 2x + C]_1^4$

$= [4 \times 4^3 + 2 \times 4^2 - 2 \times 4 + C] - [4 \times 1^3 + 2 \times 1^2 - 2 \times 1 + C]$

$= [256 + 32 - 8 + C] - [4 + 2 - 2 + C]$

$= [280] - [4]$

$= 276$

Because the Cs will **always** cancel out, you could omit the Cs when integrating, as shown below:

$= [4x^3 + 2x^2 - 2x]_1^4$

$= [4 \times 4^3 + 2 \times 4^2 - 2 \times 4] - [4 \times 1^3 + 2 \times 1^2 - 2 \times 1]$

$= [256 + 32 - 8] - [4 + 2 - 2]$

$= [280] - [4]$

$= 276$

## Exercise 9C: *Integrate the following.*

**1.** $\int_1^4 \frac{4}{x^2}\, dx$

**2.** $\int_1^2 \frac{2}{x^5}\, dx$

**3.** $\int_1^3 \frac{3}{5x^2}\, dx$

**4.** $\int_1^2 \frac{3}{5x^4}\, dx$

**5.** $\int_2^4 (x^2 + 3 - \frac{2}{x^3})\, dx$

**6.** $\int_1^3 (6 + \frac{1}{2x^2})\, dx$

## 9.5 Finding $y$ When Given $\frac{dy}{dx}$

The rules are as follows:

a. Integrate $\dfrac{dy}{dx}$;

b. Substitute values of $x$ and $y$ to find C.

For example:

..................................................................................................

7. $\dfrac{dy}{dx} = 4x - 3$

   (a) Find an expression for $y$ in terms of $x$ given that $x = 3$ when $y = -2$.

   (b) Hence find $y$ when $x = 6$.

   (a) Integrate:    $y = \int (4x - 3)\, dx$

$$= 2x^2 - 3x + C$$

Substitute $x = 3$ and $y = -2$:

$$y = 2x^2 - 3x + C$$
$$-2 = 2(3)^2 - 3(3) + C$$
$$-2 = 18 - 9 + C$$
$$-2 = 9 + C$$
$$-2 - 9 = C$$
$$-11 = C$$

Thus:    $y = 2x^2 - 3x - 11$

   (b) Substitute $x = 6$ to get:

$$y = 2(6)^2 - 3(6) - 11$$
$$y = 72 - 18 - 11$$
$$y = 43$$

..................................................................................................

8. The gradient function of a curve is $6x^2 - 4x$. Find:

   (a) the equation of the curve given that it passes through $(2, -3)$.

   (b) hence find where the curve crosses the line $x = -1$.

   (a) The gradient function is $\dfrac{dy}{dx}$.

To find the equation of the curve you need to integrate $\dfrac{dy}{dx}$.

Integrate:    $y = \int (6x^2 - 4x)\, dx$

$$= 2x^3 - 2x^2 + C$$

Substitute $x = 2$ and $y = -3$ to give:

$$y = 2x^3 - 2x^2 + C$$
$$-3 = 2(2)^3 - 2(2)^2 + C$$
$$-3 = 16 - 8 + C$$
$$-3 = 8 + C$$
$$-3 - 8 = C$$
$$-11 = C$$

Thus:    $y = 2x^3 - 2x^2 - 11$

   (b) Substitute $x = -1$ to get:

$$y = 2(-1)^3 - 2(-1)^2 - 11$$
$$y = -2 - 2 - 11$$
$$y = -15$$

Answer: $(-1, -15)$

## Exercise 9D

1. $\dfrac{dy}{dx} = 6x - 3$

   (a) Find an expression for $y$ in terms of $x$ given that $x = 1$ when $y = 3$.

   (b) Hence find $y$ when $x = 4$.

2. $\dfrac{dy}{dx} = 4 + 2x$

   (a) Find an expression for $y$ in terms of $x$ given that $x = -2$ when $y = 1$.

   (b) Hence find $y$ when $x = 2$.

3. $\dfrac{dy}{dx} = 3x^2 - 4x$

   (a) Find an expression for $y$ in terms of $x$ given that $x = 1$ when $y = -4$.

   (b) Hence find $y$ when $x = -3$.

4. $\dfrac{dy}{dx} = 6x + x^2$

   (a) an expression for $y$ in terms of $x$ given that $x = -1$ when $y = -3$.

   (b) Hence find $y$ when $x = 3$.

5. The gradient function of a curve is $\dfrac{4}{x^2}$

   (a) Find the equation of the curve given that it passes through $(1, 2)$.

   (b) Hence find where the curve crosses the line $x = -2$.

6. The gradient function of a curve is $6x^2 - 2x + 5$

   (a) Find the equation of the curve given that it passes through $(3, 1)$.

   (b) Hence find where the curve crosses the line $x = 4$.

7. The gradient function of a curve is $3x + 4$

   (a) Find the equation of the curve given that it passes through $(1, 2)$.

   (b) Hence find where the curve crosses the line $x = -2$.

8. The gradient function of a curve is $6 - 2x + 3x^2$

   (a) Find the equation of the curve given that it passes through $(-2, 4)$.

   (b) Hence find where the curve crosses the line $x = 6$.

# CHAPTER 10: AREA

## 10.1 The Area Under A Curve

Look at the curve below.

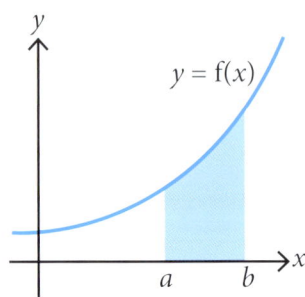

You can find the shaded area under the curve $y = f(x)$ between the lines $x = a$ and $x = b$ by integrating $y = f(x)$ between $a$ and $b$:

Area $= \int_a^b f(x)\, dx$

The rules are as follows:

a. Integrate the equation of the curve (ignoring C as the Cs will cancel);

b. Substitute the values $x = b$ and $x = a$ and subtract;

c. Always give the positive value of the answer.

For example:

1. Find the area under the curve $y = x^2 - x - 12$ between the lines $x = 0$ and $x = 2$.

Area $= \int_0^2 (x^2 - x - 12)\, dx$

$= {}_0^2[\frac{1}{3} x^3 - \frac{1}{2} x^2 - 12x]$

$= [\frac{1}{3}(8) - \frac{1}{2}(4) - 12(2)] - [0 - 0 - 0]$

$= [2\frac{2}{3} - 2 - 24] - [0]$

$= -23\frac{1}{3} - 0$

$= -23\frac{1}{3}$

Answer: The area is $23\frac{1}{3}$

Note that:
- There are no units for the area.
- The curve $y = x^2 - x - 12$ is a quadratic curve and, since the $x^2$ term is positive, it will be a U shape. Thus the negative sign in the area indicates that the part of the curve between $x = 0$ and $x = 2$ is below the $x$-axis.

## Exercise 10A

1. Find the area under the curve $y = x^2 - 7x + 10$ between the lines $x = 0$ and $x = 2$.

2. Find the area under the curve $y = 12 - 7x + x^2$ between the lines $x = 0$ and $x = 2$.

3. Find the area under the curve $y = 2x^2 + 7x - 4$ between the lines $x = -2$ and $x = 0$.

4. Find the area under the curve $y = 3x^2 - 10x - 8$ between the lines $x = 0$ and $x = 3$.

5. Find the area under the curve $y = x^2 + 2x - 24$ between the lines $x = 1$ and $x = 2$.

6. Find the area under the curve $y = 2x^2 - 11x - 6$ between the lines $x = 2$ and $x = 4$.

7. Find the area under the curve $y = x^2 + x - 6$ between the lines $x = 0$ and $x = 1$.

8. Find the area under the curve $y = 4x^2 - 11x + 10$ between the lines $x = 0$ and $x = 2$.

9. Find the area under the curve $y = 12 - 20x + 3x^2$ between the lines $x = 1$ and $x = 2$.

10. Find the area under the curve $y = 3x^2 - 5x - 3$ between the lines $x = 0$ and $x = 2$.

11. Find the area under the curve $y = 2x^2 - 3x - 20$ between the lines $x = 0$ and $x = 3$

12. Find the area under the curve $y = 2x^2 + 9x - 5$ between the lines $x = -2$ and $x = 0$.

13. Find the area under the curve $y = x^2 + 2x - 8$ between the lines $x = 0$ and $x = 2$.

14. Find the area under the curve $y = 2x^2 - 5x - 25$ between the lines $x = 1$ and $x = 2$.

15. Find the area under the curve $y = 3x^2 - 2x - 8$ between the lines $x = 0$ and $x = 2$.

## 10.2 The Area Between A Quadratic Curve And The $x$-axis

The rules are as follows:

a. Find where the curve crosses the $x$-axis by putting $y = 0$;

b. Integrate the equation of the curve between these two values.

For example:

3. (a) Sketch the curve $y = x^2 + 3x - 10$.
   (b) Find the area between the curve $y = x^2 + 3x - 10$ and the $x$-axis.

The curve crosses the $x$-axis when $y = 0$.
So: $x^2 + 3x - 10 = 0$
$(x + 5)(x - 2) = 0$
Thus: $x = -5$ and $x = 2$

The curve crosses the $y$-axis when $x = 0$.
So: $y = (0)^2 + 3(0) - 10$
$y = -10$

You find the turning point by differentiating:
$y = x^2 + 3x - 10$

$\frac{dy}{dx} = 2x + 3$

$\frac{dy}{dx} = 2x + 3 = 0$

$2x = -3$

$x = -1\frac{1}{2}$

Since $\frac{d^2y}{dx^2} = 2$ we know it is a minimum.

Substituting $x = -1\frac{1}{2}$ into $y = x^2 + 3x - 10$ gives:

$y = -12\frac{1}{4}$.

You can then sketch the curve as follows:

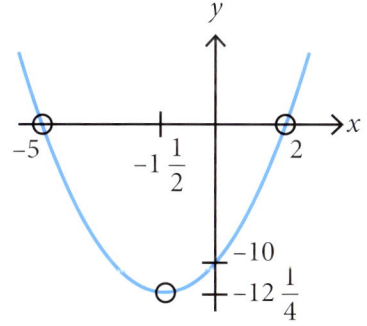

Area $= \int_{-5}^{2} (x^2 + 3x - 10)\ dx$

$= \ _{-5}^{\ \ 2}[\frac{1}{3}x^3 + \frac{3}{2}x^2 - 10x]$

$= [\frac{1}{3}(8) + \frac{3}{2}(4) - 10(2)] - [\frac{1}{3}(-125) + \frac{3}{2}(25) - 10(-5)]$

$= [2\frac{2}{3} + 6 - 20] - [-41\frac{2}{3} + 37\frac{1}{2} + 50]$

$= [-11\frac{1}{3}] - [45\frac{5}{6}]$

$= -57\frac{1}{6}$

Answer: The area is $57\frac{1}{6}$.

## 10.3 The Area Between A Cubic Curve And The $x$-axis

The rules are similar for a cubic curve. For example:

4. (a) Sketch the curve $y = 2x^3 - 3x^2 - 72x$, giving answers to 2 decimal places where appropriate.
   (b) Find the area between the curve $y = 2x^3 - 3x^2 - 72x$ and the negative $x$-axis.

The curve crosses the $x$-axis when $y = 0$.
So: $y = 2x^3 - 3x^2 - 72x = 0$
$x(2x^2 - 3x - 72) = 0$
So either: $x = 0$
or $2x^2 - 3x - 72 = 0$

You solve $2x^2 - 3x - 72 = 0$ by using the quadratic formula $\frac{-b \pm \sqrt{b^2 - 4ac}}{2a}$:
where $a = 2, b = -3, c = -72$

So: $x = \frac{3 \pm \sqrt{(-3)^2 - (4 \times 2 \times -72)}}{2 \times 2}$

$x = \frac{3 \pm \sqrt{585}}{4}$

$x = \frac{3 + \sqrt{585}}{4}$ or $\frac{3 - \sqrt{585}}{4}$

So: $x = 6.80$ or $-5.30$, to 2 decimal places.

Thus the curve crosses the $x$-axis at $(0, 0)$, $(6.80, 0)$ and $(-5.30, 0)$.

The turning points are when $\frac{dy}{dx} = 0$.

Since: $y = 2x^3 - 3x^2 - 72x$

So: $\frac{dy}{dx} = 6x^2 - 6x - 72 = 0$

Dividing through by 6 gives:
$x^2 - x - 12 = 0$
$(x - 4)(x + 3) = 0$
So either: $x - 4 = 0$
$x = 4$
or: $x + 3 = 0$
$x = -3$

You now find $y$ by substituting $x = 4$ or $-3$ into the equation for $y$:
$y = 2x^3 - 3x^2 - 72x$
When $x = 4$: $y = -208$
So this turning point is at $(4, -208)$.

When $x = -3$: $y = 135$
So this turning point is at $(-3, 135)$.

Now work out what type each turning point is by getting $\frac{d^2y}{dx^2}$:

$$\frac{dy}{dx} = 6x^2 - 6x - 72$$

$$\frac{d^2y}{dx^2} = 12x - 6$$

When $x = 4$:    $\frac{d^2y}{dx^2} = 42$ and so it is a minimum.

When $x = -3$:    $\frac{d^2y}{dx^2} = -42$ and so it is a maximum.

You can now sketch the curve:

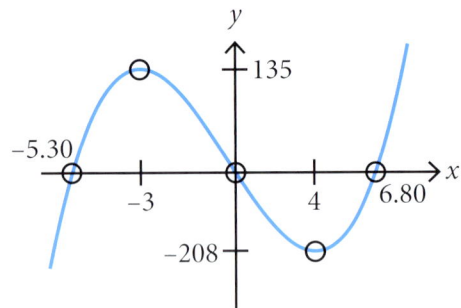

To find the area between the curve $y = 2x^3 - 3x^2 - 72x$ and the negative $x$-axis you must integrate $y = 2x^3 - 3x^2 - 72x$ between $x = -5.30$ and 0 as below:

Area    $= \int_{-5.30}^{0} (2x^3 - 3x^2 - 72x)\, dx$

$= {}_{-5.30}^{\quad 0}[\frac{1}{2}x^4 - x^3 - 36x^2]$

$= [0] - [394.524 + 148.877 - 1011.24]$

$= [0] - [-467.839]$

$= 467.84$

Answer: The area is 467.84.

## Exercise 10B

1. (a) Sketch the curve $y = x^2 - 8x + 12$.
   (b) Find the area between this curve and the $x$-axis.

2. (a) Sketch the curve $y = x^2 - x - 20$.
   (b) Find the area between this curve and the $x$-axis.

3. (a) Sketch the curve $y = -x^2 + x + 6$.
   (b) Find the area between this curve and the $x$-axis.

4. (a) Sketch the curve $y = -2x^2 - 3x + 20$.
   (b) Find the area between this curve and the $x$-axis.

## Exercise 10B...

5. (a) Sketch the curve $y = 2x^3 + 9x^2 - 60x$, giving answers to 2 decimal places where appropriate.
   (b) Find the area between this curve and the positive $x$-axis.

6. (a) Sketch the curve $y = x^3 - 3x^2 - 24x$, giving answers to 2 decimal places where appropriate.
   (b) Find the area between this curve and the negative $x$-axis.

7. (a) Sketch the curve $y = x^3 - 3x^2 - 45x$, giving answers to 2 decimal places where appropriate.
   (b) Find the area between this curve and the negative $x$-axis.

8. (a) Sketch the curve $y = 2x^3 + 15x^2 - 36x$, giving answers to 2 decimal places where appropriate.
   (b) Find the area between this curve and the positive $x$-axis.

9. (a) Sketch the curve $y = x^3 - 48x$, giving answers to 2 decimal places where appropriate.
   (b) Find the area between this curve and the positive $x$-axis.

10. (a) Sketch the curve $y = 2x^3 + 9x^2 - 108x$, giving answers to 2 decimal places where appropriate.
    (b) Find the area between this curve and the positive $x$-axis.

11. (a) Sketch the curve $y = -x^3 + 6x^2 + 135x$.
    (b) Find the area between this curve and the negative $x$-axis.

## 11.1 Matrices

A matrix is a rectangular collection of numbers. For example:

a. $\begin{pmatrix} 4 & -3 \\ -6 & 2 \end{pmatrix}$ is a matrix with 2 rows and 2 columns.

This is called a $2 \times 2$ matrix.

b. $\begin{pmatrix} 4 & -3 & 5 \end{pmatrix}$ is a matrix with 1 row and 3 columns.

This is called a $1 \times 3$ matrix.

c. $\begin{pmatrix} 4 \\ 2 \\ -5 \\ -4 \end{pmatrix}$ is a matrix with 4 rows and 1 column.

This is called a $4 \times 1$ matrix.

## 11.2 Adding And Subtracting Matrices

You can only add matrices which have the same number of rows and columns. The rule for adding or subtracting matrices is:

• Add or subtract numbers in corresponding places.

For example:

1. Find $\begin{pmatrix} 6 & -2 \\ -3 & 4 \end{pmatrix} + \begin{pmatrix} -7 & 4 \\ -4 & 2 \end{pmatrix}$

Answer = $\begin{pmatrix} -1 & 2 \\ -7 & 6 \end{pmatrix}$

2. Find $\begin{pmatrix} -4 & -1 \\ 7 & 5 \end{pmatrix} - \begin{pmatrix} -3 & 8 \\ -1 & 9 \end{pmatrix}$

Answer = $\begin{pmatrix} -1 & -9 \\ 8 & -4 \end{pmatrix}$

3. Find $\begin{pmatrix} 2x & -y \\ 6 & -3v \end{pmatrix} + \begin{pmatrix} x & -5y \\ -3 & 2v \end{pmatrix}$

Answer = $\begin{pmatrix} 3x & -6y \\ 3 & -v \end{pmatrix}$

4. Find $A + B$ if $A = \begin{pmatrix} 5 & 3 \\ -2 & -4 \end{pmatrix}$ and $B = \begin{pmatrix} -2 & 6 \\ -5 & -3 \end{pmatrix}$

$A + B = \begin{pmatrix} 5 & 3 \\ -2 & -4 \end{pmatrix} + \begin{pmatrix} -2 & 6 \\ -5 & -3 \end{pmatrix} = \begin{pmatrix} 3 & 9 \\ -7 & -7 \end{pmatrix}$

1. $\begin{pmatrix} -3 \\ 4 \end{pmatrix} + \begin{pmatrix} 2 \\ -1 \end{pmatrix}$

2. $\begin{pmatrix} -6 \\ 1 \end{pmatrix} - \begin{pmatrix} -2 \\ 5 \end{pmatrix}$

3. $\begin{pmatrix} -1 & 4 \end{pmatrix} + \begin{pmatrix} 5 & -2 \end{pmatrix}$

4. $\begin{pmatrix} 2 & -3 \end{pmatrix} - \begin{pmatrix} -1 & -2 \end{pmatrix}$

5. $\begin{pmatrix} x \\ -3 \end{pmatrix} + \begin{pmatrix} -2x \\ 1 \end{pmatrix}$

6. $\begin{pmatrix} 4 & -3y \end{pmatrix} - \begin{pmatrix} 2 & y \end{pmatrix}$

7. $\begin{pmatrix} -2x \\ 3y \end{pmatrix} + \begin{pmatrix} x \\ -4y \end{pmatrix}$

8. $\begin{pmatrix} -3x & y \end{pmatrix} - \begin{pmatrix} x & -2y \end{pmatrix}$

9. $\begin{pmatrix} 1 & -5 \\ 9 & -4 \end{pmatrix} + \begin{pmatrix} -6 & -5 \\ 5 & 2 \end{pmatrix}$

10. $\begin{pmatrix} -4 & -8 \\ -3 & 4 \end{pmatrix} - \begin{pmatrix} -4 & 7 \\ -2 & -7 \end{pmatrix}$

11. $\begin{pmatrix} x & -2y \\ 8 & 4t \end{pmatrix} + \begin{pmatrix} 3x & 5y \\ -2 & -2t \end{pmatrix}$

12. $\begin{pmatrix} 6 & -2 \\ -3 & 4 \end{pmatrix} + \begin{pmatrix} -7 & 4 \\ -4 & 2 \end{pmatrix}$

13. $\begin{pmatrix} 3n & -2m \\ -3 & -6q \end{pmatrix} - \begin{pmatrix} -7n & m \\ 11 & -3q \end{pmatrix}$

14. $\begin{pmatrix} 4.6 & -2.6 \\ -3.4 & 4.7 \end{pmatrix} + \begin{pmatrix} -7.4 & 4.8 \\ -4.1 & 2.8 \end{pmatrix}$

15. $\begin{pmatrix} -2.6 & 3.5 \\ -3.1 & -4.6 \end{pmatrix} - \begin{pmatrix} -7.5 & -5.4 \\ -4.8 & 7.2 \end{pmatrix}$

16. $\begin{pmatrix} -3 & -8 \\ 9 & -4 \end{pmatrix} + \begin{pmatrix} -2 & -4 \\ -7 & 3 \end{pmatrix} - \begin{pmatrix} 3 & -7 \\ -7 & -4 \end{pmatrix}$

$A = \begin{pmatrix} -6 & 8 \\ -3 & 4 \end{pmatrix}$ $B = \begin{pmatrix} 4 & 7 \\ -2 & 6 \end{pmatrix}$ $C = \begin{pmatrix} -2 & -9 \\ 8 & 6 \end{pmatrix}$ and

$D = \begin{pmatrix} -4 & 8 \\ -6 & -2 \end{pmatrix}$. Find:

17. $A + B$

18. $B - A$

19. $A + C$

20. $D - A$

21. $B + C$

22. $D - C$

23. $A + D$

24. $C - B$

## 11.3 Multiplying And Dividing Matrices By Whole Numbers

In this case, you multiply or divide every number in the matrix by the whole number. For example:

5. $P = \begin{pmatrix} 4 & -7 \\ -6 & 2 \end{pmatrix}$ Find (a) $6P$ (b) $\frac{-1}{2}P$

(a) Multiplying all the numbers by 6 gives:

$$6P = \begin{pmatrix} 24 & -42 \\ -36 & 12 \end{pmatrix}$$

(b) Dividing all the numbers by $-2$ gives:

$$\frac{-1}{2}P = \begin{pmatrix} -2 & 3.5 \\ 3 & -1 \end{pmatrix}$$

6. $M = \begin{pmatrix} 5 & -8 \\ -4 & 5 \end{pmatrix}$ and $N = \begin{pmatrix} -2 & -6 \\ 6 & -2 \end{pmatrix}$

Find (a) $2M + 3N$ (b) $4M - \frac{1}{2}N$

(a) $\begin{pmatrix} 10 & -16 \\ -8 & 10 \end{pmatrix} + \begin{pmatrix} -6 & -18 \\ 18 & -6 \end{pmatrix} = \begin{pmatrix} 4 & -34 \\ 10 & 4 \end{pmatrix}$

(b) $\begin{pmatrix} 20 & -32 \\ -16 & 20 \end{pmatrix} - \begin{pmatrix} -1 & -3 \\ 3 & -1 \end{pmatrix} = \begin{pmatrix} 21 & -29 \\ -19 & 21 \end{pmatrix}$

## Exercise 11B

$A = \begin{pmatrix} 5 & 6 \\ -2 & 4 \end{pmatrix}$ $B = \begin{pmatrix} -3 & -2 \\ 6 & -5 \end{pmatrix}$ $C = \begin{pmatrix} 1 & -4 \\ 3 & -6 \end{pmatrix}$

$D = \begin{pmatrix} 3 & -5 \\ -5 & 3 \end{pmatrix}$ $E = \begin{pmatrix} -9 & 8 \\ 3 & -6 \end{pmatrix}$

Find:

1. $5A$
2. $3B$
3. $-5C$
4. $8D$
5. $7E$
6. $\frac{1}{2}A$
7. $\frac{1}{10}D$
8. $\frac{1}{2}B$
9. $2A + B$
10. $3C - D$
11. $2E + 4C$
12. $5B - 3A$
13. $2A + D - E$
14. $3E - 2C + A$
15. $A + B - C - D$

## Exercise 11B...

$F = \begin{pmatrix} -2 \\ 5 \end{pmatrix}$ $G = (3 \ -4)$ $H = \begin{pmatrix} 2 \\ -7 \end{pmatrix}$ $J = (-1 \ -5)$

Find:

16. $3F$
17. $2G$
18. $4H$
19. $-2J$
20. $\frac{1}{2}F$
21. $\frac{3}{4}G$
22. $3(F - H)$
23. $\frac{1}{2}(G + J)$

## 11.4 Solving Matrix Equations

To solve matrix equations, follow the same rules as used to solve algebraic linear equations, i.e. separate the variable from the numbers. For example, solve the following:

7. $X + \begin{pmatrix} -2 & 7 \\ 5 & -3 \end{pmatrix} = \begin{pmatrix} 4 & -1 \\ 2 & -5 \end{pmatrix}$

Subtracting $\begin{pmatrix} -2 & 7 \\ 5 & -3 \end{pmatrix}$ from both sides gives:

$X = \begin{pmatrix} 4 & -1 \\ 2 & -5 \end{pmatrix} - \begin{pmatrix} -2 & 7 \\ 5 & -3 \end{pmatrix}$

Then subtract each corresponding entry as before to get:

$X = \begin{pmatrix} 6 & -8 \\ -3 & -2 \end{pmatrix}$

8. $\begin{pmatrix} 2 & -4 \\ 5 & -3 \end{pmatrix} - 2X = \begin{pmatrix} 9 & 4 \\ 6 & -5 \end{pmatrix}$

Adding $2X$ to both sides gives:

$\begin{pmatrix} 2 & -4 \\ 5 & -3 \end{pmatrix} = \begin{pmatrix} 9 & 4 \\ 6 & -5 \end{pmatrix} + 2X$

Subtracting $\begin{pmatrix} 9 & 4 \\ 6 & -5 \end{pmatrix}$ from both sides gives:

$\begin{pmatrix} 2 & -4 \\ 5 & -3 \end{pmatrix} - \begin{pmatrix} 9 & 4 \\ 6 & -5 \end{pmatrix} = 2X$

Then subtract each corresponding entry as before to get:

$2X = \begin{pmatrix} -7 & -8 \\ -1 & 2 \end{pmatrix}$

Then divide every entry by 2 to get:

$X = \begin{pmatrix} -3.5 & -4 \\ -0.5 & 1 \end{pmatrix}$

## Exercise 11C: *Solve the following.*

1. $X - \begin{pmatrix} -2 & 7 \\ 5 & 3 \end{pmatrix} = \begin{pmatrix} 4 & -2 \\ 5 & 9 \end{pmatrix}$

2. $X + \begin{pmatrix} -3 & 5 \\ 4 & -2 \end{pmatrix} = \begin{pmatrix} 6 & -2 \\ 9 & -4 \end{pmatrix}$

3. $X + (-7\ 4\ 5) = (9\ -2\ 6)$

4. $X - \begin{pmatrix} -7 \\ 2 \end{pmatrix} = \begin{pmatrix} 4 \\ -6 \end{pmatrix}$

5. $2X - \begin{pmatrix} 3 & 4 \\ -5 & 2 \end{pmatrix} = \begin{pmatrix} 7 & -2 \\ 9 & -6 \end{pmatrix}$

6. $3X + \begin{pmatrix} -2 & 5 \\ 6 & -1 \end{pmatrix} = \begin{pmatrix} 7 & -1 \\ 9 & -7 \end{pmatrix}$

7. $\begin{pmatrix} 4 & -2 \\ 6 & 3 \end{pmatrix} + 4X = \begin{pmatrix} 8 & -6 \\ 2 & 15 \end{pmatrix}$

8. $\begin{pmatrix} 7 & -3 \\ -5 & 4 \end{pmatrix} - 2X = \begin{pmatrix} 3 & -9 \\ 7 & -10 \end{pmatrix}$

9. $5X + \begin{pmatrix} -2 & 7 \\ 5 & -3 \end{pmatrix} = \begin{pmatrix} 8 & 2 \\ -10 & -8 \end{pmatrix}$

10. $\begin{pmatrix} 7 & 4 \\ -3 & 2 \end{pmatrix} - 2X = \begin{pmatrix} 1 & -2 \\ 5 & -4 \end{pmatrix}$

## 11.5 Multiplying Matrices By Matrices

Two matrices A and B can only be multiplied together to give AB if the number of **columns** in A equals the number of **rows** in B. The **order** of the answer (ie the number of rows and columns in the answer matrix) will be the number of rows in A × the number of columns in B.

The rules for multiplying two matrices is to multiply each row into each column by:

a. multiplying each pair of numbers in turn and then

b. adding these answers.

For example:

9. Find: $\begin{pmatrix} -2 & 3 \\ 4 & 2 \end{pmatrix} \begin{pmatrix} 1 \\ 4 \end{pmatrix}$

$\begin{pmatrix} -2 & 3 \\ 4 & 2 \end{pmatrix} \begin{pmatrix} 1 \\ 4 \end{pmatrix} = \begin{pmatrix} -2\times1 + 3\times4 \\ 4\times1 + 2\times4 \end{pmatrix}$

$\qquad 2\times2 \qquad 2\times1 \ = \qquad 2\times1$

$= \begin{pmatrix} -2 + 12 \\ 4 + 8 \end{pmatrix} = \begin{pmatrix} 10 \\ 12 \end{pmatrix}$

10. Find: $(-3\ 4)\begin{pmatrix} 2 \\ -5 \end{pmatrix}$

$(-3\ 4)\begin{pmatrix} 2 \\ -5 \end{pmatrix} = (-3\times2 + 4\times-5) = (-6 - 20) = (-26)$

$\quad 1\times2 \quad 2\times1 \ = \qquad 1\times1$

Note that you must put brackets round the −26 as it is a matrix and not just an integer.

11. Find: $\begin{pmatrix} 1 \\ 4 \end{pmatrix} (-2\ -3)$

$\begin{pmatrix} 1 \\ 4 \end{pmatrix} (-2\ -3) = \begin{pmatrix} 1\times-2 & 1\times-3 \\ 4\times-2 & 4\times-3 \end{pmatrix} = \begin{pmatrix} -2 & -3 \\ -8 & -12 \end{pmatrix}$

$\quad 2\times1 \qquad 1\times2 \quad = \qquad 2\times2$

12. $A = \begin{pmatrix} -3 & 4 \\ 5 & 2 \end{pmatrix}$ $B = \begin{pmatrix} 1 & -2 \\ 3 & -4 \end{pmatrix}$ Find: (a) AB (b) BA

(a) $\begin{pmatrix} -3 & 4 \\ 5 & 2 \end{pmatrix} \begin{pmatrix} 1 & -2 \\ 3 & -4 \end{pmatrix} = \begin{pmatrix} -3+12 & 6-16 \\ 5+6 & -10-8 \end{pmatrix}$

$\quad 2\times2 \qquad 2\times2 \quad = \qquad 2\times2$

$= \begin{pmatrix} 9 & -10 \\ 11 & -18 \end{pmatrix}$

(b) $\begin{pmatrix} 1 & -2 \\ 3 & -4 \end{pmatrix} \begin{pmatrix} -3 & 4 \\ 5 & 2 \end{pmatrix} = \begin{pmatrix} -3-10 & 4-4 \\ -9-20 & 12-8 \end{pmatrix}$

$\quad 2\times2 \qquad 2\times2 \quad = \qquad 2\times2$

$= \begin{pmatrix} -13 & 0 \\ -29 & 4 \end{pmatrix}$

This shows us that in matrix multiplication, AB ≠ BA.

13. $C = \begin{pmatrix} -2 & 3 \\ 5 & 2 \end{pmatrix}$ Find $C^2$.

$C^2 = \begin{pmatrix} -2 & 3 \\ 5 & 2 \end{pmatrix} \begin{pmatrix} -2 & 3 \\ 5 & 2 \end{pmatrix} = \begin{pmatrix} 4+15 & 6+6 \\ -10+10 & 15+4 \end{pmatrix}$

$= \begin{pmatrix} 19 & 0 \\ 0 & 19 \end{pmatrix}$

Note that there is **no** shortcut in finding $C^2$. You do **not** square each entry.

## Exercise 11D: *Work out the following.*

1. $(-2 \ 4) \begin{pmatrix} 5 \\ -3 \end{pmatrix}$

2. $\begin{pmatrix} 4 \\ 2 \end{pmatrix} (-2 \ 4)$

3. $\begin{pmatrix} -2 & 4 \\ 5 & 2 \end{pmatrix} \begin{pmatrix} 1 \\ 4 \end{pmatrix}$

4. $(-1 \ -3) \begin{pmatrix} -5 \\ 2 \end{pmatrix}$

5. $\begin{pmatrix} 2 \\ -3 \end{pmatrix} (-5 \ 3)$

6. $\begin{pmatrix} -1 & 4 \\ 5 & 2 \end{pmatrix} \begin{pmatrix} 2 \\ -3 \end{pmatrix}$

7. $(-2 \ -5) \begin{pmatrix} -2 \\ 4 \end{pmatrix}$

8. $\begin{pmatrix} -3 \\ 5 \end{pmatrix} (4 \ -2)$

9. $\begin{pmatrix} 3 & -2 \\ -1 & 4 \end{pmatrix} \begin{pmatrix} -2 \\ 7 \end{pmatrix}$

$A = \begin{pmatrix} -2 & 5 \\ 4 & 3 \end{pmatrix}$ $B = \begin{pmatrix} 1 & -2 \\ -3 & 5 \end{pmatrix}$ $C = \begin{pmatrix} -2 & 5 \\ 3 & -4 \end{pmatrix}$. Find:

10. AB      13. BA      16. $A^2$

11. AC      14. CA      17. $B^2$

12. BC      15. CB      18. $C^2$

## 11.6 Determinant Of A Matrix

The **determinant** of a matrix is a number and is calculated as follows. If the matrix $A = \begin{pmatrix} a & b \\ c & d \end{pmatrix}$ then the determinant of A is given by:

det A = ad – bc

You must **not** put brackets around this answer as it is a number and not a matrix. For example:

14. Calculate the determinant of A, if $A = \begin{pmatrix} 3 & -8 \\ 7 & -4 \end{pmatrix}$.

$$\text{det } A = 3 \times (-4) - (-8) \times 7$$
$$= -12 - (-56)$$
$$= -12 + 56$$
$$= 44$$

## Exercise 11E: *Find the determinant of the following matrices:*

1. $\begin{pmatrix} 5 & 7 \\ 4 & 2 \end{pmatrix}$     6. $\begin{pmatrix} 4 & 5 \\ -1 & -3 \end{pmatrix}$

2. $\begin{pmatrix} 8 & -6 \\ 3 & 5 \end{pmatrix}$     7. $\begin{pmatrix} 5 & -4 \\ -2 & 5 \end{pmatrix}$

3. $\begin{pmatrix} -4 & 5 \\ 3 & -3 \end{pmatrix}$     8. $\begin{pmatrix} 4 & -3 \\ -2 & -4 \end{pmatrix}$

4. $\begin{pmatrix} 7 & -6 \\ -5 & -2 \end{pmatrix}$     9. $\begin{pmatrix} 5 & -4 \\ -3 & 6 \end{pmatrix}$

5. $\begin{pmatrix} 6 & -6 \\ 3 & 9 \end{pmatrix}$     10. $\begin{pmatrix} 4 & -4 \\ -3 & -1 \end{pmatrix}$

## 11.7 The Unit Matrix

The unit matrix is called **I** (for **i**dentity matrix). It is defined as:

$$I = \begin{pmatrix} 1 & 0 \\ 0 & 1 \end{pmatrix}$$

When any matrix A is multiplied by I, or when I is multiplied by any matrix A, the answer is **always** A. In other words, AI = IA = A. For example:

15. If $A = \begin{pmatrix} 3 & -5 \\ -2 & 6 \end{pmatrix}$, find (a) AI (b) IA.

(a) $AI = \begin{pmatrix} 3 & -5 \\ -2 & 6 \end{pmatrix} \begin{pmatrix} 1 & 0 \\ 0 & 1 \end{pmatrix} = \begin{pmatrix} 3 & -5 \\ -2 & 6 \end{pmatrix}$

(b) $IA = \begin{pmatrix} 1 & 0 \\ 0 & 1 \end{pmatrix} \begin{pmatrix} 3 & -5 \\ -2 & 6 \end{pmatrix} = \begin{pmatrix} 3 & -5 \\ -2 & 6 \end{pmatrix}$

## 11.8 Inverse Of A Matrix

The inverse of any matrix A is called $A^{-1}$. Whenever any matrix A is multiplied by its inverse $A^{-1}$, or vice–versa, the answer is always I. In other words, $AA^{-1} = A^{-1}A = I$. The inverse of a matrix is calculated as follows.

If $A = \begin{pmatrix} a & b \\ c & d \end{pmatrix}$ then the inverse of A is given by:

$$A^{-1} = \frac{1}{\text{det } A} \begin{pmatrix} d & -b \\ -c & a \end{pmatrix}$$

For example:

16. Find the inverse of the following matrices:

(a) $A = \begin{pmatrix} 5 & 7 \\ -4 & 3 \end{pmatrix}$     (b) $B = \begin{pmatrix} -3 & -2 \\ -5 & -3 \end{pmatrix}$

(a)  $A = \begin{pmatrix} 5 & 7 \\ -4 & 3 \end{pmatrix}$

det A = 15 − (−28) = 15 + 28 = 43

$A^{-1} = \dfrac{1}{43} \begin{pmatrix} 3 & -7 \\ 4 & 5 \end{pmatrix}$

You should **not** work out the bracket.

(b)  $B = \begin{pmatrix} -3 & -2 \\ -5 & -3 \end{pmatrix}$

det B = 9 − 10 = −1

$B^{-1} = \dfrac{-1}{1} \begin{pmatrix} -3 & 2 \\ 5 & -3 \end{pmatrix} = -1 \begin{pmatrix} -3 & 2 \\ 5 & -3 \end{pmatrix}$

$= \begin{pmatrix} 3 & -2 \\ -5 & 3 \end{pmatrix}$

You **should** work out the bracket when the term outside is −1.

17. Show that the matrix $C = \begin{pmatrix} 5 & -4 \\ 10 & -8 \end{pmatrix}$ has no inverse.

det C = −40 − (−40) = 0

$C^{-1} = \dfrac{1}{0} \begin{pmatrix} -8 & 4 \\ -10 & 5 \end{pmatrix}$

You cannot divide 1 by 0. Therefore C has no inverse.

## Exercise 11F: *Find the inverse of the following matrices.*

1. $\begin{pmatrix} 3 & -6 \\ 7 & 2 \end{pmatrix}$
9. $\begin{pmatrix} -3 & 4 \\ 5 & 2 \end{pmatrix}$

2. $\begin{pmatrix} 3 & -2 \\ 5 & -4 \end{pmatrix}$
10. $\begin{pmatrix} -2 & -3 \\ 3 & 5 \end{pmatrix}$

3. $\begin{pmatrix} -2 & 4 \\ 5 & 2 \end{pmatrix}$
11. $\begin{pmatrix} -5 & 4 \\ 3 & -2 \end{pmatrix}$

4. $\begin{pmatrix} -3 & 5 \\ 4 & -2 \end{pmatrix}$
12. $\begin{pmatrix} 1 & -2 \\ 5 & 3 \end{pmatrix}$

5. $\begin{pmatrix} -2 & 5 \\ 3 & -4 \end{pmatrix}$
13. $\begin{pmatrix} -2 & 4 \\ -5 & 3 \end{pmatrix}$

6. $\begin{pmatrix} 5 & -2 \\ -8 & 3 \end{pmatrix}$
14. $\begin{pmatrix} -1 & 5 \\ 7 & -2 \end{pmatrix}$

7. $\begin{pmatrix} -2 & 6 \\ 4 & 3 \end{pmatrix}$
15. $\begin{pmatrix} 6 & -2 \\ 7 & 4 \end{pmatrix}$

8. $\begin{pmatrix} 1 & -3 \\ 5 & 4 \end{pmatrix}$
16. $\begin{pmatrix} -2 & 5 \\ 4 & -3 \end{pmatrix}$

17. Explain why the matrix $\begin{pmatrix} -2 & -5 \\ 4 & 10 \end{pmatrix}$ has no inverse.

## Exercise 11F..

18. Explain why the matrix $\begin{pmatrix} 8 & -6 \\ -4 & 3 \end{pmatrix}$ has no inverse.

19. The matrix $\begin{pmatrix} 4 & \mathbf{a} \\ 6 & 9 \end{pmatrix}$ has no inverse. Find **a**.

20. The matrix $\begin{pmatrix} -3 & 5 \\ 4 & \mathbf{q} \end{pmatrix}$ has no inverse. Find **q**.

## 11.9 Solving Harder Matrix Equations

You can use the inverse of a matrix to solve matrix equations of the form AX = B as follows:

a.  Find the inverse of A;

b.  Multiply A⁻¹ by B **in this order.**

This method works because:

AX = B

Multiplying both sides by A⁻¹ gives:

A⁻¹ AX = A⁻¹ B

But:  A⁻¹ A = I

So:  IX = A⁻¹ B

But:  IX = X

So:  X = A⁻¹ B

For example:

18. $A = \begin{pmatrix} -2 & 5 \\ 3 & -4 \end{pmatrix}$  $B = \begin{pmatrix} 1 & -2 \\ 4 & -6 \end{pmatrix}$  $C = \begin{pmatrix} -3 \\ 7 \end{pmatrix}$  Solve:

(a) AX = C (b) BX = A

(a)  AX = C

X = A⁻¹ C

det A = 8 − 15 = −7

So:  $A^{-1} = \dfrac{-1}{7} \begin{pmatrix} -4 & -5 \\ -3 & -2 \end{pmatrix}$

So:  $X = \dfrac{-1}{7} \begin{pmatrix} -4 & -5 \\ -3 & -2 \end{pmatrix} \begin{pmatrix} -3 \\ 7 \end{pmatrix}$
     *2×2      2×1*

$= \dfrac{-1}{7} \begin{pmatrix} 12 - 35 \\ 9 - 14 \end{pmatrix}$
     *2×1*

$= \dfrac{-1}{7} \begin{pmatrix} -23 \\ -5 \end{pmatrix}$

You can leave your answer in this form.

(b)  BX = A

X = B⁻¹ A

det B = −6 + 8 = 2

So: $\qquad B^{-1} = \dfrac{1}{2} \begin{pmatrix} -6 & 2 \\ -4 & 1 \end{pmatrix}$

So: $\qquad X = \dfrac{1}{2} \begin{pmatrix} -6 & 2 \\ -4 & 1 \end{pmatrix} \begin{pmatrix} -2 & 5 \\ 3 & -4 \end{pmatrix}$

$\qquad\qquad\qquad 2\times2 \qquad\quad 2\times2$

$\qquad\qquad = \dfrac{1}{2} \begin{pmatrix} 18 & -38 \\ 11 & -24 \end{pmatrix}$

$\qquad\qquad\qquad\qquad 2\times2$

$\qquad\qquad = \begin{pmatrix} 9 & -19 \\ 5\frac{1}{2} & -12 \end{pmatrix}$

## Exercise 11G

$A = \begin{pmatrix} 2 & 5 \\ 4 & 3 \end{pmatrix} \quad B = \begin{pmatrix} 4 & -2 \\ 5 & -4 \end{pmatrix} \quad C = \begin{pmatrix} -2 & 7 \\ 3 & -4 \end{pmatrix}$

$D = \begin{pmatrix} -7 \\ 4 \end{pmatrix} \qquad E = \begin{pmatrix} 1 \\ -3 \end{pmatrix}$

Solve the following:

1. AX = D
2. BX = E
3. CX = D
4. AX = E
5. AX = B
6. CX = A
7. BX = C

8. AX = C
9. CX = B
10. BX = A
11. AX + B = C
12. BX – D = E
13. CX –2A = 3B
14. AX + 3D = 2E

## 11.10 Solving Two Simultaneous Equations Using Matrices

You can use matrices to solve simultaneous equations by rewriting the two equations as one matrix equation, i.e. AX = B where

a. A is the matrix with the coefficients of $x$ and $y$ from each equation;

b. $X = \begin{pmatrix} x \\ y \end{pmatrix}$;

c. B is the matrix with the constants from each equation;

d. Find the inverse of A;

e. Multiply $A^{-1}$ by B **in this order**;

f. Write out the answers for $x$ and $y$.

For example:

19. Solve the following simultaneous equations using matrices:

(a) $4x – 3y = 19$
$\qquad 2x + 5y = -10$

(b) $3x + y – 6 = 0$
$\qquad x – 2y – 9 = 0$

(a) $A = \begin{pmatrix} 4 & -3 \\ 2 & 5 \end{pmatrix} \quad X = \begin{pmatrix} x \\ y \end{pmatrix} \quad B = \begin{pmatrix} 19 \\ -10 \end{pmatrix}$

$\qquad\qquad AX = B$
$\qquad\qquad X = A^{-1} B$
$\qquad\quad det\ A = 20 – (-6) = 20 + 6 = 26$

So: $\qquad A^{-1} = \dfrac{1}{26} \begin{pmatrix} 5 & 3 \\ -2 & 4 \end{pmatrix}$

So: $\qquad X = \dfrac{1}{26} \begin{pmatrix} 5 & 3 \\ -2 & 4 \end{pmatrix} \begin{pmatrix} 19 \\ -10 \end{pmatrix}$

$\qquad\qquad = \dfrac{1}{26} \begin{pmatrix} 95 – 30 \\ -38 – 40 \end{pmatrix}$

$\qquad\qquad = \dfrac{1}{26} \begin{pmatrix} 65 \\ -78 \end{pmatrix}$

$\qquad\qquad = \begin{pmatrix} 2\frac{1}{2} \\ -3 \end{pmatrix}$

Therefore $x = 2\dfrac{1}{2}$ and $y = -3$

(b) You must first re-write the simultaneous equations:

$\qquad\qquad 3x + y = 6$
$\qquad\qquad x – 2y = 9$

$A = \begin{pmatrix} 3 & 1 \\ 1 & -2 \end{pmatrix} \quad X = \begin{pmatrix} x \\ y \end{pmatrix} \quad B = \begin{pmatrix} 6 \\ 9 \end{pmatrix}$

$\qquad\qquad AX = B$
$\qquad\qquad X = A^{-1} B$
$\qquad\quad det\ A = -6 – 1 = -7$

So: $\qquad A^{-1} = \dfrac{-1}{7} \begin{pmatrix} -2 & -1 \\ -1 & 3 \end{pmatrix}$

So: $\qquad X = \dfrac{-1}{7} \begin{pmatrix} -2 & -1 \\ -1 & 3 \end{pmatrix} \begin{pmatrix} 6 \\ 9 \end{pmatrix}$

$\qquad\qquad = \dfrac{-1}{7} \begin{pmatrix} -12 – 9 \\ -6 + 27 \end{pmatrix}$

$\qquad\qquad = \dfrac{-1}{7} \begin{pmatrix} -21 \\ 21 \end{pmatrix}$

$\qquad\qquad = \begin{pmatrix} 3 \\ -3 \end{pmatrix}$

Therefore $x = 3$ and $y = -3$.

## Exercise 11H: *Solve the following simultaneous equations using matrices.*

1.  $2x + 3y = 2$        $x + 4y = -4$
2.  $4x - 3y = -23$        $x + 2y = 8$
3.  $2x + 5y = -4$        $-3x - y = -7$
4.  $4x - 2y = -2$        $2x + 7y = 31$
5.  $3x - 5y - 11 = 0$        $x + 4y + 19 = 0$
6.  $2x - 9y = 40$        $3x + y = 2$
7.  $4x - 3y = -24$        $x - 5y = -23$
8.  $6x + 3y = -3$        $2x - 5y = -37$
9.  $2x + 3y - 4 = 0$        $x - 5y - 15 = 0$
10. $4x - 2y = 6$        $3x + 9y = -69$
11. $3x - y = 1$        $2x + 3y = 19$
12. $2x + 4y = 24$        $x - 5y = -9$
13. $-2x + 5y = -18$        $3x - 4y = 20$
14. $-x + 2y = 13$        $-2x - 3y = -9$
15. $4x - y = -5$        $2x + 3y = -13$
16. $2x - 5y = 18$        $-x + 4y = -12$
17. $3x - 2y = -9$        $2x + 5y = 13$
18. $3x + 4y = -22$        $-2x - 5y = 24$
19. $2x - 7y = 20$        $3x + 8y = -7$
20. $-4x + 2y = 4$        $2x - 5y = 14$
21. $3x + 2y = -6$        $2x - 5y = 34$
22. $4x + 3y = -6$        $x - 2y = -7$
23. $2x - 5y = 22$        $3x - 2y = 11$
24. $-4x + 3y = -1$        $-2x - 5y = 19$
25. $2x - 7y = 24$        $3x + 2y = 11$

55

# CHAPTER 12: LOGARITHMS

## 12.1 Definition Of A Logarithm

Consider the following example: $10^2 = 100$. In this case:
- 10 is called the **base**;
- 2 is called the **index**.

The logarithm of a number is defined as: **The index, or power, to which you would raise the base to get the number.** So we can define $\log_{10} 100 = 2$ since $10^2 = 100$.

Here are some further examples:

$$\log_2 8 = 3$$
since: $$2^3 = 8$$

$$\log_4 0.25 = -1$$
since: $$4^{-1} = \frac{1}{4} = 0.25$$

$$\log_7 7 = 1$$
since: $$7^1 = 7$$

Note that $\log_a a = 1$ for any number, **a**, since $a^1 = 1$.

### Exercise 12A: *Work out the following.*

1. $\log_2 4$
2. $\log_2 32$
3. $\log_2 0.5$
4. $\log_3 27$
5. $\log_3 81$
6. $\log_3 1$
7. $\log_4 16$
8. $\log_5 125$
9. $\log_{10} 1000000$
10. $\log_{10} 0.001$

## 12.2 Logs To Base 10

Logs to base 10 are generally written **without** the base highlighted, i.e. **log 4 means $\log_{10} 4$**. However, all other bases must be specifically written.

Since logs are simply powers, or indices, to which you would raise the base to get the number, then the laws of indices are also the laws of logs, i.e.:

**Law 1** $\quad \log(ab) = \log a + \log b$

**Law 2** $\quad \log\left(\frac{a}{b}\right) = \log a - \log b$

**Law 3** $\quad \log a^n = n \log a$

For example:

1. Write the following in terms $x$, $y$ and/or $z$ where $\log a = x$, $\log b = y$ and $\log c = z$.

   (a) $\quad \log bc$
   (b) $\quad \log \frac{c}{b}$
   (c) $\quad \log a^7$

   (d) $\quad \log \frac{a^4 b^2}{c^3}$
   (e) $\quad \log \sqrt{\frac{a}{c}}$

You can simplify each of these logarithms by rewriting them using the three laws listed previously.

(a) $\quad\quad \log bc = \log b + \log c$ (using law 1)
So: $\quad\quad \log bc = y + z$

(b) $\quad\quad \log \frac{c}{b} = \log c - \log b$ (using law 2)
So: $\quad\quad \log \frac{c}{b} = z - y$

(c) $\quad\quad \log a^7 = 7 \log a$ (using law 3)
So: $\quad\quad \log a^7 = 7x$

(d) $\quad \log \frac{a^4 b^2}{c^3} = \log a^4 + \log b^2 - \log c^3$
(using laws 1 and 2)

$\quad\quad\quad\quad = 4 \log a + 2 \log b - 3 \log c$
(using law 3)

$\quad\quad\quad\quad = 4x + 2y - 3z$

(e) $\quad \log \sqrt{\frac{a}{c}}$

You must first re-write the square root in index form:

$$\log \sqrt{\frac{a}{c}} = \log \left(\frac{a}{c}\right)^{1/2}$$

Then $\log \left(\frac{a}{c}\right)^{1/2} = \frac{1}{2} \log \left(\frac{a}{c}\right)$ (using law 3)

$$= \frac{1}{2} (\log a - \log c) \text{ (using law 2)}$$

$$= \frac{1}{2} (x - z) \text{ or } \frac{1}{2}x - \frac{1}{2}z$$

### Exercise 12B: *Write the following in terms $x$, $y$ and/or $z$ where $\log a = x$, $\log b = y$ and $\log c = z$.*

1. $\log ab$
2. $\log \frac{a}{b}$
3. $\log a^2 b$
4. $\log \frac{b}{c^3}$
5. $\log \sqrt{\frac{a}{b}}$
6. $\log \sqrt{\frac{b}{c}}$
7. $\log \frac{a^3 b}{c}$
8. $\log \frac{ab^4}{c^5}$
9. $\log \sqrt{\frac{a}{c^3}}$
10. $\log \sqrt[4]{\frac{a^2 c}{b}}$

## 12.3 Logarithms For Any Base

The general definition of a logarithm for any base is:

**If $a^x = N$, then $x = \log_a N$**

You need to know how to solve general log equations. The rules are as follows:

a. Use the second part of the general definition to find the values of two of the unknowns.

b. Use the first part of the general definition to find the missing value.

For example:

2. Find the value of **a** if (a) $\log_a 49 = 2$ (b) $\log_a 0.2 = -1$.

(a) The second part of the general definition states that:
$$\log_a N = x$$
Since: $\log_a 49 = 2$
So: $N = 49$, $x = 2$ and $a = a$

The first part of the general definition states that:
$$a^x = N$$
Therefore: $a^2 = 49$
$a = \sqrt{49}$
$a = 7$

(b) The second part of the general definition states that:
$$\log_a N = x$$
Since: $\log_a 0.2 = -1$
So: $N = 0.2$, $x = -1$ and $a = a$

The first part of the general definition states that:
$$a^x = N$$
Therefore: $a^{-1} = 0.2$
So: $\dfrac{1}{a} = \dfrac{1}{5}$
$a = 5$

**Exercise 12C**: *Find the value of a in each case.*

1. $\log_a 8 = 3$
2. $\log_a 0.25 = -1$
3. $\log_a 36 = 2$
4. $\log_a 9 = 2$
5. $\log_a 625 = 4$
6. $\log_a 32 = 5$
7. $\log_a 27 = 3$
8. $\log_a 125 = 3$
9. $\log_a 16 = 4$
10. $\log_a 64 = 3$
11. $\log_a 128 = 7$
12. $\log_a 216 = 3$

You can use the same method to find the number, where the log and the base are known. The rules are the same:

a. Use the second part of the general definition to find the values of two of the unknowns.

b. Use the first part of the general definition to find the missing value.

For example:

3. Find b if (a) $\log_9 b = 2$ (b) $\log_8 b = -3$

(a) The second part of the general definition states that:
$$\log_a N = x$$
Since: $\log_9 b = 2$
So: $a = 9$, $x = 2$ and $N = b$

The first part of the general definition states that:
$$a^x = N$$
Therefore: $9^2 = b$
$b = 81$

(b) The second part of the general definition states that:
$$\log_a N = x$$
Since: $\log_8 b = -3$
So: $a = 8$, $x = -3$ and $N = b$

The first part of the general definition states that:
$$a^x = N$$
Therefore: $8^{-3} = b$
So: $b = \left(\dfrac{1}{8}\right)^3$
$b = \dfrac{1}{512}$

**Exercise 12D**: *Find the value of b in each case.*

1. $\log_3 b = 4$
2. $\log_2 b = 8$
3. $\log_5 b = 2$
4. $\log_7 b = 3$
5. $\log_3 b = 2$
6. $\log_2 b = 3$
7. $\log_4 b = 2$
8. $\log_6 b = 2$
9. $\log_5 b = 3$
10. $\log_4 b = 3$
11. $\log_5 b = -1$
12. $\log_2 b = 5$
13. $\log_6 b = 3$
14. $\log_3 b = -2$
15. $\log_4 b = \dfrac{3}{2}$

## 12.4 Working Out Logs Of Numbers To Any Base

In this case, you want to know the actual value of a logarithm given in the form $\log_a N$. For example:

....................................................................................

4.  Work out the value of $\log_3 81$

    You know that:       $\log_a N = x$
    and you want:      $\log_3 81$
    So:                   $a = 3$ and $N = 81$

    Now use the first part of the general definition to get:
    $$a^x = N$$
    Substituting:        $3^x = 81$
    And so:            $x = 4$

> ### Exercise 12E: *Work out the value of the following.*

1.  $\log_5 25$
2.  $\log_6 216$
3.  $\log_2 16$
4.  $\log_3 27$
5.  $\log_2 32$
6.  $\log_8 64$
7.  $\log_3 9$
8.  $\log_4 32$
9.  $\log_6 36$
10. $\log_8 4$
11. $\log_2 8$

## 12.5 Writing Logs Of Numbers In Terms Of Other Logs Of Prime Numbers

You can find the log of a third value, if you know the logs of two of its prime factors. The rules are as follows:

a.  Rewrite each number in terms of the prime factors;

b.  Use the appropriate law of logs;

c.  Then replace them with the values of the logs of the prime factors as appropriate.

For example:

....................................................................................

5.  If $\log 3 = p$ and $\log 5 = q$ express the following in terms of $p$ and $q$: (a) $\log 45$ (b) $\log 0.6$ (c) $\log 81$.

    (a) Write 45 as a product of prime factors, i.e. keep dividing 45 by 3 and then 5 until you get 1:

    ```
    3 | 45
    3 | 15
    5 |  5
         1
    ```

So:               $45 = 3 \times 3 \times 5$
                     $45 = 3^2 \times 5$

So:      $\log 45 = \log(3^2 \times 5)$
$$= \log 3^2 + \log 5 \quad \text{(using law 1)}$$
$$= 2\log 3 + \log 5 \quad \text{(using law 3)}$$
$$= 2p + q$$

(b) Since 0.6 is less than 1 you must use division to get 0.6:

i.e.           $0.6 = \dfrac{3}{5}$

So      $\log 0.6 = \log \dfrac{3}{5}$
$$= \log 3 - \log 5 \quad \text{(using law 2)}$$
$$= p - q$$

(c) Keep dividing 81 by 3 until you get 1:

```
3 | 81
3 | 27
3 |  9
3 |  3
     1
```

So:               $81 = 3 \times 3 \times 3 \times 3$
                     $81 = 3^4$

So:      $\log 81 = \log 3^4$
$$= 4\log 3 \quad \text{(using law 3)}$$
$$= 4p$$

> ### Exercise 12F

1.  If $\log 3 = p$ and $\log 2 = q$ express the following in terms of $p$ and $q$:
    (a) $\log 6$
    (b) $\log 1.5$
    (c) $\log 8$
    (d) $\log 72$

2.  If $\log 2 = p$ and $\log 7 = q$ express the following in terms of $p$ and $q$:
    (a) $\log 3.5$
    (b) $\log 28$
    (c) $\log 16$
    (d) $\log 98$

3.  If $\log 3 = p$ and $\log 11 = q$ express the following in terms of $p$ and $q$:
    (a) $\log 33$
    (b) $\log 99$
    (c) $\log 27$
    (d) $\log 121$

4.  If $\log 2 = p$ and $\log 3 = q$ express the following in terms of $p$ and $q$:
    (a) $\log 6$
    (b) $\log 32$
    (c) $\log 48$
    (d) $\log 1.5$

## Exercise 12F...

5. If log 2 = p and log 5 = q express the following in terms of p and q:
   (a)   log 10
   (b)   log 2.5
   (c)   log 100
   (d)   log 125

6. If log 2 = p and log 11 = q express the following in terms of p and q:
   (a)   log 22
   (b)   log 5.5
   (c)   log 64
   (d)   log 44

7. If log 7 = p and log 5 = q express the following in terms of p and q:
   (a)   log 35
   (b)   log 1.4
   (c)   log 175
   (d)   log 343

## 12.6 Writing Logs of Numbers Given To Different Bases In Terms Of Logs Of Prime Numbers

You can do the same thing for logs that are expressed in bases other than 10. For example:

6. If $\log_7 5 = p$ and $\log_7 2 = q$ express the following in terms of p and q: (a) $\log_7 10$ (b) $\log_7 35$ (c) $\log_7 3.5$ (d) $\log_7 140$.

The rules for solving these is as follows:

a.   Rewrite each number in terms of 5, 2 and/or 7;

b.   Use the appropriate law of logs;

c.   Then replace $\log_7 5 = p$, $\log_7 2 = q$ and $\log_7 7 = 1$ as appropriate.

(a)
$$10 = 2 \times 5$$
So:   $\log_7 10 = \log_7 (2 \times 5)$
$$= \log_7 2 + \log_7 5 \ \text{(using law 1)}$$
$$= p + q$$

(b)
$$35 = 5 \times 7$$
So:   $\log_7 35 = \log_7 (5 \times 7)$
$$= \log_7 5 + \log_7 7 \ \text{(using law 1)}$$
$$= p + 1$$

(c)
$$3.5 = \frac{7}{2}$$
So:   $\log_7 3.5 = \log_7 \frac{3}{2}$
$$= \log_7 7 - \log_7 2 \ \text{(using law 2)}$$
$$= 1 - q$$

(d)
$$
\begin{array}{r|l}
2 & 140 \\
2 & 70 \\
5 & 35 \\
7 & 7 \\
& 1
\end{array}
$$

So:   $140 = 2 \times 2 \times 5 \times 7$
$$140 = 2^2 \times 5 \times 7$$

So:   $\log_7 140 = \log_7 (2^2 \times 5 \times 7)$
$$= \log_7 2^2 + \log_7 5 + \log_7 7$$
$$\text{(using law 1)}$$
$$= 2\log_7 2 + \log_7 5 + \log_7 7$$
$$\text{(using law 3)}$$
$$= 2q + p + 1$$

## Exercise 12G

1. If $\log_3 2 = p$ and $\log_3 5 = q$ express the following in terms of p and q:
   (a)   $\log_3 10$
   (b)   $\log_3 20$
   (c)   $\log_3 50$
   (d)   $\log_3 6$
   (e)   $\log_3 45$
   (f)   $\log_3 2.5$

2. If $\log_2 3 = p$ and $\log_2 7 = q$ express the following in terms of p and q:
   (a)   $\log_2 21$
   (b)   $\log_2 63$
   (c)   $\log_2 147$
   (d)   $\log_2 24$
   (e)   $\log_2 28$

3. If $\log_5 2 = p$ and $\log_5 7 = q$ express the following in terms of p and q:
   (a)   $\log_5 3.5$
   (b)   $\log_5 28$
   (c)   $\log_5 98$
   (d)   $\log_5 10$
   (e)   $\log_5 175$
   (f)   $\log_5 70$

4. If $\log_4 5 = p$ and $\log_4 7 = q$ express the following in terms of p and q:
   (a)   $\log_4 35$
   (b)   $\log_4 1.4$
   (c)   $\log_4 175$
   (d)   $\log_4 20$
   (e)   $\log_4 112$

5. If $\log_6 2 = p$ and $\log_6 11 = q$ express the following in terms of p and q:
   (a)   $\log_6 22$
   (b)   $\log_6 5.5$
   (c)   $\log_6 12$
   (d)   $\log_6 44$
   (e)   $\log_6 242$
   (f)   $\log_6 132$

6. If $\log_7 3 = p$ and $\log_7 5 = q$ express the following in terms of p and q:
   (a)   $\log_7 15$
   (b)   $\log_7 21$
   (c)   $\log_7 35$
   (d)   $\log_7 45$
   (e)   $\log_7 0.6$

## Exercise 12G...

7. If $\log_9 7 = p$ and $\log_9 11 = q$ express the following in terms of p and q:
   (a) $\log_9 77$
   (b) $\log_9 63$
   (c) $\log_9 99$
   (d) $\log_9 539$
   (e) $\log_9 \dfrac{9}{49}$

8. If $\log_3 2 = p$ and $\log_3 11 = q$ express the following in terms of p and q:
   (a) $\log_3 6$
   (b) $\log_3 99$
   (c) $\log_3 5.5$
   (d) $\log_3 44$
   (e) $\log_3 2.75$
   (f) $\log_3 66$

9. If $\log_3 5 = p$ and $\log_3 7 = q$ express the following in terms of p and q:
   (a) $\log_3 35$
   (b) $\log_3 45$
   (c) $\log_3 21$
   (d) $\log_3 1.4$
   (e) $\log_3 105$

## 13.1 Solving Index Equations

You can use law 3 of logarithms to solve index equations. The rules are as follows:

a.  Take logs of both sides;

b.  Use law 3 to change the equation into a linear equation;

c.  Solve the linear equation.

For example:

1.  Solve (a) $7^x = 45$  (b) $8^{-x} = 1.96$

(a)
$$7^x = 45$$
$$\log 7^x = \log 45$$
$$x \log 7 = \log 45 \text{  (using law 3)}$$
$$x = \frac{\log 45}{\log 7}$$
$$x = 1.956...$$
$$x = 1.96 \text{ to 3 significant figures}$$

(b)
$$8^{-x} = 1.96$$
$$\log 8^{-x} = \log 1.96$$
$$-x \log 8 = \log 1.96 \text{  (using law 3)}$$
$$x = \frac{-\log 1.96}{\log 8}$$
$$x = -0.3236...$$
$$x = -0.324 \text{ to 3 significant figures}$$

**Exercise 13A**: *Solve the following, giving your answers correct to 3 significant figures.*

1.  $4^x = 7$
2.  $7^{-x} = 5$
3.  $5^x = 3$
4.  $9^x = 4$
5.  $4^{-x} = 10$
6.  $6^x = 15$
7.  $8^x = 20$
8.  $5^{-x} = 30$
9.  $3^x = 16$
10. $2^x = 35$
11. $3^{-x} = 8$
12. $12^x = 5$

## 13.2 More Complex Index Equations

You can use the same method for more complex indices. The rules are the same:

a.  Take logs of both sides;

b.  Use law 3 to change the equation into a linear equation;

c.  Solve the linear equation.

For example:

2.  Solve (a) $6^{2x-1} = 5$  (b) $4^{1-\frac{1}{3}x} = 11$

(a)
$$6^{2x-1} = 5$$
$$\log 6^{2x-1} = \log 5$$
$$(2x - 1) \log 6 = \log 5 \text{  (using law 3)}$$

Note: You must include the bracket around $2x - 1$ as there are two algebraic terms.

$$2x - 1 = \frac{\log 5}{\log 6}$$
$$2x - 1 = 0.8982$$
$$2x = 0.8982 + 1$$
$$2x = 1.8982$$
$$x = 0.9491$$
$$x = 0.949 \text{ to 3 significant figures}$$

(b)
$$4^{1-\frac{1}{3}x} = 11$$
$$\log 4^{1-\frac{1}{3}x} = \log 11$$
$$\left(1 - \frac{1}{3} x\right) \log 4 = \log 11 \text{  (using law 3)}$$

Note: You must include the bracket around $1 - \frac{1}{3} x$ as there are 2 algebraic terms.

$$1 - \frac{1}{3} x = \frac{\log 11}{\log 4}$$
$$1 - \frac{1}{3} x = 1.7297$$
$$-\frac{1}{3} x = 1.7297 - 1$$
$$-\frac{1}{3} x = 0.7297$$

Multiply both sides by $-3$ to get:
$$x = -2.1891$$
$$x = -2.19 \text{ to 3 significant figures}$$

**Exercise 13B**: *Solve the following, giving your answers correct to 3 significant figures.*

1.  $7^{3x+2} = 9$
2.  $4^{5x-2} = 6$
3.  $2^{1-2x} = 5$
4.  $3^{4-\frac{1}{2}x} = 8$
5.  $9^{3x} = 7$
6.  $6^{5+\frac{1}{4}x} = 8$
7.  $3^{4x-1} = 12$
8.  $5^{2-5x} = 9$
9.  $4^{3x+2} = 15$
10. $2^{1+\frac{3}{4}x} = 9$

## 13.3 Further Index Equations

You can use the same method when each side of the equation has an index with the same unknown. The rules are the same:

a. Take logs of both sides,

b. Use law 3 to change the equation into a linear equation,

c. Solve the linear equation.

For example:

3. Solve (a) $4^{3x-1} = 7^{x+2}$ (b) $4^{1-2x} = 3^{4x-1}$

(a)
$$4^{3x-1} = 7^{x+2}$$
$$\log 4^{3x-1} = \log 7^{x+2}$$
$$(3x-1)\log 4 = (x+2)\log 7 \text{ (using law 3)}$$

Note: You must include both brackets as there are two algebraic terms on each side.

Work out each bracket by multiplying to get:
$$3x\log 4 - \log 4 = x\log 7 + 2\log 7$$
$$3x\log 4 - x\log 7 = 2\log 7 + \log 4$$
$$x(3\log 4 - \log 7) = 2\log 7 + \log 4$$
$$0.961x = 2.292$$
$$x = \frac{2.292}{0.961}$$
$$x = 2.385$$
$$x = 2.39 \text{ to 3 significant figures}$$

(b)
$$4^{1-2x} = 3^{4x-1}$$
$$\log 4^{1-2x} = \log 3^{4x-1}$$
$$(1-2x)\log 4 = (4x-1)\log 3 \text{ (using law 3)}$$

Note: You must include both brackets as there are two algebraic terms on each side.

Work out each bracket by multiplying to get:
$$\log 4 - 2x\log 4 = 4x\log 3 - \log 3$$
$$\log 4 + \log 3 = 4x\log 3 + 2x\log 4$$
$$\log 4 + \log 3 = x(4\log 3 + 2\log 4)$$
$$1.079 = 3.113x$$
$$x = \frac{1.079}{3.113}$$
$$x = 0.3466$$
$$x = 0.347 \text{ to 3 significant figures}$$

**Exercise 13C**: *Solve the following, giving your answers correct to 3 significant figures.*

1. $5^{2x-1} = 3^{x+4}$
2. $4^{3x+2} = 7^{x-5}$
3. $2^{1-x} = 5^{x+2}$
4. $5^{1-3x} = 8^{4-x}$
5. $9^{3x+2} = 7^{1-x}$
6. $4^{x-2} = 3^{4-x}$
7. $6^{2x-1} = 3^{x+4}$
8. $6^{5x-2} = 2^{3x+5}$
9. $4^{1-3x} = 3^{x+2}$
10. $6^{2x+5} = 2^{5x-2}$

## 14.1 Solving Problems Using Log/Log Graphs

We can use log/log graphs to create straight-line graphs and hence solve problems. For example:

1. A formula for $N$ is: $N = aV^b$. Values of $N$ and $V$ are given in the table below:

| $V$ | $N$ |
|------|-------|
| 3.5 | 13.38 |
| 6.4 | 28.62 |
| 8.2 | 39.11 |
| 9.5 | 47.08 |
| 11.8 | 61.87 |

(a) Find the value of (i) $b$ (ii) $a$.
(b) Using these values find (i) $N$ when $V = 5.4$ (ii) $V$ when $N = 75$.

We can solve this question by using logs.

(a)           $N = aV^b$

Taking logs of both sides gives:
$$\log N = \log aV^b$$

Using the rules of logs gives:
$$\log N = \log a + \log V^b$$
$$\log N = \log a + b \log V$$

We can rewrite this as:
$$\log N = b \log V + \log a$$

This is the equation of a straight line matching up with $y = mx + c$ as shown:

$$\log N = b \log V + \log a$$
$$\quad y \ = \ mx \ + \ c$$

We can then:
a. work out values for $\log N$ and $\log V$ to 3 decimal places using the values given in the table.
b. draw the straight line graph putting the $\log N$ values on the $y$-axis and the $\log V$ values on the $x$-axis.
c. work out the gradient of the straight line to get the value of $b$.
d. substitute values for $N, V$ and $b$ into $N = aV^b$ to get the value of $a$.

The values for $\log N$ and $\log V$ to 3 decimal places are given in the following table.

| $V$ | $N$ | $\log V$ | $\log N$ |
|------|-------|----------|----------|
| 3.5 | 13.38 | 0.544 | 1.126 |
| 6.4 | 28.62 | 0.806 | 1.457 |
| 8.2 | 39.11 | 0.914 | 1.592 |
| 9.5 | 47.08 | 0.978 | 1.673 |
| 11.8 | 61.87 | 1.072 | 1.791 |

We now draw the straight line graph:

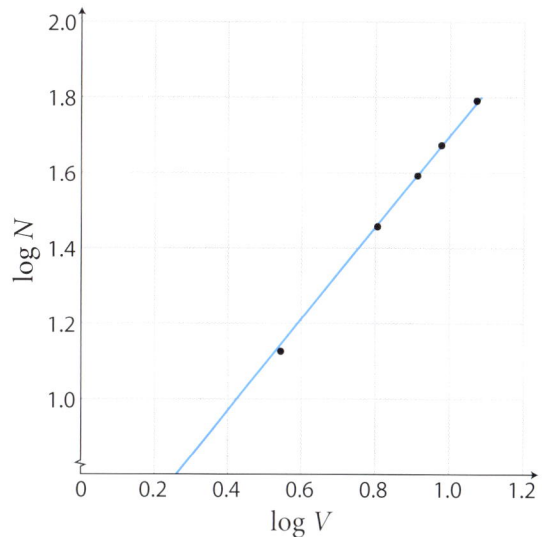

(i) We can now work out the gradient of the straight line to get the value of $b$ to 2 decimal places using the gradient formula:

$$\frac{y_2 - y_1}{x_2 - x_1}$$

We can choose any two points on the line. Taking (0.544, 1.126) and (1.072, 1.791) gives:

$$\frac{1.791 - 1.126}{1.072 - 0.544} = \frac{0.654}{0.528} = 1.26$$

So $b = 1.26$ to 2 decimal places.

(ii) We now substitute values for $N$, $V$ and $b$ into $N = aV^b$ to get the value of $a$. Again, we can choose any point on the line. So taking $N = 13.38$, $V = 3.5$ and $b = 1.26$ gives:

$$N = aVb$$
$$13.38 = a(3.5)^{1.26}$$

So:    $13.38 = 4.848a$

Giving:    $a = \dfrac{13.38}{4.848}$

So:    $a = 2.76$

We can now write the equation as $N = 2.76V^{1.26}$.

and use this to answer (b).

(b) (i) Substituting $V = 5.4$ into $N = 2.76V^{1.26}$ gives:
$N = 2.76(5.4)^{1.26} = 23.11$.

(ii) Substituting $N = 75$ into $N = 2.76V^{1.26}$ gives:
$2.76V^{1.26} = 75$

So $V^{1.26} = \dfrac{75}{2.76} = 27.174$

We can solve this equation by either taking logs:

$$\log V^{1.26} = \log 27.174$$
$$1.26 \log V = \log 27.174$$
$$\log V = \frac{\log 27.174}{1.26}$$
$$\log V = 1.1382$$
$$V = 13.75$$

or by taking the root:

$$V^{1.26} = 27.174$$
$$V = \sqrt[1.26]{27.174}$$
$$V = 13.75$$

Note that $N = 75$ is greater than any of the $N$ values given in the table and plotted on the graph. So we are making an assumption that the formula holds for values of $N$ greater than 61.87.

## Exercise 14A

1. $V = at^n$.
Values of $t$ and $V$ are given in the table below.

| $t$ | $V$ |
| --- | --- |
| 14 | 34.3 |
| 18 | 42.47 |
| 25 | 56.15 |
| 32 | 69.26 |
| 44 | 90.79 |

(a) Find the value of (i) $n$ (ii) $a$.
(b) Using these values find (i) $V$ when $t = 21$ (ii) $t$ when $V = 76.99$.

2. $W = cd^k$.
Values of $d$ and $W$ are given in the table below.

| $d$ | $W$ |
| --- | --- |
| 74 | 3.96 |
| 95 | 3.57 |
| 129 | 3.14 |
| 154 | 2.91 |
| 196 | 2.63 |

## Exercise 14A...

(a) Find the value of (i) $k$ (ii) $c$.
(b) Using these values find (i) $W$ when $d = 140$ (ii) $d$ when $W = 4.27$, stating the assumption you are making.

3. $G = vy^t$.
Values of $y$ and $G$ are given in the table below.

| $y$ | $G$ |
| --- | --- |
| 9.24 | 162.23 |
| 12.56 | 278.46 |
| 20.48 | 658.39 |
| 34.52 | 1650.25 |
| 40.66 | 2201.3 |

(a) Find the value of (i) $t$ (ii) $v$.

(b) Using these values find (i) $G$ when $y = 11.54$ (ii) $y$ when $G = 1012.27$.

4. $H = rf^q$.
Values of $f$ and $H$ are given in the table below.

| $f$ | $H$ |
| --- | --- |
| 30 | 8.32 |
| 35 | 8.93 |
| 45 | 10.02 |
| 62 | 11.62 |
| 78 | 12.91 |

(a) Find the value of (i) $q$ (ii) $r$.
(b) Using these values find (i) $H$ when $f = 82$, stating the assumption you are making. (ii) $f$ when $H = 8.57$.

5. $y = Ax^n$.
Values of $x$ and $y$ are given in the table below.

| $x$ | $y$ |
| --- | --- |
| 6.2 | 4.9 |
| 8.4 | 3.94 |
| 12 | 3.05 |
| 14.2 | 2.7 |
| 18 | 2.28 |

(a) Find the value of (i) $n$ (ii) $A$.
(b) Using these values find (i) $y$ when $x = 11$ (ii) $x$ when $y = 2.42$.

## Exercise 14A...

**6** $D = ax^b$.
Values of $x$ and $D$ are given in the table below.

| $x$ | $D$ |
|---|---|
| 9 | 100.46 |
| 14 | 89.95 |
| 26 | 77.06 |
| 35 | 71.54 |
| 48 | 66.11 |

**(a)** Find the value of (i) $b$ (ii) $a$.

**(b)** Using these values find (i) $D$ when $x = 31$ (ii) $x$ when $D = 106.97$, stating the assumption you are making.

## 14.2 Log/Log Graphs In Context

Log/log questions may be given in the context of a problem to be solved. For example:

..................................................

**2.** Willow measures the curved surface areas ($A$ cm$^3$) and height ($h$ cm) of different solids. The values for five of them are given in the table below.

| $h$ | $A$ |
|---|---|
| 6.4 | 45.81 |
| 9.5 | 75.05 |
| 12.2 | 102.6 |
| 16.4 | 148.51 |
| 22.5 | 220.52 |

Willow believes that a relationship of the form $A = bh^n$ exists where $b$ and $n$ are constants.

**(a)** Verify this relationship by drawing a suitable straight line graph, using values correct to 3 decimal places.

**(b)** Hence find the values of (i) $n$ (ii) $b$.

**(c)** Find the curved surface area of a solid with height 14 cm.

**(d)** Find the height of a solid with a curved surface area of 239 cm$^2$.

State any assumption which you make.

**(a)**
$$A = bh^n$$

Taking logs of both sides gives:
$$\log A = \log bh^n$$

Using the rules of logs gives:
$$\log A = \log b + \log h^n$$
$$\log A = \log a + n \log h$$

We can rewrite this as:
$$\log A = n \log h + \log a$$

This is the equation of a straight line matching up with $y = mx + c$ as shown:
$$\log A = n \log h + \log a$$
$$y = mx + c$$

The values for $\log h$ and $\log A$ to 3 decimal places are given in the table below.

| $h$ | $A$ | $\log h$ | $\log A$ |
|---|---|---|---|
| 6.4 | 45.81 | 0.806 | 1.661 |
| 9.5 | 75.05 | 0.978 | 1.875 |
| 12.2 | 102.6 | 1.086 | 2.011 |
| 16.4 | 148.51 | 1.215 | 2.172 |
| 22.5 | 220.52 | 1.352 | 2.343 |

We now draw the straight line graph to verify this relationship.

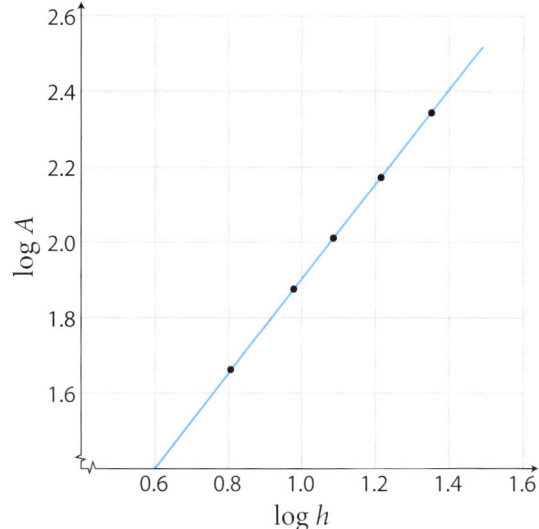

**(b)** **(i)** We can now work out the gradient of the straight line to get the value of $n$ to 2 decimal places using the gradient formula:
$$\frac{y_2 - y_1}{x_2 - x_1}$$

We can choose any two points on the line. Taking $(0.806, 1.661)$ and $(1.352, 2.343)$ gives:
$$\frac{2.343 - 1.661}{1.352 - 0.806} = \frac{0.682}{0.546} = 1.25$$

So $n = 1.25$ to 2 decimal places.

**(ii)** We now substitute values for $A$, $h$ and $n$ into $A = bh^n$ to get the value of $b$. We can choose any point on the line. Taking $A = 45.81$, $h = 6.4$ and $n = 1.25$ gives:

$$A = bh^n$$
$$45.81 = b(6.4)^{1.25}$$

So: $\quad 45.81 = 10.179b$

Giving: $\quad b = \dfrac{45.81}{10.179}$

So: $\quad b = 4.5$

We can now write the equation as $A = 4.5h^{1.25}$.

(c) Substituting $h = 14$ into $A = 4.5$ gives:
$A = 4.5(14)^{1.25} = 121.86 \text{ cm}^2$.

(d) Substituting $A = 239$ into $A = 4.5h^{1.25}$ gives:

$$4.5h^{1.25} = 239$$

So: $h^{1.25} = \dfrac{239}{4.5} = 53.11$

We can solve this equation by either taking logs:

$$\log h^{1.25} = \log 53.11$$
$$1.25 \log h = \log 53.11$$
$$\log h = \dfrac{\log 53.11}{1.25}$$
$$\log h = 1.18$$
$$h = 24$$

or by taking the root:

$$h^{1.25} = 53.11$$
$$h = \sqrt[1.25]{53.11}$$
$$h = 24$$

Assumption: We are assuming that the relationship holds for values of $A$ greater than 220.52.

## Exercise 14B

1. Quinn measures the mass ($M$ kg) and width ($w$ m) of different solids. The values of five of them are given in the table below.

| $w$ | $M$ |
|---|---|
| 5 | 10.69 |
| 12 | 29.27 |
| 20 | 52.66 |
| 24 | 64.95 |
| 33 | 93.67 |

Quinn believes that a relationship of the form $M = pw^t$
exists where $p$ and $t$ are constants.
(a) Verify this relationship by drawing a suitable straight line graph, using values correct to 3 decimal places.
(b) Hence find the values of (i) $t$ (ii) $p$.

## Exercise 14B...

(c) Find the mass of a solid with width 18 cm.
(d) Find the width of a solid with a mass of 34.94 kg.

2. Cadence records the number of tickets sold ($N$) at different shows when the price per ticket was £$P$. The results for five shows are given in the table below.

| $P$ | $N$ |
|---|---|
| 18.50 | 201 |
| 22 | 174 |
| 27.50 | 145 |
| 30 | 135 |
| 38.50 | 110 |

Cadence believes that a relationship of the form $N = aP^q$
exists where $a$ and $q$ are constants.
(a) Verify this relationship by drawing a suitable straight line graph, using values correct to 3 decimal places.
(b) Hence find the values of (i) $q$ (ii) $a$.
(c) Find the number of tickets sold when the price per ticket was £25.
(d) Find the price per ticket when 126 tickets were sold.

3. Rory records the cost of houses ($C$) in thousands of £s sold and their distance ($m$) in miles from Belfast city centre. The results for five houses are given in the table below.

| $m$ | $C$ |
|---|---|
| 8 | 404 |
| 12 | 279 |
| 18 | 192 |
| 24 | 147 |
| 32 | 113 |

Rory believes that a relationship of the form $C = am^b$
exists where $a$ and $b$ are constants.
(a) Verify this relationship by drawing a suitable straight line graph, using values correct to 3 decimal places.
(b) Hence find the values of (i) $b$ (ii) $a$.
(c) Find the cost of a house which is 14 miles from Belfast city centre.
(d) A house costs £107,000. How many miles is it from Belfast city centre?
State any assumption which you make.

## Exercise 14B...

4.  Lily is investigating the relationship between the number of passengers ($N$) on different buses to Dublin at different prices (£$P$) per passenger. The results for five buses are given in the table below.

    | $P$ | $N$ |
    |------|-----|
    | 3.50 | 82 |
    | 4.95 | 61 |
    | 6 | 51 |
    | 7.25 | 44 |
    | 8.10 | 40 |

    Lily believes that a relationship of the form
    $N = aP^q$
    exists where $a$ and $q$ are constants.
    (a)  Verify this relationship by drawing a suitable straight line graph, using values correct to 3 decimal places.
    (b)  Hence find the values of (i) $q$ (ii) $a$.
    (c)  Find the number of passengers on a bus to Dublin when the price is £5.35 per passenger.
    (d)  There are 70 passengers on a bus to Dublin. Find the price in £ per passenger.

5.  Séan records the number of litres of diesel ($D$) needed for different lengths of journeys ($T$ km). The results for five journeys are given in the table below.

    | $T$ | $D$ |
    |-------|-------|
    | 131.2 | 13.32 |
    | 216 | 21.08 |
    | 249.6 | 24.07 |
    | 294.4 | 28.02 |
    | 361.6 | 33.86 |

    Séan believes that a relationship of the form
    $D = vT^y$
    exists where $v$ and $y$ are constants
    (a)  Verify this relationship by drawing a suitable straight line graph, using values correct to 3 decimal places.
    (b)  Hence find the values of (i) $y$ (ii) $v$.
    (c)  How many litres of diesel are needed for a journey of 100 miles.
    (d)  37.15 litres of diesel are needed for a journey. How many km was this journey?
    State any assumption which you make.

# Unit 2: Mechanics

## CHAPTER 15: DISPLACEMENT/TIME AND VELOCITY/TIME GRAPHS

### 15.1 Displacement/Time Graphs

This type of graph is formed when you plot **time** along the horizontal axis and **displacement** along the vertical axis. The **gradient** of each section of the displacement/time graph tells you the **velocity** in that section. You can work out the gradient using:

$$\text{Gradient} = \frac{\text{Rise}}{\text{Run}}$$

A horizontal line segment indicates a velocity of 0 m/s (ie the body has stopped). For example:

····················································

1. Work out the velocities in each section of the displacement/time graph below.

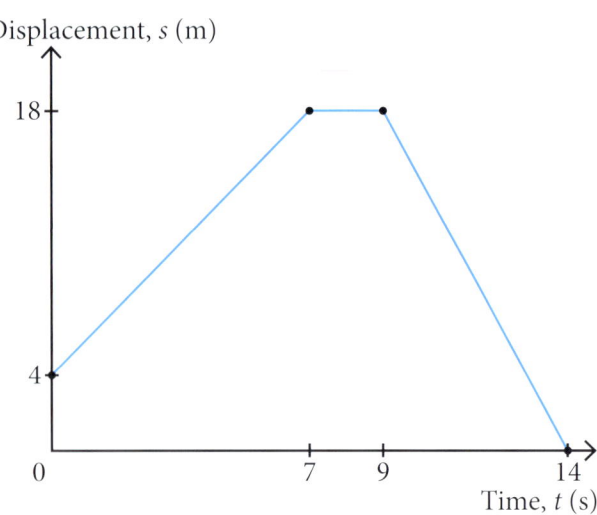

In the first section the gradient is given by:

$$\text{Gradient} = \frac{18 - 4}{7}$$

So:        $\text{Velocity} = \dfrac{14}{7} = 2 \text{ m/s}$

In the middle section the line is horizontal:

So:        $\text{Velocity} = 0 \text{ m/s}$

In the final section the gradient is given by:

$$\text{Gradient} = \frac{0 - 18}{5}$$

So:        $\text{Velocity} = \dfrac{-18}{5} = -3.6$

Which means 3.6 m/s in the opposite direction.

1.
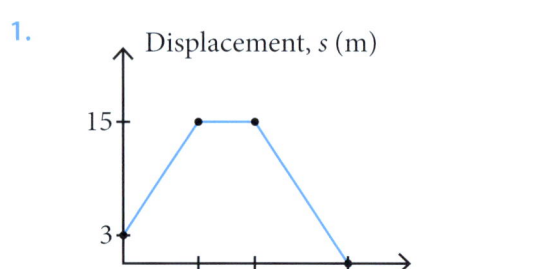

2.
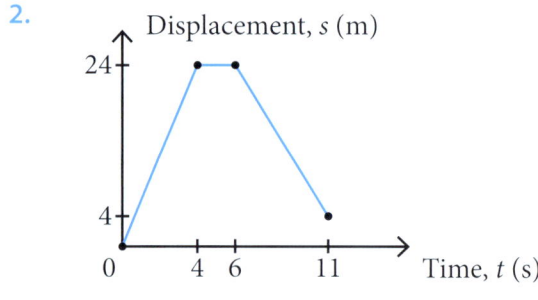

3.
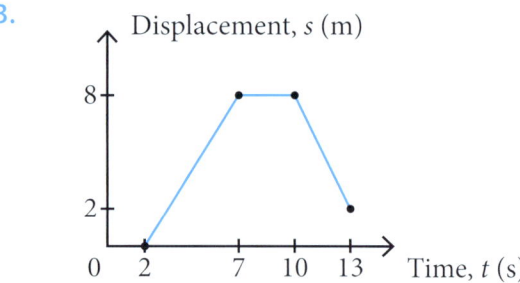

4.
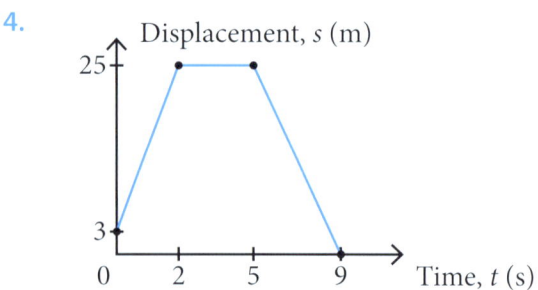

## Exercise 15A...

**5.**

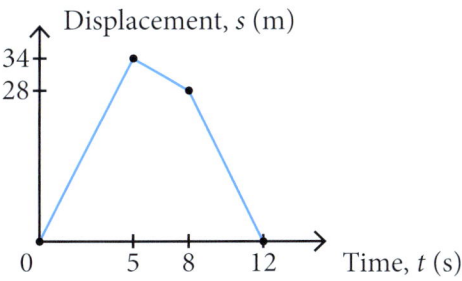

Displacement, *s* (m)

**6.**

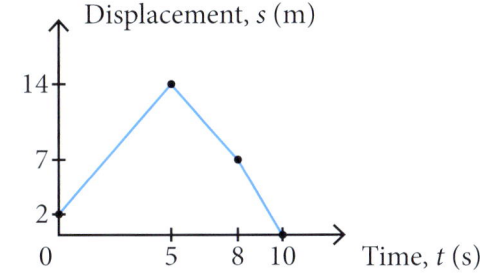

Displacement, *s* (m)

## 15.2 Velocity/Time Graphs

This type of graph is formed when you plot **time** along the horizontal axis and **velocity** along the vertical axis. The **gradient** of each section of the velocity/time graph tells you the **acceleration** in that section. You can work out the gradient using:

$$\text{Gradient} = \frac{\text{Rise}}{\text{Run}}$$

A horizontal line segment indicates an acceleration of 0 m/s² (ie the body is moving at a constant velocity). The **area under** the velocity/time graph tells you the **distance travelled** during the motion. For example:

**2.** In the velocity/time graph below, work out the
**(a)** acceleration in each section;
**(b)** total distance travelled.

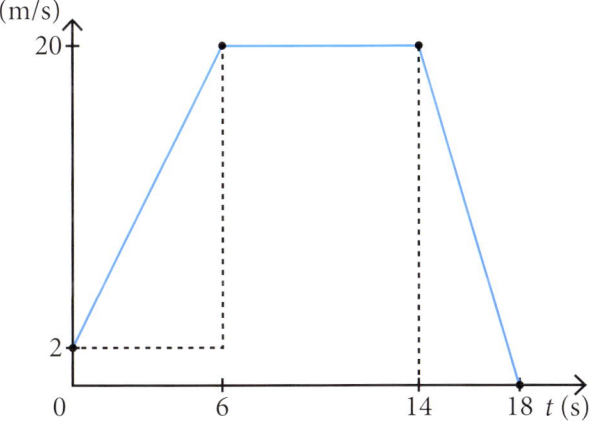

*v* (m/s)

**(a)** In the first section the gradient is given by:

$$\text{Gradient} = \frac{20 - 2}{6}$$

So: $\quad\text{Acceleration} = \dfrac{18}{6} = 3 \text{ m/s}^2$

In the middle section the line is horizontal:

So: $\quad\text{Acceleration} = 0 \text{ m/s}^2$

In the final section the gradient is given by:

$$\text{Gradient} = \frac{0 - 20}{4}$$

So: $\quad\text{Acceleration} = \dfrac{-20}{4} = -5 \text{ m/s}^2$

i.e., the body is slowing down, or decelerating.

Note: If the question had asked for the **deceleration** in the last part then the answer would be 5 m/s².

**(b)** The total distance travelled is given by the area under the velocity/time graph. You must split the area under the graph into different regular shapes as shown below:

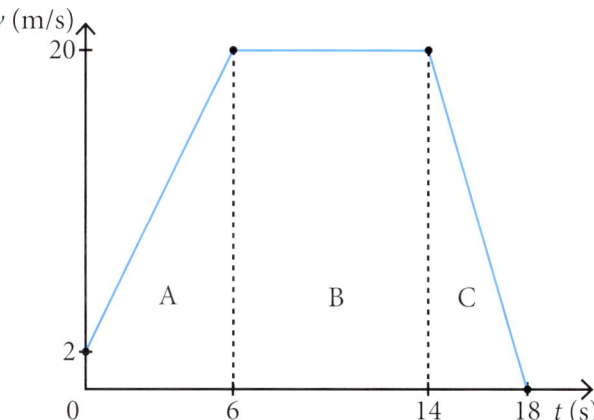

*v* (m/s)

Area A is a trapezium, so:

$$\text{Area} = \frac{1}{2}(2 + 20) \times 6$$
$$= \frac{1}{2} \times 22 \times 6$$
$$= 66$$

Area B is a rectangle, so:

$$\text{Area} = 8 \times 20$$
$$= 160$$

Area C is a triangle, so:

$$\text{Area} = \frac{1}{2} \times 4 \times 20$$
$$= 40$$

So: $\quad$ Total distance = 66 + 160 + 40
$$= 266 \text{ m}$$

## Exercise 15B

In the velocity/time graphs in questions 1 to 10, work out:
(a) the acceleration in each section of the graph;
(b) the total distance travelled.

1.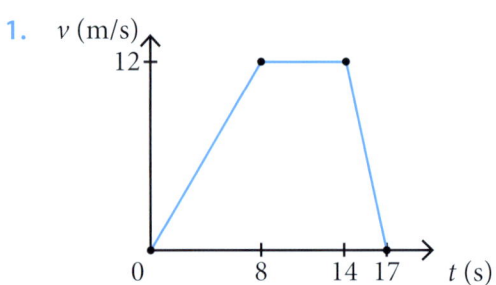

2.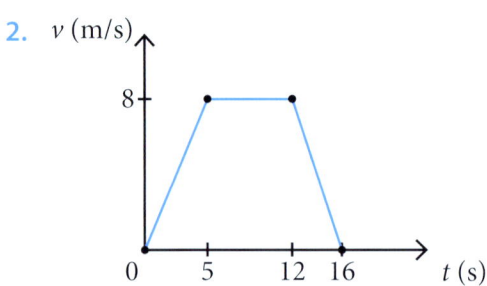

3.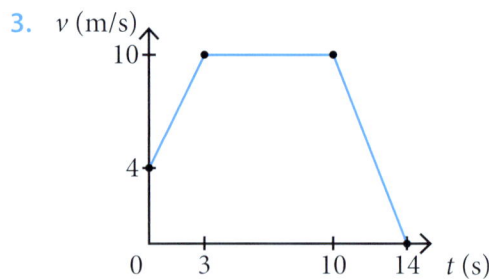

4.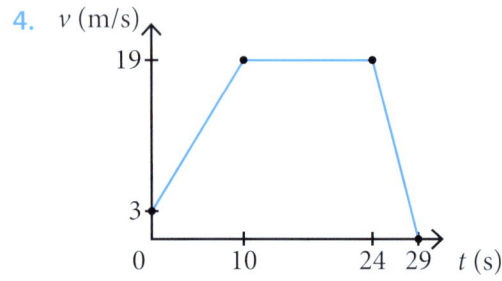

5.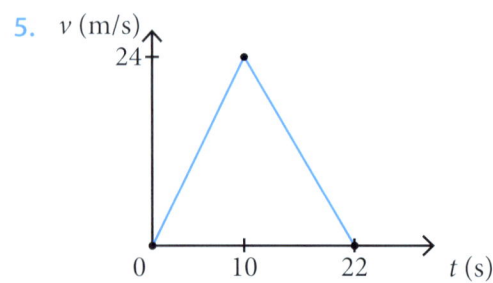

## Exercise 15B...

6.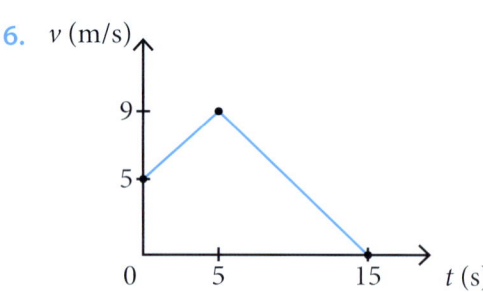

7.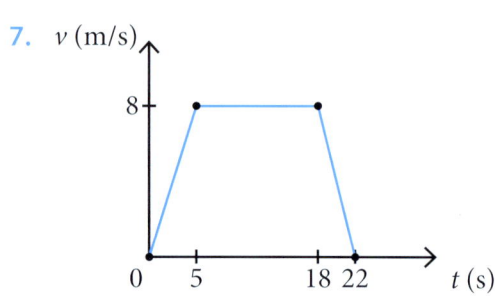

8.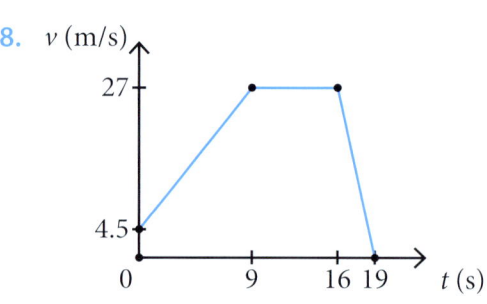

9.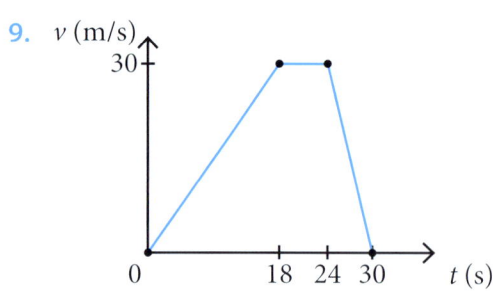

10.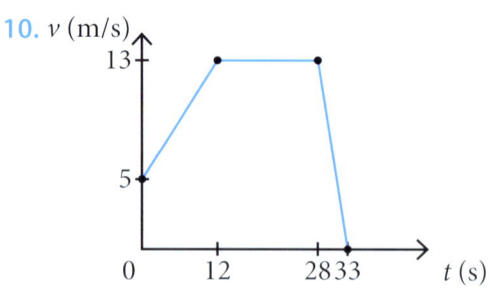

11. A body accelerates uniformly from 3 m/s to 8 m/s in 6 s. It then continues at this velocity for 10 s before uniformly decelerating to rest in a further 5 s.
    (a) Draw a velocity/time graph to show this journey.

## Exercise 15B...

(b)    Use your graph to find the (i) initial acceleration (ii) final deceleration (iii) total distance travelled.

12.    A body accelerates uniformly from 8 m/s to 20 m/s in 6 s. It then continues at this velocity for 5 s before uniformly decelerating to rest in a further 10 s.
  (a)    Draw a velocity/time graph to show this journey.
  (b)    Use your graph to find the (i) initial acceleration (ii) final deceleration (iii) total distance travelled.

13.    A body accelerates uniformly from 3 m/s to 11 m/s in 4 s. It then continues at this velocity for 6 s before uniformly decelerating to rest in a further 2 s.
  (a)    Draw a velocity/time graph to show this journey.
  (b)    Use your graph to find the (i) initial acceleration (ii) final deceleration (iii) total distance travelled.

14.    A body accelerates uniformly from 2 m/s to 9 m/s in 5 s. It then continues at this velocity for 8 s before uniformly decelerating to rest in a further 3 s.
  (a)    Draw a velocity/time graph to show this journey.
  (b)    Use your graph to find the (i) initial acceleration (ii) final deceleration (iii) total distance travelled.

15.    A body accelerates uniformly from rest to 8 m/s in 4 s. It then continues at this velocity for 7 s before uniformly decelerating to 2 m/s in a further 5 s.
  (a)    Draw a velocity/time graph to show this journey.
  (b)    Use your graph to find the (i) initial acceleration (ii) final deceleration (iii) total distance travelled.

16.    A body accelerates uniformly from 5 m/s to 12 m/s in 4 s. It then continues at this velocity for 12 s before uniformly decelerating to rest in a further 6 s.
  (a)    Draw a velocity/time graph to show this journey.
  (b)    Use your graph to find the (i) initial acceleration (ii) final deceleration (iii) total distance travelled.

## Exercise 15B...

17.    A body accelerates uniformly from rest to 20 m/s in 5 s. It then continues at this velocity for 8 s before uniformly decelerating to 4 m/s in a further 9 s.
  (a)    Draw a velocity/time graph to show this journey.
  (b)    Use your graph to find the (i) initial acceleration (ii) final deceleration (iii) total distance travelled.

### 15.3 Uniformly Accelerated Motion

Consider a body which accelerates uniformly from $u$ m/s to $v$ m/s in $t$ seconds at an acceleration of $a$ m/s$^2$ covering a distance of $s$ metres. Its velocity/time graph is shown below:

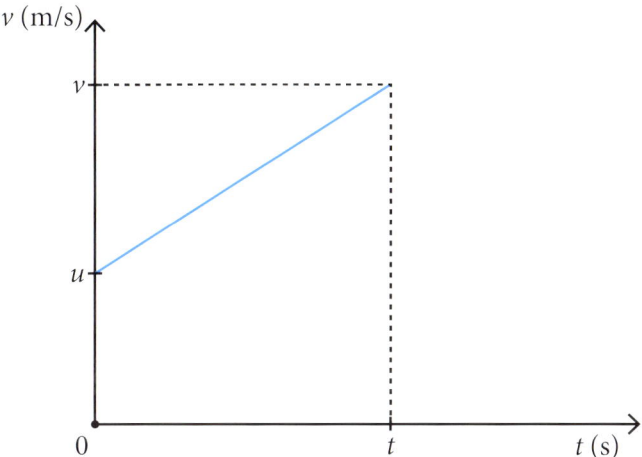

The acceleration is given by the gradient.

So:    $$a = \frac{v - u}{t}$$
$$v - u = at$$
So:    $$v = u + at \qquad \textbf{Equation 1}$$

The distance $s$ is given by the area of the trapezium.

So:    $$s = \tfrac{1}{2}t(u + v) \qquad \textbf{Equation 2}$$

You can rearrange Equation 1 to get:
$$u + at = v$$
$$at = v - u$$
$$t = \frac{v - u}{a}$$

Substituting this into Equation 2 gives:
$$s = \tfrac{1}{2}\,\frac{v - u}{a}(u + v)$$

Multiplying each side by $2a$ gives:
$$2as = (v - u)(u + v)$$
$$2as = v^2 - u^2$$
So:    $$v^2 = u^2 + 2as \qquad \textbf{Equation 3}$$

71

Substituting $v = u + at$ into Equation 2 gives:

$$s = \frac{1}{2}t(u + v)$$

$$s = \frac{1}{2}t(u + u + at)$$

$$s = \frac{1}{2}t(2u + at)$$

$$\boldsymbol{s = ut + \frac{1}{2}at^2} \qquad \textbf{Equation 4}$$

These are the four **equations of motion**. They will be used below and in chapter 16.

## 15.4 Problems Involving Two Journeys

Sometimes you need to solve problems involving two journeys. For example:

3.  Owen sets off from home walking at a constant velocity of 1.8 m/s. Two minutes later Martin sets off from home cycling from rest at a constant acceleration of 2.4 m/s² until he reaches a velocity of 12 m/s. He then continues at this velocity until he catches up with Owen. Martin then decelerates uniformly to rest in a further 4 s.
    (a)     Draw a velocity/time graph to show these journeys.
    (b)     (i) Find the time Owen has walked when Martin catches up with him. (ii) Find the distance Owen has walked when Martin catches up with him. (iii) Find the distance between Owen and Martin when Martin stops.

When answering this question, remember:
*   You must change all times to seconds.
*   You must use the equations for constant speed for Owen's journey.
*   You must use both the equations for uniform acceleration and for constant speed for Martin's journey as shown below.

(a) To plot the graph we need to work out how long Martin takes to reach his maximum speed.

For the first part of Martin's journey:
Using:     $v = u + at$     with $u = 0$, $a = 2.4$ and $v = 12$
          $12 = 2.4t$
So:       $t = \dfrac{12}{2.4} = 5$ seconds

So Martin reaches 12 m/s after 5 seconds.

Because he doesn't start until 2 minutes after Owen, i.e. 120 seconds, we plot (125, 12) on the graph.

We can now draw the graph, where $T$ is the time

Martin catches up with Owen:

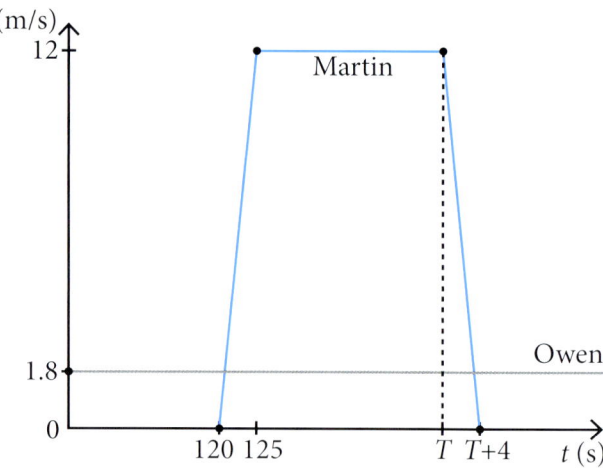

(b)     (i) Let:
        $T$ = the time when Martin catches up with Owen;
        $D$ = the distance to this point.
        Now consider Martin and Owen separately.

        **Owen** is travelling at constant speed, so:
            Distance = velocity × time
                    $s = vt$
        So:         $D = 1.8T$

        **Martin**: Consider each part of his journey separately. For the first part:
        Using:     $v^2 = u^2 + 2as$
        with:      $u = 0$, $a = 2.4$ and $v = 12$
                   $144 = 0 + 2 \times 2.4 \times s$
                   $s = \dfrac{144}{4.8} = 30$ m

        For the second part, $t = T - 125$. So:
            Distance = velocity × time
                    $s = vt$
        So:         $D = 12(T - 125)$

        Therefore the total distance travelled by Martin is:
                   $D = 12(T - 125) + 30$
                   $D = 12T - 1500 + 30$
                   $D = 12T - 1470$

        However we know that the distance travelled by Martin is equal to the distance travelled by Owen, since this is the point where they meet. Therefore:

        $12T - 1470 = 1.8T$
        $12T - 1.8T = 1470$
        $10.2T = 1470$
        $T = \dfrac{1470}{10.2}$

        So $T = 144$ s, to the nearest integer.

(ii) To find the distance Owen has walked at time $T$, substitute $T$ into either equation for $D$:

$D = 1.8T$
$D = 1.8 \times 144$
$D = 259$ m (to the nearest m)

(iii) Consider the last part of Martin's journey. You need to find the distance he travels.

Using: $s = \frac{1}{2}t(u + v)$
with: $u = 12$, $v = 0$ (because he stops)
and $t = 4$
$s = \frac{1}{2}(4)(12 + 0)$
$s = 24$ m

However, Owen is still walking, so we need to find out how far he walks in these 4 seconds:
Distance = velocity × time
$s = vt$
So: $D = 1.8 \times 4$
$D = 7.2$m

So the distance between them is:
$= s - D$
$= 24 - 7.2$
$= 16.8$ m

## Exercise 15C

1. Lily leaves home 4 minutes before Aideen and walks at a constant speed of 1.2 m/s. Aideen cycles after her accelerating from rest at 0.8 m/s² for 10s until she reaches a maximum velocity which she maintains until she overtakes Lily. She then immediately decelerates uniformly to rest 20 s after overtaking Lily, who continues to walk at 1.2 m/s.
   (a) Draw a velocity/time graph to show these journeys.
   (b) (i) Find Aideen's maximum velocity (ii) Find the distance from home when Aideen overtakes Lily. (iii) Find Aideen's deceleration. (iv) Find the distance between Aideen and Lily when Aideen stops.

2. Padraig leaves home walking at a constant velocity of 1.5 m/s. 3 minutes later Steve leaves home. He cycles from rest at an acceleration of 2 m/s² for 6 s until he reaches a maximum velocity which he maintains until he overtakes Padraig.

### Exercise 15C...

(a) Draw a velocity/time graph to show these journeys.
(b) (i) Find the time Padraig has walked when Steve catches up with him. (ii) Find the distance from home when Steve catches up with Padraig.

Steve then immediately decelerates uniformly to rest at 1.2 m/s² after overtaking Padraig, who continues to walk at 1.5 m/s. (iii) Find the distance between Steve and Padraig when Steve stops.

# CHAPTER 16: CONSTANT ACCELERATION

## 16.1 Equations Of Motion

These equations of motion were derived in Chapter 15:

1.  $v = u + at$

2.  $v^2 = u^2 + 2as$

3.  $s = ut + \frac{1}{2}at^2$

4.  $s = \frac{1}{2}t(u + v)$

where:  $u$ = initial velocity in m/s
$v$ = final velocity in m/s
$a$ = acceleration in m/s$^2$
$t$ = time in s
$s$ = distance in m

The rules for using these equations are:

- List what you know and what you want to find,
- Choose the appropriate formula.

For example:

................................................................

1.  A body moving at a velocity of 3 m/s accelerates uniformly at 2 m/s$^2$ for 5 s. Find:
    (a)   its final velocity;
    (b)   the distance it covers.

    (a)   We know:          $u = 3$
          $a = 2$
          $t = 5$

          We want to find:    $v = ?$

          So we use:    $v = u + at$
          $v = 3 + 2 \times 5$
          $v = 3 + 10$
          $v = 13$ m/s

    (b)   We know:          $u = 3$
          $a = 2$
          $t = 5$

          We want to find:    $s = ?$

          So we use:    $s = ut + \frac{1}{2}at^2$
          $s = 3(5) + \frac{1}{2}(2)(5)^2$
          $s = 15 + 25$
          $s = 40$ m

................................................................

2.  A body reaches a velocity of 24 m/s after accelerating uniformly for 8 s, during which time it travels 112 m. Find:
    (a)   its initial velocity;
    (b)   its acceleration.

(a)   We know:          $v = 24$
          $t = 8$
          $s = 112$

      We want to find:    $u = ?$

      So we use:    $s = \frac{1}{2}t(u + v)$
      $112 = \frac{1}{2} \times 8(u + 24)$
      $112 = 4(u + 24)$
      $112 = 4u + 96$
      $112 - 96 = 4u$
      $16 = 4u$
      $u = 4$ m/s

(b)   We know:          $u = 4$
          $v = 24$
          $t = 8$

      We want to find:    $a = ?$

      So we use:    $v = u + at$
      $24 = 4 + 8a$
      $20 = 8a$
      $a = 2.5$ m/s$^2$

## Exercise 16A

1.  A body accelerates uniformly from 3 m/s to 9 m/s in 4 s. Find:
    (a)   its acceleration
    (b)   the distance covered.

2.  A body accelerates uniformly from 2 m/s to 6 m/s in 6 s. Find:
    (a)   its acceleration
    (b)   the distance covered.

3.  A body accelerates uniformly for 4 s at 1.5 m/s$^2$. Its initial velocity is 8 m/s. Find:
    (a)   its final velocity
    (b)   the distance covered.

4.  A body initially moving at 10 m/s accelerates uniformly for 8 s covering 100 m. Find:
    (a)   its final velocity
    (b)   its acceleration.

5.  A body accelerates uniformly from 3 m/s to 12 m/s in covering 30 m. Find:
    (a)   the time taken
    (b)   its acceleration.

6.  A body accelerates uniformly from 6 m/s to 10 m/s at an acceleration of 0.4 m/s$^2$. Find:
    (a)   the distance covered
    (b)   the time taken.

## Exercise 16A...

7. A body reaches a velocity of 4 m/s after accelerating uniformly for 12 s and covering 36 m. Find:
   (a) its initial velocity
   (b) its acceleration.

8. A body accelerates uniformly from 4 m/s for 6 s at 3 m/s². Find:
   (a) its final velocity:
   (b) the distance travelled.

9. A body accelerates uniformly at 4 m/s² covering 152 m in reaching a velocity of 35 m/s. Find:
   (a) its initial velocity:
   (b) the time taken.

10. A body accelerates uniformly from 8 m/s for 4 s in covering 80 m. Find:
    (a) its acceleration:
    (b) its final velocity.

11. A body accelerates uniformly from 2 m/s at 3.5 m/s² in travelling 159.75 m. Find:
    (a) its final velocity:
    (b) the time taken.

12. A body accelerates uniformly at 1.5 m/s² for 2 s acquiring a velocity of 10 m/s. Find:
    (a) its initial velocity:
    (b) the distance travelled.

13. A body accelerates uniformly from 9 m/s to 30 m/s in travelling 136.5 m. Find:
    (a) its acceleration:
    (b) the time taken.

14. A body accelerates uniformly from 9.9 m/s to 33 m/s in 6.5 s. Find
    (a) its acceleration:
    (b) the distance travelled.

## 16.2 Deceleration

When a body slows down it is called a **deceleration**. A deceleration can be written as a negative acceleration. For example, if the deceleration is 2 m/s² then you would write $a = -2$ m/s².

The rules for solving problems involving deceleration are the same as before, except that you need to be careful to write the number correctly as positive or negative. The rules are:

- List what you know and what you want to find.
- Write the deceleration, if given, as a **negative** acceleration.
- Choose the appropriate formula.
- Write the deceleration, if found, as a **positive** quantity.

For example:

........................................................................................

3. A body travelling at 4 m/s comes to rest uniformly in 1.6 s. Find:
   (a) its deceleration;
   (b) the distance travelled in coming to rest.

   (a) The phrase 'coming to rest' means that the final velocity is 0 m/s. Therefore:

   We know: $u = 4$
   $v = 0$
   $t = 1.6$
   We want to find: $a = ?$

   So we use: $v = u + at$
   $0 = 4 + 1.6a$
   $-1.6a = 4$
   $a = \dfrac{4}{-1.6}$
   $a = -2.5$

   Remember the question asks us to find the **deceleration**.

   So the deceleration = 2.5 m/s²

   (b) We know: $u = 4$
   $v = 0$
   $t = 1.6$
   We want to find: $s = ?$
   So we use: $s = \frac{1}{2}t(u + v)$
   $s = \frac{1}{2} \times 1.6(4 + 0)$
   $s = 0.8 \times 4$
   $s = 3.2$ m

## Exercise 16B

1. A body travelling at 12 m/s decelerates uniformly at 3 m/s² in 2 s. Find:
   (a) the final velocity;
   (b) the distance travelled.

2. A body decelerates uniformly at 2.5 m/s² to a velocity of 7 m/s in moving 48 m. Find:
   (a) the initial velocity;
   (b) the time taken.

3. A body travelling at 12 m/s comes to rest uniformly in moving 24 m. Find:
   (a) its deceleration;
   (b) the time taken.

## Exercise 16B...

4.  A body travelling at 13 m/s slows down uniformly to 4 m/s at a deceleration of 6 m/s². Find:
    (a)    the time taken;
    (b)    the distance travelled in coming to rest.

5.  A body travelling at 3 m/s comes to rest uniformly in 2 s. Find:
    (a)    its deceleration
    (b)    the distance travelled in coming to rest.

6.  A body travelling at 14 m/s decelerates uniformly at 2 m/s² in moving 33 m. Find
    (a)    the final velocity;
    (b)    the the time taken.

7.  A body decelerates uniformly at 4 m/s² to a velocity of 2 m/s in 1.5 s. Find:
    (a)    the initial velocity;
    (b)    the distance travelled.

8.  A body travels 24 m in coming to rest uniformly in 2 s. Find:
    (a)    the initial velocity;
    (b)    its deceleration.

## 16.3 Vertical Motion

All bodies fall vertically at the same acceleration due to gravity. This acceleration is called '$g$' where **$g$ is equal to 10 m/s².**

**Bodies falling down** will **accelerate downwards** and so you take $a = 10$ m/s².

**Bodies going up** will **slow down** and so you take $a = -10$ m/s².

For example:

.......................................................................................

4.  A stone is dropped from the top of a 100 m building. Find:
    (a)    the velocity with which it hits the ground;
    (b)    the time taken;
    (c)    the distance travelled in the 4th second.

    (a)    The word 'drops' means that the initial velocity is 0. The ball is falling down and so $a = 10$.

    So we know:        $u = 0$
                       $a = 10$
                       $s = 100$
    We want to find:   $v = ?$

So we use:   $v^2 = u^2 + 2as$
             $v^2 = 0 + 2(10)(100)$
             $v^2 = 2000$
             $v = \sqrt{2000}$
             $v = 44.72$ m/s

(b)    We know:        $u = 0$
                       $a = 10$
                       $s = 100$
       We want to find:   $t = ?$

       So we use:   $s = ut + \frac{1}{2}at^2$
                    $100 = 0 + \frac{1}{2}(10)t^2$
                    $100 = 5t^2$
                    $t^2 = \frac{100}{5}$
                    $t^2 = 20$
                    $t = \sqrt{20}$
                    $t = 4.47$ s

(c)    To find the distance travelled in the 4th second:
       •    find the distance travelled after 3 s;
       •    find the distance travelled after 4 s;
       •    subtract the answers.

       First we set:       $t = 3$
       So we know:         $u = 0$
                           $a = 10$
                           $t = 3$
       We want to find:    $s = ?$

       So we use:   $s = ut + \frac{1}{2}at^2$
                    $s = 0 + \frac{1}{2}(10)(3)^2$
                    $s = 5 \times 9 = 45$ m

       Second, we set:     $t = 4$
       So we know:         $u = 0$
                           $a = 10$
                           $t = 4$
       We want to find:    $s = ?$

       So we use:   $s = ut + \frac{1}{2}at^2$
                    $s = 0 + \frac{1}{2}(10)(4)^2$
                    $s = 5 \times 16 = 80$ m

       Finally, we subtract:
       Distance travelled = 80 − 45 = 35 m

.......................................................................................

5.  A stone is thrown up from the ground with a velocity of 3.5 m/s. Find:
    (a)    how high will it reach;
    (b)    the time it takes to return to the ground;
    (c)    between which times the stone is more than 0.4 m above the ground.

(a) The stone will go up until it stops, i.e. when $v = 0$.

We know:
$$u = 3.5$$
$$v = 0$$
$$a = -10$$

We want to find: $s = ?$

So we use: $v^2 = u^2 + 2as$
$$0 = 3.5^2 - 2(10)s$$
$$20s = 12.25$$
$$s = \frac{12.25}{20}$$
$$s = 0.6125 \text{ m}$$

(b) The time taken for the stone to reach its greatest height (from 3.5 m/s to 0 m/s) is the same as the time taken for it to return to the ground (from 0 m/s to 3.5 m/s). So you work out the time taken for the stone to reach its greatest height and then double this.

We know:
$$u = 3.5$$
$$v = 0$$
$$a = -10$$

We want to find: $t = ?$

So we use: $v = u + at$
$$0 = 3.5 - 10t$$
$$10t = 3.5$$
$$t = 0.35 \text{ s}$$

This is the time to reach the greatest height. So the time for it to return to the ground is:
$$0.35 \times 2 = 0.7 \text{s}$$

(c) We need to find the times when $s = 0.4$.

We know:
$$u = 3.5$$
$$a = -10$$
$$s = 0.4$$

We want to find: $t = ?$

So we use: $s = ut + \frac{1}{2}at^2$
$$0.4 = 3.5t - \frac{1}{2} \times 10\, t^2$$
$$0.4 = 3.5t - 5t^2$$

This is a quadratic equation. You must bring all the terms to one side and then solve it using the quadratic formula. So we have:
$$5t^2 - 3.5t + 0.4 = 0$$

Thus:
$$a = 5$$
$$b = -3.5$$
$$c = 0.4$$

Using: $t = \dfrac{-b \pm \sqrt{b^2 - 4ac}}{2a}$
$$t = \frac{3.5 \pm \sqrt{3.5^2 - 4 \times 5 \times 0.4}}{2 \times 5}$$

$$t = \frac{3.5 \pm \sqrt{4.25}}{10}$$

$$t = \frac{3.5 + \sqrt{4.25}}{10} \text{ or } \frac{3.5 - \sqrt{4.25}}{10}$$

$$t = \frac{5.562}{10} \text{ or } \frac{1.438}{10}$$

$$t = 0.556 \text{ s or } 0.144 \text{ s}$$

So the answer is that the the stone is more than 0.4 m above the ground between 0.144 s and 0.556 s.

## Exercise 16C

1. A ball takes 2.5 s to drop to the floor. Find:
   (a) the velocity with which it hits the floor;
   (b) how far it falls.

2. A stone is thrown up from the floor at 14 m/s. Find:
   (a) how high it rises;
   (b) the time it takes to reach this height.

3. A ball drops 1.84 m to the floor. Find:
   (a) the velocity with which it hits the floor;
   (b) the time it takes to reach the floor.

4. A stone is thrown up from the floor at 8.3 m/s. Find:
   (a) how high it rises;
   (b) the time it takes to return to the floor.

5. A ball is thrown down from the top of a tall cliff with a velocity of 1.3 m/s. Find:
   (a) the distance travelled in the third second;
   (b) the distance travelled after 5 seconds;
   (c) its velocity after 5 seconds.

6. A stone is thrown up from the floor at 3.8 m/s. Find:
   (a) its greatest height;
   (b) the times when it is 0.5 m above the floor.

7. A ball is thrown down from the top of a tall building with a velocity of 0.4 m/s. Find:
   (a) the time taken to fall 3 m;
   (b) the further distance travelled in the next 2 s.

8. A stone is thrown up from the ground at 1.56 m/s. Find:
   (a) its speed and direction after 0.2 s;
   (b) the time to reach its greatest height;
   (c) its greatest height;
   (d) the times between which the stone is more than 8 cm above the ground.

## 16.4 Harder Questions

The same methods can be use to solve more difficult problems. For example:

6. A stone is dropped from a shelf 2 m above the ground. At the same moment another stone is thrown up from the ground at 6.2 m/s. Find:
   (a) when they pass each other;
   (b) how far above the ground they are when they pass;
   (c) the distance between them after 0.2 s.

   (a) Consider each stone separately.
   Let: $t$ = the time when they pass
   and: $h$ = the height above the ground
   The stone that drops will have fallen a distance of:
   $$s = 2 - h$$

   Firstly, consider the stone dropping.

   We know: $u = 0$
   $a = 10$ (because it is falling down)
   $s = 2 - h$
   We want to find $t = ?$ (ie, the time they pass)

   We use $s = ut + \frac{1}{2}at^2$
   $2 - h = 0 + \frac{1}{2}10t^2$
   $2 - h = 5t^2$

   Next, consider the stone thrown up.

   We know: $u = 6.2$
   $a = -10$ (because it is going up)
   $s = h$
   We want to find $t = ?$ (i.e., the time they pass)

   We use $s = ut + \frac{1}{2}at^2$
   $h = 6.2t - \frac{1}{2}10t^2$
   $h = 6.2t - 5t^2$
   $5t^2 = 6.2t - h$

   You can put the two expressions for $5t^2$ equal to get:
   $6.2t - h = 2 - h$
   which gives: $6.2t = 2$

   So: $t = \dfrac{2}{6.2}$
   $t = 0.323$ s

   (b) Since we now know $t$, we can substitute $t = 0.323$ into either equation:
   $2 - h = 5t^2$
   Rearrange: $2 - 5t^2 = h$
   $h = 2 - 5t^2$

   $h = 2 - 5(0.323)^2$
   $h = 1.48$ m

   (c) Substitute $t = 0.2$ into each equation to find the height of each stone at this time, and then subtract the answers to find the distance between them:

   Dropping stone: $h = 2 - 5t^2$
   $h = 2 - 5(0.2)^2$
   $h = 1.8$ m

   Stone going up: $h = 6.2t - 5t^2$
   $h = 6.2(0.2) - 5(0.2)^2$
   $h = 1.04$ m

   So the distance between them:
   $s = 1.8 - 1.04$
   $= 0.76$ m

7. A ball is thrown up at 6 m/s from the top of a cliff 4.6 m above the ground. Find
   (a) the greatest height above the ground that it reaches
   (b) the total time it takes it to reach the ground
   (c) the times between which it is 5.8 m above the ground

   (a) We know: $u = 6$
   $v = 0$
   $a = -10$
   We want to find: $s = ?$

   So we use: $v^2 = u^2 + 2as$
   $0 = 6^2 - 2(10)s$
   $20s = 36$
   $s = \dfrac{36}{20}$
   $s = 1.8$ m

   However, this is the height above the point it was thrown from. But it was thrown from the top of a cliff. So the greatest height above the ground is: $= 1.8 + 4.6$
   $= 6.4$ m

   (b) There are two time intervals: the time interval when the ball is moving upwards, and the time interval when it is moving downwards. You need to work out the times for both and add up the answers.

Firstly, from the top of the cliff to the greatest height:

We know:
$$u = 6$$
$$v = 0$$
$$a = -10$$

We want to find: $t = ?$

So we use $\quad v = u + at$
$$0 = 6 - 10t$$
$$10t = 6$$

So $\quad\quad t = 0.6$ s to reach the greatest height

Then, from the greatest height to the ground:

We know: $\quad u = 0$
$$a = 10$$
$$s = 6.4 \text{ (the greatest height)}$$

We want to find: $t = ?$

We use: $\quad s = ut + \frac{1}{2}at^2$
$$6.4 = (0 \times t) + (\frac{1}{2} \times 10t^2)$$
$$6.4 = \frac{1}{2} \times 10t^2$$
$$6.4 = 5t^2$$
$$1.28 = t^2$$
$$1.131 = t$$

Add the two time intervals together to get:
Total time $= 0.6 + 1.131$
$$= 1.731 \text{ s}$$

(c) The ball is thrown from the top of a cliff, so you must first subtract 4.6 from 5.8 to get $s = 1.2$.

We know:
$$u = 6$$
$$a = -10$$
$$s = 1.2$$

We want to find: $\quad\quad t = ?$

We use: $\quad\quad s = ut + \frac{1}{2}at^2$
$$1.2 = 6t + \frac{1}{2} \times -10t^2$$
$$1.2 = 6t - 5t^2$$

This is a quadratic equation. You must bring all the terms to one side and then solve it using the quadratic formula.

So we have: $5t^2 - 6t + 1.2 = 0$
Thus: $\quad\quad a = 5$
$$b = -6$$
$$c = 1.2$$

Using: $\quad\quad t = \dfrac{-b \pm \sqrt{b^2 - 4ac}}{2a}$

$$t = \dfrac{6 \pm \sqrt{6^2 - 4 \times 5 \times 1.2}}{2 \times 5}$$

$$t = \dfrac{6 \pm \sqrt{12}}{10}$$

$$t = \dfrac{6 + \sqrt{12}}{10} \text{ or } \dfrac{6 - \sqrt{12}}{10}$$

$$t = \dfrac{9.464}{10} \text{ or } \dfrac{2.536}{10}$$

Thus: $\quad\quad t = 0.946$ s or $0.254$ s

So the ball is 5.8 m above the ground at times

$t = 0.254$ s

and

$t = 0.946$ s.

## Exercise 16D

1.  A stone is dropped from a shelf 1.4 m above the ground. At the same moment another stone is thrown up from the ground at 5.3 m/s. Find:
    (a) when they pass each other;
    (b) how far above the ground they are when they pass;
    (c) the distance between them after 0.15 s.

2.  A stone falls from a cliff $h$ metres high to the ground. 0.2 s later another stone is thrown down from the cliff at 2.3 m/s. They hit the ground at the same time. Find:
    (a) the time after the first stone is thrown at which they hit the ground;
    (b) the height, $h$, of the cliff;
    (c) the velocity of each stone when they hit the ground.

3.  A ball is thrown up at 5 m/s from the top of a shed 2.8 m above the ground. Find:
    (a) the greatest height above the ground that it reaches;
    (b) the total time it takes it to reach the ground;
    (c) the velocity with which it hits the ground;
    (d) the times between which it is 3.5 m above the ground.

4.  A ball is thrown up at 3.2 m/s from the top of a cliff 8.4 m above the ground. Find:
    (a) the greatest height above the ground that it reaches;
    (b) the total time it takes it to reach the ground;
    (c) the velocity with which it hits the ground;
    (d) the times between which it is 8.6 m above the ground.

## Exercise 16D...

5.  A ball falls from a window ledge 2.3 m above the ground. 0.2 s later another stone is thrown up from the ground at 4.5 m/s. Find:
    (a)  when they pass;
    (b)  the height above the ground when they pass;
    (c)  how many seconds between the ball hitting the ground and the stone hitting the ground.

6.  A stone is dropped from a cliff 5 m above the ground. At the same moment another stone is thrown up from the ground at 8 m/s. Find:
    (a)  when they pass each other;
    (b)  how far above the ground they are when they pass;
    (c)  the distance between them after 0.4 s.

# CHAPTER 17: NEWTON'S LAWS

## 17.1 Definitions

Isaac Newton's three laws of motion are as follows:

**Law 1:** Every body remains stationary or in constant or uniform motion unless acted upon by an external force.

**Law 2:** The force is proportional to the acceleration. The force, $F$, is worked out using the formula:

$$F = ma$$

where: $m$ is the mass of the object
$a$ is the acceleration

The units of force are Newtons (N) when the mass is in kg and the acceleration is in m/s$^2$.

**Law 3:** To every action there is an equal and opposite reaction.

## 17.2 Acceleration Forces

You can use Newton's laws to solve problems involving forces and accelerating objects. For example:

1. A force 34 N causes a mass of $M$ kg to accelerate at 1.6 m/s$^2$. Find the value of $M$.

Using: $F = ma$
$34 = M \times 1.6$

So: $M = \dfrac{34}{1.6}$

$M = 21.25$ kg

## Exercise 17A

1. Find the force which will cause a mass of 8 kg to accelerate at 2.5 m/s$^2$.

2. A force 24 N causes a mass of $M$ kg to accelerate at 4 m/s$^2$. Find the value of $M$.

3. A force of 32 N is used to accelerate a mass of 6.4 kg. Find its acceleration.

4. Find the force which will cause a mass of 20 kg to accelerate at 1.2 m/s$^2$.

5. A force 28.8 N causes a mass of $M$ kg to accelerate at 3.6 m/s$^2$. Find the value of $M$.

6. A force of 21 N is used to accelerate a mass of 14 kg. Find its acceleration.

## Exercise 17A...

7. Find the force which will cause a mass of 8 kg to accelerate at 2.8 m/s$^2$.

8. A force 18 N causes a mass of $M$ kg to accelerate at 0.6 m/s$^2$. Find the value of $M$.

Sometimes you have to work out the information you need from other information you are given. For example:

2. (a) Find the force needed to accelerate a mass of 3 kg from 3 m/s to 8 m/s in 4 s.
   (b) Find the distance travelled.

   (a) To solve this question, we must first find the acceleration, and then use $F = ma$.

   We know: $u = 3$
   $t = 4$
   $v = 8$
   We want to find: $a = ?$

   So we use: $v = u + at$
   $8 = 3 + 4a$
   $4a = 5$
   $a = 1.25$ m/s$^2$
   Then: $F = ma$
   $F = 3 \times 1.25$
   $= 3.75$ N

   (b) We know: $u = 3$
   $t = 4$
   $v = 8$
   We want to find: $s = ?$

   So we use: $s = \frac{1}{2}t(u + v)$
   $s = \frac{1}{2} \times 4(3 + 8)$
   $s = 2 \times 11$
   $s = 22$ m

## Exercise 17B

1. (a) Find the force needed to accelerate a mass of 4 kg from 4 m/s to 13 m/s in 6 s.
   (b) Find the distance travelled.

2. (a) Find the force needed to accelerate a mass of 9 kg from 8 m/s to 14 m/s in travelling 22 m.
   (b) Find the time taken.

## Exercise 17B...

3. (a) Find the force needed to accelerate a mass of 6 kg to a velocity of 43 m/s in 8 s during which it travels 200 m.
   (b) Find the initial velocity.

4. (a) Find the force needed to accelerate a mass of 8 kg initially moving at a velocity of 2 m/s and travelling 97.5 m in 5 s.
   (b) Find the final velocity.

5. (a) Find the force needed to accelerate a mass of 12 kg from 13 m/s to 25 m/s during which it travels 114 m.
   (b) Find the time taken.

6. (a) Find the force needed to accelerate a mass of 16 kg from 4 m/s to 11 m/s in 5 s.
   (b) Find the distance travelled.

7. (a) Find the force needed to accelerate a mass of 6 kg initially moving at a velocity of 3 m/s which causes it to travel 189 m in 9 s.
   (b) Find the final velocity.

8. (a) Find the force needed to accelerate a mass of 15 kg to a velocity of 18 m/s in 4 s during which it travels 52 m.
   (b) Find the initial velocity.

## 17.3 Deceleration Force

You can use the same method to solve problems involving decelerating objects. For example:

3. (a) Find the force needed to bring a body of mass 7 kg moving at 14 m/s to rest in 3.5 s.
   (b) Find the distance covered.

   (a) To solve this question, we must first find the acceleration, and then use $F = ma$.

   We know: $u = 14$
   $v = 0$ (as it comes to rest)
   $t = 3.5$
   We want to find: $a = ?$
   So we use: $v = u + at$
   $0 = 14 + 3.5a$
   $-3.5a = 14$
   $a = -4$ m/s$^2$
   Then $F = ma$
   $F = 7 \times -4 = -28$ N

   Because the question asked for the force, you

must give the positive value as the answer. Therefore the answer is that the decelerating force is 28 N.

(b) We know: $u = 14$
$t = 3.5$
$v = 0$
We want to find: $s = ?$
So we use: $s = \frac{1}{2}t(u + v)$
$s = \frac{1}{2} \times 3.5(14 + 0)$
$s = 3.5 \times 7$
$s = 24.5$ m

## Exercise 17C

1. (a) Find the force needed to bring a body of mass 7 kg to rest in 2 s and in 4 m.
   (b) Find the initial velocity.

2. (a) Find the force needed to bring a body of mass 4 kg moving at 6 m/s to rest in 4.5 m.
   (b) Find the time taken.

3. (a) Find the force needed to bring a body of mass 9 kg moving at 12 m/s to rest in 3 s.
   (b) Find the distance covered.

4. (a) Find the force needed to bring a body of mass 6 kg to rest in 2 s and in 7 m.
   (b) Find the initial velocity.

5. (a) Find the force needed to bring a body of mass 8 kg moving at 5 m/s to rest in 10 m.
   (b) Find the time taken.

6. (a) Find the force needed to bring a body of mass 7 kg moving at 3 m/s to rest in 3 m.
   (b) Find the time taken.

7. (a) Find the force needed to bring a body of mass 4 kg moving at 9 m/s to rest in 3 s.
   (b) Find the distance covered.

8. (a) Find the force needed to bring a body of mass 8 kg to rest in 2 s and in 5 m.
   (b) Find the initial velocity.

9. (a) Find the force needed to bring a body of mass 6 kg moving at 6 m/s to rest in 12 m.
   (b) Find the time taken.

10. (a) Find the force needed to bring a body of mass 9 kg moving at 7 m/s to rest in 5 s.
    (b) Find the distance covered.

# CHAPTER 18: FORCES

## 18.1 Resolving Forces

A **force** is a **vector**, with both **magnitude** and **direction**. You can split a force into its two perpendicular components by using trigonometry. This process is known as 'resolving the forces'. For example:

1. Work out the horizontal and vertical component of the force shown below.

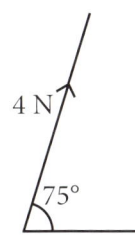

You can resolve the 4 N force into its two components (the horizontal component $R_H$ and the vertical component $R_V$) as shown below.

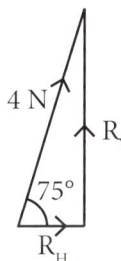

You can now work out the values of $R_H$ and $R_V$ by using trigonometry:

So:  $\sin 75 = \dfrac{R_V}{4}$

$R_V = 4 \sin 75$
$R_V = 3.86$ N

And:  $\cos 75 = \dfrac{R_H}{4}$

$R_H = 4 \cos 75$
$R_H = 1.04$ N

2. Work out the horizontal and vertical component of the force shown below.

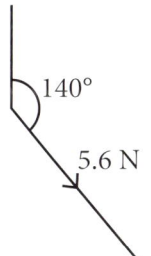

You can resolve the 5.6 N force into its two components (the horizontal component $R_H$ and the vertical component $R_V$) as shown below. You must work with the acute angle of 40° as shown.

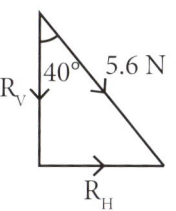

You can now work out the values of $R_H$ and $R_V$ by using trigonometry :

So:  $\sin 40 = \dfrac{R_H}{5.6}$

$R_H = 5.6 \sin 40$
$R_H = 3.60$ N

An:d  $\cos 40 = \dfrac{R_V}{5.6}$

$R_V = 5.6 \cos 40$
$R_V = 4.29$ N

**Exercise 18A**: *Work out the horizontal and vertical components of the forces shown below.*

1.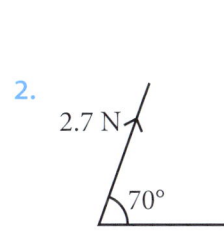

2.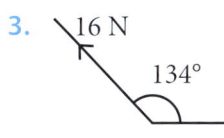

3. 16 N 134°

4. 80° 12 N

5. 14 N 64°

6.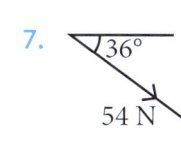

7.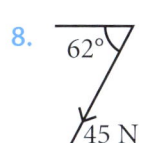

8. 62° 45 N

9. 236° 3.4 N

10. 128° 53 N

83

## 18.2 Resultant Of Parallel Forces

The **resultant** of a set of forces is the **single** force that is **equivalent** to all the **other** forces. You must give both its magnitude and also its direction since force is a vector.

To find the resultant of **parallel forces** you:

a.  Add them, if they act in the same direction.

b.  Subtract them, if they act in opposite directions.

For example:

1.  Find the resultant of the following forces:

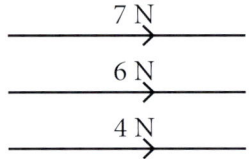

The resultant force is 7 + 6 + 4 = 17 N acting horizontally to the right.

2.  Find the resultant of the following forces:

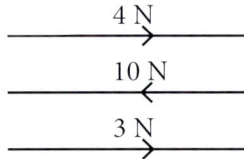

The resultant force is 10 – 4 – 3 = 3 N acting horizontally to the left.

## 18.3 Resultant Of Non-Parallel Forces Acting At A Point

When you have two or more non-parallel forces acting at a point you can find the resultant of these forces by:

a.  Resolving each force if necessary.

b.  Finding the resultant force in each of two perpendicular directions. When the forces are acting on a **horizontal plane**, you resolve the forces **horizontally** and **vertically**. When the forces are acting on an **inclined plane**, you resolve the forces **along** the plane and **perpendicular** to the plane.

c.  Finding the magnitude of the resultant force by using Pythagoras' theorem.

d.  Finding the direction of the resultant force by using trigonometry.

For example:

3.  Find the magnitude and direction of the resultant of the forces shown below:

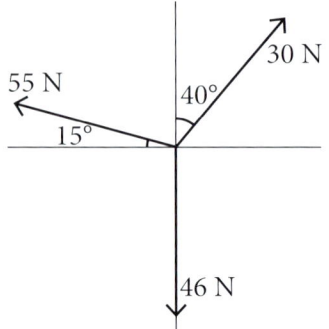

You must first resolve the 55 N and the 30 N forces into their horizontal and vertical components. You do not need to resolve the 46 N force as it is a vertical force. This gives the following:

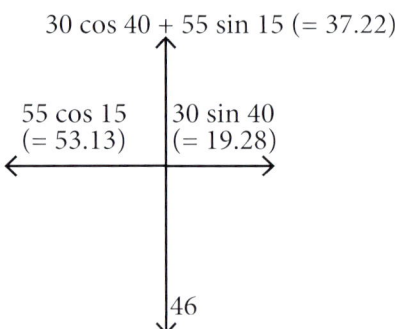

The resultant horizontal force is:
$$53.13 - 19.28 = 33.85 \text{ acting to the left}$$

The resultant vertical force is:
$$46 - 37.22 = 8.78 \text{ acting down}$$

You can then calculate the magnitude and direction of this resultant force as follows:

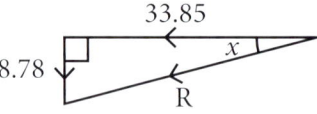

First find R:     $R^2 = 33.85^2 + 8.78^2$
$R^2 = 1222.91$
$R = \sqrt{1222.91}$
$R = 35.0$ N, to 3 significant figures

Then find $x$:    $\tan x = \dfrac{8.78}{33.85}$

$\tan x = 0.2594\ldots$
$x = 14.5°$, to 3 significant figures

So the answer is that a force of 35.0 N acting at 14.5° below the horizontal (as shown above).

1.
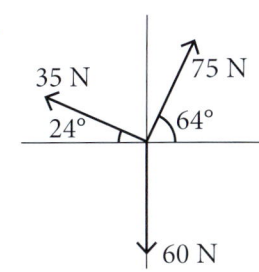

2.
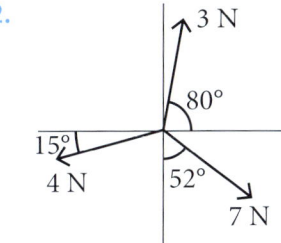

3.
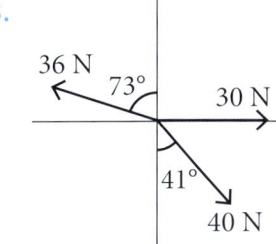

4.
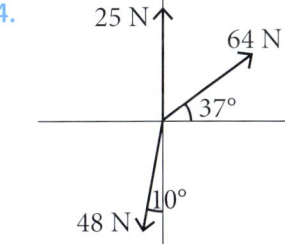

5.
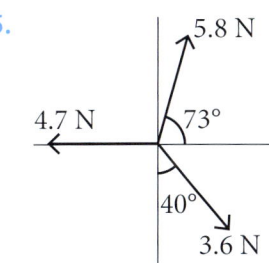

6.
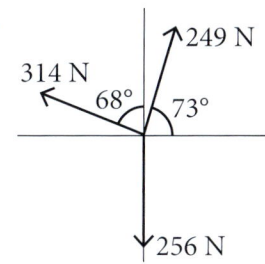

7.
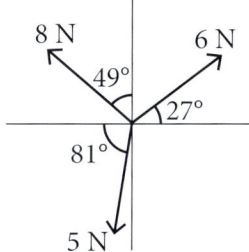

8.
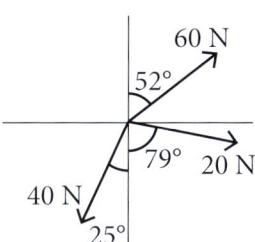

9.
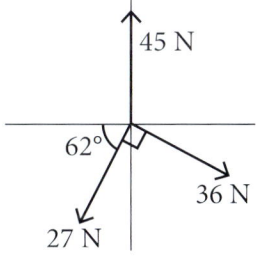

10.
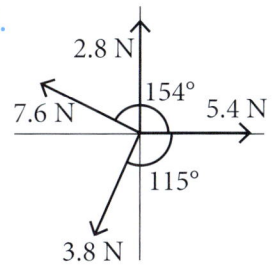

## 18.4 Resultant Of Forces Acting Along Different Sides Of A Rectangle

The rules are similar:

a. Find the resultant force horizontally and vertically.

b. Find the magnitude of the resultant force by using Pythagoras' theorem.

c. Find the direction of the resultant force by using trigonometry.

For example:

...........................................................

4. Find the magnitude and direction of the resultant of the forces shown below:

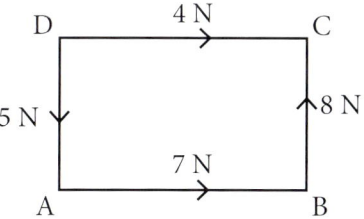

The resultant horizontal force is:
$$7 + 4 = 11 \text{ acting to the right}$$

The resultant vertical force is:
$$8 - 5 = 3 \text{ acting up}$$

You can then calculate the magnitude and direction of this resultant force as follows:

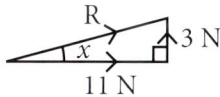

First find R:
$$R^2 = 3^2 + 11^2$$
$$R^2 = 130$$
$$R = \sqrt{130}$$
$$R = 11.4 \text{ N, to 3 significant figures}$$

Then find $x$:
$$\tan x = \frac{3}{11}$$
$$\tan x = 0.2727\ldots$$
$$x = 15.3°, \text{ to 3 significant figures}$$

So the answer is a force of 11.4 N acting at 15.3° above the horizontal (as shown above).

...........................................................

## Exercise 18C

Use the rectangle below to find the magnitude and direction of the resultant of the forces in each question below.

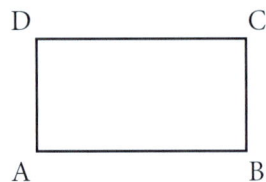

1.  7 N acting along DC and
    9 N acting along CB and
    4 N acting along AB and
    2 N acting along AD.

2.  8 N acting along DC and
    5 N acting along BC and
    3 N acting along BA and
    6 N acting along AD.

3.  16 N acting along DC and
    15 N acting along BC and
    14 N acting along BA and
    12 N acting along DA.

4.  25 N acting along DC and
    10 N acting along BC and
    30 N acting along AB and
    14 N acting along DA.

5.  7 N acting along DC and
    4 N acting along CB and
    9 N acting along BA and
    5 N acting along DA.

6.  6.8 N acting along CD and
    2.7 N acting along CB and
    3.2 N acting along AB and
    5 N acting along AD.

7.  24 N acting along DC and
    5 N acting along BC and
    13 N acting along BA and
    19 N acting along AD.

8.  16 N acting along CD and
    5.8 N acting along CB and
    9.2 N acting along BA and
    7.4 N acting along DA.

9.  25 N acting along DC and
    22 N acting along CB and
    14 N acting along BA and
    16 N acting along AD.

## Exercise 18C

10. 27 N acting along DC and
    23 N acting along BC and
    14 N acting along BA and
    35 N acting along DA.

## 18.5 Resultant Of Forces Acting Along An Inclined Plane

The rules in this case are:

a.  Find the resultant force along the plane and perpendicular to the plane.

b.  Find the magnitude of the resultant force by using Pythagoras' theorem.

c.  Find the direction of the resultant force by using trigonometry.

For example:

...........................................................................................

5.  Find the magnitude and direction of the resultant of the forces shown below.

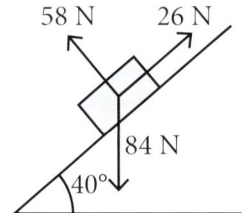

You do not need to resolve either the 58 N or the 26 N since they are already perpendicular or parallel to the plane. You resolve the 84 N force as follows:

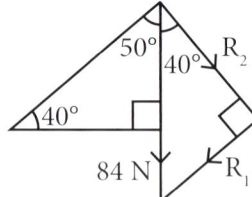

This gives:  $\sin 40 = \dfrac{R_1}{84}$

So:  $R_1 = 84 \sin 40$
     $R_1 = 53.99$ N

And:  $\cos 40 = \dfrac{R_2}{84}$

     $R_2 = 84 \cos 40$
     $R_2 = 64.35$ N

You then get:

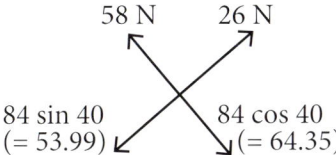

58 N    26 N

84 sin 40
(= 53.99)    84 cos 40
(= 64.35)

The resultant force along the plane is:

53.99 – 26 = 27.99 acting down the plane

The resultant force perpendicular to the plane is

64.35 – 58 = 6.35 acting down

You can then calculate the magnitude and direction of this resultant force as follows:

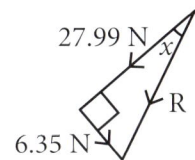

27.99 N    x
R
6.35 N

First find R:    $R^2 = 6.35^2 + 27.99^2$

$R^2 = 823.76$

$R = \sqrt{823.76}$

$R = 28.7$ N

Then find $x$:    $\tan x = \dfrac{6.35}{27.99}$

$\tan x = 0.2269\ldots$

$x = 12.8°$, to 3 significant figures

So the answer is force of 28.7 N acting at 12.8° to the plane, as shown above.

## Exercise 18D: *Find the magnitude and direction of the resultant of the forces shown below.*

**1.**

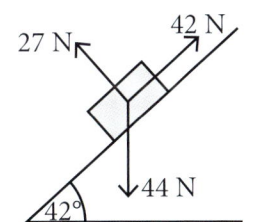

42 N    53 N

35°   60 N

**2.**

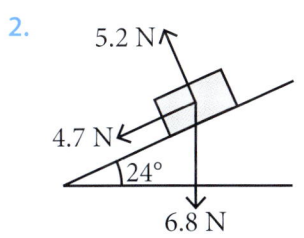

5.2 N

4.7 N

24°

6.8 N

**3.**

27 N    42 N

42°    44 N

**4.**

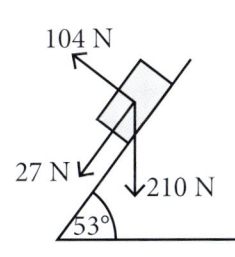

104 N

27 N    210 N

53°

## Exercise 18D...

**5.**

3.6 N    4.8 N

28°

5.2 N

**6.**

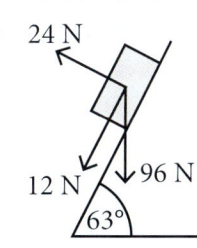

24 N

12 N    96 N

63°

## 18.6 Equilibrium Of Forces

When a set of forces is in **equilibrium** then the resultant force in each of two perpendicular directions will be **0**. You can use this fact to find unknown forces. The rules for finding unknown forces when all the forces are in equilibrium are:

a.  Resolve each force if necessary.

b.  Equate the forces in each of the two perpendicular directions.

For example:

.......................................................................................

**6.**  Find the unknown forces below, given that the forces are in equilibrium:

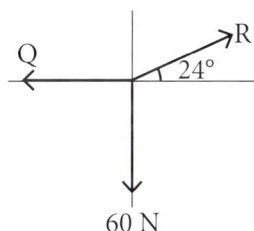

Q    R
24°
60 N

You do not need to resolve either the 60 N or the Q N forces as they are already in perpendicular directions. You resolve the RN force to get:

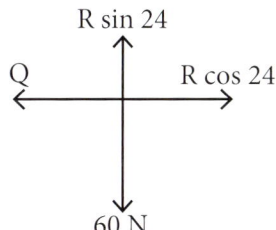

R sin 24

Q    R cos 24

60 N

You can then equate the vertical forces to get:

R sin 24 = 60

$R = \dfrac{60}{\sin 24}$

R = 147.52 N

= 147.5 N (to 1 decimal place)

You can then equate the horizontal forces to get:

Q = R cos 24
Q = 147.5 cos 24
Q = 134.77 N
Q = 134.8 N (to 1 decimal place)

**Exercise 18E**: *Find the unknown forces in the questions below, given that the forces are in equilibrium.*

**1.**

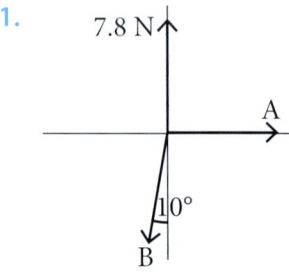

**2.**

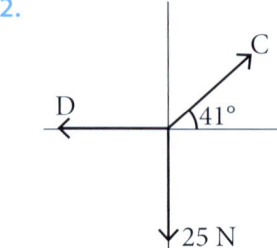

**3.**

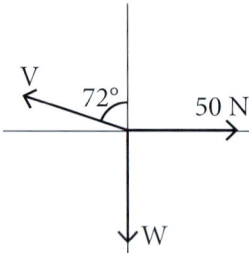

**4.**

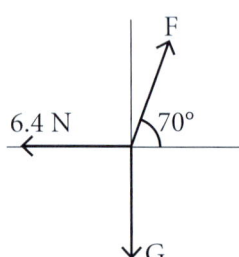

**5.**

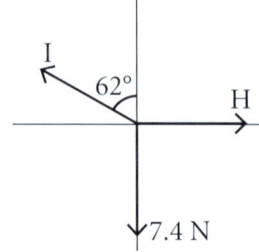

**6.**

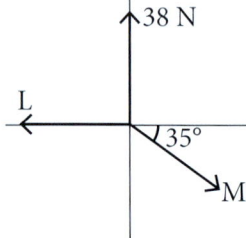

**7.**

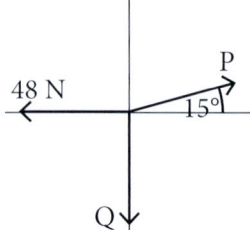

**8.**

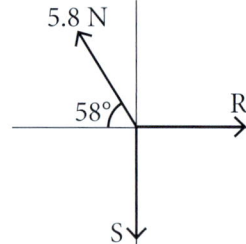

**9.**

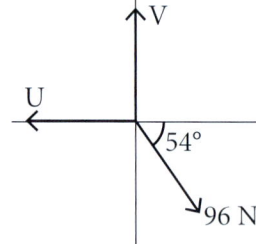

**10.**

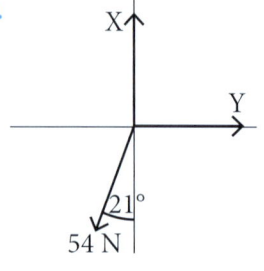

## 18.7 Forces On An Inclined Plane

You can also find unknown forces on an inclined plane, if you know that the forces are in equilibrium. For example:

**7.** Find the unknown forces in the diagram below, given that the forces are in equilibrium:

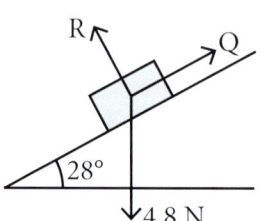

You should resolve the forces along the plane and perpendicular to the plane. Thus you do not need to resolve either R or Q. You only need to resolve the 4.8 N force to get:

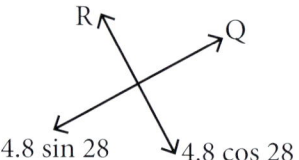

You can then equate the forces to get:

R = 4.8 cos 28
R = 4.24 N

and

Q = 4.8 sin 28
Q = 2.25 N

**Exercise 18F**: *Find the unknown forces in the questions below, given that the forces are in equilibrium:*

**1.**

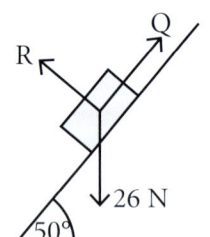

**2.**

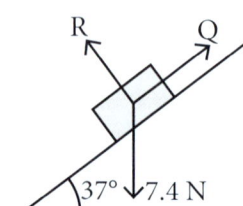

**3.**

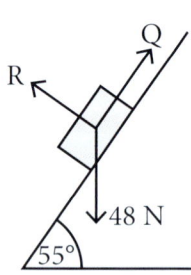

**4.**

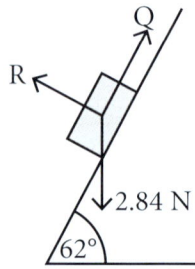

## Exercise 18F...

**5.**

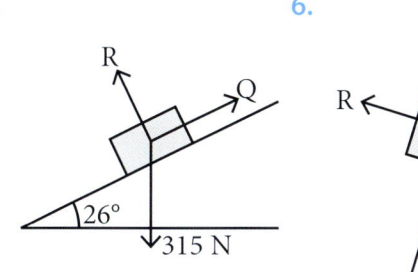

**6.**

$$Q(\frac{\cos 20° \sin 65°}{\cos 65°} + \sin 20°) = 60$$

$$Q = 60 \div (\frac{\cos 20° \sin 65°}{\cos 65°} + \sin 20°)$$

$$Q = 25.45 \text{ N}$$

Substitute this value back into [3] to find P:

$$P = \frac{Q \cos 20°}{\cos 65°}$$

$$P = \frac{25.45 \cos 20°}{\cos 65°}$$

$$P = 56.6 \text{ N}$$

## 18.8 Harder Questions

You may be asked more difficult questions involving equilibrium where you have to combine the ideas already studied in this chapter. For example:

8. Find the unknown forces below, given that the forces are in equilibrium:

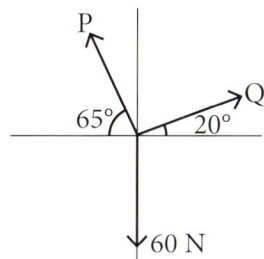

You do not need to resolve the 60 N force as it acts vertically. You resolve the two unknown forces to get:

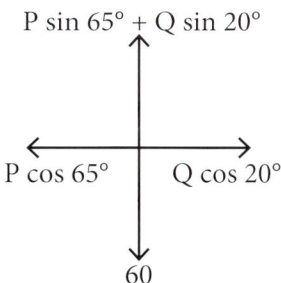

You can then equate the vertical forces to get:
$$60 = P \sin 65° + Q \sin 20° \quad [1]$$

And you can equate the horizontal forces to get:
$$P \cos 65° = Q \cos 20° \quad [2]$$

You can rearrange [2] to get:
$$P = \frac{Q \cos 20°}{\cos 65°} \quad [3]$$

Susbtituting [3] into [1] gives:

$$Q(\frac{\cos 20° \sin 65°}{\cos 65°}) + Q \sin 20° = 60$$

## Exercise 18G: Find the unknown forces in the questions below, given that the forces are in equilibrium:

**1.**

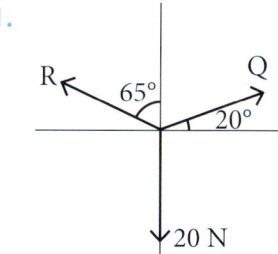

**4.**

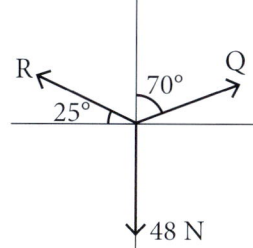

**2.**

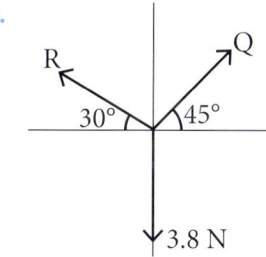

**5.**

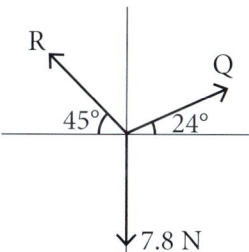

**3.**

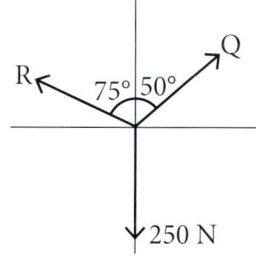

**6.**

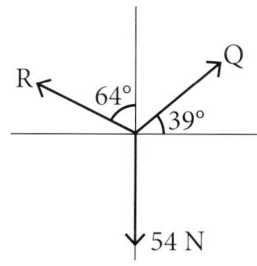

# CHAPTER 19: VECTORS

## 19.1 Magnitude and Direction

**Vectors** are quantities with both **magnitude** and **direction**. For example force, acceleration, velocity and displacement are all vectors.

**Scalars** are quantities with **only magnitude**. For example, mass, time, speed and distance are all scalars.

Vectors can be written in the form **a i + b j** where **i** and **j** denote unit vectors parallel to a set of standard $x$-$y$ axes.

Look at the vector a**i** + b**j** below:

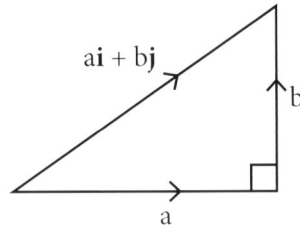

You can find the **magnitude of the vector** R, by using Pythagoras' theorem as follows:

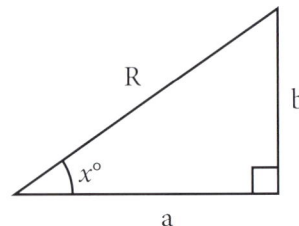

$$R^2 = a^2 + b^2$$
$$R = \sqrt{a^2 + b^2}$$

You can find the direction by using trigonometry as follows:

$$\tan x = \frac{b}{a}$$

So:
$$x = \tan^{-1} \frac{b}{a}$$

For example:

1. Find the magnitude and direction of the force −7**i** − 4**j**.

First, draw the vector:

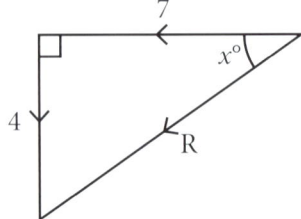

Magnitude:
$$R = \sqrt{(-7)^2 + (-4)^2}$$
$$R = \sqrt{65} = 8.06 \text{ N}$$

Direction:
$$\tan x = \frac{4}{7}$$
$$x = \tan^{-1} \frac{4}{7}$$
$$x = 29.7° \text{ with the horizontal.}$$

1. 4**i** + 5**j**
2. 7**i** − 2**j**
3. −3**i** + 6**j**
4. 8**i** + 15**j**
5. −**i** + 3**j**
6. 5**i** + 2**j**
7. 12**i** − 5**j**
8. 4**i** + 2**j**
9. 5**i** + 6**j**
10. 7**i** − 3**j**

## 19.2 Finding Speed And Distance

The **speed** of a body is the magnitude of the velocity. The **distance** a body travels is the magnitude of the displacement. For example:

2. A body moves with a velocity of (6**i** − 7**j**) m/s. Find its speed.

Magnitude:
$$R = \sqrt{6^2 + (-7)^2}$$
$$R = \sqrt{85}$$
$$R = 9.22 \text{ m/s}$$

3. A body has displacement (− 4**i** + 2**j**) m from O. Find its distance from O.

Magnitude:
$$R = \sqrt{(-4)^2 + 2^2}$$
$$R = \sqrt{20}$$
$$R = 4.47 \text{ m}$$

## Exercise 19B

1. A body moves with a velocity of (6**i** − 8**j**) m/s. Find its speed.

2. A body moves with a velocity of (−4**i** + 7**j**) m/s. Find its speed.

3. A body moves with a velocity of (−2**i** − 8**j**) m/s. Find its speed.

4. A body has displacement (−**i** + 2**j**) m from O. Find its distance from O.

## Exercise 19B...

5. A body has displacement (24**i** – 10**j**) m from O. Find its distance from O.

6. A body has displacement (9**i** + 7**j**) m from O. Find its distance from O.

## 19.3 Resultant Of Forces

You can find the resultant of forces written as vectors by adding the **i** components together and adding the **j** components together. For example:

4. The 3 forces (4**i** – 6**j**) N, (–2**i** + 5**j**) N and (–3**i** + 4**j**) N act on a body. Find the resultant of these forces.

$$
\begin{array}{r}
4\mathbf{i} - 6\mathbf{j} \\
-2\mathbf{i} + 5\mathbf{j} \\
+ \ \underline{-3\mathbf{i} + 4\mathbf{j}} \\
-\ \mathbf{i} + 3\mathbf{j}
\end{array}
$$

So the answer is (– **i** + 3**j**) N

## Exercise 19C

1. The 3 forces (4**i** – 2**j**) N, (5**i** + 3**j**) N and (– 3**i** +**j**) N act on a body. Find the resultant of these forces.

2. The 3 forces (**i** + 3**j**) N, (–4**i** – 6**j**) N and (–2**i** + 5**j**) N act on a body. Find the resultant of these forces.

3. The 3 forces (3**i** – 2**j**) N, (–**i** – 3**j**) N and (–7**i** + 4**j**) N act on a body. Find the resultant of these forces.

4. The 3 forces (**i** – 2**j**) N, (–3**i** + 4**j**) N and (2**i** – **j**) N act on a body.Find the resultant of these forces.

5. The 3 forces (2**i** + 5**j**) N, (4**i** – 6**j**) N and (–3**i** + **j**) N act on a body. Find the resultant of these forces.

6. The 3 forces (**i** – 3**j**) N, (–2**i** + 4**j**) N and (5**i** – 2**j**) N act on a body. Find the resultant of these forces.

7. The 3 forces (–3**i** – 5**j**) N, (2**i** – 3**j**) N and (–**i** + 4**j**) N act on a body. Find the resultant of these forces.

8. The 3 forces (–**i** – 4**j**) N, (3**i** – **j**) N and (–5**i** + 3**j**) N act on a body. Find the resultant of these forces.

9. The 3 forces (4**i** + 2**j**) N, (–**i** + 6**j**) N and (3**i** – 5**j**) N act on a body. Find the resultant of these forces.

10. The 3 forces (–3**i** + 4**j**) N, (5**i** + 2**j**) N and (–**i** + 6**j**) N act on a body. Find the resultant of these forces.

## 19.4 Finding An Unknown Force When You Are Given The Resultant Force

Sometimes you know the resultant force, and need to find an unknown force. The rules are:

a. Add the forces you are given.

b. Subtract this answer from the resultant force.

For example:

5. The forces **P** N, (–**i** + 6**j**) N and (3**i** – 5**j**) N act on a body. The resultant of these forces is (7**i** – 3**j**) N. Find **P**.

Add the forces:

$$
\begin{array}{r}
-\mathbf{i} + 6\mathbf{j} \\
+ \ \underline{3\mathbf{i} - 5\mathbf{j}} \\
2\mathbf{i} + \mathbf{j}
\end{array}
$$

Subtract the total from the resultant:

$$
\begin{array}{r}
7\mathbf{i} - 3\mathbf{j} \\
- \ \underline{2\mathbf{i} + \mathbf{j}} \\
5\mathbf{i} - 4\mathbf{j}
\end{array}
$$

So the answer is  (5**i** – 4**j**) N

## Exercise 19D

1. The forces **P** N, (3**i** + **j**) N and (– 2**i** + 4**j**) N act on a body.The resultant of these forces is (2**i** + 3**j**) N. Find **P**.

2. The forces **P** N, (5**i** + 2**j**) N and (**i** – 6**j**) N act on a body. The resultant of these forces is 3**i** N. Find **P**.

3. The forces **P** N, (2**i** – 4**j**) N and (– **i** + 7**j**) N act on a body. The resultant of these forces is (2**i** + 8**j**) N. Find **P**.

4. The forces **P** N, (**i** + 3**j**) N and (2**i** – 4**j**) N act on a body. The resultant of these forces is (–**i** – 3**j**) N. Find **P**.

5. The forces **P** N, (4**i** – 2**j**) N and (–3**i** + **j**) N act on a body. The resultant of these forces is (4**i** + 7**j**) N. Find **P**.

6. The forces **P** N, (4**i** – 5**j**) N and (–2**i** + 6**j**) N act on a body. The resultant of these forces is 4**j** N. Find **P**.

7. The forces **P** N, (–3**i** – 2**j**) N and (**i** – 4**j**) N act on a body. The resultant of these forces is (3**i** – 7**j**) N. Find **P**.

## Exercise 19D

8. The forces **P** N, (4**i** – 3**j**) N and (–**i** – 2**j**) N act on a body. The resultant of these forces is (3**i** – 7**j**) N. Find **P**.

9. The forces **P** N, (–2**i** + **j**) N and (3**i** – 5**j**) N act on a body. The resultant of these forces is (5**i** – **j**) N. Find **P**.

10. The forces **P** N, (6**i** – 2**j**) N and (–4**i** + 5**j**) N act on a body. The resultant of these forces is (–**i** + 2**j**) N. Find **P**.

## 19.5 Newton's Second Law

Newton's second law can be written in vector form as:

$$\boldsymbol{F} = m\boldsymbol{a}$$

For example:

6. The forces (6**i** – 2**j**) N and (–4**i** + 5**j**) N act on a body of mass 5 kg. Find the acceleration.

To answer this question, you need to:
- Find the resultant force.
- Use $\boldsymbol{F} = m\boldsymbol{a}$.

Resultant:       6**i** – 2**j**
            +  –4**i** + 5**j**
                   2**i** + 3**j**

Use:        $\boldsymbol{F} = m\boldsymbol{a}$
        2**i** + 3**j** = 5**a**

So:        $\boldsymbol{a} = \dfrac{1}{5}(2\boldsymbol{i} + 3\boldsymbol{j})$ m/s$^2$

7. The forces (3**i** – 5**j**) N and **P** N act on a body of mass 2kg. The acceleration is (2**i** + 5**j**) m/s$^2$. Find **P**.

To answer this question, you need to:
- Find the resultant force using $\boldsymbol{F} = m\boldsymbol{a}$.
- Subtract the known force from the resultant force.

Use:        $\boldsymbol{F} = m\boldsymbol{a}$
        $\boldsymbol{F} = 2(2\boldsymbol{i} + 5\boldsymbol{j})$
        $\boldsymbol{F} = 4\boldsymbol{i} + 10\boldsymbol{j}$

Then subtract:   4**i** + 10**j**
            –  3**i** – 5**j**
                   **i** + 15**j**

So the answer is (**i** + 15**j**) N

## Exercise 19E

1. The forces (3**i** – 2**j**) N and (2**i** – 13**j**) N act on a body of mass 5kg. Find the acceleration.

2. The forces (–5**i** – **j**) N and **P** N act on a body of mass 3 kg. The acceleration is (–2**i** + **j**) m/s$^2$. Find **P**.

3. The forces (5**i** – 2**j**) N and (–11**i** – 10**j**) N act on a body of mass 6 kg. Find the acceleration.

4. The forces (30**i** – 15**j**) N and **P** N act on a body of mass 7 kg. The acceleration is (4**i** – 3**j**) m/s$^2$. Find **P**.

5. The forces (4**i** +7**j**) N and (–12**i** + 5**j**) N act on a body of mass 4 kg. Find the acceleration.

6. The forces (39**i** + 10**j**) N and **P** N act on a body of mass 9 kg. The acceleration is (4**i** + 2**j**) m/s$^2$. Find **P**.

7. The forces (2**i** – **j**) N and (–4**i** + 7**j**) N act on a body of mass 2 kg. Find the acceleration.

8. The forces (9**i** + 2**j**) N and **P** N act on a body of mass 3 kg. The acceleration is (2**i** – **j**) m/s$^2$. Find **P**.

9. The forces (4**i** – 9**j**) N and (5**i** + 15**j**) N act on a body of mass 3 kg. Find the acceleration.

10. The forces (–3**i** – 15**j**) N and **P** N act on a body of mass 5 kg. The acceleration is (–**i** – 2**j**) m/s$^2$. Find **P**.

## 19.6 Constantly Accelerated Motion

You can use the following equations of motion written in vector form:

$$\boldsymbol{v} = \boldsymbol{u} + \boldsymbol{a}t$$
$$\boldsymbol{s} = \boldsymbol{u}t + \tfrac{1}{2}\boldsymbol{a}t^2$$
$$\boldsymbol{s} = \tfrac{1}{2}t(\boldsymbol{u} + \boldsymbol{v})$$

For example:

8. A body of mass 6 kg moving with a velocity of (3**i** + 2**j**) m/s accelerates at (7**i** – 2**j**) m/s$^2$ for 3 s. Find:
   (a) the force producing the acceleration;
   (b) the final velocity;
   (c) the displacement after 3 s.

   (a)  Use:        $\boldsymbol{F} = m\boldsymbol{a}$
               $\boldsymbol{F} = 6(7\boldsymbol{i} – 2\boldsymbol{j})$
               $\boldsymbol{F} = (42\boldsymbol{i} – 12\boldsymbol{j})$ N

(b)    We know:               $u = 3\mathbf{i} + 2\mathbf{j}$
                              $a = 7\mathbf{i} - 2\mathbf{j}$
                              $t = 3$
       We want to find:       $v = ?$

       So we use:   $v = u + at$
                    $v = (3\mathbf{i} + 2\mathbf{j}) + 3(7\mathbf{i} - 2\mathbf{j})$
                    $v = 3\mathbf{i} + 2\mathbf{j} + 21\mathbf{i} - 6\mathbf{j}$
                    $v = (24\mathbf{i} - 4\mathbf{j})$ m/s

(c)    We know:               $u = 3\mathbf{i} + 2\mathbf{j}$
                              $a = 7\mathbf{i} - 2\mathbf{j}$
                              $t = 3$
       We want to find:       $s = ?$

       So we use:   $s = ut + \tfrac{1}{2}at^2$
                    $s = 3(3\mathbf{i} + 2\mathbf{j}) + \tfrac{1}{2}(9)(7\mathbf{i} - 2\mathbf{j})$
                    $s = 9\mathbf{i} + 6\mathbf{j} + 4.5(7\mathbf{i} - 2\mathbf{j})$
                    $s = 9\mathbf{i} + 6\mathbf{j} + 31.5\mathbf{i} - 9\mathbf{j}$
                    $s = (40.5\mathbf{i} - 3\mathbf{j})$ m

## Exercise 19F

1.  A body of mass 4 kg moving with a velocity of $(3\mathbf{i} - 2\mathbf{j})$ m/s accelerates at $(\mathbf{i} - 3\mathbf{j})$ m/s$^2$ for 3 s. Find:
    (a)    the force producing the acceleration.
    (b)    the final velocity.
    (c)    the displacement after 3 s.

2.  A body of mass 5 kg moving with a velocity of $(-\mathbf{i} + 2\mathbf{j})$ m/s is acted upon by a force of $(10\mathbf{i} + 10\mathbf{j})$ N and accelerates for 2 s. Find:
    (a)    the acceleration.
    (b)    the final velocity.
    (c)    the displacement after 2 s.

3.  A body of mass 2 kg accelerates at $(\mathbf{i} + 3\mathbf{j})$ m/s$^2$ for 6 s reaching a final velocity of $(4\mathbf{i} + 14\mathbf{j})$ m/s. Find:
    (a)    the force producing the acceleration.
    (b)    the inital velocity.
    (c)    the displacement after 6 s.

4.  A body of mass 8 kg moving with a velocity of $(4\mathbf{i} - 3\mathbf{j})$ m/s is acted upon by a force of $-60\mathbf{j}$ N and accelerates for 4 s. Find:
    (a)    the acceleration.
    (b)    the final velocity.
    (c)    the displacement after 4 s.

5.  A body of mass 6 kg accelerates at $(-2\mathbf{i} - 5\mathbf{j})$ m/s$^2$ for 3 s reaching a final velocity of $(-3\mathbf{i} - 11\mathbf{j})$ m/s. Find:
    (a)    the force producing the acceleration.
    (b)    the inital velocity.
    (c)    the displacement after 3 s.

## Exercise 19F...

6.  A body of mass 3 kg moving with a velocity of $(-2\mathbf{i} - 5\mathbf{j})$ m/s is acted upon by a force of $(7.5\mathbf{i} + 37.5\mathbf{j})$ N and accelerates for 5 s. Find:
    (a)    the acceleration.
    (b)    the final velocity.
    (c)    the displacement after 5 s.

7.  A body of mass 7 kg accelerates at $(-2\mathbf{i} + \mathbf{j})$ m/s$^2$ for 4 s and travels a displacement of $-4\mathbf{j}$ m. Find:
    (a)    the force producing the acceleration.
    (b)    the initial velocity.
    (c)    the final velocity.

8.  A body of mass 10 kg moving with a velocity of $(-\mathbf{i} + 3\mathbf{j})$ m/s is acted upon by a force of $(40\mathbf{i} + 20\mathbf{j})$ N and accelerates for 2 s. Find:
    (a)    the acceleration.
    (b)    the final velocity.
    (c)    the displacement after 2 s.

9.  A body of mass 4 kg accelerates at $(-2\mathbf{i} + 4\mathbf{j})$ m/s$^2$ for 2 s and travels a displacement of $(6\mathbf{i} + 4\mathbf{j})$ m. Find:
    (a)    the force producing the acceleration.
    (b)    the initial velocity.
    (c)    the final velocity.

10. A body of mass 2 kg is acted upon by a force of $(-60\mathbf{i} + 36\mathbf{j})$ N and accelerates for 6 s reaching a final velocity of $(-8\mathbf{i} + 12\mathbf{j})$ m/s. Find:
    (a)    the acceleration.
    (b)    the initial velocity.
    (c)    the displacement after 6 s.

## 19.7 Further Problems

The same methods can be used to solve more complex problems. For example:

9.  A body is moving parallel to the vector $3\mathbf{i} - 4\mathbf{j}$ with a speed of 65 m/s. Find its velocity.

    To answer this question, you need to:
    • Find the magnitude of the parallel vector.
    • Work out how many times greater the speed is than this magnitude.

    The magnitude of the parallel vector is:
    $$R = \sqrt{3^2 + (-4)^2}$$
    $$R = \sqrt{25}$$
    $$R = 5$$

Next, find how many times the speed is greater than this magnitude:

$$\frac{65}{5} = 13$$

So the velocity is 13 times the vector i.e.:

Velocity = 13(3**i** – 4**j**)
= (39**i** – 52**j**) m/s

## Exercise 19G

1. A body is moving parallel to the vector 5**i** – 12**j** with a speed of 26 m/s. Find its velocity.

2. A body is moving parallel to the vector –3**i** + 4**j** with a speed of 30 m/s. Find its velocity.

3. A body is moving parallel to the vector 15**i** + 8**j** with a speed of 51 m/s. Find its velocity.

4. A body is moving parallel to the vector –7**i** – 24**j** with a speed of 75 m/s. Find its velocity.

5. A body is moving parallel to the vector 4**i** + 3**j** with a speed of 45 m/s. Find its velocity.

6. A body is moving parallel to the vector –12**i** + 5**j** with a speed of 39 m/s. Find its velocity.

# CHAPTER 20: FRICTION

## 20.1 The Concept Of Friction

Friction is a **force** which always acts on rough surfaces. Friction always opposes the direction of motion in which a body is moving, or the direction of motion in which it would move. Friction can only prevent motion up to a limiting value after which motion will take place.

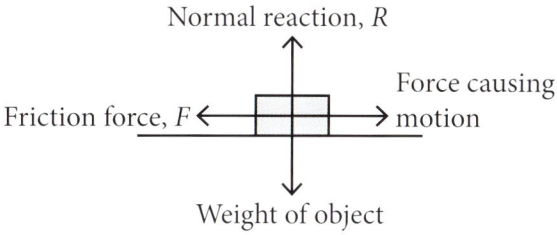

## 20.2 Bodies Just About To Move – Horizontal Motion

Remember, friction always acts **opposite** to the direction in which the body would move. The rules for solving this type of problem are:

a.   Resolve forces **horizontally** and **vertically**.

b.   Equate the resolved forces in each direction (because you know that the block is just about to move).

For example:

......................................................................................

1.   A block mass 6 kg rests on a rough horizontal plane. A horizontal force of 32 N will just cause the block to start to move. Find:
   (a)   the friction force;
   (b)   the normal reaction.

   (a)   First, sketch the forces:

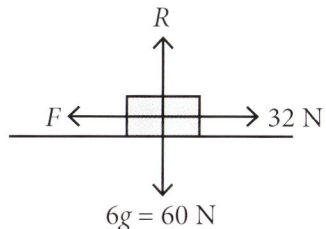

       Resolving horizontally:
         $F = 32$ N

   (b)   Resolving vertically:
         $R = 6g = 60$ N

......................................................................................

### Exercise 20A

1.   A block of mass 4 kg rests on a rough horizontal plane. A horizontal force of 25 N will just cause the block to start to move. Find:
   (a)   the friction force;
   (b)   the normal reaction.

2.   A block of mass 2.8 kg rests on a rough horizontal plane. A horizontal force of 18 N will just cause the block to start to move. Find:
   (a)   the friction force;
   (b)   the normal reaction.

3.   A block of mass 4.8 kg rests on a rough horizontal plane. A horizontal force of 25 N will just cause the block to start to move. Find:
   (a)   the friction force;
   (b)   the normal reaction.

## 20.3 Bodies Just About To Move – Inclined Plane

When the block lies on an inclined plane, the rules are similar:

a.   Resolve forces **along** the plane and **perpendicular** to the plane.

b.   Equate the resolved forces in each direction (because you know that the block is just about to move).

For example:

......................................................................................

2.   A block of mass 4 kg rests on a rough plane inclined at 25° to the horizontal. It is just about to move. Find:
   (a)   the friction force;
   (b)   the normal reaction.

   (a)   If it is just about to move then friction will act **up** the slope. Thus the forces are as follows:

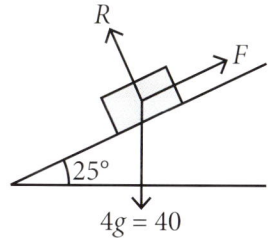

       We need to resolve the forces, as shown in the following diagram.

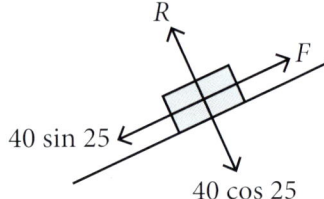

Resolving along the plane of the slope:
$$F = 40 \sin 25$$
$$= 16.90 \text{ N}$$

(b)  Resolving perpendicular to the plane:
$$R = 40 \cos 25$$
$$= 36.25 \text{ N}$$

3.  A block of mass 5 kg is at rest on a rough plane inclined at 30° to the horizontal. The frictional force on the block is 12.99 N. Find the least force needed to:
(a)  move it up the plane
(b)  stop it falling down the plane.

(a)  If the force is to move the block **up** the plane then friction will act **down** the plane. Let the force be called $P$. Thus the forces are as follows:

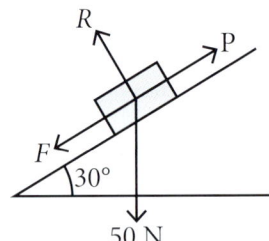

We need to resolve the forces, as shown below:

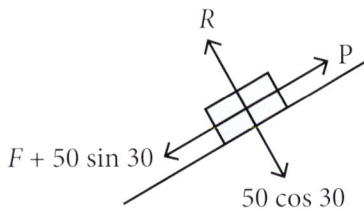

Resolving perpendicular to the plane:
$$R = 50 \cos 30$$
$$R = 43.3 \text{ N}$$

Resolving along the plane:
$$P = F + 50 \sin 30$$
So:
$$P = 12.99 + 25$$
$$P = 37.99 \text{ N}$$

(b)  If the force is to stop the block falling **down** the plane then friction will act **up** the slope. Let the force be called $P$. Thus the forces are as follows:

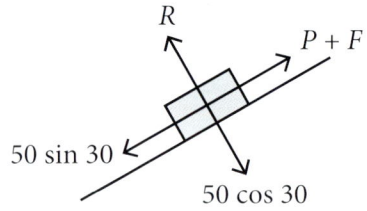

Resolving perpendicular to the plane:
$$R = 50 \cos 30$$
$$= 43.3 \text{ N}$$

(b)  Resolving along the plane:
$$P + F = 50 \sin 30$$
$$P + F = 25$$
So:  $P + 12.99 = 25$
$$P = 25 - 12.99$$
$$P = 12.01 \text{ N}$$

## Exercise 20B

1.  A block of mass 8 kg is at rest on a rough plane inclined at 20° to the horizontal. It is just about to move. Find:
(a)  the frictional force on the block;
(b)  the normal reaction.

2.  A block of mass 12 kg is at rest on a rough plane inclined at 42° to the horizontal. It is just about to move. Find:
(a)  the frictional force on the block;
(b)  the normal reaction.

3.  A block of mass 6 kg is at rest on a rough plane inclined at 24° to the horizontal. The frictional force on the block is 3.9 N. Find the least force needed to:
(a)  move it up the plane;
(b)  stop it falling down the plane.

4.  A block of mass 8 kg is at rest on a rough plane inclined at 32° to the horizontal. The frictional force on the block is 10.17 N. Find the least force needed to:
(a)  move it up the plane;
(b)  stop it falling down the plane.

5.  A block of mass 5.6 kg is at rest on a rough plane inclined at 15° to the horizontal. The frictional force on the block is 2.46 N. Find the least force needed to:
(a)  move it up the plane;
(b)  stop it falling down the plane.

6.  A block of mass 2.8 kg is at rest on a rough plane inclined at 35° to the horizontal. The frictional force on the block is 6.58 N. Find the

## Exercise 20B...

least force needed to:
(a) move it up the plane;
(b) stop it falling down the plane.

7. A block of mass 14 kg is at rest on a rough plane inclined at 22° to the horizontal. The frictional force on the block is 18.88 N. Find the least force needed to:
   (a) move it up the plane;
   (b) stop it falling down the plane.

8. A block of mass 3.7 kg is at rest on a rough plane inclined at 26° to the horizontal. The frictional force on the block is 5.19 N. Find the least force needed to:
   (a) move it up the plane;
   (b) stop it falling down the plane.

9. A block of mass 4.3 kg is at rest on a rough plane inclined at 14° to the horizontal. The frictional force on the block is 2.5 N. Find the least force needed to:
   (a) move it up the plane;
   (b) stop it falling down the plane.

10. A block mass 7.8 kg is at rest on a rough plane inclined at 34° to the horizontal. The frictional force on the block is 23.55 N. Find the least force needed to:
    (a) move it up the plane;
    (b) stop it falling down the plane.

## 20.4 Bodies Moving – Horizontal Motion

Friction always acts opposite to the direction in which the body moves. The rules for finding the resultant acceleration of such a body are:

a. Resolve forces horizontally and vertically.

b. Equate the resolved forces vertically.

c. Find the resultant horizontal force.

d. Use $F = ma$.

For example:

......................................................................

4. A block of mass 7.6 kg is initially at rest. It is pulled along a rough horizontal plane by a horizontal force of 58 N. The frictional force on the block is 6 N per kg of mass. Find:
   (a) the acceleration;
   (b) the time it takes to reach a velocity of 4 m/s.

(a) We must first find the friction force. The frictional force is 6 N per kg of mass
$= 6 \times 7.6 = 45.6$ N.

Now we can sketch the forces and resolve them horizontally:

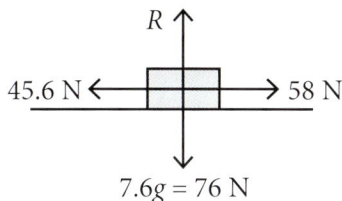

$$7.6g = 76 \text{ N}$$

Resultant horizontal force:
$$= 58 - 45.6$$
$$= 12.4 \text{ N}$$

Find the acceleration:
$$F = ma$$
$$12.4 = 7.6a$$
$$a = \frac{12.4}{7.6}$$
$$= 1.63 \text{ m/s}^2$$

(b) We know:
$$u = 0$$
$$a = 1.63$$
$$v = 4$$

We want to find: $t = ?$
So we use:
$$v = u + at$$
$$4 = 0 + 1.63t$$
$$t = \frac{4}{1.63}$$
$$t = 2.45 \text{ s}$$

## Exercise 20C

1. A block of mass 3.4 kg is initially at rest. It is pulled along a rough horizontal plane by a horizontal force of 42 N. The frictional force on the block is 2.7 N per kg of mass. Find:
   (a) the acceleration;
   (b) the time it takes to reach a velocity of 2.5 m/s.

2. A block of mass 7.2 kg accelerates from 2 m/s to 26 m/s in 8 s on a rough horizontal plane when acted upon by a horizontal force of 48 N. Find:
   (a) the frictional force on the block;
   (b) the distance travelled.

3. A block of mass 6 kg is initially at rest. It is pulled along a rough horizontal plane by a horizontal force of 72 N. The frictional force on the block is 4.8 N per kg of mass. Find:
   (a) the acceleration;
   (b) the time it takes to travel 5.4 m.

## Exercise 20C...

4. A block of mass 2.8 kg accelerates from 4 m/s and travels 32 m in 4 s on a rough horizontal plane when acted upon by a horizontal force of 26 N. Find:
   (a) the frictional force on the block;
   (b) the final velocity.

5. A block of mass 24 kg is initially at rest. It is pulled along a rough horizontal plane by a horizontal force of 176 N. The frictional force on the block is 5.8 N per kg of mass. Find:
   (a) the acceleration;
   (b) the distance travelled in 5 s.

6. A block of mass 4.3 kg accelerates from 6 m/s to 56 m/s in travelling 310 m on a rough horizontal plane when acted upon by a horizontal force of 52 N. Find:
   (a) the frictional force on the block;
   (b) the time taken.

7. A block of mass 4.8 kg is initially at rest. It is pulled along a rough horizontal plane by a horizontal force of 37 N. The frictional force on the block is 7.2 N per kg of mass:
   (a) the acceleration;
   (b) the velocity when it has travelled 8.2 m.

8. A block of mass 5.8 kg accelerates reaching a velocity of 27 m/s in 6 s while travelling 90 m on a rough horizontal plane when acted upon by a horizontal force of 68 N. Find:
   (a) the frictional force on the block;
   (b) the initial velocity.

9. A block mass 7.6 kg is initially at rest. It is pulled along a rough horizontal plane by a horizontal force of 58 N. The frictional force on the block is 6 N per kg of mass. Find:
   (a) the acceleration;
   (b) the velocity after 4 s.

10. A block of mass 8 kg is initially at rest. It is pulled along a rough horizontal plane by a horizontal force of 44 N. The frictional force on the block is 4 N per kg of mass. Find:
    (a) the acceleration;
    (b) the distance travelled in 5 s.

11. A block of mass 3.7 kg accelerates from 7 m/s and travels 504 m in 12 s on a rough horizontal plane when acted upon by a horizontal force of 40 N. Find:
    (a) the frictional force on the block;

## Exercise 20C...

   (b) the final velocity.

12. A body of mass 8 kg rests on a rough horizontal plane. The frictional force on the body is 23.8 N. It is just about to move when a force of P N is applied at 20° to the horizontal. Find the value of P.

13. A body of mass 8.4 kg is pulled along a rough horizontal plane by a force of 48 N acting at 35° to the horizontal at an acceleration of 2 m/s². Find the frictional force on the body.

14. A body of mass $M$ kg rests on a rough horizontal plane. The frictional force on the body is 17.64 N. The body moves with an acceleration of 2 m/s² when a force of 35 N is applied at 16° to the horizontal. Find the value of $M$.

15. A body of mass 6.5 kg is pulled along a rough horizontal plane by a force of 56 N acting at 24° to the horizontal at an acceleration of $a$ m/s². The frictional force on the body is 29.57 N. Find the value of $a$.

## 20.5 Bodies Moving – Inclined Plane

The same principles can be applied to bodies moving on inclined planes. For example:

5. A block of mass 7.2 kg rests on a rough plane inclined at 36° to the horizontal. A force of 64 N parallel to, and acting up, the plane is applied to the body and it accelerates uniformly to a velocity of 6 m/s in 3 s. Find the frictional force.

First, sketch the forces:

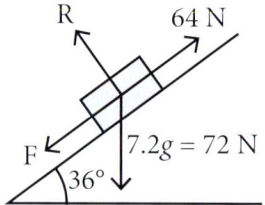

You must first find the acceleration as follows.

We know:
$$u = 0$$
$$v = 6$$
$$t = 3$$

We want to find:
$$a = ?$$

So we use:
$$v = u + at$$
$$6 = 0 + 3a$$
$$a = 2 \text{ m/s}^2$$

You must now resolve the forces, as shown:

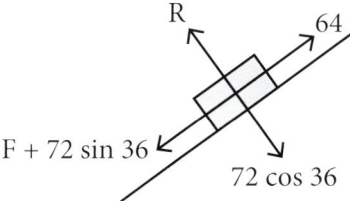

So the resultant force along the plane:
$$= 64 - F - 72 \sin 36$$

Using:
$$F = ma$$
$$64 - F - 72 \sin 36 = 7.2 \times 2$$
$$64 - F - 42.3 = 14.4$$
$$21.7 - F = 14.4$$
$$21.7 - 14.4 = F$$
$$F = 7.3 \text{ N}$$

## Exercise 20D

1. A block of mass 6 kg is at rest on a rough plane inclined at 40° to the horizontal. A force of 84 N parallel to, and acting up, the plane is applied to the body. It accelerates uniformly, travelling 5 m in 2.5 s. Find the frictional force.

2. A block of mass 6.2 kg is at rest on a rough plane inclined at 36° to the horizontal. A force of 52 N parallel to, and acting up, the plane is applied to the body. It accelerates uniformly to a velocity of 6 m/s in 5 s. Find the frictional force.

3. A block of mass 5.8 kg is at rest on a rough plane inclined at 24° to the horizontal. A force of $P$ N parallel to, and acting up, the plane is applied to the body. It accelerates uniformly to a velocity of 3 m/s in travelling 2.25 m. The frictional force is 36.03 N. Find $P$.

4. A block of mass 3.9 kg is at rest on a rough plane inclined at 35° to the horizontal. A force of $P$ N parallel to, and acting up, the plane is applied to the body. It accelerates uniformly, travelling 5 m in 2 s. The frictional force is 24.28 N. Find $P$.

5. A block of mass 4.5 kg is at rest on a rough plane inclined at 40° to the horizontal. A force of 54 N parallel to, and acting up, the plane is applied to the body. It accelerates uniformly to a velocity of 9.6 m/s in 3 s. Find the frictional force.

6. A block of mass 9 kg is at rest on a rough plane inclined at 56° to the horizontal. A force of 95 N parallel to, and acting up, the plane is applied to

## Exercise 20D...

the body. It accelerates uniformly to a velocity of 2.1 m/s in travelling 1.575 m. Find the frictional force.

7. A block of mass 7 kg is at rest on a rough plane inclined at 25° to the horizontal. A force of $P$ N parallel to, and acting up, the plane is applied to the body. It accelerates uniformly, travelling 3 m in 2 s. The frictional force is 29.18 N. Find $P$.

8. A block of mass 8 kg is at rest on a rough plane inclined at 42° to the horizontal. A force of 78 N parallel to, and acting up, the plane is applied to the body. It accelerates uniformly to a velocity of 2.8 m/s in 1.4 s. Find the frictional force.

9. A block of mass 5.6 kg is at rest on a rough plane inclined at 26° to the horizontal. A force of $P$ N parallel to, and acting up, the plane is applied to the body. It accelerates uniformly to a velocity of 3 m/s in travelling 7.5 m. The frictional force is 22.15 N. Find $P$.

10. A block of mass 4.8 kg is at rest on a rough plane inclined at 33° to the horizontal. A force of 49 N parallel to, and acting up, the plane is applied to the body. It accelerates uniformly, travelling 80 cm in 2 s. Find the frictional force.

# CHAPTER 21: CONNECTED BODIES

## 21.1 The Concept of Connected Bodies

Sometimes you have to deal with problems of forces acting on two connected bodies. The rules for solving this type of problem are:

a. Consider the two bodies separately.

b. Use $F = ma$.

For example:

1. A van of mass 1100 kg tows a trailer of mass 560 kg by means of a light horizontal tow bar. The tractive force produced by the van's engine is 3960 N. The van and trailer travel along a straight horizontal road as shown below and accelerate at 1.6 m/s². The resistance to motion of the van is 950 N. Find:
   (a) the resistance to motion of the trailer;
   (b) the magnitude of the tension in the tow bar.

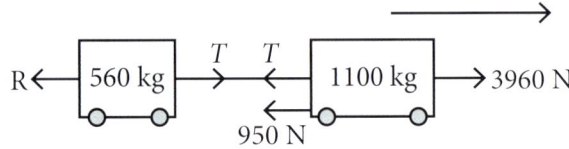

Let $T$ = the magnitude of the tension in the tow bar and $R$ = the resistance to motion of the trailer.

First consider the van:
$$F = ma$$
$$3960 - 950 - T = 1100 \times 1.6$$
$$3010 - T = 1760$$
$$3010 - 1760 = T$$
$$T = 1250 \text{ N}$$

Next consider the trailer:
$$F = ma$$
$$T - R = 560 \times 1.6$$
$$1250 - R = 560 \times 1.6$$
$$1250 - R = 896$$
$$1250 - 896 = R$$
$$R = 354 \text{ N}$$

So the answers are (a) 354 N (b) 1250 N.

2. A van of mass 1050 kg tows a trailer of mass 520 kg by means of a light horizontal tow bar. The tractive force produced by the van's engine is 3750 N. The van and trailer travel along a straight horizontal road as shown in the diagram. The resistance to motion of the van is 860 N and the resistance to motion of the trailer is 425 N. Find:

(a) the acceleration;
(b) the magnitude of the tension in the tow bar.

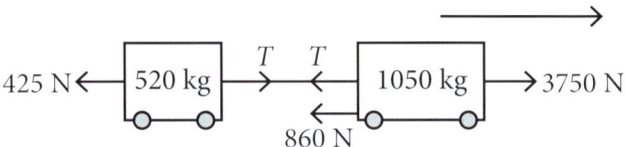

Let $T$ = the magnitude of the tension in the tow bar and $a$ = the acceleration.

First consider the van:
$$F = ma$$
$$3750 - 860 - T = 1050a$$
$$2890 - T = 1050a$$

Next consider the trailer:
$$F = ma$$
$$T - 425 = 520a$$

You can add these equations to get rid of the $T$:
$$2890 - T = 1050a$$
$$+ \quad \underline{T - 425 = \quad 520a}$$
$$2465 = 1570a$$
$$a = \frac{2465}{1570}$$
$$a = 1.57 \text{ m/s}^2$$

Substituting $a$ into either equation will give $T$:
$$T - 425 = 520a$$
$$T - 425 = 520 \times 1.57$$
$$T - 425 = 816.4$$
$$T = 816.4 + 425$$
$$T = 1241.4 \text{ N}$$

So the answers are (a) 1.57 m/s² (b) 1241.4 N.

## Exercise 21A

1. A van of mass 1060 kg tows a trailer of mass $M$ kg by means of a light horizontal tow bar. The tractive force produced by the van's engine is 3160 N. The van and trailer travel along a straight horizontal road. The resistance to motion of the van is 925 N and the resistance to motion of the trailer is 435 N. The magnitude of the tension in the tow bar is 980 N. Find:
   (a) the acceleration;
   (b) $M$.

2. A van of mass 1160 kg tows a trailer of mass 480 kg by means of a light horizontal tow bar. The tractive force produced by the van's engine is 3680 N. The van and trailer travel along a

## Exercise 21A...

straight horizontal road. The resistance to motion of the van is 925 N and the resistance to motion of the trailer is 385 N. Find:

(a) the acceleration;

(b) the magnitude of the tension in the tow bar.

3. A van of mass 1080 kg tows a trailer of mass 450 kg by means of a light horizontal tow bar. The tractive force produced by the van's engine is 3750 N. The van and trailer travel along a straight horizontal road and accelerate at 1.3 m/s$^2$. The resistance to motion of the van is 924 N. Find:

(a) the resistance to motion of the trailer;

(b) the magnitude of the tension in the tow bar.

4. A van of mass 1120 kg tows a trailer of mass 385 kg by means of a light horizontal tow bar. The tractive force produced by the van's engine is 3880 N. The van and trailer travel along a straight horizontal road and accelerate at 1.25 m/s$^2$. The resistance to motion of the trailer is 575 N. Find:

(a) the resistance to motion of the van;

(b) the magnitude of the tension in the tow bar.

5. A van of mass 1200 kg tows a trailer of mass $M$ kg by means of a light horizontal tow bar. The tractive force produced by the van's engine is $P$ N. The van and trailer travel along a straight horizontal road and accelerate at 1.4 m/s$^2$. The resistance to motion of the van is 845 N and the resistance to motion of the trailer is 620 N. The magnitude of the tension in the tow bar is 975 N. Find:

(a) $P$;

(b) $M$.

6 A van of mass $M$ kg tows a trailer of mass $m$ kg by means of a light horizontal tow bar. The tractive force produced by the van's engine is 3440 N. The van and trailer travel along a straight horizontal road and accelerate at 1.15 m/s$^2$. The resistance to motion of the van is 920 N and the resistance to motion of the trailer is 546 N. The magnitude of the tension in the tow bar is 864 N. Find:

(a) $M$;

(b) $m$.

## Exercise 21A...

7. A van of mass 980 kg tows a trailer of mass 420 kg by means of a light horizontal tow bar. The tractive force produced by the van's engine is 3050 N. The van and trailer travel along a straight horizontal road. The resistance to motion of the van is 825 N. The magnitude of the tension in the tow bar is 910 N. Find:

(a) the acceleration;

(b) the resistance to motion of the van.

8. A van of mass $M$ kg tows a trailer of mass 375 kg by means of a light horizontal tow bar. The tractive force produced by the van's engine is 3220 N. The van and trailer travel along a straight horizontal road and accelerate at 1.08 m/s$^2$. The resistance to motion of the van is 810 N and the resistance to motion of the trailer is 380 N. Find:

(a) $M$;

(b) the magnitude of the tension in the tow bar.

## 21.2 Resistance Per Mass

Sometimes the resistance to the motion is given **per mass**. To find the **total** resistance you would then multiply this figure by the mass. For example:

........................................................................

3. The resistance to the motion of a car of mass 960 kg is 0.642 N per kg of mass. Find the total resistance.

Total resistance = 960 × 0.642 = 616.32 N

........................................................................

4. A van of mass 1125 kg tows a trailer of mass 540 kg by means of a light horizontal tow bar. The tractive force produced by the van's engine is 3250 N. The van and trailer travel along a straight horizontal road as shown below. The resistance to motion of the van is 0.86 N per kg of mass and the resistance to motion of the trailer is 0.82 N per kg of mass. Find:

(a) the acceleration;

(b) the magnitude of the tension in the tow bar.

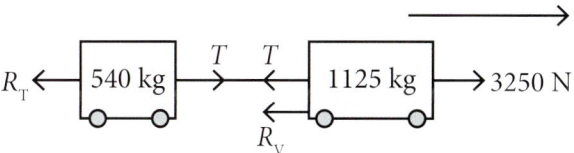

Let $T$ = the magnitude of the tension in the tow bar and $a$ = the acceleration.

First consider the van. Total resistance $R_V$ is:
$$0.86 \times 1125 = 967.5 \text{ N}$$
Using: $F = ma$
$$3250 - 967.5 - T = 1125a$$
$$2282.5 - T = 1125a$$

Next consider the trailer. Total resistance $R_T$ is:
$$0.82 \times 540 = 442.8 \text{ N}$$
Using: $F = ma$
$$T - 442.8 = 540a$$

You can add these equations to get rid of the $T$:
$$2282.5 - T = 1125a$$
$$+ \quad T - 442.8 = 540a$$
$$1839.7 = 1665a$$
$$a = \frac{1839.7}{1665}$$
$$a = 1.105 \text{ m/s}^2$$

Substituting a into either equation will give $T$:
$$T - 442.8 = 540a$$
$$T - 442.8 = 540 \times 1.105$$
$$T - 442.8 = 596.7$$
$$T = 596.7 + 442.8$$
$$T = 1039.5 \text{ N}$$

So the answers are (a) 1.11 m/s² (to 3 s.f.) and (b) 1040 N (to 3 s.f.).

## Exercise 21B

1. A van of mass 1140 kg tows a trailer of mass 540 kg by means of a light horizontal tow bar. The tractive force produced by the van's engine is 3460 N. The van and trailer travel along a straight horizontal road. The resistance to motion of the van is 0.88 N per kg of mass and the resistance to motion of the trailer is 0.83 N per kg of mass. Find:
   (a) the acceleration;
   (b) the magnitude of the tension in the tow bar.

2. A van of mass 1025 kg tows a trailer of mass 496 kg by means of a light horizontal tow bar. The tractive force produced by the van's engine is 3375 N. The van and trailer travel along a straight horizontal road. The resistance to motion of the van is 0.92 N per kg of mass and the resistance to motion of the trailer is 0.87 N per kg of mass. Find:
   (a) the acceleration;
   (b) the magnitude of the tension in the tow bar.

## Exercise 21B

3. A van of mass 986 kg tows a trailer of mass 424 kg by means of a light horizontal tow bar. The tractive force produced by the van's engine is 3215 N. The van and trailer travel along a straight horizontal road and accelerate at 1.2 m/s². The resistance to motion of the van is 0.92 N per kg of mass. Find:
   (a) the magnitude of the tension in the tow bar;
   (b) the resistance to motion of the trailer per kg of mass.

4. A van of mass 1024 kg tows a trailer of mass 414 kg by means of a light horizontal tow bar. The tractive force produced by the van's engine is 3540 N. The van and trailer travel along a straight horizontal road and accelerate at 0.96 m/s². The resistance to motion of the trailer is 1.12 N per kg of mass. Find:
   (a) the magnitude of the tension in the tow bar;
   (b) the resistance to motion of the van per kg of mass.

5. A van of mass 1156 kg tows a trailer of mass $M$ kg by means of a light horizontal tow bar. The tractive force produced by the van's engine is $P$ N. The van and trailer travel along a straight horizontal road and accelerate at 1.28 m/s². The resistance to motion of the van is 0.84 N per kg of mass and the resistance to motion of the trailer is 0.8 N per kg of mass. The magnitude of the tension in the tow bar is 920 N. Find:
   (a) $P$;
   (b) $M$.

6. A van of mass $M$ kg tows a trailer of mass $m$ kg by means of a light horizontal tow bar. The tractive force produced by the van's engine is 3356 N. The van and trailer travel along a straight horizontal road and accelerate at 1.08 m/s². The resistance to motion of the van is 1.05 N per kg of mass and the resistance to motion of the trailer is 0.96 N per kg of mass. The magnitude of the tension in the tow bar is 875 N. Find:
   (a) $M$;
   (b) $m$.

7. A van of mass 976 kg tows a trailer of mass 448 kg by means of a light horizontal tow bar.

## Exercise 21B

the tension in the tow bar.

The tractive force produced by the van's engine is 3164 N. The van and trailer travel along a straight horizontal road. The resistance to motion of the van is 1.02 N per kg of mass. The magnitude of the tension in the tow bar is 920 N. Find:

(a) the acceleration;

(b) the resistance to motion of the trailer per kg of mass.

8. A van of mass $M$ kg tows a trailer of mass 386 kg by means of a light horizontal tow bar. The tractive force produced by the van's engine is 3274 N. The van and trailer travel along a straight horizontal road and accelerate at 1.12 m/s². The resistance to motion of the van is 0.86 N per kg of mass and the resistance to motion of the trailer is 0.82 N per kg of mass. Find:

(a) $M$;

(b) the magnitude of the tension in the tow bar.

## 21.3 Resistance Per Mass – Harder Questions

Often you are asked more difficult questions involving resistance per mass. For example:

5. A car of mass 1400 kg tows a trailer of mass 600 kg at a constant speed of 14 m/s. The resistance to motion of the car is 1.3 N per kg of mass and the resistance to motion of the trailer is 0.9 N per kg of mass. Find:

(a) the tractive force of the car's engine;

(b) the magnitude of the tension in the tow bar.

After travelling for a short time, the car accelerates at 0.2 m/s². Find:

(c) the new magnitude of the tension in the tow bar;

(d) the new tractive force of the engine.

The tow bar then breaks.

(e) Find the deceleration of the trailer.

First, sketch all the forces:

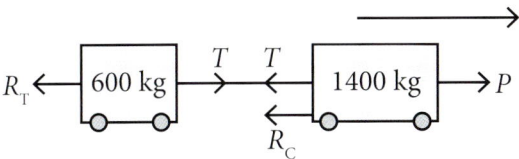

Let the tractive force = $P$ and $T$ = the magnitude of

(a) The car (and thus the trailer) are moving at a constant speed. So you must equate the forces. Total resistance of the car $R_C$ is:
$$1.3 \times 1400 = 1820 \text{ N}$$

Total resistance of the trailer $R_T$ is:
$$0.9 \times 600 = 540 \text{ N}$$

You should consider the whole system. Note that in doing so, the tensions cancel each other out. Since the system is travelling at a constant speed, the tractive force of the engine is equal to the sum of the resistances of the car and trailer:
$$P = 540 + 1820$$
$$P = 2360 \text{ N}$$

(b) Since the system is travelling at a constant speed, the tension must be equal to the resistance of the trailer.
$$T = 540 \text{ N from part (a)}$$

(c) In this part of the question, the car is accelerating. So you must use $F = ma$.

First consider the car:
Using: $\qquad F = ma$
$$P - (1820 + T) = 1400 \times 0.2$$
$$P - 1820 - T = 280$$
$$P - T = 2100$$

Then consider the trailer:
Using $\qquad F = ma$
$$T - 540 = 600 \times 0.2$$
$$T - 540 = 120$$
$$T = 660 \text{ N}$$

(d) Substituting the value of $T$ from part (c):
$$P - T = 2100$$
$$P - 660 = 2100$$
$$P = 2760 \text{ N}$$

So the tractive force of the engine is 2760 N

(e) If the tow bar breaks then the only force acting on the trailer is –540 N – from part (c) – which will slow it down. Note that the force is negative as it acts opposite to the direction of travel.

Using: $\qquad F = ma$
$$-540 = 600a$$
$$a = \frac{-540}{600}$$
$$a = -0.9 \text{ m/s}^2$$

Be careful: the question asked for the **dec**eleration. So the deceleration is 0.9 m/s².

## Exercise 21C

1. A car of mass 1500 kg tows a trailer of mass 450 kg at a steady speed. The resistance to motion of the car is 1.25 N per kg of mass and the resistance to motion of the trailer is 0.84 N per kg of mass. Find:
   (a) the tractive force of the car's engine;
   (b) the magnitude of the tension in the tow bar.

   After travelling for a short time, the car accelerates at 0.15 m/s². Find:
   (c) the new magnitude of the tension in the tow bar;
   (d) the new tractive force of the engine.
   (e) If the tow bar breaks, find the deceleration of the trailer.

2. A car of mass 1350 kg tows a trailer of mass 540 kg at a constant speed. The resistance to motion of the car is 1.4 N per kg of mass and the resistance to motion of the trailer is 0.95 N per kg of mass. Find:
   (a) the tractive force of the car's engine;
   (b) the magnitude of the tension in the tow bar.

   After travelling for a short time, the car accelerates at 0.3 m/s². Find:
   (c) the new magnitude of the tension in the tow bar;
   (d) the new tractive force of the engine.
   (e) If the tow bar breaks, find the deceleration of the trailer.

3. A car of mass 1200 kg tows a caravan of mass 1500 kg at a steady speed. The resistance to motion of the car is 1.6 N per kg of mass and the resistance to motion of the caravan is 1.8 N per kg of mass. Find:
   (a) the tractive force of the car's engine;
   (b) the magnitude of the tension in the tow bar.

   After travelling for a short time, the car accelerates at 0.28 m/s². Find:
   (c) the new magnitude of the tension in the tow bar;
   (d) the new tractive force of the engine.
   (e) If the tow bar breaks, find the deceleration of the caravan.

4. A car of mass 1100 kg tows a caravan of mass 1400 kg at an acceleration of 0.4 m/s². The

## Exercise 21C...

resistance to motion of the car is 1.3 N per kg of mass and the resistance to motion of the caravan is 1.6 N per kg of mass. The car and caravan start from rest. Find:
   (a) the tractive force of the car's engine;
   (b) the magnitude of the tension in the tow bar;
   (c) the distance travelled in 6 s;
   (d) the velocity of the car after it has travelled 5 m.
   (e) As soon as the car has travelled 5 m the tow bar breaks. Find the additional distance the caravan travels before it comes to rest.

5. A van of mass 1170 kg tows a trailer of mass 520 kg by means of a light horizontal tow bar. The tractive force produced by the van's engine is 3756 N. The van and trailer accelerate uniformly from rest to 20 m/s in 16 s.
   (a) Find the acceleration.
   The resistance to motion of the van is 0.78 N per kg of mass. Find:
   (b) the total resistance to the motion of the van and trailer;
   (c) the resistance to the motion of the van;
   (d) the resistance to the motion of the trailer;
   (e) the magnitude of the tension in the tow bar.
   The van and trailer then travel at a constant speed of 20 m/s and after some time the tow bar breaks.
   (f) Find the time that it takes for the trailer to come to rest.

6. A van of mass 1156 kg tows a trailer of mass 480 kg by means of a light horizontal tow bar. The tractive force produced by the van's engine is $P$ N. The van and trailer accelerate uniformly from rest to 6 m/s in travelling 11.25 m.
   (a) Find the acceleration.

   The resistance to motion of the van is 0.92 N per kg of mass and the resistance to motion of the trailer is 0.85 N per kg of mass. Find:
   (b) the total resistance to the motion of the van and trailer;
   (c) the magnitude of the tension in the tow bar;
   (d) the value of $P$.

## Exercise 21C...

The van and trailer then travel at a constant speed of 6 m/s and after some time the tow bar breaks. Find:

(e)   the time before the trailer comes to rest;

(f)   the additional distance travelled before the trailer comes to rest.

## 21.4 Pulleys

Problems can also involve bodies that are connected by strings that pass over a pulley. In this case, the tensions in the connecting string act in the same direction. To solve this type of question, we need to use these rules:

a.   Consider each particle separately.

b.   Use $F = ma$ for each one.

For example:

.................................................................

6.   Two bodies of mass 0.3 kg and 0.1 kg are connected by a light inextensible string which passes over a smooth fixed pulley as shown.

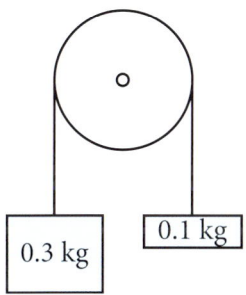

The system is released from rest with the bodies hanging vertically. Calculate:
(a)   the acceleration of the system;
(b)   the tension in the string;
(c)   the force exerted by the string on the pulley when the bodies are in motion.

First, mark all the forces on the diagram. Once the system is released, the 0.3 kg particle will move down as it is heavier, while the 0.1 kg particle will move up. The tension in the string acts away from each particle and is the same (you would call it $T$). The weight of each particle is found using $F = ma$ where $a$ = the acceleration due to gravity = 10 m/s$^2$.

So the weight of the 0.3 kg particle is:
$0.3 \times 10 = 3$ N.

and the weight of the 0.1 kg particle is:
$0.1 \times 10 = 1$ N.

These forces are shown in the following diagram.

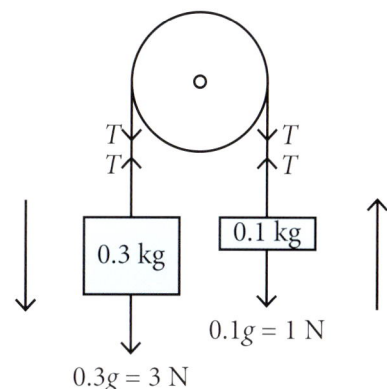

$$0.3g = 3 \text{ N}$$
$$0.1g = 1 \text{ N}$$

(a)   First consider the 0.3 kg particle:
Using:       $F = ma$
$$3 - T = 0.3a$$

Then consider the 0.1 kg particle:
$$T - 1 = 0.1a$$

You can then solve these simultaneous equations by adding them to get rid of the $T$s.

$$3 - T = 0.3a$$
$$+ \quad \underline{T - 1 = 0.1a}$$
$$2 = 0.4a$$
$$a = 5 \text{ m/s}^2$$

(b)   You can find the tension by substituting the acceleration into either equation:
$$T - 1 = 0.1a$$
$$T - 1 = 0.5$$
$$T = 1.5 \text{ N}$$

(c)   The force exerted by the string on the pulley when the bodies are in motion will be the sum of the tensions:
$$1.5 + 1.5 = 3 \text{ N}$$

## Exercise 21D

1.   Two bodies of mass 0.9 kg and 0.4 kg are connected by a light inextensible string which passes over a smooth fixed pulley. The system is released from rest with the bodies hanging vertically. Calculate:
(a)   the acceleration of the system;
(b)   the tension in the string;
(c)   the force exerted by the string on the pulley when the bodies are in motion.

2.   Two bodies of mass 1.2 kg and 0.8 kg are connected by a light inextensible string which passes over a smooth fixed pulley. The system is released from rest with the bodies hanging vertically. Calculate:
(a)   the acceleration of the system;

## Exercise 21D

   (b)   the tension in the string;
   (c)   the force exerted by the string on the pulley when the bodies are in motion.

3.  Two bodies of mass 0.3 kg and 0.2 kg are connected by a light inextensible string which passes over a smooth fixed pulley. The system is released from rest with the bodies hanging vertically. Calculate:
   (a)   the acceleration of the system;
   (b)   the tension in the string;
   (c)   the force exerted by the string on the pulley when the bodies are in motion.

4.  Two bodies of mass 0.7 kg and 0.5 kg are connected by a light inextensible string which passes over a smooth fixed pulley. The system is released from rest with the bodies hanging vertically. Calculate:
   (a)   the acceleration of the system;
   (b)   the tension in the string;
   (c)   the force exerted by the string on the pulley when the bodies are in motion.

5.  Two bodies of mass 1.5 kg and 1 kg are connected by a light inextensible string which passes over a smooth fixed pulley. The system is released from rest with the bodies hanging vertically. Calculate:
   (a)   the acceleration of the system;
   (b)   the tension in the string;
   (c)   the force exerted by the string on the pulley when the bodies are in motion.

6.  Two bodies of mass 1.1 kg and 0.5 kg are connected by a light inextensible string which passes over a smooth fixed pulley. The system is released from rest with the bodies hanging vertically. Calculate:
   (a)   the acceleration of the system;
   (b)   the tension in the string;
   (c)   the force exerted by the string on the pulley when the bodies are in motion.

7.  Two bodies of mass 0.5 kg and 0.3 kg are connected by a light inextensible string which passes over a smooth fixed pulley. The system is released from rest with the bodies hanging vertically. Calculate:
   (a)   the acceleration of the system;
   (b)   the tension in the string;
   (c)   the force exerted by the string on the pulley when the bodies are in motion.

## Exercise 21D...

8.  Two bodies of mass 70 kg and 30 kg are connected by a light inextensible string which passes over a smooth fixed pulley. The system is released from rest with the bodies hanging vertically. Calculate:
   (a)   the acceleration of the system;
   (b)   the tension in the string;
   (c)   the force exerted by the string on the pulley when the bodies are in motion.

## 21.5 Pulleys – Harder Questions

Questions involving pulleys can feature more complex situations. For example:

7.  Two bodies A and B of mass 0.7 kg and 0.2 kg respectively are connected by a light inextensible string which passes over a smooth fixed pulley as shown in the diagram. Particle A is 0.72 m above the ground. The system is released from rest with the bodies hanging vertically. Calculate:
   (a)   the acceleration of the system;
   (b)   the tension in the string;
   (c)   the force exerted by the string on the pulley when the bodies are in motion.

When A hits the ground the string becomes slack and B continues to rise. Assuming that B does not reach the pulley, find:
   (d)   the speed of the bodies at the instant A hits the ground;
   (e)   the additional distance B rises after A hits the ground;
   (f)   the time that elapses between A hitting the ground and the string becoming taut again.

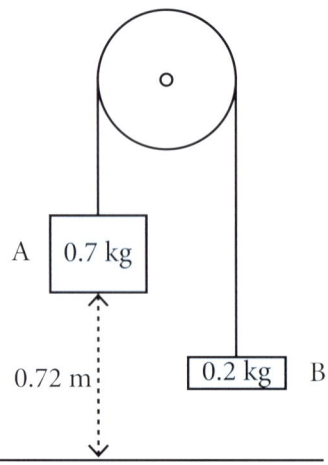

Parts (a) (b) and (c) are worked out as before. The weight of the 0.7 kg particle is:
$0.7 \times 10 = 7$ N

and the weight of the 0.2 kg particle is:
$0.2 \times 10 = 1$ N

Let the tension in the string be $T$. These forces are shown in the diagram below. Since A is heavier than B, it will move downwards, and B will move upwards.

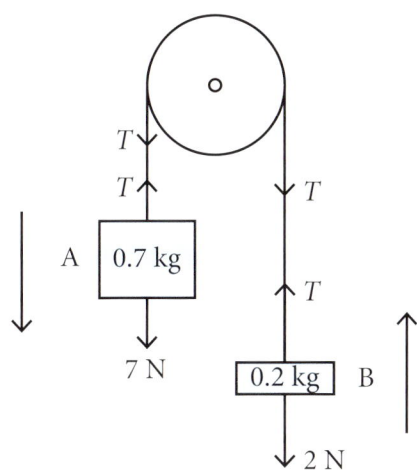

(a) First consider particle A:
Using:  $F = ma$
$7 - T = 0.7a$

Then consider particle B:
Using:  $F = ma$
$T - 2 = 0.2a$

Adding these equations together gives:
$5 = 0.9a$
$a = \dfrac{5}{0.9}$
$a = 5.56$ m/s$^2$

(b) Substitute a into either equation to get $T$:
$T - 2 = 0.2a$
$T - 2 = 0.2 \times 5.56$
$T - 2 = 1.112$
$T = 3.11$ N

(c) The force on pulley is the sum of the tensions:
$= 2 \times 3.112$
$= 6.224$ N

(d) The system is released from rest.
So we know that:
$u = 0$
$a = 5.56$
$s = 0.72$
We want to find:  $v = ?$

So we use:  $v^2 = u^2 + 2as$
$v^2 = 0 + 2(5.56)(0.72)$
$v^2 = 8.0064$
$v = \sqrt{8.0064}$
$v = 2.83$ m/s

(e) After A hits the ground the string becomes slack and B continues to rise. The acceleration slowing B down is the acceleration due to gravity which is $-10$ m/s$^2$. The initial speed of B after A hits the ground equals the speed of the bodies at the instant A hits the ground $= 2.83$ m/s. B will rise until it stops, i.e. until $v = 0$. So we know that:
$u = 2.83$
$a = -10$
$v = 0$
We want to find:  $s = ?$

So we use:  $v^2 = u^2 + 2as$
$0 = 2.83^2 - 2(10)s$
$20s = 8.009$ kg
$s = 0.4$ m

(f) After B stops it will then begin to fall down again under gravity until it reaches the speed of 2.83 m/s. At this point the string will become taut again. You need to find the time taken until B stops and then double this (since it moved up, and then down again, after A hit the ground).
So we know:  $u = 2.83$
$a = -10$
$v = 0$
We want to find:  $t = ?$

So we use:  $v = u + at$
$0 = 2.83 - 10t$
$10t = 2.83$
$t = 0.283$ s

So the time that elapses between A hitting the ground and the string becoming taut again is:
$0.283 \times 2 = 0.566$ s

# Exercise 21E

1. Two bodies A and B of mass 0.6 kg and 0.4 kg respectively are connected by a light inextensible string which passes over a smooth fixed pulley. Particle A is 1.2 m above the ground. The system is released from rest with the bodies hanging vertically. Calculate:
   (a) the acceleration of the system;
   (b) the tension in the string;

## Exercise 21E

(c)  the force exerted by the string on the pulley when the bodies are in motion.

When A hits the ground the string becomes slack and B continues to rise. Assuming that B does not reach the pulley find:

(d)  the time it takes for A to hit the ground;

(e)  the speed of the bodies at the instant A hits the ground;

(f)  the additional distance B rises after A hits the ground;

(g)  the time that elapses between A hitting the ground and the string becoming taut again.

2.  Two bodies A and B of mass 2.6 kg and 1.4 kg respectively are connected by a light inextensible string which passes over a smooth fixed pulley. The system is released from rest with the bodies hanging vertically. Calculate:

(a)  the acceleration of the system;

(b)  the tension in the string;

(c)  the force exerted by the string on the pulley when the bodies are in motion.

A hits the ground after 1.2 s. When A hits the ground the string becomes slack and B continues to rise. Assuming that B does not reach the pulley find:

(d)  the distance that A falls to the ground;

(e)  the speed of the bodies at the instant A hits the ground;

(f)  the additional distance B rises after A hits the ground;

(g)  the time that elapses between A hitting the ground and the string becoming taut again.

3.  Two bodies A and B of mass 0.7 kg and 0.3 kg respectively are connected by a light inextensible string which passes over a smooth fixed pulley. The system is released from rest with the bodies hanging vertically. Calculate:

(a)  the acceleration of the system;

(b)  the tension in the string;

(c)  the force exerted by the string on the pulley when the bodies are in motion.

A hits the ground after 1.5 s. When A hits the ground the string becomes slack and B continues to rise. Assuming that B does not reach the pulley find:

(d)  the distance that A falls to the ground;

(e)  the speed of the bodies at the instant A hits the ground;

(f)  the additional distance B rises after A hits the ground;

(g)  the time that elapses between A hitting the ground and the string becoming taut again.

4.  Two bodies A and B of mass 3.6 kg and 1.4 kg respectively are connected by a light inextensible string which passes over a smooth fixed pulley. Particle A is 0.75 m above the ground. The system is released from rest with the bodies hanging vertically. Calculate:

(a)  the acceleration of the system;

(b)  the tension in the string;

(c)  the force exerted by the string on the pulley when the bodies are in motion.

When A hits the ground the string becomes slack and B continues to rise. Assuming that B does not reach the pulley find:

(d)  the time it takes for A to hit the ground;

(e)  the speed of the bodies at the instant A hits the ground;

(f)  the additional distance B rises after A hits the ground;

(g)  the time that elapses between A hitting the ground and the string becoming taut again.

5.  Two bodies A and B of mass 1.3 kg and 0.7 kg respectively are connected by a light inextensible string which passes over a smooth fixed pulley. The system is released from rest with the bodies hanging vertically. Calculate:

(a)  the acceleration of the system;

(b)  the tension in the string;

(c)  the force exerted by the string on the pulley when the bodies are in motion.

A hits the ground after 0.8 s. When A hits the ground the string becomes slack and B continues to rise. Assuming that B does not reach the pulley find:

(d)  the distance that A falls to the ground;

(e)  the speed of the bodies at the instant A hits the ground;

(f)  the additional distance B rises after A hits the ground;

(g)  the time that elapses between A hitting the ground and the string becoming taut again.

6.  Two bodies A and B of mass 3.7 kg and 1.3 kg respectively are connected by a light inextensible string which passes over a smooth fixed pulley. The system is released from rest

## Exercise 21E...

with the bodies hanging vertically. Calculate:
- **(a)** the acceleration of the system;
- **(b)** the tension in the string;
- **(c)** the force exerted by the string on the pulley when the bodies are in motion.

A hits the ground after 0.4 s. When A hits the ground the string becomes slack and B continues to rise. Assuming that B does not reach the pulley find:
- **(d)** the distance that A falls to the ground;
- **(e)** the speed of the bodies at the instant A hits the ground;
- **(f)** the time that elapses between A hitting the ground and the string becoming taut again.

7.  Two bodies A and B of mass 1.5 kg and 0.5 kg respectively are connected by a light inextensible string which passes over a smooth fixed pulley. The system is released from rest with the bodies hanging vertically. Calculate:
- **(a)** the acceleration of the system;
- **(b)** the tension in the string;
- **(c)** the force exerted by the string on the pulley when the bodies are in motion.

A hits the ground at 6 m/s. When A hits the ground the string becomes slack and B continues to rise. Assuming that B does not reach the pulley find:
- **(d)** the time it takes for A to hit the ground;
- **(e)** the distance that A falls to the ground;
- **(f)** the time that elapses between A hitting the ground and the string becoming taut again.

8.  Two bodies A and B of mass 2.4 kg and 0.6 kg respectively are connected by a light inextensible string which passes over a smooth fixed pulley. The system is released from rest with the bodies hanging vertically. Calculate:
- **(a)** the acceleration of the system;
- **(b)** the tension in the string;
- **(c)** the force exerted by the string on the pulley when the bodies are in motion.

A hits the ground at 3 m/s. When A hits the ground the string becomes slack and B continues to rise. Assuming that B does not reach the pulley find:
- **(d)** the time it takes for A to hit the ground;
- **(e)** the distance that A falls to the ground;
- **(f)** the time that elapses between A hitting the ground and the string becoming taut again.

## 21.6 Pulleys Where One Body Is On A Horizontal Table

You can also be asked to deal with problems involving pulleys, where only one object hangs vertically and the other is on a horizontal surface. The rules for solving this problem are similar to before:

a.  Consider each particle separately;

b.  Use $F = ma$.

For example:

8.  Two bodies of mass 4 kg and 6 kg are connected by a light inextensible string which passes over a smooth fixed pulley. The 4 kg body lies on a smooth horizontal table and the 6 kg body hangs vertically as shown in the diagram.

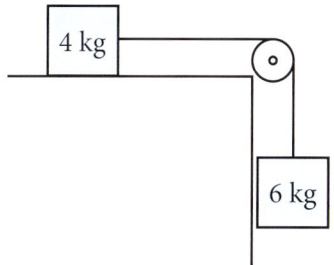

The system is released from rest. Calculate:
- **(a)** the acceleration of the system;
- **(b)** the tension in the string;
- **(c)** the force exerted by the string on the pulley when the bodies are in motion.

Because the table is smooth there is no friction acting on the 4 kg body. When the system is released from rest the 6 kg body will move downwards and the 4 kg body will move to the right. Mark all the forces acting on the bodies on the diagram:

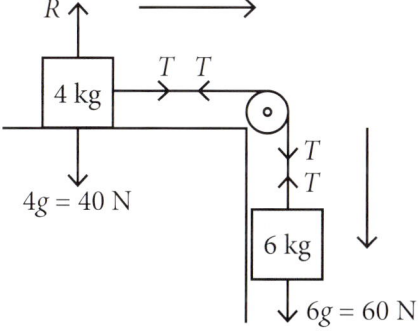

- **(a)** First, consider the 6 kg particle:
$$F = ma$$
$$60 - T = 6a$$

Next consider the 4 kg particle:
$$F = ma$$
$$T = 4a$$

(Note that neither the reaction $R$ nor the 40 N weight affect the horizontal motion as they are perpendicular to the line of motion.)

You can solve these simultaneous equations by adding them to get rid of the $T$s:

$$60 - T = 6a$$
$$+ \qquad T = 4a$$
$$60 = 10a$$
$$a = 6 \text{ m/s}^2$$

(b) You can find the tension by substituting into either equation:
$$T = 4a$$
$$T = 4 \times 6$$
$$= 24 \text{ N}$$

(c) The two tensions act on the pulley. Since these tensions are vectors you must add them nose-to-tail and then work out the resultant force.

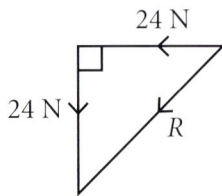

$$R^2 = 24^2 + 24^2$$
$$R^2 = 576 + 576$$
$$R^2 = 1152$$
$$R = \sqrt{1152}$$
$$R = 33.94….$$

So: $\qquad R = 33.9$ N to 3 significant figures

## Exercise 21F

1. Two bodies of mass 7 kg and 8 kg are connected by a light inextensible string which passes over a smooth fixed pulley. The 7 kg body lies on a smooth horizontal table and the 8 kg body hangs vertically. The system is released from rest. Calculate:
   (a) the acceleration of the system correct to 3 significant figures;
   (b) the tension in the string correct to 3 significant figures;
   (c) the force exerted by the string on the pulley when the bodies are in motion.

1. Two bodies of mass 7 kg and 8 kg are connected by a light inextensible string which passes over a smooth fixed pulley. The 7 kg

## Exercise 21F

body lies on a smooth horizontal table and the 8 kg body hangs vertically. The system is released from rest. Calculate:
   (a) the acceleration of the system correct to 3 significant figures;
   (b) the tension in the string correct to 3 significant figures;
   (c) the force exerted by the string on the pulley when the bodies are in motion.

2. Two bodies of mass 2 kg and 5 kg are connected by a light inextensible string which passes over a smooth fixed pulley. The 2 kg body lies on a smooth horizontal table and the 5 kg body hangs vertically. The system is released from rest. Calculate:
   (a) the acceleration of the system correct to 3 significant figures;
   (b) the tension in the string correct to 3 significant figures;
   (c) the force exerted by the string on the pulley when the bodies are in motion.

3. Two bodies of mass 3 kg and 8 kg are connected by a light inextensible string which passes over a smooth fixed pulley. The 3 kg body lies on a smooth horizontal table and the 8 kg body hangs vertically. The system is released from rest. Calculate:
   (a) the acceleration of the system correct to 3 significant figures;
   (b) the tension in the string correct to 3 significant figures;
   (c) the force exerted by the string on the pulley when the bodies are in motion.

4. Two bodies of mass 0.4 kg and 0.7 kg are connected by a light inextensible string which passes over a smooth fixed pulley. The 0.4 kg body lies on a smooth horizontal table and the 0.7 kg body hangs vertically. The system is released from rest. Calculate:
   (a) the acceleration of the system correct to 3 significant figures;
   (b) the tension in the string correct to 3 significant figures;
   (c) the force exerted by the string on the pulley when the bodies are in motion.

5. Two bodies of mass 2.4 kg and 3.2 kg are connected by a light inextensible string which passes over a smooth fixed pulley. The 2.4 kg

body lies on a smooth horizontal table and the 3.2 kg body hangs vertically. The system is released from rest. Calculate:

(a) the acceleration of the system correct to 3 significant figures;

(b) the tension in the string correct to 3 significant figures;

(c) the force exerted by the string on the pulley when the bodies are in motion.

6. Two bodies of mass 16 kg and 22 kg are connected by a light inextensible string which passes over a smooth fixed pulley. The 16 kg body lies on a smooth horizontal table and the 22 kg body hangs vertically. The system is released from rest. Calculate:

(a) the acceleration of the system correct to 3 significant figures;

(b) the tension in the string correct to 3 significant figures;

(c) the force exerted by the string on the pulley when the bodies are in motion.

7. Two bodies of mass 4.5 kg and 6 kg are connected by a light inextensible string which passes over a smooth fixed pulley. The 4.5 kg body lies on a smooth horizontal table and the 6 kg body hangs vertically. The system is released from rest. Calculate:

(a) the acceleration of the system correct to 3 significant figures;

(b) the tension in the string correct to 3 significant figures;

(c) the force exerted by the string on the pulley when the bodies are in motion.

8. Two bodies of mass 0.8 kg and 1.2 kg are connected by a light inextensible string which passes over a smooth fixed pulley. The 0.8 kg body lies on a smooth horizontal table and the 1.2 kg body hangs vertically. The system is released from rest. Calculate:

(a) the acceleration of the system;

(b) the tension in the string;

(c) the force exerted by the string on the pulley when the bodies are in motion.

9. Two bodies of mass 7 kg and 9 kg are connected by a light inextensible string which passes over a smooth fixed pulley. The 7 kg body lies on a smooth horizontal table and the 9 kg body hangs vertically. The system is

released from rest. Calculate:

(a) the acceleration of the system;

(b) the tension in the string;

(c) the force exerted by the string on the pulley when the bodies are in motion.

10. Two bodies of mass 48 kg and 60 kg are connected by a light inextensible string which passes over a smooth fixed pulley. The 48 kg body lies on a smooth horizontal table and the 60 kg body hangs vertically. The system is released from rest. Calculate:

(a) the acceleration of the system correct to 3 significant figures;

(b) the tension in the string correct to 4 significant figures;

(c) the force exerted by the string on the pulley when the bodies are in motion.

## 21.7 Pulleys Where One Body Is On A Horizontal Table – Harder Questions

You can be asked more complex questions involving pulleys and horizontal surfaces, which often require you to take friction into account. The rules for solving this type of problem are:

a. Consider each particle separately.

b. Then use $F = ma$.

For example:

........................................................................

9. Two bodies A and B, of mass 0.8 kg and 1.4 kg respectively, are connected by a light inextensible string which passes over a smooth fixed pulley. Particle A lies on a rough horizontal table and particle B hangs vertically exactly 0.75 m above the ground as shown in the diagram.

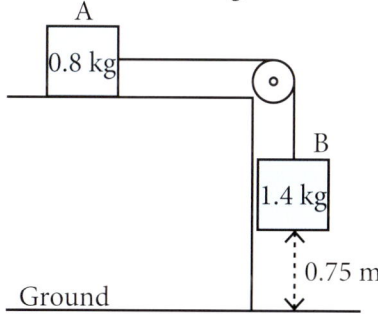

The frictional force acting on the table is 3.68 N. The system is released from rest. Calculate:

(a) the acceleration of the system;

(b)    the tension in the string;

(c)    the velocity with which particle B strikes the ground.

After particle B strikes the ground particle A continues to move. Assuming A does not reach the pulley find:

(d)    the time it takes A to stop;

(e)    the distance A travels before stopping.

Because the table is rough there is friction acting on the 4 kg body. When the system is released from rest the 1.4 kg body will move downwards and the 0.8 kg body will move to the right. You need to mark all the forces acting on the bodies, including the frictional force, $F$, acting on the 0.8 kg body:

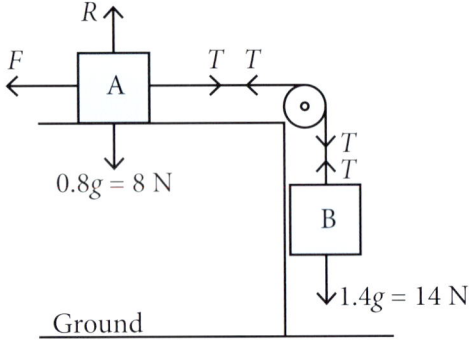

(a)    First consider the 1.4 kg particle (B):
$$F = ma$$
$$14 - T = 1.4a$$

Then consider the 0.8 kg particle (A):
$$F = ma$$
$$T - 3.68 = 0.8a$$

You can then solve these simultaneous equations by adding them to get rid of the $T$s:

$$14 - T = 1.4a$$
$$+ \ \underline{T - 3.68 = 0.8a}$$
$$10.32 = 2.2a$$

$$a = \frac{10.32}{2.2}$$
$$a = 4.6909..... \text{ m/s}^2$$
$$a = 4.69 \text{ m/s}^2 \text{ to 3 significant figures}$$

(b)    You can find the tension by substituting into either equation:
$$T - 3.68 = 0.8a$$
$$T - 3.68 = 0.8 \times 4.6909$$
$$T - 3.68 = 3.7527$$
$$T = 3.7527 + 3.68$$
$$T = 7.43 \text{ N to 3 significant figures}$$

(c)    You need to use the appropriate equation of motion.

We know:    $u = 0$ (since the system is released from rest)
$$a = 4.6909$$
$$s = 0.75$$

We want to find:    $v = ?$

So we use:    $v^2 = u^2 + 2as$
$$v^2 = 0 + 2 \times 4.6909 \times 0.75$$
$$v^2 = 7.0364$$
$$v = \sqrt{7.0364}$$
$$v = 2.6526....$$
$$v = 2.65 \text{ m/s to 3 significant figures}$$

(d)    At the moment the 1.4 kg body hits the ground, the 0.8 kg body is moving at 2.6526 m/s. When it hits the ground the string will become slack and so there will be no tension pulling the 0.8 kg body. The only horizontal force acting on the 0.8 kg body will be the frictional force, as shown below, which will slow it down.

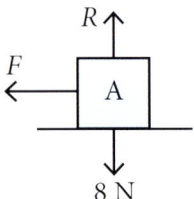

This gives:    $F = ma$
$$-3.68 = 0.8a$$

So:    $a = \dfrac{-3.68}{0.8}$
$$a = -4.6 \text{ m/s}^2$$

Thus we know the following:
$$u = 2.6526$$
$$a = -4.6$$
$$v = 0 \text{ (when it stops the velocity is 0)}$$

We want to find:    $t = ?$

So we use:    $v = u + at$
$$0 = 2.6526 - 4.6t$$
$$4.6t = 2.6526$$
$$t = \frac{2.6526}{4.6}$$
$$= 0.5767....$$
$$t = 0.577 \text{ s to 3 significant figures}$$

(e)    To find the distance travelled, we know:
$$u = 2.6526$$
$$a = -4.6$$
$$v = 0$$

We want to find:    $s = ?$

112

So we use: $v^2 = u^2 + 2as$

$$0 = 2.6526^2 - 2 \times 4.6 \times s$$
$$0 = 7.0363 - 9.2s$$
$$9.2s = 7.0363$$
$$s = \frac{7.0363}{9.2}$$
$$s = 0.7648....$$
$$s = 0.765 \text{ m to 3 significant figures}$$

## Exercise 21G

1. Two bodies A and B, of mass 2 kg and 5 kg respectively, are connected by a light inextensible string which passes over a smooth fixed pulley. Body A lies on a rough horizontal table and body B hangs vertically. The frictional force acting on body A is 16 N. The system is released from rest. Calculate:
   (a)    the acceleration of the system;
   (b)    the tension in the string.

   B hits the ground after 0.48 s. Calculate:
   (c)    the velocity with which body B strikes the ground.

   After body B strikes the ground body A continues to move. Assuming A does not reach the pulley find:
   (d)    the time it takes A to stop;
   (e)    the distance A travels before stopping.

2. Two bodies A and B, of mass 0.4 kg and 0.7 kg respectively, are connected by a light inextensible string which passes over a smooth fixed pulley. Body A lies on a rough horizontal table and body B hangs vertically exactly 0.64 m above the ground. The frictional force acting on body A is 1.5 N. The system is released from rest. Calculate:
   (a)    the acceleration of the system;
   (b)    the tension in the string;
   (c)    the velocity with which body B strikes the ground.

   After body B strikes the ground body A continues to move. Assuming A does not reach the pulley find:
   (d)    the time it takes A to stop;
   (e)    the distance A travels before stopping.

3. Two bodies A and B, of mass 16 kg and 24 kg respectively, are connected by a light inextensible string which passes over a smooth fixed pulley. Body A lies on a rough horizontal table and body B hangs vertically. The frictional force acting on body A is 96 N. The system is released from rest. Calculate:

## Exercise 21G...

   (a)    the acceleration of the system;
   (b)    the tension in the string.

   B hits the ground after 0.42 s. Calculate:
   (c)    the velocity with which body B strikes the ground.

   After body B strikes the ground body A continues to move. Assuming A does not reach the pulley find:
   (d)    the time it takes A to stop;
   (e)    the distance A travels before stopping.

4. Two bodies A and B, of mass 1.3 kg and 1.8 kg respectively, are connected by a light inextensible string which passes over a smooth fixed pulley. Body A lies on a rough horizontal table and body B hangs vertically exactly 1.2 m above the ground. The frictional force acting on body A is 5.2 N. The system is released from rest. Calculate:
   (a)    the acceleration of the system;
   (b)    the tension in the string;
   (c)    the velocity with which body B strikes the ground.

   After body B strikes the ground body A continues to move. Assuming A does not reach the pulley find:
   (d)    the time it takes A to stop;
   (e)    the distance A travels before stopping.

5. Two bodies A and B, of mass 45 kg and 60 kg respectively, are connected by a light inextensible string which passes over a smooth fixed pulley. Body A lies on a rough horizontal table and body B hangs vertically. The frictional force acting on body A is 135 N. The system is released from rest. Calculate:
   (a)    the acceleration of the system;
   (b)    the tension in the string.

   B hits the ground after 0.24 s. Calculate:
   (c)    the velocity with which body B strikes the ground.

   After body B strikes the ground body A continues to move. Assuming A does not reach the pulley find:
   (d)    the time it takes A to stop;
   (e)    the distance A travels before stopping.

6. Two bodies A and B, of mass 18 kg and 21 kg respectively, are connected by a light inextensible string which passes over a smooth fixed pulley. Body A lies on a rough horizontal table and

body B hangs vertically exactly 0.45 m above the ground. The frictional force acting on body A is 54 N. The system is released from rest. Calculate:
(a) the acceleration of the system;
(b) the tension in the string;
(c) the velocity with which body B strikes the ground.

After body B strikes the ground body A continues to move. Assuming A does not reach the pulley find:
(d) the time it takes A to stop;
(e) the distance A travels before stopping.

7. Two bodies A and B, of mass 0.64 kg and 0.72 kg respectively, are connected by a light inextensible string which passes over a smooth fixed pulley. Body A lies on a rough horizontal table and body B hangs vertically. The frictional force acting on body A is 2.688 N. The system is released from rest. Calculate:
(a) the acceleration of the system;
(b) the tension in the string;

B hits the ground after 0.76 s. Calculate:
(c) the velocity with which body B strikes the ground.

After body B strikes the ground body A continues to move. Assuming A does not reach the pulley find:
(d) the time it takes A to stop;
(e) the distance A travels before stopping.

8. Two bodies A and B, of mass 9 kg and 12 kg respectively, are connected by a light inextensible string which passes over a smooth fixed pulley. Body A lies on a rough horizontal table and body B hangs vertically exactly 0.85 m above the ground. The frictional force acting on body A is 32.4 N. The system is released from rest. Calculate:
(a) the acceleration of the system;
(b) the tension in the string;
(c) the velocity with which body B strikes the ground.

After body B strikes the ground body A continues to move. Assuming A does not reach the pulley find:
(d) the time it takes A to stop;
(e) the distance A travels before stopping.

9. Two bodies A and B, of mass 36 kg and 42 kg respectively, are connected by a light inextensible string which passes over a smooth fixed pulley. Body A lies on a rough horizontal table and body B hangs vertically. The frictional force acting on body A is 154.29 N. The system is released from rest. Calculate:
(a) the acceleration of the system;
(b) the tension in the string;

B hits the ground after 0.76 s. Calculate:
(c) the velocity with which body B strikes the ground.

After body B strikes the ground body A continues to move. Assuming A does not reach the pulley find:
(d) the time it takes A to stop;
(e) the distance A travels before stopping.

10. Two bodies A and B, of mass 2.4 kg and 2.9 kg respectively, are connected by a light inextensible string which passes over a smooth fixed pulley. Body A lies on a rough horizontal table and body B hangs vertically exactly 1.16 m above the ground. The frictional force acting on body A is 17.28 N. The system is released from rest. Calculate:
(a) the acceleration of the system;
(b) the tension in the string;
(c) the velocity with which body B strikes the ground.

After body B strikes the ground body A continues to move. Assuming A does not reach the pulley find:
(d) the time it takes A to stop;
(e) the distance A travels before stopping.

# CHAPTER 22: MOMENTS

## 22.1 The Principle Of Moments

The **moment** of a force measures the **turning effect** of the force. The moment is proportional to both the force and the perpendicular distance from the turning point. It can be calculated as follows:

moment = force × perpendicular distance

The **Principle of Moments** states that:

When a system is in equilibrium then the sum of all the clockwise moments about any point is equal to the sum of all the anti-clockwise moments about this point.

## 22.2 Finding Two Unknown Forces

The rules when finding two unknown forces are:

a. Take moments about the point where one of these forces acts;

b. Equate the vertical forces.

For example:

---

1. AB is a uniform rod of length 8 m and mass 4.8 kg. It rests on two supports, one at C where AC = 1.6 m and the other at D where DB = 2 m. Find the reactions at C and D.

   First, mark all the forces on a diagram. AB is a uniform rod and so the weight acts at the centre of AB. Therefore the weight = $4.8g = 48$ N.

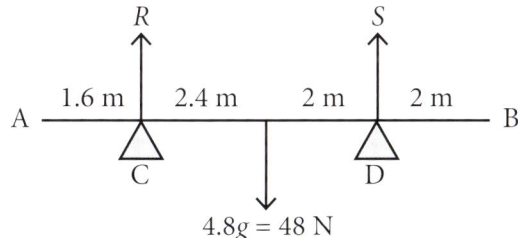

   Taking moments about C gives:
   $$S \times 4.4 = 48 \times 2.4$$
   $$4.4S = 115.2$$
   $$S = \frac{115.2}{4.4}$$
   $$S = 26.2 \text{ N}$$

   Equating forces gives:
   $$R + S = 48$$
   $$R + 26.2 = 48$$
   $$R = 48 - 26.2$$
   $$R = 21.8 \text{ N}$$

1. AB is a uniform rod of length 12 m and mass 8 kg. It rests on two supports, one at A and the other at C where CB = 2 m. Find the reactions at A and C.

2. AB is a uniform rod of length 10 m and mass 5 kg. It rests on two supports, one at C where AC = 2 m and the other at D where DB = 2.5 m. Find the reactions at C and D.

3. AB is a uniform rod of length 18 m and mass 6 kg. It rests on two supports, one at C where AC = 2 m and the other at B. Find the reactions at C and B.

4. AB is a uniform rod of length 24 m and mass 12 kg. It rests on two supports, one at C where AC = 7 m and the other at D where DB = 9 m. Find the reactions at C and D.

5. AB is a uniform rod of length 16 m and mass 5.6 kg. It rests on two supports, one at A and the other at C where CB = 3.5 m. Find the reactions at A and C.

6. AB is a uniform rod of length 10 m and mass 2.6 kg. It rests on two supports, one at C where AC = 2.4 m and the other at D where DB = 3.3 m. Find the reactions at C and D.

7. AB is a uniform rod of length 12 m and mass 0.8 kg. It rests on two supports, one at C where AC = 1.2 m and the other at D where DB = 2.3 m. Find the reactions at C and D.

8. AB is a uniform rod of length 14 m and mass 3.6 kg. It rests on two supports, one at C where AC = 1.5 m and the other at D where DB = 3 m. Find the reactions at C and D.

Some questions feature rods suspended from strings, rather than resting on supports. They can be answered in the same way. For example:

---

2. A uniform rod AB of length 18 m and mass 7.8 kg is held horizontally in equilibrium by two strings, one at C where AC = 2 m and the other at D where DB = 6 m. Find the tensions in the two strings.

   Mark all the forces on a diagram.

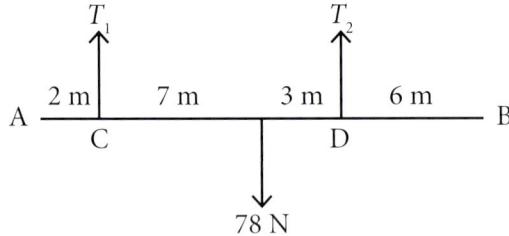

Taking moments about C gives:
$$T_2 \times 10 = 78 \times 7$$
$$10T_2 = 546$$
$$T_2 = 54.6 \text{ N}$$

Equating forces gives:
$$T_1 + T_2 = 78$$
$$T_1 + 54.6 = 78$$
$$T_1 = 78 - 54.6$$
$$T_1 = 23.4 \text{ N}$$

## Exercise 22B

1. A uniform rod AB of length 16 m and mass 5 kg is held horizontally in equilibrium by two strings, one at A and the other at C where AC = 14 m. Find the tensions in the two strings.

2. A uniform rod AB of length 28 m and mass 8 kg is held horizontally in equilibrium by two strings, one at C where AC = 2 m and the other at D where DB = 9 m. Find the tensions in the two strings.

3. A uniform rod AB of length 10 m and mass 2.4 kg is held horizontally in equilibrium by two strings, one at C where AC = 2 m and the other at B. Find the tensions in the two strings.

4. A uniform rod AB of length 12 m and mass 5.6 kg is held horizontally in equilibrium by two strings, one at A and the other at C where AC = 10 m. Find the tensions in the two strings.

5. A uniform rod AB of length 16 m and mass 0.9 kg is held horizontally in equilibrium by two strings, one at C where AC = 3 m and the other at D where DB = 6 m. Find the tensions in the two strings.

6. A uniform rod AB of length 8 m and mass 1.6 kg is held horizontally in equilibrium by two strings, one at C where AC = 1.5 m and the other at B. Find the tensions in the two strings.

7. A uniform rod AB of length 24 m and mass 3 kg is held horizontally in equilibrium by

two strings, one at A and the other at C where AC = 14.5 m. Find the tensions in the two strings.

8. A uniform rod AB of length 8 m and mass 24 kg is held horizontally in equilibrium by two strings, one at C where AC = 2.4 m and the other at D where DB = 2.2 m. Find the tensions in the two strings.

9. A uniform rod AB of length 32 m and mass 4 kg is held horizontally in equilibrium by two strings, one at C where AC = 3 m and the other at D where DB = 12 m. Find the tensions in the two strings.

10. A uniform rod AB of length 30 m and mass 3.6 kg is held horizontally in equilibrium by two strings, one at C where AC = 7 m and the other at B. Find the tensions in the two strings.

## 22.3 Finding An Unknown Force And A Distance

If a distance is unknown, you can use these rules:

a. Equate the vertical force;

b. Take moments about the point where one of these forces acts.

For example:

3. AB is a uniform rod of length 16 m and mass 5.5 kg. It rests on two supports, one at C where AC = 1.6 m and the other at D where DB = 0.8 m. Find how far from C a mass of 3.2 kg should be placed so that the reaction at C will be twice the reaction at D.

First, draw a diagram.

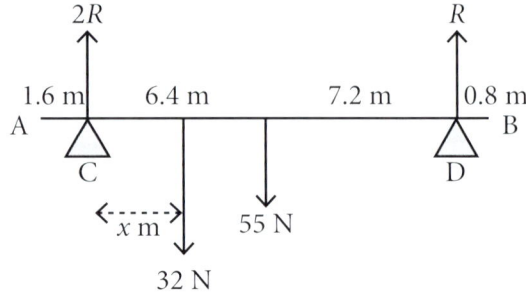

Equating forces gives:
$$2R + R = 32 + 55$$
$$3R = 87$$
$$R = 29$$

Taking moments about C gives:
$$32x + 55 \times 6.4 = 29 \times 13.6$$
$$32x + 352 = 394.4$$
$$32x = 394.4 - 352$$
$$32x = 42.4$$
$$x = 1.325$$

So the answer is: 1.325 m from C.

## Exercise 22C

1. AB is a uniform rod of length 13 m and mass 2.4 kg. It rests on two supports, one at C where AC = 2 m and the other at D where DB = 3.2 m. Find how far from C a mass of 1.8 kg should be placed so that the reaction at D will be twice the reaction at C.

2. AB is a uniform rod of length 20 m and mass 1.8 kg. It rests on two supports, one at C where AC = 3 m and the other at D where DB = 6 m. Find how far from C a mass of 1.2 kg should be placed so that the reaction at D will be twice the reaction at C.

3. AB is a uniform rod of length 16 m and mass 3.8 kg. It rests on two supports, one at C where AC = 3.5 m and the other at D where DB = 5.6 m. Find how far from C a mass of 3.4 kg should be placed so that the reaction at D will be twice the reaction at C.

4. AB is a uniform rod of length 18 m and mass 4 kg. It rests on two supports, one at C where AC = 2 m and the other at D where DB = 6 m. Find how far from C a mass of 1.4 kg should be placed so that the reaction at D will be three times the reaction at C.

5. AB is a uniform rod of length 26 m and mass 2.8 kg. It rests on two supports, one at C where AC = 4 m and the other at D where DB = 11 m. Find how far from C a mass of 1.7 kg should be placed so that the reaction at D will be twice the reaction at C.

6. AB is a uniform rod of length 8 m and mass 4.6 kg. It rests on two supports, one at C where AC = 1.7 m and the other at D where DB = 2.8 m. Find how far from C a mass of 3.8 kg should be placed so that the reaction at D will be twice the reaction at C.

## 22.4 A Rod Just Starting To Tilt

Consider the diagram below, where AB is a uniform rod of mass 3 kg. It rests on two supports, one at C and the other at D. A weight $W$ N is placed at D.

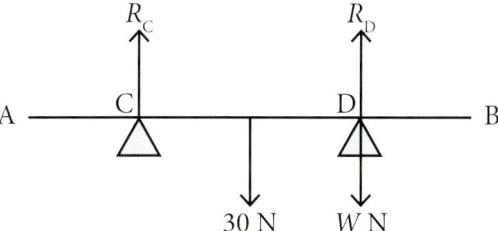

As $W$ is moved towards B the reactions change, with the reaction at D increasing as $W$ approaches it and the reaction at C decreasing. There might come a time when the rod will **just start to tilt** about the reaction at D. At this moment the reaction at C will be 0, as shown below.

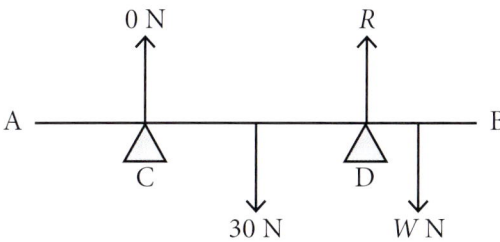

These types of problem can often be solved by taking moments around the pivot point. For example:

4. AB is a uniform rod of length 8 m and mass 5.6 kg. It rests on two supports, one at C where AC = 1.6 m and the other at D where DB = 1.3 m. Find the largest mass that can be placed at B without the rod tilting.

Call the mass $M$ kg. The reaction at C will be 0. Mark all the forces on a diagram.

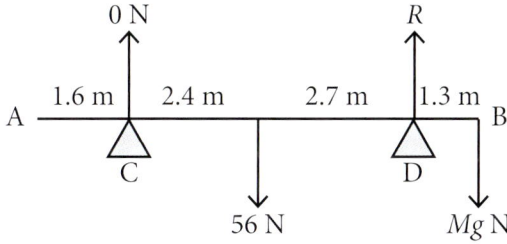

You should take moments about D so that you don't need to work out the reaction R. Taking moments about D gives:
$$10M \times 1.3 = 56 \times 2.7$$
$$13M = 151.2$$
$$M = 11.6 \text{ kg}$$

5.  AB is a uniform rod of length 14 m and mass 2.4 kg. It rests on two supports, one at C where AC = 3 m and the other at D where DB = 3.2 m. Find how far from B a mass of 3.6 kg should be placed so that the rod will just start to tilt.

Call the distance from the 3.6 kg mass to D $x$ metres. The reaction at C will be 0.

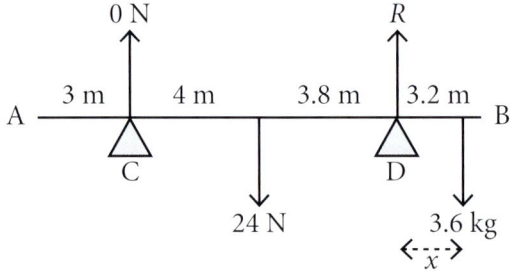

You should take moments about D so that you don't need to work out the reaction $R$. Taking moments about D gives:

$$36x = 24 \times 3.8$$
$$36x = 91.2$$
$$x = 2.53 \text{ m}$$

However, this is the distance of the mass from D. The distance from B will then be:
$$3.2 - 2.53 = 0.67 \text{ m}$$

## Exercise 22D

1.  AB is a uniform rod of length 12 m and mass 4.2 kg. It rests on two supports, one at C where AC = 2.5 m and the other at D where DB = 1.2 m. Find the largest mass that can be placed at B without the rod tilting.

2.  AB is a uniform rod of length 18 m and mass 3.5 kg. It rests on two supports, one at C where AC = 2 m and the other at D where DB = 3 m. Find how far from B a mass of 8.4 kg should be placed so that the rod will just start to tilt.

3.  AB is a uniform rod of length 6 m and mass 4.6 kg. It rests on two supports, one at C where AC = 1.2 m and the other at D where DB = 0.8 m. Find the largest mass that can be placed at B without the rod tilting.

4.  AB is a uniform rod of length 24 m and mass 3.2 kg. It rests on two supports, one at C where AC = 4 m and the other at D where DB = 9 m. Find how far from B a mass of 2.6 kg should be placed so that the rod will just start to tilt.

## Exercise 22D...

5.  AB is a uniform rod of length 10 m and mass 4.9 kg. It rests on two supports, one at C where AC = 2 m and the other at D where DB = 3.6 m. Find the largest mass that can be placed at B without the rod tilting.

6.  AB is a uniform rod of length 28 m and mass 5.2 kg. It rests on two supports, one at C where AC = 4 m and the other at D where DB = 10.5 m. Find how far from B a mass of 4.3 kg should be placed so that the rod will just start to tilt.

7.  A uniform rod AB of mass 2 kg and length 6 cm rests on two supports at C and D where AC = 2 cm and DB = 1.5 cm. Find:
    (a)  the reactions at each support;
    (b)  the least mass that should be placed at A to cause the rod to tilt.

# Unit 3: Statistics

## CHAPTER 23: BIVARIATE ANALYSIS

### 23.1 Correlation

**Bivariate analysis** refers to the analysis of two sets of data in order to see if there is a link or connection between them. This link or connection is called the **correlation**. There are two types of correlation:

- **Positive correlation** is when as one variable increases (or decreases) the other increases (or decreases). The graph below shows an example of positive correlation.

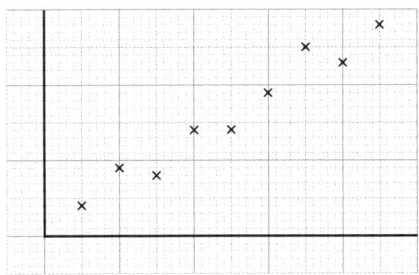

- **Negative correlation** is when as one variable increases (or decreases) the other decreases (or increases). The graph below shows an example of negative correlation.

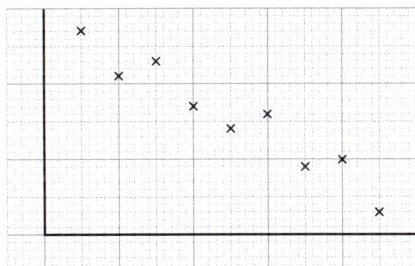

One way to see if there is correlation between two variables is to plot the variables on graph paper, as shown above. Another way to find out if there is correlation is to calculate the Spearman's Rank Correlation Coefficient as outlined below.

### 23.2 Spearman's Rank Correlation Coefficient, *r*

The rules for calculating Spearman's Rank Correlation Coefficient are as follows:

a. Each piece of data in each variable is given a rank depending on its position in the data. You can either

rank from the smallest to largest (smallest piece of data 1, the next smallest piece of data 2 and so on) or you can rank the largest to smallest (largest piece of data 1, the next largest piece of data 2 and so on): it does not matter which, as long as they are in order. Do this for each of the two variables.

b. Work out the differences, *d*, between corresponding ranks assigned to each data pair.

c. Calculate Spearman's Rank Correlation Coefficient:

$$r = 1 - \frac{6\Sigma d^2}{n(n^2 - 1)}$$

where:     $\Sigma d^2$ = the sum of all the $d^2$
                 $n$ = the number of pairs of data

You then use Spearman's Rank Correlation Coefficient, *r*, to determine if there is any correlation , and if so what type of correlation, as follows:

- **$0 < r \leq 1$** indicates **positive** correlation (1 would mean perfect positive correlation)

- **$-1 \leq r < 0$** indicates **negative** correlation (−1 would mean perfect negative correlation)

For example:

1. The table below shows pairs of data.
   (a)   Calculate Spearman's Rank Correlation Coefficient for all the data.
   (b)   What can you say about the correlation?

| **A** | 74 | 82 | 78 | 72 | 79 |
|---|---|---|---|---|---|
| **B** | 34 | 42 | 37 | 39 | 45 |

(a)   To answer this question, you must first rank each piece of data for A and then rank each piece of data for B. We will rank starting with the smallest piece of data. Therefore for A we would rank as follows:

72 rank 1
74 rank 2
78 rank 3
79 rank 4
82 rank 5

And for rank B:

34 rank 1
37 rank 2
39 rank 3
42 rank 4
45 rank 5

This gives us the following table:

| A | 74 | 82 | 78 | 72 | 79 |
|---|---|---|---|---|---|
| Rank A | 2 | 5 | 3 | 1 | 4 |
| B | 34 | 42 | 37 | 39 | 45 |
| Rank B | 1 | 4 | 2 | 3 | 5 |

Next, you must work out the difference in the corresponding ranks, i.e. Rank A – Rank B. This gives:

| Rank A | 2 | 5 | 3 | 1 | 4 |
|---|---|---|---|---|---|
| Rank B | 1 | 4 | 2 | 3 | 5 |
| Difference $d$ | 1 | 1 | 1 | −2 | −1 |

Next, you must square these differences. This gives:

| $d$ | 1 | 1 | 1 | −2 | −1 |
|---|---|---|---|---|---|
| $d^2$ | 1 | 1 | 1 | 4 | 1 |

Then you must add these differences. This gives:
$$\Sigma d^2 = 1 + 1 + 1 + 4 + 1$$
$$= 8$$

Then calculate Spearman's Rank Correlation Coefficient, where $n = 5$:

$$r = 1 - \frac{6\Sigma d^2}{n(n^2 - 1)}$$

$$r = 1 - \frac{6 \times 8}{5 \times 24}$$

$$r = 1 - \frac{48}{120}$$

$$r = 0.6$$

(b) As 0.6 is positive this shows there is **positive** correlation.

## 23.3 Tied Ranks In Spearman's Rank Correlation Coefficient

Where two or more of the data are the same then you need to use **tied ranks**. For example, when working with the following data:

| A | 50 | 45 | 50 | 53 |
|---|---|---|---|---|

we would rank starting with the smallest piece of data,

i.e. 45 is rank 1. The first 50 should be rank 2, but it is tied with the other 50 which should be rank 3. In this case you take the mean of the ranks for both the 50s, i.e.:

45 rank 1
50 rank 2.5
50 rank 2.5
53 rank 4

Sometimes, more than two pieces of data are paired. For example, when working with this data:

| A | 50 | 45 | 50 | 50 |
|---|---|---|---|---|

we would again rank starting with the smallest piece of data, i.e. 45 is rank 1. The first 50 should be rank 2 but it is tied with the second 50 which should be rank 3 **and** the third 50 which should be rank 4. In this case you take the mean of the ranks for all three 50s, i.e.:

45 rank 1
50 rank 3
50 rank 3
50 rank 3

You can use this approach if you have to calculate Spearman's Rank Correlation Coefficient for tied data. For example:

2. The table below shows pairs of data.
   (a) Calculate Spearman's Rank Correlation Coefficient for all the data.
   (b) What can you say about the correlation?

| A | 5.6 | 4.2 | 9.3 | 6.4 | 4.2 | 3.8 | 7.5 | 5.2 |
|---|---|---|---|---|---|---|---|---|
| B | 54 | 52 | 22 | 35 | 54 | 61 | 32 | 36 |

(a) As before, you must first rank each piece of data for A and then rank each piece of data for B. This gives:

| A | 5.6 | 4.2 | 9.3 | 6.4 | 4.2 | 3.8 | 7.5 | 5.2 |
|---|---|---|---|---|---|---|---|---|
| Rank A | 5 | 2.5 | 8 | 6 | 2.5 | 1 | 7 | 4 |
| B | 54 | 52 | 22 | 35 | 54 | 61 | 32 | 36 |
| Rank B | 6.5 | 5 | 1 | 3 | 6.5 | 8 | 2 | 4 |

Next, you must work out the difference in the corresponding ranks. This gives:

| Rank A | 5 | 2.5 | 8 | 6 | 2.5 | 1 | 7 | 4 |
|---|---|---|---|---|---|---|---|---|
| Rank B | 6.5 | 5 | 1 | 3 | 6.5 | 8 | 2 | 4 |
| $d$ | −1.5 | −2.5 | 7 | 3 | −4 | −7 | 5 | 0 |

Next, you must square these differences. This gives:

| $d$ | −1.5 | −2.5 | 7 | 3 | −4 | −7 | 5 | 0 |
|---|---|---|---|---|---|---|---|---|
| $d^2$ | 2.25 | 6.25 | 49 | 9 | 16 | 49 | 25 | 0 |

Then you must add these differences. This gives:
$$\Sigma d^2 = 156.5$$

You then calculate Spearman's Rank Correlation Coefficient, where $n = 8$:

$$r = 1 - \frac{6\Sigma d^2}{n(n^2 - 1)}$$

$$r = 1 - \frac{6 \times 156.5}{8 \times 63}$$

$$r = 1 - \frac{939}{504}$$

$$r = -0.863$$

(b)  As this value is less than 0 this shows there is **negative** correlation.

.................................................................

3.  The table below shows pairs of data.
  (a)  Calculate Spearman's Rank Correlation Coefficient for all the data.
  (b)  What can you say about the correlation?

| A | 43 | 45 | 34 | 41 | 50 | 37 | 39 |
|---|----|----|----|----|----|----|----|
| B | 99 | 99 | 92 | 87 | 99 | 84 | 95 |

(a)  There are three 99s. These should be ranked 5, 6 and 7. So you rank each of them as 6, i.e. the mean of 5, 6 and 7. So we have:

| A | 43 | 45 | 34 | 41 | 50 | 37 | 39 |
|---|----|----|----|----|----|----|----|
| Rank A | 5 | 6 | 1 | 4 | 7 | 2 | 3 |
| B | 99 | 99 | 92 | 87 | 99 | 84 | 95 |
| Rank B | 6 | 6 | 3 | 2 | 6 | 1 | 4 |

And calculate the differences, and square them:

| Rank A | 5 | 6 | 1 | 4 | 7 | 2 | 3 |
|--------|---|---|---|---|---|---|---|
| Rank B | 6 | 6 | 3 | 2 | 6 | 1 | 4 |
| $d$ | −1 | 0 | −2 | 2 | 1 | 1 | −1 |
| $d^2$ | 1 | 0 | 4 | 4 | 1 | 1 | 1 |

Adding these differences gives:
$$\Sigma d^2 = 12$$

Then calculate Spearman's Rank Correlation Coefficient, where $n = 7$:

$$r = 1 - \frac{6\Sigma d^2}{n(n^2 - 1)}$$

$$r = 1 - \frac{6 \times 12}{7 \times 48}$$

$$r = 1 - \frac{72}{336}$$

$$r = 0.786$$

(b)  As 0.786 is positive, this shows there is **positive** correlation.

## Exercise 23A

For each of the following:
(a)  Calculate Spearman's Rank Correlation Coefficient for all the data.
(b)  Comment on the correlation.

1.
| A | 61 | 56 | 52 | 64 | 56 | 58 | 43 | 48 |
|---|----|----|----|----|----|----|----|----|
| B | 68 | 65 | 68 | 71 | 74 | 62 | 58 | 54 |

2.
| A | 5.6 | 5.1 | 4.8 | 4.6 | 5.8 | 5.4 | 4.8 | 4.3 |
|---|-----|-----|-----|-----|-----|-----|-----|-----|
| B | 5.3 | 5.2 | 4.6 | 4.1 | 5.2 | 4.9 | 4.5 | 4.3 |

3.
| A | 63 | 48 | 52 | 73 | 84 | 69 |
|---|----|----|----|----|----|----|
| B | 42 | 46 | 47 | 38 | 38 | 48 |

4.
| A | 82 | 64 | 82 | 84 | 68 | 74 | 82 | 73 |
|---|----|----|----|----|----|----|----|----|
| B | 9 | 3 | 15 | 13 | 8 | 10 | 8 | 4 |

5.
| A | 4.6 | 3.6 | 3.4 | 4.8 | 4.2 | 4.3 | 3.4 | 3.8 |
|---|-----|-----|-----|-----|-----|-----|-----|-----|
| B | 44 | 74 | 69 | 52 | 57 | 44 | 62 | 42 |

6.
| A | 36 | 34 | 45 | 28 | 56 | 39 | 44 | 52 |
|---|----|----|----|----|----|----|----|----|
| B | 5.2 | 5.7 | 4.3 | 5.6 | 4.6 | 5.4 | 5 | 4.5 |

7.
| A | 4.5 | 4.2 | 3.2 | 4.7 | 2.4 | 4.4 | 3.5 | 2.6 |
|---|-----|-----|-----|-----|-----|-----|-----|-----|
| B | 68 | 84 | 73 | 81 | 64 | 81 | 81 | 56 |

8.
| A | 58 | 69 | 61 | 56 | 67 | 58 | 64 | 72 |
|---|----|----|----|----|----|----|----|----|
| B | 52 | 43 | 52 | 55 | 48 | 59 | 57 | 45 |

9.
| A | 41 | 38 | 55 | 36 | 52 | 41 | 48 | 41 |
|---|----|----|----|----|----|----|----|----|
| B | 76 | 73 | 94 | 83 | 86 | 76 | 89 | 79 |

10.
| A | 25 | 14 | 28 | 11 | 22 | 26 | 19 | 14 |
|---|----|----|----|----|----|----|----|----|
| B | 8 | 18 | 4 | 16 | 2 | 3 | 6 | 17 |

## 23.4 Scatter Graphs

You draw a scatter graph by plotting the data for one variable on the horizontal axis and the data for the other variable on the vertical axis. You can draw a **line of best fit** on the scatter graph if there is correlation. The rules for drawing a line of best fit are as follows:

a.  Work out the mean for each of the two sets of data.

b.  Draw an envelope around the points plotted.

c.  Plot the point showing the mean for each of the two sets of data.

d.  Draw a straight line passing through this point with roughly the same number of points on each side and roughly parallel to the sides of the envelope.

You can find the equation of the line of best fit by using these rules:

a.  Take 2 points that lie on the line of best fit (it is a good idea to use the point which is the mean for each of the two sets of data).

b.  Find the gradient, $m$, of the line of best fit by using:

$$m = \frac{y_2 - y_1}{x_2 - x_1}$$

Substitute the $x$-coordinate and the $y$-coordinate of one of the points into $y = mx + c$ to find the value of $c$.

For example:

.............................................................................

4.  The table below shows the marks of 6 pupils in English and Maths:

| Maths | 43 | 48 | 57 | 52 | 54 | 48 |
|---|---|---|---|---|---|---|
| English | 72 | 86 | 88 | 75 | 94 | 79 |

(a)  Draw a scatter graph to show this data with the English marks on the vertical axis and the Maths marks on the horizontal axis.

(b)  Draw the line of best fit.

(c)  Determine the equation of the line of best fit.

(d)  Calculate Spearman's Rank Correlation Coefficient.

(e)  What significance do you attach to the value of Spearman's Rank Correlation Coefficient?

(a)  Plot these points on graph paper (see part b).

(b)  First draw an envelope around the points that you plotted (the dotted line below). Then find the mean English and the mean Maths scores:

English:      Total = 494
              Mean = 494 ÷ 6 = 82.3

Maths:        Total = 302
              Mean = 302 ÷ 6 = 50.3

You must plot these on the graph and draw the line of best fit through the point (50.3, 82.3):

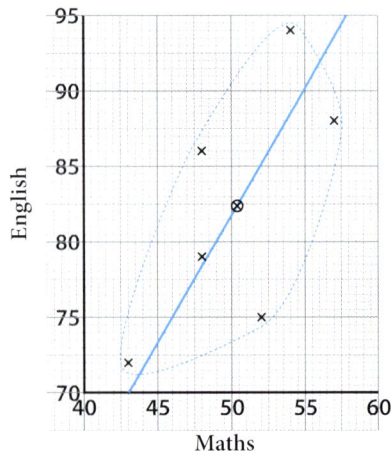

Maths

(c)  You need to choose 2 points on the line of best fit in order to work out the gradient. Let us choose (50.3, 82.3) and (43, 70). Then:

$$m = \frac{y_2 - y_1}{x_2 - x_1}$$

$$m = \frac{82.3 - 70}{50.3 - 43}$$

$$m = \frac{12.3}{7.3}$$

$$m = 1.68$$

So:      $y = mx + c$
         $y = 1.68x + c$

You can now substitute one of these points into this equation to work out $c$. Let us choose (43, 70).

So $x = 43$ and $y = 70$ giving:

$$y = 1.68x + c$$
$$70 = 1.68 \times 43 + c$$
$$70 = 72.24 + c$$

So:      $c = -2.24$

So the equation of the line of best fit is:

$$y = 1.68x - 2.24$$

(d)

| English | 72 | 86 | 88 | 75 | 94 | 79 |
|---|---|---|---|---|---|---|
| Rank English | 1 | 4 | 5 | 2 | 6 | 3 |
| Maths | 43 | 48 | 57 | 52 | 54 | 48 |
| Rank Maths | 1 | 2.5 | 6 | 4 | 5 | 2.5 |

| Rank English | 1 | 4 | 5 | 2 | 6 | 3 |
|---|---|---|---|---|---|---|
| Rank Maths | 1 | 2.5 | 6 | 4 | 5 | 2.5 |
| $d$ | 0 | 1.5 | −1 | −2 | 1 | 0.5 |

| $d$ | 0 | 1.5 | −1 | −2 | 1 | 0.5 |
|---|---|---|---|---|---|---|
| $d^2$ | 0 | 2.25 | 1 | 4 | 1 | 0.25 |

$\Sigma d^2 = 8.5$

$n = 6$

So  $r = 1 - \dfrac{6\Sigma d^2}{n(n^2 - 1)}$

$r = 1 - \dfrac{6 \times 8.5}{6 \times 35}$

$r = 1 - \dfrac{51}{336}$

$r = 0.757$

(e)  As 0.757 is positive this shows there is **positive** correlation.

## Exercise 23B

1. The table below shows the marks of 5 pupils in History and French.

| French | 53 | 59 | 56 | 64 | 62 |
|---|---|---|---|---|---|
| History | 77 | 86 | 74 | 83 | 94 |

   (a) Draw a scatter graph to show this data with the History marks on the vertical axis and the French marks on the horizontal axis.
   (b) Draw the line of best fit.
   (c) Determine the equation of the line of best fit.
   (d) Calculate Spearman's Rank Correlation Coefficient.
   (e) What significance do you attach to the value of Spearman's Rank Correlation Coefficient?

2. The table below shows the masses and lengths of 7 objects.

| Length (cm) | 32 | 36 | 14 | 22 | 17 | 32 | 25 |
|---|---|---|---|---|---|---|---|
| Mass kg | 5.1 | 5.4 | 4.2 | 4.7 | 3.6 | 5.3 | 3.2 |

   (a) Draw a scatter graph to show this data with the masses on the vertical axis and the lengths on the horizontal axis.
   (b) Draw the line of best fit.
   (c) Determine the equation of the line of best fit.
   (d) Calculate Spearman's Rank Correlation Coefficient.
   (e) What significance do you attach to the value of Spearman's Rank Correlation Coefficient?

3. The table below shows the areas and volumes of 8 objects.

| Area (cm²) | 94 | 81 | 91 | 86 | 96 | 96 | 74 | 85 |
|---|---|---|---|---|---|---|---|---|
| Volume (cm³) | 451 | 438 | 444 | 425 | 456 | 452 | 423 | 412 |

   (a) Draw a scatter graph to show this data with the volume on the vertical axis and the area on the horizontal axis.
   (b) Draw the line of best fit.
   (c) Determine the equation of the line of best fit.
   (d) Calculate Spearman's Rank Correlation Coefficient.
   (e) What significance do you attach to the value of Spearman's Rank Correlation Coefficient?

## Exercise 23B...

4. The table below shows the densities and volumes of 7 objects.

| Volume (cm³) | 115 | 97 | 115 | 111 | 123 | 94 | 104 |
|---|---|---|---|---|---|---|---|
| Density (kg/cm³) | 5.2 | 5.6 | 4.5 | 5.6 | 4.8 | 6.8 | 6.2 |

   (a) Draw a scatter graph to show this data with the density on the vertical axis and the volume on the horizontal axis.
   (b) Draw the line of best fit.
   (c) Determine the equation of the line of best fit.
   (d) Calculate Spearman's Rank Correlation Coefficient.
   (e) What significance do you attach to the value of Spearman's Rank Correlation Coefficient?

5. The table below shows the perimeters and areas of 7 objects.

| Perimeter (cm) | 52 | 61 | 55 | 58 | 64 | 48 | 46 |
|---|---|---|---|---|---|---|---|
| Area (cm²) | 77 | 94 | 86 | 81 | 88 | 81 | 74 |

   (a) Draw a scatter graph to show this data with the area on the vertical axis and the perimeter on the horizontal axis.
   (b) Draw the line of best fit.
   (c) Determine the equation of the line of best fit.
   (d) Calculate Spearman's Rank Correlation Coefficient.
   (e) What significance do you attach to the value of Spearman's Rank Correlation Coefficient?

6. The table below shows the masses and lengths of 9 objects.

| Mass (kg) | 3.5 | 12 | 19 | 25.5 | 31 | 28.5 | 24 | 7.5 | 15 |
|---|---|---|---|---|---|---|---|---|---|
| Length (cm) | 1.5 | 2.5 | 4.7 | 4.5 | 6.7 | 5.7 | 6.3 | 2.5 | 3.7 |

   (a) Draw a scatter graph to show this data with the length on the vertical axis and the mass on the horizontal axis.
   (b) Draw the line of best fit.
   (c) Determine the equation of the line of best fit.
   (d) Calculate Spearman's Rank Correlation Coefficient.

## Exercise 23B...

(e)     What significance do you attach to the value of Spearman's Rank Correlation Coefficient?

7.  The table below shows the average speed of a car and the time taken for 8 journeys.

| Time taken (hours) | 7.6 | 8.7 | 6.4 | 8.3 | 7.1 | 8.1 | 7.3 | 6.8 |
|---|---|---|---|---|---|---|---|---|
| Average speed (mph) | 40 | 36 | 52 | 32 | 62 | 45 | 48 | 56 |

(a)     Draw a scatter graph to show this data with the average speed on the vertical axis and the time taken on the horizontal axis.
(b)     Draw the line of best fit.
(c)     Determine the equation of the line of best fit.
(d)     Calculate Spearman's Rank Correlation Coefficient.
(e)     What significance do you attach to the value of Spearman's Rank Correlation Coefficient?

8.  The table below shows the temperature and rainfall at 6 different places.

| Rainfall (mm) | 12 | 26 | 13 | 21 | 21 | 9 |
|---|---|---|---|---|---|---|
| Temperature (°C) | 8 | 12 | 7 | 9 | 14 | 5 |

(a)     Draw a scatter graph to show this data with the temperature on the vertical axis and the rainfall on the horizontal axis.
(b)     Draw the line of best fit.
(c)     Determine the equation of the line of best fit.
(d)     Calculate Spearman's Rank Correlation Coefficient.
(e)     What significance do you attach to the value of Spearman's Rank Correlation Coefficient?

9.  The table below shows the areas and widths of 8 objects.

| Width (cm) | 31 | 40 | 50 | 24 | 51 | 43 | 32 | 47 |
|---|---|---|---|---|---|---|---|---|
| Area (cm²) | 31 | 46 | 76 | 24 | 71 | 61 | 41 | 58 |

(a)     Draw a scatter graph to show this data with the area on the vertical axis and the width on the horizontal axis.
(b)     Draw the line of best fit.

## Exercise 23B...

(c)     Determine the equation of the line of best fit.
(d)     Calculate Spearman's Rank Correlation Coefficient.
(e)     What significance do you attach to the value of Spearman's Rank Correlation Coefficient?

10. The table below shows the perimeters and areas of 7 objects.

| Perimeter (cm) | 43 | 45 | 34 | 41 | 50 | 37 | 39 |
|---|---|---|---|---|---|---|---|
| Area (cm²) | 99 | 97 | 92 | 87 | 99 | 84 | 95 |

(a)     Draw a scatter graph to show this data with the area on the vertical axis and the perimeter on the horizontal axis.
(b)     Draw the line of best fit.
(c)     Determine the equation of the line of best fit.
(d)     Calculate Spearman's Rank Correlation Coefficient.
(e)     What significance do you attach to the value of Spearman's Rank Correlation?

## 24.1 Mean And Standard Deviation Of A List Of Numbers

The **mean** is one of three different statistical averages (the others being the **median** and the **mode**). The **standard deviation** is a measure of how 'spread' the data is. The standard deviation uses all the data. The formulae for calculating the mean and standard deviation of a list of numbers are:

**Mean** $\qquad\qquad \bar{x} = \dfrac{\Sigma x}{n}$

**Standard Deviation** $\qquad s = \sqrt{\dfrac{\Sigma x^2}{n} - (\bar{x})^2}$

where $\quad n$ = the number of figures in the list
$\qquad\;\; \Sigma x$ = the sum of all the $x$s
$\qquad\;\; \Sigma x^2$ = the sum of all the $x^2$s

The rules for calculating the **mean** are:

a. Add up all the numbers;

b. Divide by how many numbers there are.

The rules for calculating the **standard deviation** are:

a. Square all the numbers;

b. Add up the squares;

c. Divide the total of the squares by how many numbers there are;

d. Subtract the square of the mean;

e. Take the square root of your answer.

For example:

..................................................................................

1. Find the mean and standard deviation of these data: 6.4, 3.8, 4.7, 5.3 and 4.8.

So we have:

| $x$ | $x^2$ |
|---|---|
| 6.4 | 40.96 |
| 3.8 | 14.44 |
| 4.7 | 22.09 |
| 5.3 | 28.09 |
| 4.8 | 23.04 |
| Total = 25.0 | Total = 128.62 |

Mean $\qquad\qquad\qquad \bar{x} = \dfrac{\Sigma x}{n}$

$\qquad\qquad\qquad\qquad\quad = \dfrac{25}{5} = 5$

Standard Deviation $\qquad s = \sqrt{\dfrac{\Sigma x^2}{n} - (\bar{x})^2}$

$\qquad\qquad\qquad\qquad\quad = \sqrt{\dfrac{128.62}{5} - 5^2}$

$\qquad\qquad\qquad\qquad\quad = \sqrt{0.724}$

$\qquad\qquad\qquad\qquad\quad = 0.851$

**Exercise 24A**: *Find the mean and standard deviation of the following.*

1. 14, 11, 16, 13

2. 9.4, 6.8, 5.2, 7.3, 4.9

3. 127, 114, 138, 121, 134

4. £5.24, £3.66, £9.24, £4.54

5. 15, 11, 14, 12, 10, 9, 8, 12

6. 7, 11, 13, 8, 6, 7, 9, 5

7. 18, 22, 23, 25, 26, 27, 28, 29

8. 14, 15, 17, 19, 21, 22, 22, 23, 24, 26

## 24.2 Mean And Standard Deviation Of A Frequency Distribution

The formulae for calculating the mean and standard deviation of a frequency distribution are:

**Mean** $\qquad\qquad \bar{x} = \dfrac{\Sigma fx}{n}$

**Standard Deviation** $\qquad s = \sqrt{\dfrac{\Sigma fx^2}{n} - (\bar{x})^2}$

where $\quad n$ = the number of figures in the list, or $\Sigma f$
$\qquad\;\; \Sigma fx$ = the sum of all the $fx$s
$\qquad\;\; \Sigma fx^2$ = the sum of all the $fx^2$s

The rules for calculating the **mean** of a frequency distribution are:

a. Multiply $f$ by $x$ to get $fx$ for each number;

b. Add up all the $fx$s;

c. Divide $\Sigma fx$ by the sum of the frequencies.

The rules for calculating the **standard deviation** of a frequency distribution are:

a. Multiply $fx$ by $x$ to get $fx^2$ for each number;

b. Add up all the $fx^2$;

c. Divide $\Sigma fx^2$ by the sum of the frequencies;

d. Subtract the square of the mean;

e.  Take the square root of your answer.

For example:

2.  Find the mean and standard deviation of the following frequency distribution:

| $x$ | $f$ |
|---|---|
| 1 | 2 |
| 2 | 7 |
| 3 | 4 |
| 4 | 5 |

Calculate $fx$ and $fx^2$, so we have:

| $x$ | $f$ | $fx$ | $fx^2$ |
|---|---|---|---|
| 1 | 2 | 2 | 2 |
| 2 | 7 | 14 | 28 |
| 3 | 4 | 12 | 36 |
| 4 | 5 | 20 | 80 |
|  | Total = 18 | Total = 48 | Total = 146 |

Mean

$$\overline{x} = \frac{\Sigma fx}{n}$$

$$= \frac{48}{18} = \frac{8}{3} \text{ or } 2\tfrac{2}{3}$$

Standard Deviation

$$s = \sqrt{\frac{\Sigma fx^2}{n} - (\overline{x})^2}$$

$$= \sqrt{\frac{146 - (2\tfrac{2}{3})^2}{18}}$$

$$= \sqrt{1}$$

$$= 1$$

**Exercise 24B**: *Find the mean and standard deviation of the following.*

1.

| $x$ | $f$ |
|---|---|
| 1 | 6 |
| 2 | 9 |
| 3 | 4 |
| 4 | 1 |

2.

| $x$ | $f$ |
|---|---|
| 2 | 7 |
| 4 | 11 |
| 6 | 10 |
| 8 | 2 |

3.

| $x$ | $f$ |
|---|---|
| 0 | 6 |
| 3 | 9 |
| 6 | 8 |
| 9 | 2 |

4.

| $x$ | $f$ |
|---|---|
| 1 | 16 |
| 2 | 22 |
| 3 | 7 |
| 4 | 5 |

**Exercise 24B...**

5.  The number of children in different families, as shown in the table below.

| Number of children | Frequency |
|---|---|
| 0 | 7 |
| 1 | 4 |
| 2 | 9 |
| 3 | 8 |
| 4 | 5 |
| 5 | 3 |
| 6 | 4 |

6.  The scores in mental maths tests, as shown in the table below.

| Score | Frequency |
|---|---|
| 2 | 3 |
| 3 | 3 |
| 4 | 2 |
| 5 | 5 |
| 6 | 4 |
| 7 | 1 |
| 8 | 2 |
| 9 | 4 |
| 10 | 1 |

7.  The number of children in each class in school, as shown in the table below.

| Number of children in each class | Frequency |
|---|---|
| 23 | 4 |
| 24 | 3 |
| 25 | 5 |
| 26 | 8 |
| 27 | 2 |
| 28 | 4 |
| 29 | 5 |
| 30 | 1 |

8.  The ages of children in a Sunday School, as shown in the table below.

| Age (years) | Frequency |
|---|---|
| 5 | 12 |
| 6 | 17 |
| 7 | 13 |
| 8 | 11 |
| 9 | 12 |
| 10 | 11 |
| 11 | 12 |
| 12 | 12 |

## Exercise 24B...

9. The weights of objects, to the nearest kg, as shown in the table below.

| Weight (kg) | Frequency |
|---|---|
| 4 | 3 |
| 5 | 7 |
| 6 | 9 |
| 7 | 12 |
| 8 | 14 |
| 9 | 5 |

10. The number of text messages sent by teenagers in one day, as shown in the table below.

| Number of text messages | Frequency |
|---|---|
| 12 | 8 |
| 13 | 11 |
| 14 | 6 |
| 15 | 2 |
| 16 | 4 |
| 17 | 9 |

## 24.3 Mean And Standard Deviation Of A Grouped Frequency Distribution

If you have a grouped frequency distribution, you need do an additional step:

a. Take $x$ to be the mid-value of each group;

b. Repeat the process used with the frequency distribution.

You can work out the mid-value of a group by adding the limits and then dividing by 2. Thus the mid-value of the group 15–29 is 22 since $15 + 29 = 44$ and $44 \div 2 = 22$. Note that a calculation of the mean or standard deviation from a grouped distribution list is only an **estimate** because the original data is **not known**.

For example:

3. Find the estimate of the mean and standard deviation of the grouped frequency distribution below:

| Group | Frequency |
|---|---|
| $1 < M \leq 4$ | 7 |
| $4 < M \leq 10$ | 4 |
| $10 < M \leq 11$ | 9 |
| $11 < M \leq 18$ | 3 |

Taking $x$ to be the mid-values gives the following:

| Group | $f$ | $x$ | $fx$ | $fx^2$ |
|---|---|---|---|---|
| $1 < M \leq 4$ | 7 | 2.5 | 17.5 | 43.75 |
| $4 < M \leq 10$ | 4 | 7 | 28 | 196 |
| $10 < M \leq 11$ | 9 | 10.5 | 94.5 | 992.25 |
| $11 < M \leq 18$ | 3 | 14.5 | 43.5 | 630.75 |
| | Total $= 23$ | | Total $= 183.5$ | Total $= 1862.75$ |

Mean
$$\bar{x} = \frac{\Sigma fx}{n}$$
$$= \frac{183.5}{23} = 7.98 \text{ to 3 s.f.}$$

Standard Deviation
$$s = \sqrt{\frac{\Sigma fx^2}{n} - (\bar{x})^2}$$
$$= \sqrt{\frac{1862.75}{23} - 7.98^2}$$
$$= \sqrt{17.3} = 4.16$$

## Exercise 24C: Find the estimate of the mean and standard deviation of the following.

1. The distances, in km, run by an athlete on training runs, as shown below.

| Distance ($l$ km) | Frequency |
|---|---|
| $1 < l \leq 6$ | 7 |
| $6 < l \leq 11$ | 9 |
| $11 < l \leq 16$ | 4 |
| $16 < l \leq 21$ | 5 |

2. The numbers of books on each of 50 shelves in a library, as shown below.

| Numbers of books | Frequency |
|---|---|
| 0 – 8 | 14 |
| 9 – 16 | 21 |
| 17 – 20 | 11 |
| 21 – 25 | 4 |

3. The width of books, in cm, on a library shelf, as shown below.

| Width ($w$ cm) | Frequency |
|---|---|
| $2 < w \leq 4$ | 3 |
| $4 < w \leq 6$ | 8 |
| $6 < w \leq 8$ | 4 |
| $8 < w \leq 10$ | 5 |

4. The marks of pupils in a test, as shown below.

| Marks | Frequency |
|---|---|
| 1 – 10 | 4 |
| 11 – 20 | 8 |
| 21 – 30 | 9 |
| 31 – 40 | 14 |
| 41 – 50 | 15 |

5. The ages of people on an excursion, as shown below.

| Age ($a$ years) | Frequency |
|---|---|
| $1 \leq a < 6$ | 8 |
| $6 \leq a < 11$ | 14 |
| $11 \leq a < 16$ | 9 |
| $16 \leq a < 21$ | 10 |
| $21 \leq a < 26$ | 9 |

6. Lengths of objects are recorded and rounded to the nearest cm. The table shows the rounded lengths of these objects.

| Length (cm) | Frequency |
|---|---|
| 1 – 5 | 13 |
| 6 – 8 | 11 |
| 9 – 16 | 7 |
| 17 – 20 | 9 |

7. Heights of objects are recorded and rounded to the nearest m. The table shows the rounded heights of these objects.

| Height (m) | Frequency |
|---|---|
| 1 – 9 | 8 |
| 10 – 14 | 15 |
| 15 – 20 | 6 |
| 21 – 30 | 4 |

8. The lengths of objects, in cm, as shown below.

| Length ($l$ cm) | Frequency |
|---|---|
| $0 < l \leq 10$ | 7 |
| $10 < l \leq 12$ | 9 |
| $12 < l \leq 20$ | 14 |
| $20 < l \leq 24$ | 10 |

9. The times taken to complete a race, as shown below.

| Time ($t$ mins) | Frequency |
|---|---|
| $2 < t \leq 5$ | 16 |
| $5 < t \leq 9$ | 22 |
| $9 < t \leq 14$ | 14 |
| $14 < t \leq 16$ | 8 |

10. The heights of objects, in m to the nearest m, as shown below.

| Height (m) | Frequency |
|---|---|
| 1 – 5 | 7 |
| 6 – 10 | 4 |
| 11 – 15 | 12 |
| 16 – 20 | 18 |
| 21 – 25 | 9 |

11. The widths of shapes, as shown below.

| Width ($w$ cm) | Frequency |
|---|---|
| $0 < w \leq 10$ | 3 |
| $10 < w \leq 15$ | 4 |
| $15 < w \leq 20$ | 8 |
| $20 < w \leq 24$ | 12 |
| $24 < w \leq 30$ | 10 |
| $30 < w \leq 40$ | 3 |

12. The volumes of shapes, as shown below.

| Volume ($V$ litres) | Frequency |
|---|---|
| $1 < V \leq 8$ | 3 |
| $8 < V \leq 12$ | 16 |
| $12 < V \leq 18$ | 22 |
| $18 < V \leq 20$ | 34 |
| $20 < V \leq 27$ | 24 |
| $27 < V \leq 40$ | 1 |

13. The masses of objects, in kg to the nearest kg, as shown below.

| Mass (kg) | Frequency |
|---|---|
| 1 – 7 | 6 |
| 8 – 14 | 11 |
| 15 – 21 | 14 |
| 22 – 28 | 9 |
| 29 – 35 | 10 |

14. The areas of fields in hectares, as shown below.

| Area ($A$ hectares) | Frequency |
|---|---|
| $1 < A \leq 9$ | 3 |
| $9 < A \leq 17$ | 5 |
| $17 < A \leq 25$ | 4 |
| $25 < A \leq 33$ | 6 |
| $33 < A \leq 41$ | 2 |

## 24.4 Harder Problems

Sometimes you are given incomplete data with which to work. For example:

**4.** The frequency table below shows the marks in a test.

| Marks | Frequency |
|-------|-----------|
| 1 – 5 | 8 |
| 6 – 7 | |
| 8 – 13 | 12 |
| 14 – 16 | 12 |
| 17 – 22 | 4 |

The mean mark is 9.98. Find:
(a)   the frequency for the 6 – 7 group;
(b)   the standard deviation.

(a)   To solve this problem you must:
- Call the missing frequency $n$.
- Work out the mid-values of each group ($x$).
- Multiply the mid-values by the frequency to get $fx$.
- Add up all the $fx$s.
- Divide $\Sigma fx$ by the sum of the frequencies to get the mean.
- Form an equation and solve it to find the missing frequency.

So we have:

| Mark | Frequency $f$ | Mid-value $x$ | $fx$ |
|------|------|------|------|
| 1 – 5 | 8 | 3 | 24 |
| 6 – 7 | $n$ | 6.5 | 6.5$n$ |
| 8 – 13 | 12 | 10.5 | 126 |
| 14 – 16 | 12 | 15 | 180 |
| 17 – 22 | 4 | 19.5 | 78 |
| | Total = 36 + $n$ | | Total = 408 + 6.5$n$ |

The mean:

$$\bar{x} = \frac{\Sigma fx}{n}$$

$$= \frac{408 + 6.5n}{36 + n} = 9.98$$

Cross multiplying gives:

$$9.98(36 + n) = 408 + 6.5n$$
$$359.28 + 9.98n = 408 + 6.5n$$
$$9.98n - 6.5n = 408 - 359.28$$
$$3.48n = 48.72$$

$$n = \frac{48.72}{3.48} = 14$$

So the missing frequency, $n = 14$

(b)   You can now replace $n$ with 14 and find the standard deviation as before. So we have:

| Mark | Frequency $f$ | Mid-value $x$ | $fx$ | $fx^2$ |
|------|------|------|------|------|
| 1 – 5 | 8 | 3 | 24 | 72 |
| 6 – 7 | **14** | 6.5 | 91 | 591.5 |
| 8 – 13 | 12 | 10.5 | 126 | 1323 |
| 14 – 16 | 12 | 15 | 180 | 2700 |
| 17 – 22 | 4 | 19.5 | 78 | 1521 |
| | Total = 50 | | | Total = 6207.5 |

Standard Deviation:   $s = \sqrt{\dfrac{\Sigma fx^2}{n} - (\bar{x})^2}$

$$= \sqrt{\frac{6207.5}{50} - 9.98^2}$$

$$= \sqrt{24.5496}$$

$$= 4.95$$

## Exercise 24D

**1.** The frequency table below shows the lengths of objects, in cm, rounded to the nearest cm.

| Length (cm) | Frequency |
|-------------|-----------|
| 2 – 5 | 3 |
| 6 – 15 | 7 |
| 16 – 18 | |
| 19 – 23 | 4 |
| 24 – 36 | 15 |

The mean length is 20.125 cm. Find:
(a)   the missing frequency ;
(b)   the standard deviation.

**2.** The frequency table below shows the amount spent, in £s, rounded to the nearest £, by shoppers at a supermarket till in one day.

| Amount spent (£) | Frequency |
|------------------|-----------|
| 35 – 44 | 4 |
| 45 – 50 | 17 |
| 51 – 60 | 36 |
| 61 – 80 | |
| 81 – 84 | 9 |

The mean amount spent is £58.6625. Find:
(a)   the missing frequency;
(b)   the standard deviation.

3. The frequency table below shows the amounts of pocket money, in £s, for pupils at a school.

| Pocket money (£) | Frequency |
|---|---|
| 2 – 2.60 | 3 |
| 2.61 – 3.39 | 7 |
| 3.40 – 5 | 14 |
| 5.01 – 5.99 | |
| 6 – 10 | 14 |

The mean amount of pocket money is £5.294. Find:
(a) the missing frequency
(b) the standard deviation.

4. The frequency table below shows the widths of metal rods, in cm to the nearest cm.

| Width (cm) | Frequency |
|---|---|
| 2 – 6 | |
| 7 – 11 | 14 |
| 12 – 14 | 11 |
| 15 – 18 | 9 |
| 19 – 26 | 12 |

The mean width is 14.07 cm. Find:
(a) the missing frequency;
(b) the standard deviation.

5. The frequency table below shows the lengths of journeys, in km to the nearest km, made by John in a month.

| Length (km) | Frequency |
|---|---|
| 10 – 30 | 17 |
| 31 – 35 | 24 |
| 36 – 40 | 16 |
| 41 – 50 | |
| 51 – 70 | 18 |

The mean length is 39.665 km. Find:
(a) the missing frequency;
(b) the standard deviation.

6. The frequency table below shows the masses of objects, in kg to the nearest kg.

| Mass (kg) | Frequency |
|---|---|
| 1 – 5 | |
| 6 – 8 | 14 |
| 9 – 13 | 9 |
| 14 – 16 | 22 |

The mean mass is 10.84 kg. Find:
(a) the missing frequency;
(b) the standard deviation.

7. The frequency table below shows the lengths of objects, $l$, in m.

| Length $l$ (m) | Frequency |
|---|---|
| $1 < l \le 6$ | 8 |
| $6 < l \le 12$ | 4 |
| $12 < l \le 23$ | |
| $23 < l \le 30$ | 9 |

The mean length is 14.9 m. Find:
(a) the missing frequency;
(b) the standard deviation.

8. The perimeters of shapes, $P$, in cm, are shown below.

| Perimeter $P$,(cm) | Frequency |
|---|---|
| $5 < P \le 8$ | 7 |
| $8 < P \le 14$ | 4 |
| $14 < P \le 26$ | 3 |
| $26 < P \le 30$ | |
| $30 < P \le 32$ | 8 |

The mean perimeter is 19.26 cm. Find:
(a) the missing frequency;
(b) the standard deviation.

9. The frequency table below shows the capacities of bottles, in ml to the nearest ml.

| Capacity (ml) | Frequency |
|---|---|
| 1 – 80 | 17 |
| 81 – 120 | |
| 121 – 200 | 14 |
| 201 – 240 | 13 |

The mean capacity is 128.1 ml. Find:
(a) the missing frequency;
(b) the standard deviation.

## 24.5 Further Problems

Sometimes other information is missing and you have to use different techniques. For example:

......................................................................

5. The lengths of 9 objects have mean 8.4 cm and standard deviation 1.6 cm. A tenth object is 9.5 cm long. Find:
(a) the mean, and
(b) the standard deviation
of all ten objects.

(a) To find the mean, you use these rules:
- Find the total of the 9 objects.
- Add the tenth length.
- Find the mean of the 10 lengths.

Total of 9 objects $= 9 \times 8.4 = 75.6$
Total of 10 objects $= 75.6 + 9.5 = 85.1$
Mean of 10 objects $= 85.1 \div 10 = 8.51$ cm

(b) To find the standard deviation, you use these rules:
- Find the $\Sigma x^2$ for the 9 lengths.
- Add on the square of the tenth length.
- Find the standard deviation of the 10 lengths.

So, for the nine objects:

Standard deviation $\quad s = \sqrt{\dfrac{\Sigma x^2}{n} - (\bar{x})^2}$

$$1.6 = \sqrt{\dfrac{\Sigma x^2}{9} - 8.4^2}$$

Squaring both sides gives:

$$2.56 = \dfrac{\Sigma x^2}{9} - 70.56$$

So: $\quad \dfrac{\Sigma x^2}{9} = 2.56 + 70.56$

$$\dfrac{\Sigma x^2}{9} = 73.12$$

Multiplying both sides by 9 gives:

$$\Sigma x^2 = 73.12 \times 9$$
$$= 658.08$$

Then, for the 10 objects:

$$\Sigma x^2 = 658.08 + 9.5^2$$
$$\Sigma x^2 = 748.33$$

So the standard deviation is given by:

$$s = \sqrt{\dfrac{\Sigma x^2}{n} - (\bar{x})^2}$$
$$= \sqrt{\dfrac{748.33}{10} - 8.51^2}$$
$$= \sqrt{2.4129}$$
$$= 1.55 \text{ cm}$$

6. The mean and standard deviation of the wages for 25 employees in a factory are £176 and £18.40. The mean and standard deviation of the wages for 15 employees in an adjacent office are £142 and £20.60. Find:
(a) the mean, and
(b) the standard deviation
of the wages for all the workers.

(a) To find the mean, use this process:
- Find the total of the factory wages.
- Find the total of the office wages.
- Find the total of the wages for all the workers.
- Find the mean of the wages for all the workers.

So, for the factory workers:
Total wage $= 176 \times 25 = £4400$

And for the office workers:
Total wage $= 142 \times 15 = £2130$

Therefore, for all the workers:
Total wage $= £4400 + £2130 = £6530$

So:
$$\text{Mean wage} = \dfrac{6530}{40} = £163.25$$

(b) To find the standard deviation, use this process:
- Find the $\Sigma x^2$ for the factory workers.
- Find the $\Sigma x^2$ for the office workers.
- Find the $\Sigma x^2$ for all the workers.
- Find the standard deviation for all the workers.

So, for the factory workers:

Standard deviation $\quad s = \sqrt{\dfrac{\Sigma x^2}{n} - (\bar{x})^2}$

$$18.40 = \sqrt{\dfrac{\Sigma x^2}{25} - 176^2}$$

Squaring both sides gives:

$$338.56 = \dfrac{\Sigma x^2}{25} - 30976$$

So: $\quad \dfrac{\Sigma x^2}{25} = 338.56 + 30976$

$$\dfrac{\Sigma x^2}{25} = 31314.56$$

Multiplying both sides by 25 gives:

$$\Sigma x^2 = 782864$$

Then, for the office workers:

Standard deviation $\quad s = \sqrt{\dfrac{\Sigma x^2}{n} - (\bar{x})^2}$

$$20.60 = \sqrt{\dfrac{\Sigma x^2}{15} - 142^2}$$

Squaring both sides gives:

$$424.36 = \dfrac{\Sigma x^2}{15} - 20164$$

So: $\quad \dfrac{\Sigma x^2}{15} = 424.36 + 20164$

$$\dfrac{\Sigma x^2}{15} = 20588.36$$

Multiplying both sides by 15 gives:

$$\Sigma x^2 = 308825.4$$

Therefore, for all the workers:

$$\Sigma x^2 = 782864 + 308825.4$$
$$= 1091689.4$$

So the standard deviation is given by:

$$s = \sqrt{\frac{\Sigma x^2}{n} - (\overline{x})^2}$$

$$= \sqrt{\frac{1091689.4}{40} - 163.25^2}$$

$$= \sqrt{641.6725}$$

$$= £25.33$$

## Exercise 24E

1. The mean and standard deviation of 8 masses are 46 kg and 4 kg. A ninth mass is 40 kg. Find the mean and standard deviation of all nine masses.

2. The mean and standard deviation of 12 marks in a test are 53 and 8. A pupil who missed the test then scored 56 marks. Find the mean and standard deviation of all 13 marks.

3. There are 18 girls and 10 boys in a class. The mean and standard deviation of the marks of the girls are 46 and 5. The mean and standard deviation of the marks of the boys are 38 and 8. Find the mean and standard deviation of the whole class.

4. A company employs full time and part time staff. There are 24 full time and 10 part time staff. The mean and standard deviation of the wages of the full time staff are £235.60 and £18.40. The mean and standard deviation of the wages of all the employees are £221.47 and £27.87. Find the mean and standard deviation of the part time staff.

5. The lengths of 25 objects were recorded. The mean and standard deviation of these lengths were 5.04 cm and 0.41 cm. A sample of 10 objects was chosen from these 25 objects. The mean and standard deviation of the lengths in the sample were 4.8 cm and 0.3 cm. Find the mean and standard deviation of the lengths of the 15 objects not in the sample.

6. The mean and standard deviation of the marks of 15 boys in a class test were 64 and 7. The mean and standard deviation of the marks of 10 girls in this class test were 68 and 5. Find the mean and standard deviation of the whole class.

7. The mean and standard deviation of the marks of 30 pupils in an exam were 54 and 6. It was then discovered that one of the pupils had cheated and his mark of 47 was then excluded from the data. Find the mean and standard deviation of the remaining 29 pupils.

## Exercise 24E

8. The mean and standard deviation of 20 diameters of circles are 47 cm and 8 cm. The mean and standard deviation of another set of 30 diameters of circles are 52 cm and 6 cm. Find the mean and standard deviation of all 50 diameters.

## 24.6 Transforming Sets Of Data

Sometimes you are asked to transform data, i.e. when every figure is modified in some way. For example:

7. Consider the set of values: 1, 2, 3, 4, 5. What happens to the mean and standard deviation of these figures when:
   (a) 6 is added to each figure?
   (b) each figure is trebled?
   (c) each figure is divided by 4 and then 2 is subtracted?

The mean and standard deviation of these figures can be found as follows:

| $x$ | $x^2$ |
|---|---|
| 1 | 1 |
| 2 | 4 |
| 3 | 9 |
| 4 | 16 |
| 5 | 25 |
| Total = 15 | Total = 55 |

Mean:   $\overline{x} = \dfrac{\Sigma x}{n}$

$$= \frac{15}{5} = 3$$

Standard deviation:   $s = \sqrt{\dfrac{\Sigma x^2}{n} - (\overline{x})^2}$

$$= \sqrt{\frac{55}{5} - 3^2}$$

$$= \sqrt{2}$$

$$= 1.414$$

(a)   Adding 6 to each figure:

| $x$ | $x^2$ |
|---|---|
| 7 | 49 |
| 8 | 64 |
| 9 | 81 |
| 10 | 100 |
| 11 | 121 |
| Total = 45 | Total = 415 |

Mean $\quad \bar{x} = \dfrac{45}{5} = 9$

Standard deviation $\quad s = \sqrt{\dfrac{415}{5} - 9^2}$

$$= \sqrt{2}$$
$$= 1.414$$

Note that:
- The mean is **6 more** than the original mean.
- The standard deviation is the **same** as the original standard deviation.

(b) Trebling each figure:

| $x$ | $x^2$ |
|---|---|
| 3 | 9 |
| 6 | 36 |
| 9 | 81 |
| 12 | 144 |
| 15 | 225 |
| Total = 45 | Total = 495 |

Mean $\quad \bar{x} = \dfrac{45}{5} = 9$

Standard deviation $\quad s = \sqrt{\dfrac{495}{5} - 9^2}$

$$= \sqrt{18}$$
$$= 3\sqrt{2}$$
$$= 4.24$$

Note that:
- The mean is **3 times** the original mean.
- The standard deviation is **3 times** the original standard deviation.

(c) Dividing each figure by 4 and then subtracting 2:

| $x$ | $x^2$ |
|---|---|
| −1.75 | 3.0625 |
| −1.5 | 2.25 |
| −1.25 | 1.5625 |
| −1 | 1 |
| −0.75 | 0.5625 |
| Total = −6.25 | Total = 8.4375 |

Mean $\quad \bar{x} = \dfrac{-6.25}{5} = -1.25$

Standard deviation $\quad s = \sqrt{\dfrac{8.4375}{5} - (-1.25)^2}$

$$= \sqrt{0.125}$$
$$= \tfrac{1}{4}\sqrt{2}$$

Note that:
- The mean is the original mean **divided by 4 and then 2 subtracted**.
- The standard deviation is the original standard deviation **divided by 4**.

The previous example shows that the following are the rules for transforming data.

For changes to the **mean**, if the mean of a set of data is $\bar{x}$, then:

- Adding $y$ to all the figures changes the mean to $\bar{x} + y$.
- Subtracting $y$ from all the figures changes the mean to $\bar{x} - y$.
- Multiplying all the figures by $y$ changes the mean to $y\bar{x}$.
- Dividing all the figures by $y$ changes the mean to $\dfrac{\bar{x}}{y}$.

For changes to the **standard deviation**, if the standard deviation of a set of data is $s$, then:

- Adding $y$ to all the figures leaves the standard deviation unchanged.
- Subtracting $y$ from all the figures leaves the standard deviation unchanged.
- Multiplying all the figures by $y$ changes the standard deviation to $ys$.
- Dividing all the figures by $y$ changes the standard deviation to $\dfrac{s}{y}$.

These rules can be used to find answers more conveniently than in the previous example. For example:

8. The scores in a test have mean 54 and standard deviation 5.6. Find the new mean and new standard deviation when all the figures are:
   (a) increased by 7;
   (b) halved;
   (c) tripled and then decreased by 7.

   (a) New mean = 54 + 7 = 61
       New standard deviation = 5.6 (i.e. unchanged)

   (b) New mean = $\dfrac{54}{2} = 27$
       New standard deviation = $\dfrac{5.6}{2} = 2.8$

   (c) New mean = 54 × 3 − 7 = 155
       New standard deviation = 5.6 × 3 = 16.8

## Exercise 24F

1. The scores in a test have mean 46 and standard deviation 4.7. Find the new mean and new standard deviation when all the figures are:
   (a) increased by 6;
   (b) doubled;
   (c) halved and then 3 subtracted.

## Exercise 24F...

2. The heights of a set of objects have mean 15.2 cm and standard deviation 2.8 cm. Find the new mean and new standard deviation when all the figures are:
   (a) multiplied by 4;
   (b) reduced by 5;
   (c) halved and then 7 added.

3. The ages of people in a club have mean 54 years and standard deviation 2.9 years. Find the new mean and new standard deviation when all the ages are:
   (a) divided by 4;
   (b) increased by 10;
   (c) multiplied by 5 and then reduced by 2.

4. The times that substances take to dissolve were recorded with mean 1.4 minutes and standard deviation 0.24 minutes. Find the new mean and new standard deviation in minutes when all the times are:
   (a) reduced by 30 seconds;
   (b) tripled;
   (c) halved and then increased by 15 seconds.

5. The lengths of a set of objects have mean 5.2 m and standard deviation 1.2 m. Find the new mean and new standard deviation in metres when all the lengths are:
   (a) increased by 60 cm;
   (b) halved;
   (c) tripled and then reduced by 20 cm.

6. The radii of a set of circles have mean 8.4 cm and standard deviation 2.31 cm. Find the new mean and new standard deviation when all the radii are:
   (a) reduced by 2.5 cm;
   (b) multiplied by 4;
   (c) divided by 3 and then increased by 1.4 cm.

7. The IQs of people in a club were measured. The mean IQ was 114 and the standard deviation of the IQs was 18. Find the new mean and new standard deviation when all the IQs were:
   (a) increased by 23;
   (b) divided by 3;
   (c) doubled and then reduced by 15.

## Exercise 24F...

8. The distances pupils walk to school have mean 2.8 km and standard deviation 0.3 km. Find the new mean and new standard deviation in km when all the distances are:
   (a) reduced by 600 m;
   (b) doubled;
   (c) divided by 4 and then increased by 200 m.

9. The goals scored in a football tournament have mean 2.43 and standard deviation 0.27. Find the new mean and new standard deviation when all the goals are:
   (a) increased by 5;
   (b) divided by 9;
   (c) tripled and then reduced by 4.

10. The volumes of a set of liquids have mean 3.4 litres and standard deviation 0.8 litres. Find the new mean and new standard deviation in litres when all the volumes are:
    (a) reduced by 800 ml;
    (b) doubled;
    (c) divided by 5 and then increased by 150 ml.

# CHAPTER 25: PROBABILITY

## 25.1 The Rules Of Probability

**Probability** is the study of how likely it is that one or more events will happen. A probability is expressed as a value between 0 (definitely won't happen) and 1 (definitely will happen). You need to know the following three rules of probability:

### The AND rule for independent events

Two events, A and B, are **independent** if the outcome of A does not affect the outcome of B. If P(A) is the probability that event A happens and P(B) is the probability that event B happens and A and B are independent then:

$$P(A \text{ and } B) = P(A) \times P(B)$$

### The OR rule for mutually exclusive events

Two events, A and B, are **mutually exclusive** if A and B cannot occur at the same time. If P(A) is the probability that event A happens and P(B) is the probability that event B happens and A and B are mutually exclusive then:

$$P(A \text{ or } B) = P(A) + P(B)$$

### The NOT rule

If P(A) is the probability that event A happens then the probability that event A does not happen is given by:

$$P(\text{not } A) = 1 - P(A)$$

## 25.2 Tree Diagrams

A **tree diagram** can be used to work out probabilities. The following examples show how to construct and use a tree diagram:

1.  A box contains 8 red and 6 blue marbles. 3 marbles are selected at random one after the other without replacement.
    (a)   Draw a tree diagram to show all the possible outcomes.
    (b)   Hence find the probability that (i) the first 3 marbles selected are red, blue and blue in that order; (ii) 2 red and 1 blue are selected, and (iii) at least 1 blue is selected.

    (a)   When drawing a tree diagram, remember that the probabilities on each pair of branches on the tree diagram must always add up to 1. In this example, it is easier to express the probabilities as fractions. Because we are not

replacing the marbles in the box after they have been selected, the first set of branches is expressed as a probability out of 14 marbles, the second out of 13 marbles and the third out of 12 marbles. Hence we have:

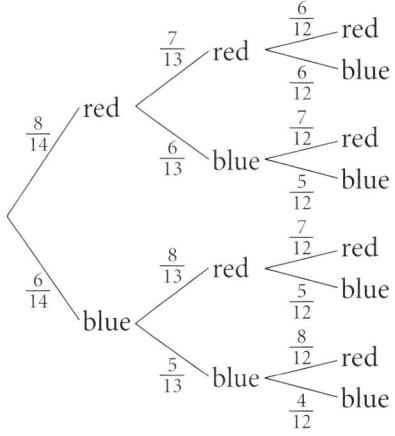

We can use the tree diagram to calculate the probability of any combination occurring.

(b) (i) Using the AND rule:
$$P(R \text{ and } B \text{ and } B) = \frac{8}{14} \times \frac{6}{13} \times \frac{5}{12}$$
$$= \frac{10}{91}$$

(ii) You should write out all the possible combinations first. Thus we could have:

R and R and B, or

R and B and R, or

B and R and R

You should then work out the probability for each of these combinations by multiplying (i.e., using the AND rule):

$$P(R \text{ and } R \text{ and } B) = \frac{8}{14} \times \frac{7}{13} \times \frac{6}{12}$$
$$= \frac{2}{13}$$

$$P(R \text{ and } B \text{ and } R) = \frac{8}{14} \times \frac{6}{13} \times \frac{7}{12}$$
$$= \frac{2}{13}$$

$$P(B \text{ and } R \text{ and } R) = \frac{6}{14} \times \frac{8}{13} \times \frac{7}{12}$$
$$= \frac{2}{13}$$

Because you want the probability that **any** of these combinations will happen, you should then add each of these probabilities (i.e., using the OR rule) to get:

$$P(\text{2 R and 1 B}) = \frac{2}{13} + \frac{2}{13} + \frac{2}{13}$$

$$= \frac{6}{13}$$

(iii) It is quicker to find the probability that *no* blues are selected and then subtract this probability from 1 (i.e., using the NOT rule) to find the probability that *at least* 1 blue is selected. So we have:

$$P(\text{no B}) = P(\text{R and R and R})$$

$$= \frac{8}{14} \times \frac{7}{13} \times \frac{6}{12}$$

$$= \frac{2}{13}$$

So P(at least 1 B) $= 1 - \frac{2}{13} = \frac{11}{13}$

..............................................................

2. The probability it is sunny is 0.74. If it is sunny then the probability that Yasmin goes for a walk is 0.85. Otherwise the probability that Yasmin goes for a walk is 0.28.
   (a)    Draw a tree diagram to show all the possible outcomes.
   (b)    Hence find the probability that (i) it is sunny and Yasmin goes for a walk, and (ii) Yasmin goes for a walk.

   (a)    As before, we draw the tree diagram showing the probabilities given in the question:

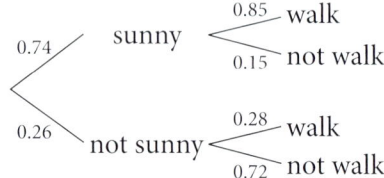

   (b)    (i) P(it is sunny and Yasmin goes for a walk)
          $= 0.74 \times 0.85$
          $= 0.629$

   (ii) There are two possible scenarios that result in Yasmin going for a walk:

   P(it is sunny and Yasmin goes for a walk)
          $= 0.74 \times 0.85$
          $= 0.629$

   or:

   P(not sunny and Yasmin goes for a walk)
          $= 0.26 \times 0.28$
          $= 0.0728$

So: P(Yasmin goes for a walk)
          $= 0.629 + 0.0728$
          $= 0.7018$

## Exercise 25A

1. The probability traffic lights are red is 0.5. The probability traffic lights are amber is 0.2. The probability traffic lights are green is 0.3. A car approaches two sets of traffic lights.
   (a)    Draw a tree diagram to show all the possible outcomes.
   (b)    Hence find the probability that: (i) one set of traffic lights is red and the other set of traffic lights is green; (ii) both traffic lights are different; (iii) at least one set of traffic lights is green.

2. A box contains 12 green and 18 yellow discs. Two discs are selected at random, one after the other, and replaced each time.
   (a)    Draw a tree diagram to show all the possible outcomes.
   (b)    Hence find the probability that: (i) the first disc is green and the second is yellow; (ii) both are green; (iii) one is green and the other is yellow.

3. The probability Maureen eats chips is 0.76. If Maureen eats chips then the probability she eats a burger is 0.6. Otherwise the probability she eats a burger is 0.48.
   (a)    Draw a tree diagram to show all the possible outcomes.
   (b)    Hence find the probability that: (i) she eats chips and a burger; (ii) she eats a burger.

4. The probability that Oisin decides to study French is 0.7. If Oisin studies French then the probability that he decides to study German is 0.28. Otherwise the probability he decides to study German is 0.62.
   (a)    Draw a tree diagram to show all the possible outcomes.
   (b)    Hence find the probability that: (i) he decides to study French and German; (ii) he decides to study German.

5. There are 15 boys and 12 girls in a class. Three pupils are selected at random.
   (a)    Draw a tree diagram to show all the possible outcomes.

## Exercise 25A

(b) Hence find the probability that: (i) a girl and then a boy and then a girl are selected; (ii) at least one boy is selected; (iii) more girls than boys are selected.

6. The probability that Veronica buys a dog is 0.81. If Veronica buys a dog then the probability that she buys a cat is 0.62. Otherwise the probability that she buys a cat is 0.68.
   (a) Draw a tree diagram to show all the possible outcomes.
   (b) Hence find the probability that: (i) she doesn't buy a dog but she buys a cat; (ii) she buys a cat.

7. Box A contains six 20p coins and four 50p coins. Box B contains three 20p coins and seven 50p coins. A coin is chosen at random from box A and placed in box B. A coin is then chosen at random from box B.
   (a) Draw a tree diagram to show all the possible outcomes.
   (b) Hence find the probability that: (i) a 20p coin is chosen from box B; (ii) a coin of the same value is chosen each time.

8. The probability that Clodagh goes to Belfast by train is 0.44. If Clodagh goes to Belfast by train then the probability that she visits *Titanic Belfast* is 0.35. Otherwise the probability that she visits *Titanic Belfast* is 0.42.
   (a) Draw a tree diagram to show all the possible outcomes.
   (b) Hence find the probability that: (i) she goes to Belfast by train and she visits *Titanic Belfast*; (ii) she visits *Titanic Belfast*.

## 25.3 Venn Diagrams

A **Venn diagram** uses circles to show how different sets overlap each other. The rules for drawing a Venn diagram with two sets are as follows:

a. Begin by filling in the intersection of the two circles.

b. Then fill in the other parts of each circle.

c. Fill in outside the two circles for those values that are in neither set.

For example:

3. There are 42 girls in Year 13.
   23 play netball.
   17 play hockey.
   8 play neither netball nor hockey.
   (a) Draw a Venn diagram to show this information.
   (b) Hence use the Venn diagram to find how many girls play both netball and hockey.
   (c) A girl is chosen at random. Find the probability she (i) plays both netball and hockey; (ii) plays netball but not hockey.

(a) Let $x$ = the number of girls who play both netball and hockey. Thus we can say:

$(23 - x)$ girls play netball but not hockey, and $(17 - x)$ girls play hockey but not netball.

We can therefore draw the Venn diagram:

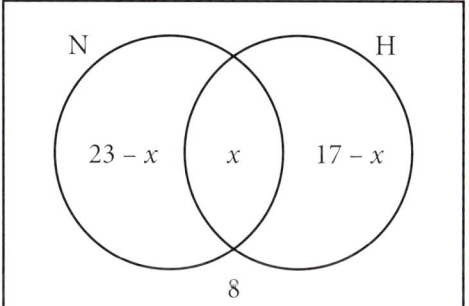

(b) The total number of girls is 42. The four parts of the Venn diagram must add up to this total.

Thus:     $42 = (23 - x) + x + (17 - x) + 8$
So:        $42 = 48 - x$
So:         $x = 48 - 42$
                = 6 girls who play both

(c) (i) There are 42 girls in total. 6 girls play both netball and hockey. So:

P(girl plays both netball and hockey)
$= \dfrac{6}{42} = \dfrac{1}{7}$

(ii) $23 - 6 = 17$ girls play netball but not hockey.

So: P(girl plays netball but not hockey) $= \dfrac{17}{42}$

You can also draw Venn diagrams with three circles.

4. There are 35 students in a class:
   2 students study Physics, Chemistry and Biology.
   6 students study Physics and Biology.
   9 students study Physics and Chemistry.
   5 students study Biology and Chemistry.
   18 students study Physics.
   21 students study Chemistry.
   10 students study Biology.
   (a) Draw a Venn diagram to show this information.
   (b) A student is chosen at random. Find the probability (i) that he/she studies only Physics; (ii) that he/she studies Chemistry but not Biology.

   (a)

   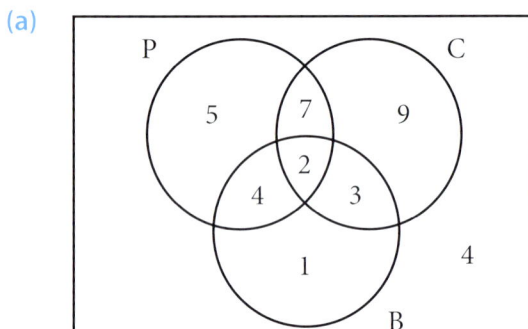

   (b) (i) 5 students study only Physics. So:

   $$P(\text{only Physics}) = \frac{5}{35} \text{ or } \frac{1}{7}$$

   (ii) From the Venn diagram, the number of students studying Chemistry but not Biology = 7 + 9 = 16. So:

   $$P(\text{Chemistry but not Biology}) = \frac{16}{35}$$

## Exercise 25B

1. There are 18 boys in a youth club.
   8 play rugby.
   12 play football.
   4 play neither rugby nor football.
   (a) Draw a Venn diagram to show this information.
   (b) Hence use the Venn diagram to find how many boys play both rugby and football.
   (c) A boy is chosen at random. Find the probability he: (i) plays both rugby and football; (ii) plays rugby but not football.

2. There are 31 boys in a form class.
   17 study Irish.
   19 study Spanish.
   3 study neither Irish nor Spanish.

## Exercise 25B

   (a) Draw a Venn diagram to show this information.
   (b) Hence use the Venn diagram to find how many boys study both Irish and Spanish.
   (c) A boy is chosen at random. Find the probability he: (i) studies only Irish; (ii) does not study Spanish.

3. There are 33 girls on a trip to a concert.
   18 buy a CD.
   21 buy a T-shirt.
   8 buy neither a CD nor a T-shirt.
   (a) Draw a Venn diagram to show this information.
   (b) Hence use the Venn diagram to find how many girls bought both a CD and a T-shirt.
   (c) A girl is chosen at random. Find the probability she: (i) buys neither a CD nor a T-shirt; (ii) buys both a CD and a T-shirt.

4. There are 55 books on a bookshelf.
   26 are hardback.
   8 are hardback romantic books.
   15 are neither hardback nor romantic.
   (a) Draw a Venn diagram to show this information.
   (b) Hence use the Venn diagram to find how many books are: (i) romantic but not hardback; (ii) romantic.
   (c) A book is chosen at random. Find the probability it is: (i) a hardback; (ii) neither hardback nor romantic.

5. There are 31 girls in a games club.
   21 play chess.
   13 play chess and draughts.
   4 play neither chess nor draughts.
   (a) Draw a Venn diagram to show this information.
   (b) Hence use the Venn diagram to find how many girls play only draughts.
   (c) A girl is chosen at random. Find the probability she plays: (i) both chess and draughts; (ii) only draughts.

6. 61 boys go to after-school activities.
   23 go to art club.
   25 go to computer club.
   22 go to neither art club nor computer club.

## Exercise 25B...

(a) Draw a Venn diagram to show this information.

(b) Hence use the Venn diagram to find how many boys go to both art club and computer club.

(c) A boy is chosen at random. Find the probability he goes to: (i) only the art club; (ii) both art club and computer club.

7. 36 people go out together for a meal.
22 have a starter.
22 have a dessert.
3 have neither a starter nor a dessert.

(a) Draw a Venn diagram to show this information.

(b) Hence use the Venn diagram to find how many have both a starter and a dessert

(c) A person is chosen at random. Find the probability the person has: (i) a starter; (ii) both a starter and a dessert.

8. There are 27 pupils in a class.
13 wear glasses.
7 are left-handed.
4 are left-handed and wear glasses.

(a) Draw a Venn diagram to show this information.

(b) Hence use the Venn diagram to find how many pupils are not left-handed and do not wear glasses.

(c) A pupil is chosen at random. Find the probability the pupil: (i) is left-handed and wear glasses; (ii) wears glasses but is not left-handed; (iii) is left-handed but does not wear glasses.

9. 32 people were asked how they drink coffee.
21 said they took milk with their coffee.
8 said they took milk and sugar with their coffee.
7 said they took neither milk nor sugar with their coffee.

(a) Draw a Venn diagram to show this information.

(b) Hence use the Venn diagram to find how many took sugar with their coffee .

(c) One of these people was chosen at random. Find the probability the person took: (i) milk and sugar with their coffee; (ii) sugar but not milk with their coffee; (iii) neither milk nor sugar with their coffee.

## Exercise 25B...

10. 60 teenagers were asked how they helped at home.
24 said they tidied up their rooms.
23 said they helped wash the dishes.
22 said they neither tidied up their rooms nor helped wash the dishes.

(a) Draw a Venn diagram to show this information.

(b) Hence use the Venn diagram to find how many tidied up their rooms and helped wash the dishes.

(c) One of these teenagers was chosen at random. Find the probability the teenager: (i) tidied up their room and helped wash the dishes; (ii) helped wash the dishes but did not tidy up their room; (iii) tidied up their room but did not help wash the dishes.

11. There are 55 teenagers in a youth club.
6 teenagers have a dog, cat and rabbit.
15 teenagers have a dog and cat.
10 teenagers have a dog and rabbit.
9 teenagers have a cat and rabbit.
33 teenagers have a dog.
30 teenagers have a cat.
15 teenagers have a rabbit.

(a) Draw a Venn diagram to show this information.

(b) A teenager is chosen at random. Find the probability that the teenager has: (i) a rabbit but not a cat; (ii) none of these pets.

12. 37 ladies in a club were discussing where they had been on holiday.
2 had been to Spain, France and Italy.
6 had been to Spain and France.
5 had been to Spain and Italy.
3 had been to France and Italy.
20 had been to Spain.
14 had been to France.
11 had been to Italy.

(a) Draw a Venn diagram to show this information.

(b) A lady is chosen at random. Find the probability that she has been to (i) Spain but not Italy; (ii) France and Italy but not Spain.

## 25.4 Conditional Probability

Conditional probability is when the probability of the second event is conditional on the first event having happened. The rules for conditional probability are:

a. **P(A|B)** means the probability that A will happen given that B has happened:

$$P(A|B) = \frac{P(A \text{ and } B)}{P(B)}$$

b. **P(B|A)** means the probability that B will happen given that A has happened:

$$P(B|A) = \frac{P(A \text{ and } B)}{P(A)}$$

For example:

.................................................................

5.  The probability a girl in a school plays netball is $\frac{5}{9}$.

    The probability a girl in a school plays hockey is $\frac{28}{45}$.

    The probability a girl in a school plays neither netball nor hockey is $\frac{2}{45}$.

    (a) Draw a Venn diagram to find the probability that a girl plays both netball and football.

    (b) Hence find the probability that a girl chosen at random plays (i) netball, given that she plays hockey; (ii) hockey, given that she plays netball.

    (a) Let the probability that a girl plays both netball and football be $p$.

    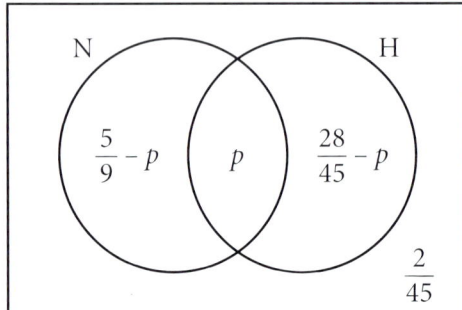

    Total of probabilities inside the Venn diagram

    $$= \frac{5}{9} - p + p + \frac{28}{45} - p + \frac{2}{45}$$

    $$= 1\frac{2}{9} - p$$

    But the total of the probabilities must add up to 1.

    So:   $1\frac{2}{9} - p = 1$

    Therefore:   $p = \frac{2}{9}$

(b) We know:

$P(\text{girl plays netball}) = \frac{5}{9}$

$P(\text{girl plays hockey}) = \frac{28}{45}$

$P(\text{girl plays netball and hockey}) = \frac{2}{9}$

(i) P(netball, given that she plays hockey)

$$= \frac{P(\text{girl plays netball and hockey})}{P(\text{girl plays hockey})}$$

$$= \frac{2}{9} \div \frac{28}{45}$$

$$= \frac{5}{14}$$

(ii) P(hockey, given that she plays netball)

$$= \frac{P(\text{girl plays netball and hockey})}{P(\text{girl plays netball})}$$

$$= \frac{2}{9} \div \frac{5}{9}$$

$$= \frac{2}{5}$$

.................................................................

6.  The probability that a boy chosen at random from Year 11 plays rugby is 0.6. If he plays rugby the probability that he plays football is 0.56. Otherwise the probability that he plays football is 0.73.

    (a) Draw a tree diagram to show all the possible outcomes.

    (b) Hence find the probability a boy chosen at random from Year 11 plays (i) rugby and football; (ii) football; (iii) rugby, if he plays football.

    (a)

    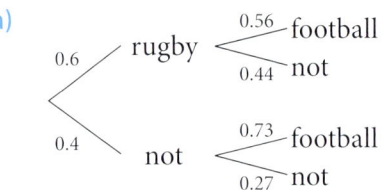

    (b) (i) P(boy plays rugby and football)
    = P(rugby) × P(football)
    = 0.6 × 0.56
    = 0.336

    (ii) P(boy plays football) = P(boy plays rugby and football) or P(boy does not play rugby and plays football)
    = 0.336 + (0.4 × 0.73)
    = 0.628

(iii) P(plays rugby if he plays football)

$$= \frac{\text{P(plays rugby and football)}}{\text{P(plays football)}}$$

$$= 0.336 \div 0.628$$

$$= 0.535$$

7. The probability Alan reads a book is $\frac{2}{7}$.

The probability he reads a magazine is $\frac{8}{13}$.

The probability he reads a book and a magazine is $\frac{12}{77}$.

Find the probability that Alan reads:
(a) a book if he reads a magazine;
(b) a magazine if he reads a book.

(a) P(reads a book if he reads a magazine)

$$= \frac{\text{P(reads a book and a magazine)}}{\text{P(reads a magazine)}}$$

$$= \frac{12}{77} \div \frac{8}{13}$$

$$= \frac{39}{154}$$

(b) P(reads a magazine if he reads a book)

$$= \frac{\text{P(reads a book and a magazine)}}{\text{P(reads a book)}}$$

$$= \frac{12}{77} \div \frac{2}{7}$$

$$= \frac{6}{11}$$

## Exercise 25C

1. 33 pupils go on a sports weekend.
   18 swim.
   14 play football.
   9 neither swim nor play football.
   (a) Draw a Venn diagram to find how many pupils swim and play football.
   (b) Hence find the probability: (i) a pupil swims but does not play football; (ii) a pupil swims given that he plays football; (iii) a pupil plays football given that he swims.

2. There are 34 pupils in a Year 12 form class.
   13 study History.
   22 study Geography.
   4 study neither History nor Geography.
   (a) Draw a Venn diagram to find how many pupils study both History and Geography.
   (b) Hence find the probability a pupil (i) studies only Geography; (ii) studies

## Exercise 25C

History given that they study Geography; (iii) studies Geography given that they study History.

3. There are 40 cars in a car park.
   23 are foreign-made.
   7 are red foreign-made cars.
   8 are neither red nor foreign made cars.
   (a) Draw a Venn diagram to find how many cars are red.
   (b) Hence find the probability a car (i) is red; (ii) is red given that it is foreign-made; (iii) is foreign-made given that it is red.

4. There are 39 people in a canteen.
   22 order chips.
   20 order ice cream.
   4 order neither chips nor ice cream.
   (a) Draw a Venn diagram to find how many order chips and ice cream.
   (b) Hence find the probability a person orders (i) chips or ice cream; (ii) chips given that she orders ice cream; (iii) ice cream given that she orders chips.

5. The probability Rory plays rugby is $\frac{4}{7}$.

   The probability Rory plays snooker is $\frac{2}{5}$.

   The probability Rory plays rugby and snooker is $\frac{1}{3}$.

   Find the probability Rory plays (i) rugby if he plays snooker; (ii) snooker if he plays rugby.

6. The probability it rains is 0.7. If it rains the probability Rachel goes for a swim is 0.84. Otherwise the probability Rachel goes for a swim is 0.35.
   (a) Draw a tree diagram to show all the possible outcomes.
   (b) Hence find the probability: (i) it rains and Rachel goes for a swim; (ii) Rachel goes for a swim; (iii) Rachel goes for a swim if it rains; (iv) it rains if Rachel goes for a swim.

7. The probability Caoimhe is late going for a train is 0.64. If Caoimhe is late the probability the train is late is 0.15. Otherwise the probability the train is late is 0.8.
   (a) Draw a tree diagram to show all the possible outcomes.

## Exercise 25C...

(b) Hence find the probability: (i) Caoimhe is late and the train is late; (ii) the train is late; (iii) Caoimhe is late if the train is late; (iv) the train is late if Caoimhe is late.

8. The probability David revises for his exam is $\frac{7}{9}$.

   If David revises the probability he passes is $\frac{4}{5}$.

   Otherwise the probability he passes is $\frac{1}{10}$.

   (a) Draw a tree diagram to show all the possible outcomes.
   (b) Hence find the probability: (i) David revises and he passes; (ii) David passes; (iii) David passes if he revises.

9. The probability of getting chips for dinner is $\frac{2}{9}$.

   The probability of getting ice cream for dessert is $\frac{1}{3}$.

   The probability of getting chips and ice cream is $\frac{1}{30}$.

   Show that it is more likely that you get ice cream given that you get chips rather than getting chips given that you get ice cream.

10. 91 pupils are in Year 12.
    46 of them went to a rock concert.
    35 of them went to a country concert.
    17 of them went to neither a rock concert nor a country concert.
    (a) Draw a Venn diagram to find how many pupils went to both concerts.
    (b) Hence find the probability a pupil chosen at random (i) goes to both a rock concert and a country concert; (ii) goes to the rock concert if the pupil went to the country concert.

11. The probability a car is British built is 0.56.
    The probability a car is blue is 0.4.
    The probability a car is a blue British-built car is 0.35.
    A car is chosen at random. Find the probability that:
    (a) the car is British-built if it is blue;
    (b) the car is blue if the car is British-built.

## Exercise 25C...

12. The probability that Sinéad passes Maths is 0.6.
    The probability Sinéad passes Further Maths is 0.45.
    The probability Sinéad passes both is 0.35.
    Find the probability Sinéad passes:
    (a) Maths if she passes Further Maths;
    (b) Further Maths if she passes Maths.

13. The probability Colin catches the flu is $\frac{3}{5}$.

    The probability Colin develops a chest infection is $\frac{4}{7}$.

    The probability Colin catches the flu and develops a chest infection is $\frac{4}{11}$.

    Find the probability Colin:
    (a) catches the flu if he develops a chest infection;
    (b) develops a chest infection if he catches the flu.

## 25.5 Harder Questions

Sometimes you are given some probabilities and have to work out others from these. For example:

8. The probability A and B happen is $\frac{8}{27}$.

   The probability B happens is $\frac{7}{9}$.

   The probability B happens given that A happens is $\frac{4}{9}$.

   Find:
   (a) The probability A happens given that B happens.
   (b) The probability A happens.

   (a) P(A happens given that B happens)
   $$= \frac{P(A \text{ and } B \text{ happen})}{P(B \text{ happens})}$$
   $$= \frac{8}{27} \div \frac{7}{9}$$
   $$= \frac{8}{21}$$

   (b) P(B happens given that A happens)
   $$= \frac{P(A \text{ and } B \text{ happen})}{P(A \text{ happens})}$$

   So: $\frac{4}{9} = \frac{8}{27} \div P(A \text{ happens})$

   So: $P(A \text{ happens}) = \frac{8}{27} \div \frac{4}{9}$
   $$= \frac{2}{3}$$

9. The probability A happens given that B happens is 0.72.
The probability B happens is 0.5.
The probability A happens is 0.9.
Find:
(a) the probability A and B happen
(b) the probability B happens given that A happens.

(a) P(A happens given that B happens)

$$= \frac{P(A \text{ and } B \text{ happen})}{P(B \text{ happens})}$$

So: $\qquad 0.72 = \dfrac{P(A \text{ and } B \text{ happen})}{0.5}$

So: P(A and B happen) = $0.72 \times 0.5$
$\qquad\qquad\qquad\qquad = 0.36$

(b) P(B happens given that A happens)

$$= \frac{P(A \text{ and } B \text{ happen})}{P(A \text{ happens})}$$

$$= \frac{0.36}{0.9}$$

$$= 0.4$$

## Exercise 25D

1. The probability A and B happen is 0.24. The probability B happens is 0.3. The probability B happens given that A happens is 0.48. Find:
   (a) the probability A happens given that B happens;
   (b) the probability A happens.

2. The probability A happens given that B happens is 0.88. The probability B happens is 0.25. The probability A happens is 0.4. Find:
   (a) the probability A and B happen;
   (b) the probability B happens given that A happens.

3. The probability A happens given that B happens is 0.32. The probability A and B happen is 0.16. The probability B happens given that A happens is 0.2. Find:
   (a) the probability B happens;
   (b) the probability A happens.

4. The probability A and B happen is 0.15. The probability B happens is 0.3. The probability B happens given that A happens is 0.75. Find:
   (a) the probability A happens given that B happens;
   (b) the probability A happens.

## Exercise 25D

5. The probability A happens given that B happens is 0.7. The probability A and B happen is 0.42. The probability A happens is 0.8. Find:
   (a) the probability B happens;
   (b) the probability B happens given that A happens.

6. The probability A happens given that B happens is $\dfrac{22}{35}$. The probability B happens is $\dfrac{4}{11}$. The probability A happens is $\dfrac{2}{5}$. Find:
   (a) the probability A and B happen;
   (b) the probability B happens given that A happens.

7. The probability A and B happen is 0.049. The probability B happens is 0.25. The probability B happens given that A happens is 0.14. Find:
   (a) the probability A happens given that B happens;
   (b) the probability A happens.

8. The probability A happens given that B happens is 0.256. The probability B happens is 0.15. The probability A happens is 0.24. Find:
   (a) the probability A and B happen;
   (b) the probability B happens given that A happens.

9. The probability A happens given that B happens is 0.896. The probability A and B happen is 0.2688. The probability B happens given that A happens is 0.84. Find:
   (a) the probability B happens;
   (b) the probability A happens.

10. The probability A and B happen is 0.3648. The probability B happens is 0.48. The probability B happens given that A happens is 0.608. Find:
    (a) the probability A happens given that B happens;
    (b) the probability A happens.

11. The probability A happens given that B happens is $\dfrac{5}{12}$. The probability A and B happen is $\dfrac{5}{32}$. The probability A happens is $\dfrac{7}{12}$. Find:
    (a) the probability B happens;
    (b) the probability B happens given that A happens.

## Exercise 25D...

12. The probability A happens given that B happens is $\frac{7}{12}$. The probability B happens is $\frac{5}{6}$. The probability A happens is $\frac{11}{12}$. Find:

    (a) the probability A and B happen;
    (b) the probability B happens given that A happens.

13. The probability A happens given that B happens is $\frac{39}{154}$. The probability A and B happen is $\frac{12}{77}$. The probability B happens given that A happens is $\frac{6}{11}$. Find:

    (a) the probability B happens;
    (b) the probability A happens.

## 25.6 'OR' Rule When Outcomes Are Not Mutually Exclusive

Where the outcomes A and B are not mutually exclusive then the probability of getting either A or B is given by:

P(A or B) = P(A) + P(B) – P(A and B)

This is written in set notation on the formula sheet as:

$P(A \cup B) = P(A) + P(B) - P(A \cap B)$

For example:

..................................................................

10. There are 100 pupils in a year group.
    64 study Chemistry.
    52 study Biology.
    36 study both Chemistry and Biology.
    A pupil is taken at random.
    Find the probability the pupil studies Chemistry or Biology.

    $P(\text{Chemistry}) = \frac{64}{100}$

    $P(\text{Biology}) = \frac{52}{100}$

    $P(\text{Chemistry and Biology}) = \frac{36}{100}$

    P(Chemistry or Biology) = P(Chemistry) + P(Biology) – P(Chemistry and Biology)

    So P(Chemistry or Biology)

    $= \frac{64}{100} + \frac{52}{100} - \frac{36}{100} = \frac{80}{100}$ or $\frac{4}{5}$ or 0.8.

## Exercise 25E

1. There are 40 people in a sports club.
   24 play football.
   17 play tennis.
   14 play both.
   A person is taken at random.
   Find the probability the person plays football or tennis.

2. There are 28 pupils in a class.
   18 have a dog.
   14 have a cat.
   23 have a dog or a cat.
   A pupil is taken at random.
   Find the probability the pupil has both a dog and a cat.

3. 200 people were surveyed.
   164 have a mobile phone.
   132 have a tablet.
   121 have both.
   A person is taken at random.
   Find the probability the person has a mobile phone or a tablet.

4. 56 people were at a reception lunch.
   50 chose either salad or chips with their main course.
   23 chose salad.
   41 chose chips.
   A person is taken at random.
   Find the probability the person chose both salad and chips.

5. 68 people were surveyed.
   42 drank tea or coffee.
   34 drank tea and coffee.
   26 drank tea.
   A person is taken at random.
   Find the probability the person drank coffee.

6. 30 people are in a gym for an afternoon session.
   29 go to body pump or spinning.
   14 go to body pump.
   7 go to both.
   A person is taken at random.
   Find the probability the person goes to spinning.

# CHAPTER 26: BINOMIAL DISTRIBUTION

## 26.1 Binomial Expansion

A **binomial** is an expression that is the sum of two terms, for example $p + q$.

A **binomial expansion** is the algebraic expansion of **powers** of a binomial, for example $(p + q)^2$.

A **binomial distribution** is the relationship between probabilities and the binomial expansion.

In chapter 1 we learned how to expand three brackets. We can now extend this process to expand powers of a bracket. We already know the expansions:

$(p + q)^1 = p + q$

$(p + q)^2 = p^2 + 2pq + q^2$

$(p + q)^3 = p^3 + 3p^2q + 3pq^2 + q^3$

We can now work out further expansions as follows:

$(p + q)^4 = (p + q)(p + q)^3$

$\quad = p(p^3 + 3p^2q + 3pq^2 + q^3) + q(p^3 + 3p^2q + 3pq^2 + q^3)$

$\quad = \quad p^4 + 3p^3q + 3p^2q^2 + \quad pq^3$

$\quad + \qquad p^3q + 3p^2q^2 + 3pq^3 + q^4$

$\qquad \overline{p^4 + 4p^3q + 6p^2q^2 + 4pq^3 + q^4}$

$(p + q)^5 = (p + q)(p + q)^4$

$\quad = p(p^4 + 4p^3q + 6p^2q^2 + 4pq^3 + q^1) + q(p^4 + 4p^3q$
$\quad + 6p^2q^2 + 4pq^3 + q^4)$

$\quad = \quad p^5 + 4p^4q + \quad 6p^3q^2 + \quad 6p^2q^3 + \quad pq^4$

$\quad + \qquad p^4q + \quad 4p^3q^2 + \quad 6p^2q^3 + 4pq^4 + q^5$

$\qquad \overline{p^5 + 5p^4q + 10p^3q^2 + 10p^2q^3 + 5pq^4 + q^5}$

Let us look at all these expansions together.

$(p + q)^1 = p + q$

$(p + q)^2 = p^2 + 2pq + q^2$

$(p + q)^3 = p^3 + 3p^2q + 3pq^2 + q^3$

$(p + q)^4 = p^4 + 4p^3q + 6p^2q^2 + 4pq^3 + q^4$

$(p + q)^5 = p^5 + 5p^4q + 10p^3q^2 + 10p^2q^3 + 5pq^4 + q^5$

The coefficients are:

$(p + q)^1 = 1 \; 1$

$(p + q)^2 = 1 \; 2 \; 1$

$(p + q)^3 = 1 \; 3 \; 3 \; 1$

$(p + q)^4 = 1 \; 4 \; 6 \; 4 \; 1$

$(p + q)^5 = 1 \; 5 \; 10 \; 10 \; 5 \; 1$

## 26.2 Pascal's Triangle

**Blaise Pascal** was a very famous French mathematician and philosopher who lived from 1623 to 1662. One of his most famous quotes combined the logic of probability with philosophy: "*Belief [in a deity] is a wise wager. Granted that faith cannot be proved, what harm will come to you if you gamble on its truth and it proves false? If you gain, you gain all; if you lose, you lose nothing. Wager, then, without hesitation, that He exists.*"

Pascal came up with a way to work out the coefficients of all the powers of $(p + q)$. He set the coefficients in a triangle known as **Pascal's triangle**. The CCEA specification only requires us to be able to expand as far as $(p + q)^8$. The diagram below shows Pascal's triangle up to power 8.

```
            1   1
          1   2   1
        1   3   3   1
      1   4   6   4   1
    1   5  10  10   5   1
  1   6  15  20  15   6   1
1   7  21  35  35  21   7   1
1   8  28  56  70  56  28   8   1
```

To work out any coefficient you simply add the two numbers above it in the previous line. For example:

Line 5:

$\quad 5 = 1 + 4, 10 = 4 + 6$, etc.

Line 8:

$\quad 8 = 1 + 7, 28 = 7 + 21, 56 = 21 + 35, 70 = 35 + 35$, etc.

In each expansion the powers of $p$ decrease in ones, from the power of the expansion to zero power, i.e.:

The powers of $p$ in $(p + q)^2$ are 2, 1 and 0.
The powers of $p$ in $(p + q)^3$ are 3, 2, 1 and 0.
The powers of $p$ in $(p + q)^4$ are 4, 3, 2, 1 and 0.
The powers of $p$ in $(p + q)^5$ are 5, 4, 3, 2, 1 and 0.

Also, in each expansion the powers of $q$ increase in ones from zero to the power of the expansion, i.e.:

The powers of $q$ in $(p + q)^2$ are 0, 1 and 2.
The powers of $q$ in $(p + q)^3$ are 0, 1, 2 and 3.
The powers of $q$ in $(p + q)^4$ are 0, 1, 2, 3 and 4.
The powers of $p$ in $(p + q)^5$ are 0, 1, 2, 3, 4 and 5.

We can now use Pascal's triangle to work out the remainder of the expansions. These are:

$(p + q)^6 =$
$p^6 + 6p^5q + 15p^4q^2 + 20p^3q^3 + 15p^2q^4 + 6pq^5 + q^6$

$(p + q)^7 =$
$p^7 + 7p^6q + 21p^5q^2 + 35p^4q^3 + 35p^3q^4 + 21p^2q^5 + 7pq^6 + q^7$

$(p + q)^8 =$
$p^8 + 8p^7q + 28p^6q^2 + 56p^5q^3 + 70p^4q^4 + 56p^3q^5 + 28p^2q^6 + 8pq^7 + q^8$

## 26.3 Binomial Distribution

We can now apply the binomial expansion to work out probability. Let:

$p$ = the probability of an event happening;

$q$ = the probability of an event not happening, i.e. = $1 - p$.

Then to work out the probability that an event happens $r$ times out of a total of $n$ times we substitute appropriate values into the $r$th term in the expansion. For example:

1. The probability Roger beats Novak in a tennis match is 0.76. They play 6 tennis matches. Work out the probability Roger beats Novak in 4 of these matches.

   We need to use the expansion $(p + q)^6$. We need the term including $p^4$. This term will also then include the term $q^2$. Row 6 of Pascal's triangle tells us that the coefficient of this term will be 15. So the term we need is $15p^4q^2$. We can then write down the values of $p$, $q$ and $n$:

   $p = 0.76$
   $q = 1 - 0.76 = 0.24$
   $n = 6$

   So:   $P(4) = 15p^4q^2 = 15(0.76)^4(0.24)^2$
   $= 0.2882492 = 0.29$ to 2 decimal places

### Exercise 26A

1. A box contains a large number of black balls and white balls. The probability of taking a black ball at random from the box is 0.84. Cadence takes 6 balls. Work out the probability that she takes 4 black balls.

2. A bag contains a large number of cards, some of which are blank and some of which are numbered. The probability of taking a numbered card is ²⁄₅. Ciaran takes 5 cards. Work out the probability that he takes 3 numbered cards.

3. There are a large number of bananas in a crate. The probability that a banana taken at random is bad is 15%. Willow takes 7 bananas. Work out the probability that she takes 2 bad bananas.

### Exercise 26A...

4. The probability of getting a 5 on a biased dice is ²⁄₉. Ronan tosses this biased dice 4 times. Work out the probability that he gets 5 three times.

5. The probability that Lily visits her granny on any day is 0.8. Work out the probability that she visits her granny on 5 days during a week.

6. The probability a boy has a birthday on a Saturday is ¹⁄₇. 8 boys are taken at random. Work out the probability that 3 of these boys have a birthday on a Saturday.

7. 4% of light bulbs in a batch are faulty. 5 are taken from the batch at random. Work out the probability that 2 of them are faulty.

## 26.4 Harder Questions

Binomial distributions can allow us to solve more complex problems. For example:

2. The probability Arlene goes to a class in her gym is 90%. There are 8 classes this week. Work out the probability that:
   (a) Arlene goes to 3 of them;
   (b) Arlene goes to at least 6 classes;
   (c) Arlene goes to at most 1 class.

   We need to use the expansion $(p + q)^8$.

   (a) We need the term including $p^3$. This term will also then include the term $q^5$. Row 8 of Pascal's triangle tells us that the coefficient of this term will be 56. So the term we need is $56p^3q^5$. We can then write down the values of $p$, $q$ and $n$:
   $p = 90\% = 0.9$ (Always work in decimals or fractions but not percentages)
   $q = 1 - 0.9 = 0.1$
   $n = 8$
   So:      $P(3) = 56p^3q^5 = 56(0.9)^3(0.1)^5$
   $= 0.000408$
   $= 0.00041$ to 2 significant figures

   (b) The phrase 'at least 6' means 6 or 7 or 8. So we need the terms including $p^6$, $p^7$ and $p^8$. These terms will also then include the term $q^2$, $q$ and then only the $p^8$ term. Row 8 of Pascal's triangle tells us that the coefficients of these terms will be 28, 8 and 1. So the terms we need are $28p^6q^2$, $8p^7q$ and $p^8$. We can then write down the values of $p$ and $q$:

$p = 0.9$
$q = 0.1$

So: P(at least 6) $= 28p^6q^2 + 8p^7q + p^8$
$= 28(0.9)^6(0.1)^2 + 8(0.9)^7(0.1) + (0.9)^8$
$= 0.9619… = 0.96$ to 2 significant figures

(c) The phrase 'at most 1' means 0 or 1. So the terms we need are $q^8 + 8pq^7$. Hence:
$p = 0.9$
$q = 0.1$

So: P(at most 1) $= (0.1)^8 + 8(0.9)(0.1)^7$
$= 0.00000073$ to 2 significant figures

## Exercise 26B

1. A box contains a large number of balls. 10% are red, 20% are green, 30% are pink and 40% are silver. 8 people each take a ball in turn at random, note its colour and then replace it in the box. Work out the probability, to 3 significant figures, that:
   (a) 5 of the balls are red;
   (b) at least 2 of the balls are silver;
   (c) at most 1 ball is green.

2. 36% of the people on a cruise are Irish. 8 people on the cruise are selected at random. Work out the probability, to 3 significant figures, that:
   (a) 2 of them are Irish;
   (b) at least 1 is Irish;
   (c) half are Irish.

3. The ratio of men to women in a night class is 2:3. 5 people are selected at random. Work out the probability, to 3 significant figures, that:
   (a) 2 of them are women;
   (b) at least 4 are women;
   (c) more women than men are taken.

4. The probability that a bus is late is 0.12. Willow travels on 4 buses per day. Work out the probability that:
   (a) none is late, to 1 decimal place;
   (b) 3 are late, to 2 significant figures;
   (c) at most 2 are late, to 3 significant figures.

5. 85% of seeds sown by Quinn germinate. A sample of 7 seeds is taken at random. Work out the probability, to 3 significant figures, that:
   (a) 1 will germinate;
   (b) at least 5 will germinate;
   (c) 3 will not germinate.

# CHAPTER 27: NORMAL DISTRIBUTION

## 27.1 Definitions

Consider tossing a coin 4 times. We can work out the probabilities of getting 0 heads, 1 head, 2 heads, 3 heads and 4 heads.

### 0 Heads
There is only one possible outcome:
    TTTT
So P(0H) = ½ × ½ × ½ × ½ = ¹⁄₁₆

### 1 Head
There are 4 possible outcomes:
    HTTT
    THTT
    TTHT
    TTTH
The probability of each of these outcomes is ¹⁄₁₆.
So P(1H) = ⁴⁄₁₆

### 2 Heads
There are 6 possible outcomes:
    HHTT
    HTHT
    HTTH
    THHT
    THTH
    TTHH
The probability of each of these outcomes is ¹⁄₁₆.
So P(2H) = ⁶⁄₁₆

### 3 Heads
There are 4 possible outcomes:
    HHHT
    HHTH
    HTHH
    THHH
The probability of each of these outcomes is ¹⁄₁₆.
So P(3H) = ⁴⁄₁₆

### 4 Heads
There is only one possible outcome:
    HHHH
P(4H) = ¹⁄₁₆

We can now draw these probabilities on a probability curve. The probability curve is a bell shape as shown in the diagram. Note how the probability curve is symmetrical about the mean. In this example, the mean of 0, 1, 2, 3 and 4 is 10 ÷ 5 = 2, marked with a dotted line.

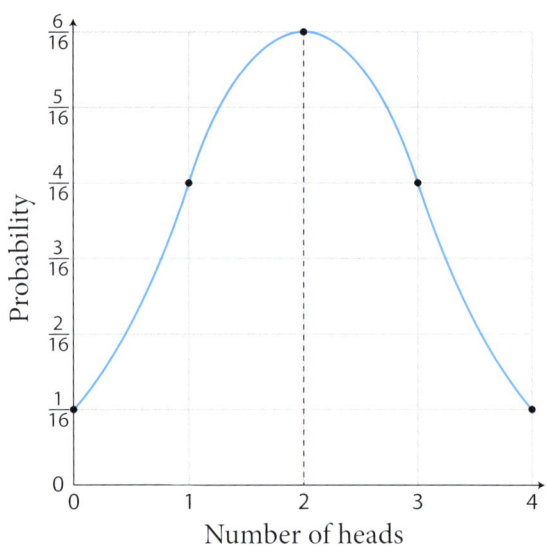

The curve we have drawn is called a **normal probability curve**. The curve is:
• bell shaped;
• symmetrical about the mean;
• has a total area underneath it of 1.

All normal distributions have the same properties and can be represented by similar normal probability curves.

## 27.2 Standardised Normal Distributions

We can standardise all normal distributions by changing the actual scores, $x$, to standard scores, $z$ using the relationship:

$$z = \frac{x - \mu}{\sigma}$$

where:   $\mu$ = the mean of the distribution
         $\sigma$ = the standard deviation of the distribution

The mean of every normal distribution would then have a $z$ score of 0. The normal probability table on the next page gives the areas under the curve and to the left of $z$ for different values of $z$. It only gives the area for positive values of $z$. However, we can find the areas for negative values of $z$ because the curve is symmetrical. In this case the table gives us the area under the curve and to the right of the negative value of $z$.

# Normal Probability Table

| z | 0.00 | 0.01 | 0.02 | 0.03 | 0.04 | 0.05 | 0.06 | 0.07 | 0.08 | 0.09 |
|---|------|------|------|------|------|------|------|------|------|------|
| 0.0 | 0.5000 | 0.5040 | 0.5080 | 0.5120 | 0.5160 | 0.5199 | 0.5239 | 0.5279 | 0.5319 | 0.5359 |
| 0.1 | 0.5398 | 0.5438 | 0.5478 | 0.5517 | 0.5557 | 0.5596 | 0.5636 | 0.5675 | 0.5714 | 0.5753 |
| 0.2 | 0.5793 | 0.5832 | 0.5871 | 0.5910 | 0.5948 | 0.5987 | 0.6026 | 0.6064 | 0.6103 | 0.6141 |
| 0.3 | 0.6179 | 0.6217 | 0.6255 | 0.6293 | 0.6331 | 0.6368 | 0.6406 | 0.6443 | 0.6480 | 0.6517 |
| 0.4 | 0.6554 | 0.6591 | 0.6628 | 0.6664 | 0.6700 | 0.6736 | 0.6772 | 0.6808 | 0.6844 | 0.6879 |
| 0.5 | 0.6915 | 0.6950 | 0.6985 | 0.7019 | 0.7054 | 0.7088 | 0.7123 | 0.7157 | 0.7190 | 0.7224 |
| 0.6 | 0.7257 | 0.7291 | 0.7324 | 0.7357 | 0.7389 | 0.7422 | 0.7454 | 0.7486 | 0.7517 | 0.7549 |
| 0.7 | 0.7580 | 0.7611 | 0.7642 | 0.7673 | 0.7704 | 0.7734 | 0.7764 | 0.7794 | 0.7823 | 0.7852 |
| 0.8 | 0.7881 | 0.7910 | 0.7939 | 0.7967 | 0.7995 | 0.8023 | 0.8051 | 0.8078 | 0.8106 | 0.8133 |
| 0.9 | 0.8159 | 0.8186 | 0.8212 | 0.8238 | 0.8264 | 0.8289 | 0.8315 | 0.8340 | 0.8365 | 0.8389 |
| 1.0 | 0.8413 | 0.8438 | 0.8461 | 0.8485 | 0.8508 | 0.8531 | 0.8554 | 0.8577 | 0.8599 | 0.8621 |
| 1.1 | 0.8643 | 0.8665 | 0.8686 | 0.8708 | 0.8729 | 0.8749 | 0.8770 | 0.8790 | 0.8810 | 0.8830 |
| 1.2 | 0.8849 | 0.8869 | 0.8888 | 0.8907 | 0.8925 | 0.8944 | 0.8962 | 0.8980 | 0.8997 | 0.9015 |
| 1.3 | 0.9032 | 0.9049 | 0.9066 | 0.9082 | 0.9099 | 0.9115 | 0.9131 | 0.9147 | 0.9162 | 0.9177 |
| 1.4 | 0.9192 | 0.9207 | 0.9222 | 0.9236 | 0.9251 | 0.9265 | 0.9279 | 0.9292 | 0.9306 | 0.9319 |
| 1.5 | 0.9332 | 0.9345 | 0.9357 | 0.9370 | 0.9382 | 0.9394 | 0.9406 | 0.9418 | 0.9429 | 0.9441 |
| 1.6 | 0.9452 | 0.9463 | 0.9474 | 0.9484 | 0.9495 | 0.9505 | 0.9515 | 0.9525 | 0.9535 | 0.9545 |
| 1.7 | 0.9554 | 0.9564 | 0.9573 | 0.9582 | 0.9591 | 0.9599 | 0.9608 | 0.9616 | 0.9625 | 0.9633 |
| 1.8 | 0.9641 | 0.9649 | 0.9656 | 0.9664 | 0.9671 | 0.9678 | 0.9686 | 0.9693 | 0.9699 | 0.9706 |
| 1.9 | 0.9713 | 0.9719 | 0.9726 | 0.9732 | 0.9738 | 0.9744 | 0.9750 | 0.9756 | 0.9761 | 0.9767 |
| 2.0 | 0.9772 | 0.9778 | 0.9783 | 0.9788 | 0.9793 | 0.9798 | 0.9803 | 0.9808 | 0.9812 | 0.9817 |
| 2.1 | 0.9821 | 0.9826 | 0.9830 | 0.9834 | 0.9838 | 0.9842 | 0.9846 | 0.9850 | 0.9854 | 0.9857 |
| 2.2 | 0.9861 | 0.9864 | 0.9868 | 0.9871 | 0.9875 | 0.9878 | 0.9881 | 0.9884 | 0.9887 | 0.9890 |
| 2.3 | 0.9893 | 0.9896 | 0.9898 | 0.9901 | 0.9904 | 0.9906 | 0.9909 | 0.9911 | 0.9913 | 0.9916 |
| 2.4 | 0.9918 | 0.9920 | 0.9922 | 0.9925 | 0.9927 | 0.9929 | 0.9931 | 0.9932 | 0.9934 | 0.9936 |
| 2.5 | 0.9938 | 0.9940 | 0.9941 | 0.9943 | 0.9945 | 0.9946 | 0.9948 | 0.9949 | 0.9951 | 0.9952 |
| 2.6 | 0.9953 | 0.9955 | 0.9956 | 0.9957 | 0.9959 | 0.9960 | 0.9961 | 0.9962 | 0.9963 | 0.9964 |
| 2.7 | 0.9965 | 0.9966 | 0.9967 | 0.9968 | 0.9969 | 0.9970 | 0.9971 | 0.9972 | 0.9973 | 0.9974 |
| 2.8 | 0.9974 | 0.9975 | 0.9976 | 0.9977 | 0.9977 | 0.9978 | 0.9979 | 0.9979 | 0.9980 | 0.9981 |
| 2.9 | 0.9981 | 0.9982 | 0.9982 | 0.9983 | 0.9984 | 0.9984 | 0.9985 | 0.9985 | 0.9986 | 0.9986 |
| 3.0 | 0.9987 | 0.9987 | 0.9987 | 0.9988 | 0.9988 | 0.9989 | 0.9989 | 0.9989 | 0.9990 | 0.9990 |
| 3.1 | 0.9990 | 0.9991 | 0.9991 | 0.9991 | 0.9992 | 0.9992 | 0.9992 | 0.9992 | 0.9993 | 0.9993 |
| 3.2 | 0.9993 | 0.9993 | 0.9994 | 0.9994 | 0.9994 | 0.9994 | 0.9994 | 0.9995 | 0.9995 | 0.9995 |
| 3.3 | 0.9995 | 0.9995 | 0.9995 | 0.9996 | 0.9996 | 0.9996 | 0.9996 | 0.9996 | 0.9996 | 0.9997 |
| 3.4 | 0.9997 | 0.9997 | 0.9997 | 0.9997 | 0.9997 | 0.9997 | 0.9997 | 0.9997 | 0.9997 | 0.9998 |

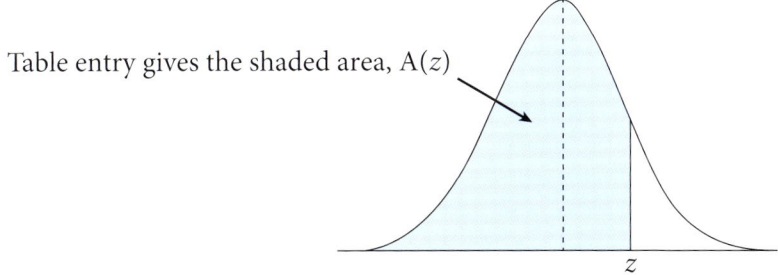

Table entry gives the shaded area, $A(z)$

For example:

....................................................................

1. Use the normal probability table to find:
   (a) P($z < 1.4$)
   (b) P($z > 1.4$)
   (c) P($z < -2.38$)
   (d) P($z > -2.38$)

   (a) For P($z < 1.4$), go down the extreme left hand column under $z$ to 1.4 and read off the value under 0.00. This is the answer we need since the area needed is the whole area to the left of 1.4.

   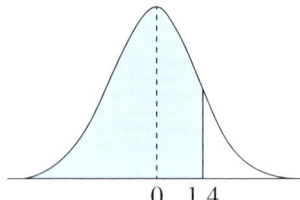

   So:  Answer = 0.9192

   (b) For P($z > 1.4$), go down the extreme left hand column under $z$ to 1.4 and read off the value under 0.00. We then have to subtract this from 1 since the area needed is the area to the right of 1.4 (remembering that the whole area under the bell shape is 1).

   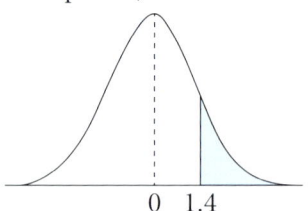

   So:  Answer = 1 − 0.9192 = 0.0808

   (c) For P($z < -2.38$), remember that the curve is symmetrical and that the table only gives the values for positive $z$. So we need to find the area corresponding to $z = 2.38$. We go down the extreme left hand column under $z$ to 2.3 and read off the value under 0.08. This gives 0.9913. This means that the area to the *right* of −2.38 is 0.9913. However we want the area to the *left* of −2.38.

   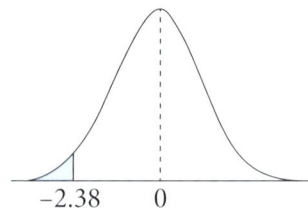

   So:  Answer = 1 − 0.9913 = 0.0087

   (d) For P ($z > -2.38$), we want the area to the right of −2.38. Again, remember that the curve is symmetrical and that the table only gives the values for positive $z$. So we need to find the area corresponding to $z = 2.38$. We go down the extreme left hand column under $z$ to 2.3 and read off the value under 0.08.

   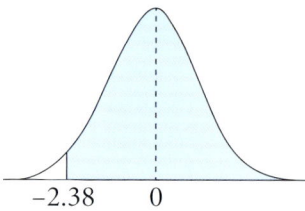

   So:  Answer = 0.9913

**Exercise 27A**: *Use the normal probability table to find the following:*

1. (a) P($z < 0.79$)     4. (a) P($z < -1$)
   (b) P($z > 0.79$)          (b) P($z > -1$)

2. (a) P($z < -2.14$)    5. (a) P($z < 1.64$)
   (b) P($z > -2.14$)        (b) P($z > 1.64$)

3. (a) P($z < 2.53$)     6. (a) P($z < 0.64$)
   (b) P($z > 2.53$)         (b) P($z > 0.64$)

## 27.3 Non-Standardised Normal Distributions

Sometimes we are given a distribution which first needs to be standardised before we can work out probabilities. For example:

....................................................................

2. The heights of objects are normally distributed with mean 10.8 cm and standard deviation 1.5 cm.
   (a) Find the probability that the height of an object chosen at random is greater than 14.4 cm.
   (b) Find the probability that the height of an object chosen at random is less than 8.7 cm.
   (c) Find the probability that the height of an object chosen at random is greater than 9.69 cm.
   (d) Find the probability that the height of an object chosen at random is less than 13.29 cm.

   (a) We must first find the value for $z$ where:
   $x = 14.4$
   $\mu = 10.8$
   $\sigma = 1.5$

Using: $z = \dfrac{x - \mu}{\sigma}$

$z = \dfrac{14.4 - 10.8}{1.5}$

$= \dfrac{3.6}{1.5}$

$= 2.4$

We then use the normal probability table as before.

So:    $A(2.4) = 0.9918$

However, we need the probability that the height of the object is *greater* than 14.4 cm.

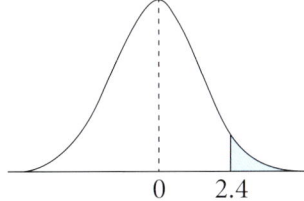

So:    Answer = $1 - 0.9918 = 0.0082$

(b)  We must first find the value for *z* where:

$x = 8.7$

$\mu = 10.8$

$\sigma = 1.5$

Using: $z = \dfrac{x - \mu}{\sigma}$

$z = \dfrac{8.7 - 10.8}{1.5}$

$= \dfrac{-2.1}{1.5}$

$= -1.4$

We then use the normal probability table as before.

So:    $A(-1.4) = 0.9192$

However, we need the probability that the height of the object is *less* than 8.7 cm.

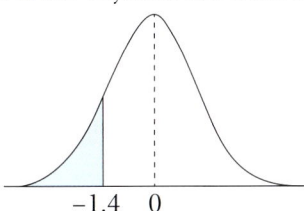

So:    Answer = $1 - 0.9192 = 0.0808$

(c)  We must first find the value for *z* where:

$x = 9.69$

$\mu = 10.8$

$\sigma = 1.5$

Using: $z = \dfrac{x - \mu}{\sigma}$

$z = \dfrac{9.69 - 10.8}{1.5}$

$= \dfrac{-1.11}{1.5}$

$= -0.74$

We then use the normal probability table as before. $A(-0.74) = A(0.74)$.

So:   $A(-0.74) = 0.7704$

We need the probability that the height of the object is greater than 9.69 cm, so this is the value we need.

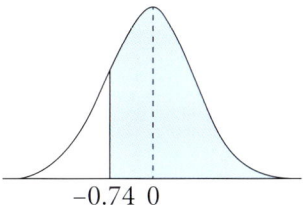

So:    Answer = 0.7704

(d)  We must first find the value for *z* where:

$x = 13.29$

$\mu = 10.8$

$\sigma = 1.5$

Using: $z = \dfrac{x - \mu}{\sigma}$

$z = \dfrac{13.29 - 10.8}{1.5}$

$= \dfrac{2.49}{1.5}$

$= 1.66$

We then use the normal probability table as before.

So:    $A(1.66) = 0.9515$

We need the probability that the height of the object is less than 13.29 cm, so this is the value we need.

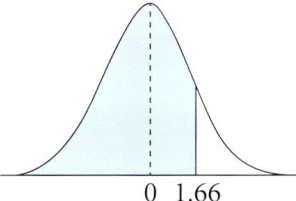

So:    Answer = 0.9515

## Exercise 27B

1. The marks in a test are normally distributed with mean 55 and standard deviation 5. Find the probability that a student taken at random scored over 63.

2. The weights of objects are normally distributed with mean 8.4 N and standard deviation 0.2 N. Find the probability that an object taken at random is lighter than 8.146 N.

3. The ages of people in a club are normally distributed with mean 14.8 years and standard deviation 2.5 years. Find the probability that a person taken at random is over 20.4 years old.

4. The marks in a test are normally distributed with mean 48 and standard deviation 1.2. Find the probability that a student taken at random scored under 44.7.

5. The weights of objects are normally distributed with mean 12.6 N and standard deviation 3.5 N. Find the probability that an object taken at random is lighter than 16.94 N.

6. The ages of people in a gym are normally distributed with mean 22.5 years and standard deviation 5.8 years. Find the probability that a person taken at random is under 30.62 years old.

7. The marks in a test are normally distributed with mean 52 and standard deviation 2.4. Find the probability that a student taken at random scored over 49.

8. The weights of objects are normally distributed with mean 36.4 N and standard deviation 4.2 N. Find the probability that an object taken at random is heavier than 47.11 N.

9. The ages of people in a club are normally distributed with mean 15.8 years and standard deviation 4.5 years. Find the probability that a person taken at random is under 12.38 years old.

10. The marks in a test are normally distributed with mean 64 and standard deviation 5.3. Find the probability that a student taken at random scored under 78.31.

11. The weights of objects are normally distributed with mean 7.4 N and standard deviation 1.35 N. Find the probability that an object taken at random is heavier than 4.16 N.

## Exercise 27B...

12. The ages of people in a night class are normally distributed with mean 21.5 years and standard deviation 6.25 years. Find the probability that a person taken at random is over 13.25 years old.

## 27.4 Normal Distributions With Groups

Sometimes the values in a set are grouped, for example into exam grades. Sometimes you are asked to use a normal distribution to determine the group a particular piece of data is in. For example:

3. The weights of a set of objects are normally distributed with mean 7 kg and standard deviation 2.5 kg. Objects with weights less than 5 kg are classified as 'small'. Objects with weights more than 10 kg are classified as 'large'. The other objects are classified as 'normal'.
   (a) Work out the probability that an object taken at random is 'large'.
   (b) Work out the probability that an object taken at random is not 'small'.

   (a) We must first find the value for $z$ where:
   $x = 10$
   $\mu = 7$
   $\sigma = 2.5$

   So: $$z = \frac{10 - 7}{2.5}$$
   $$= 1.2$$

   We then use the normal probability table as before.
   So: $A(1.2) = 0.8849$

   However, this is the probability that the object is *not* 'large'.

   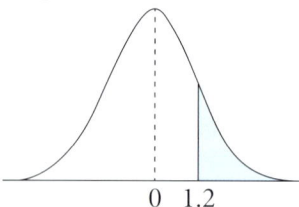

   So: Answer $= 1 - 0.8849 = 0.1151$

   (b) We must first find the value for $z$ where:
   $x = 5$
   $\mu = 7$
   $\sigma = 2.5$

So:         $z = \dfrac{5 - 7}{2.5}$

            $= -0.8$

We then use the normal probability table as before. $A(-0.8) = A(0.8)$.
So:       $A(0.8) = 0.7881$

This is the probability that the object is not 'small', so it is the value we need.

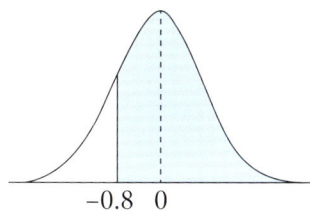

$-0.8$  $0$

So:     Answer $= 0.7881$

## Exercise 27C

1.  The marks in an exam are normally distributed with mean 62 and standard deviation 1.6. The possible grades are C, B and A. The lowest mark getting grade A is 64. Find the probability that a student taken at random gets grade A.

2.  The sizes of shirts are normally distributed with mean 14.6 and standard deviation 2.5. The shirts are classified as 'small', 'medium' and 'large'. The greatest 'small' shirt size is 10. Find the probability that a shirt taken at random is 'small'.

3.  The marks in an exam are normally distributed with mean 66 and standard deviation 8. The pass mark is 52. Find the probability that a student taken at random passes the exam.

4.  The weights of a set of objects are normally distributed with mean 8 kg and standard deviation 1.25 kg. Objects with weights less than 5 kg are classified as 'small'. Objects with weights more than 10.25 kg are classified as 'large'. The other objects are classified as 'normal'. One object is taken at random. Work out the probability that it is:
    (a)   'small';
    (b)   not 'large'.

5.  The marks in an exam are normally distributed with mean 63.8 and standard deviation 5. The possible grades are C, B and A. The minimum mark needed to get grade C is 55. The minimum mark needed to get grade B is 59. The minimum mark needed to get grade A is 70.

## Exercise 27C...

Find the probability that a student taken at random:
(a)   gets at least grade C;
(b)   gets at least grade B;
(c)   gets grade A;
(d)   does not get a grade.

6.  The marks in an exam are normally distributed with mean 64 and standard deviation 4. The pass mark is 67.
    (a)   What percentage of people pass the exam?
    (b)   If 30,000 people sat the exam how many would be expected to fail?

# Unit 4: Discrete and Decision Mathematics

## CHAPTER 28: COUNTING

### 28.1 The Multiplication And Addition Principles

Imagine you are choosing your first car and have narrowed the choice down to 2 simple considerations:

• Model – either a Skoda, Smart or a Honda, and

• Colour – either red, blue, silver or black

Thus you have 3 choices of model and 4 choices of colour. You can list out the full range of possibilities – for example a red Honda, a Silver Skoda or a blue Smart – and so on, but how can you be sure to include all of the alternatives?

The key idea is to use a **systematic** method for constructing your list. One system might be to list every possibility by model, meaning to list all the colours of one model and then go on to the next model and so on. For example:

Red Skoda, Blue Skoda, Silver Skoda, Black Skoda,
Red Smart, Blue Smart, Silver Smart, Black Smart,
Red Honda, Blue Honda, Silver Honda or Black Honda.

Equally, you could have listed the alternatives by colour first, in which case the list would look like this:

Red Skoda, Red Smart, Red Honda,
Blue Skoda, Blue Smart, Blue Honda,
Silver Skoda, Silver Smart, Silver Honda,
Black Skoda, Black Smart or Black Honda.

In either case, the number of alternatives equals:

$4 \times 3$ or $3 \times 4 = 12$

This is known as the **multiplication principle** which states that:

If    a choice is made from Option List 1 and a second choice is made from Option List 2 and

   • Option List 1 contains $N$ possibilities

   • Option List 2 contains $M$ possibilities

Then **the number of combined choices is $N \times M$ (1 from List 1 AND 1 from List 2)** .

Now suppose that a pupil is choosing GCSE subjects and is told that they must take one subject from either of two lists:

| List 1 |
| --- |
| English Language |
| English Literature |
| French |
| German |
| Spanish |

| List 2 |
| --- |
| History |
| Geography |
| Business Studies |
| ICT |

In this case, the choice is obviously the same as making a choice from an overall list of 9 subjects. This is known as the **addition principle** which states that:

If    a choice is made from either Option List 1 or from Option List 2, given there are no elements in common between the 2 lists, and

   • Option List 1 contains $N$ possibilities

   • Option List 2 contains $M$ possibilities

Then **the number of combined choices is $N + M$ (1 from List 1 OR 1 from List 2)**.

Frequently these two principles are combined in an options scenario. For example:

1. The menu for the Grand School End-of-Year Banquet comprises three courses with one choice from each, as shown below. How many possible different three-course meals are there?

| Starters |
| --- |
| Melon |
| Mussels |
| French Cheese |
| Onion Soup |
| Forest Mushrooms |

| Main Courses |
| --- |
| Steak and Onions |
| Liver and Bacon |
| Chicken Maryland |
| Spaghetti Carbonara |

OR

| Vegetarian Main Courses |
| --- |
| Stuffed Aubergines |
| Nut Roast |
| Pasta and Pine Nuts |

| Desserts |
| --- |
| Choice of Ice Creams |
| Chocolate Pudding |
| Toffee Dumplings |
| Fruit Salad |
| Stuffed Pears |
| Meringues and Peaches |

The number of possible different meals is one choice from 5 starters then either one from 4 or one from 3 main courses and finally one from 6 desserts. So the total number of possible meals is:

$5 \times (4 + 3) \times 6$
= 210 possible different meals.

## Exercise 28A

1. Freda's garden has a large flowerbed planted with border plants around the edges and bulbs and bushes in the middle. She must choose one type of border plant from a list of 7, one type of bulb from daffodils, tulips, crocuses or lilies and one type of shrub from azalea, fushia or rhododendron. How many different flowerbeds may she create?

2. Padraig makes his dinner every night. He chooses one from lettuce, spinach, green beans or peas; together with one from ham, chicken or sausage; accompanied by one of tomato sauce or burger relish. Then how many different dinners may he make?

3. To be promoted in a particular business an employee must:
   • Be recommended by one of the three supervisors, and
   • Make their excellence performance target in any one of the five responsibility areas, and
   • Either work late or come in early every day.
   In how many ways may promotion come about?

4. Belfast Slow Walking Association propose criteria for their lifetime slowness award. These are:

## Exercise 28A...

   • Traverse one of the 7 main streets slower than anyone else, and
   • Take longer than 10 minutes to walk 100 m in Bedford St, Donegal Rd or Laganside, and
   • Either walk, leap and jump around City Hall or hop along Royal Avenue.
   In how many ways might someone obtain this award?

5. An electric circuit consists of five resistors in parallel, joined in series to a further seven resistors which are joined in parallel. Along how many different routes may electricity flow in this circuit?

6. Another circuit consists of five resistors in series connected in parallel to seven resistors joined in series. Along how many different routes may electricity flow in this circuit?

7. Five roads link Quincey to Marllborough, a sea port. Four different roads link Quincey to Arlington, which is also a sea port. Arlington port is connected by two different shipping lanes to Arles port. Marlborough port is connected by three shipping lanes to La Bongais port. Arles is connected by a single motorway to Etien. La Bongais is connected by two different roads to Etien. How many different routes may a traveller take from Quincey to Etien?

8. There are 7 different small marbles in a jar, 4 different large marbles in a cup, 15 shells in a box, and 23 different playing cards in a packet. Jason picks three items – a marble, a shell and a playing card. In how many different ways may he do this?

## 28.2 Counting Arrangements

Imagine a child has forgotten the code sequence to open the digital lock on their toy treasure chest. There are four buttons – a cow, a horse, a pig and a donkey. These have to be pushed in the correct sequence to open the lid. The child begins by trying:

Cow, Horse, Pig, Donkey

Nothing happens. They then try:

Pig, Cow, Donkey, Horse

Nothing happens. They then try:

Horse, Donkey, Cow, Pig

How long can this process go on for? Close the book and attempt to write out all the combinations that the child could try. What is the best way to be sure that you have included all the possibilities? As before, it is important to use a **systematic** order to list all the possibilities.

One method is to keep the first animal the same each time until all of those possibilities have been exhausted. Then try the next animal, and so on for all four. Then, for the second, third and fourth places use the same method. If we pushed 'Horse' first, then there are three other animals to pick for the second place. Then two alternatives left for the third place. By the time three buttons have been pushed, the last choice is automatic.

This method would produce the following results:

| Cow | Horse | Pig | Donkey |
|-----|-------|--------|--------|
| Cow | Horse | Donkey | Pig |
| Cow | Pig | Donkey | Horse |
| Cow | Pig | Horse | Donkey |
| Cow | Donkey | Pig | Horse |
| Cow | Donkey | Horse | Pig |

for the first six possibilities, then:

| Horse | Cow | Pig | Donkey |
|-------|--------|--------|--------|
| Horse | Cow | Donkey | Pig |
| Horse | Pig | Donkey | Cow |
| Horse | Pig | Cow | Donkey |
| Horse | Donkey | Pig | Cow |
| Horse | Donkey | Cow | Pig |

for the second six possibilities, then:

| Pig | Horse | Cow | Donkey |
|-----|--------|--------|--------|
| Pig | Horse | Donkey | Cow |
| Pig | Cow | Donkey | Horse |
| Pig | Cow | Horse | Donkey |
| Pig | Donkey | Cow | Horse |
| Pig | Donkey | Horse | Cow |

for the third six possibilities, then finally:

| Donkey | Horse | Cow | Pig |
|--------|-------|-------|------|
| Donkey | Horse | Pig | Cow |
| Donkey | Cow | Pig | Horse |
| Donkey | Cow | Horse | Pig |
| Donkey | Pig | Cow | Horse |
| Donkey | Pig | Horse | Cow |

Thus, the total number of possible code sequences is 24.

This could have been expected since there are 4 ways to choose the first animal, followed by 3 remaining ways left to choose the second animal, then 2 remaining ways to choose the third animal. The final choice must then be the last remaining animal. This makes:

Number of sequences = $4 \times 3 \times 2 \times 1$
= 24 sequence codes.

In general, the expression:
$$n \times (n - 1) \times (n - 2) \ldots \times 3 \times 2 \times 1$$

is written as $n!$ which is said as '$n$ factorial'. So:
$$n! = n \times (n - 1) \times (n - 2) \ldots \times 3 \times 2 \times 1$$

Now suppose we wish to list all the arrangements of any two buttons chosen from the four animals above. These would be:

| Donkey | Horse |
|--------|--------|
| Donkey | Cow |
| Donkey | Pig |
| Horse | Donkey |
| Horse | Cow |
| Horse | Pig |
| Cow | Donkey |
| Cow | Horse |
| Cow | Pig |
| Pig | Donkey |
| Pig | Horse |
| Pig | Cow |

Note: it is important to remember that (Donkey, Horse) and (Horse, Donkey) are two **different** arrangements or permutations.

There are 12 arrangements in this list. This could have been expected as there are 4 ways to pick the first animal and then 3 remaining to pick the second, so the total will be $4 \times 3$ by the multiplication principle.

Note: the number of ways of arranging $r$ items from a list of $n$ items is given by the symbol ${}_{n}P_{r}$. This can be calculated on a scientific calculator. For example, the number of ways of arranging 2 items out of a list of 4 is ${}_{4}P_{2} = 12$; the number of patterns from all the letters of the word MONDAY = $6! = {}_{6}P_{6} = 720$; and the number of patterns of 3 letters from the word MONDAY = ${}_{6}P_{3} = 120$.

## Exercise 28B

1. How many different patterns may be listed from all the letters of the word 'HOUND'?

2. The four-digit security numbers for bank accounts in Byzantia are subject to an unusual

## Exercise 28B...

restriction: All four digits must be different from each other. How many possible security numbers are there for any account?

3. Lucien has 7 different favourite books on his hobby, cooking. He places them on the top of his shelf in a straight line. In how many different orders may he arrange them?

4. The stationmaster on the coastal line in Norfolk plans the loading of the train every day. If the engine pulls three carriages chosen from a selection of six, how many different arrangements of carriages are possible?

5. Filippe, the florist, plans a new shop display each day. He places six pot plants in a row at the front of his window display chosen from 10 pot plants in his premises. How many such displays may he form?

6. The new Principal of Armagh Academy decrees that every class must study three different subjects in the three periods before break every day. If Year 10 pupils have fourteen subjects in their curriculum, in how many different ways may the Principal's requirement be met?

7. The dancing final had 15 contestants taking part, and impartial observers said they all had a roughly equal chance of taking the top places. In how many different ways could the gold, silver and bronze awards be given out?

8. A mum moves her personal belongings to her new office, including six individual portraits of her children. In how many different ways may she arrange these in a row on the top of her desk?

9. A new strategy game, Alisto, involves choosing 4 objects from a list of 23. These are then placed in a row on a playing board. In how many ways may this be done?

10. A Further Maths GCSE paper consists of twelve questions. In how many different ways may these be arranged?

## 28.3 Combinations

In the previous section we discussed arrangements. A **combination** is a selection of items from a larger group in which **the order doesn't matter**.

For example, if we are asked to list all the **arrangements** of 2 items from apple, banana, cherry and damson, we will produce the following list:

| apple, banana | apple, cherry | apple, damson |
|---|---|---|
| banana, apple | banana, cherry | banana, damson |
| cherry, apple | cherry, banana | cherry, damson |
| damson, apple | damson, banana | damson, cherry |

This list contains 12 pairs. Whereas if we list all the **combinations** (or selections) of 2 items from apple, banana, cherry and damson, we will produce the following list:

| apple, banana | apple, cherry | apple, damson |
|---|---|---|
| banana, cherry | banana, damson | cherry, damson |

This list contains just 6 pairs. The reason for the difference is that in the **combination** (apple, banana) is treated as the **same** pair as (banana, apple). The order does not matter in a combination.

When listing out combinations one systematic method is to choose one item as first and then list all the selections which include it (like the first row in the second table above). When we move on to the second item, we list all the selections which include that item, but excluding the first item that we chose. And so on. For example:

2. You have a bag with five chocolate bars in it: Aero, Mars, Galaxy, Yorkie and Snickers. You offer a friend two bars from the bag. List all the combinations of bars that she could choose.

Begin with Aero and list all the selections which include it. This is the first row in the table below. Then, choose Mars and list all combinations which include it, but which exclude Aero. Then repeat with Galaxy and list all combinations which include it, but which exclude Aero and Mars. Finally, choose Yorkie and list all combinations which include it, but which exclude Aero, Mars and Galaxy. The answer is:

| Aero and Mars | Aero and Galaxy | Aero and Yorkie | Aero and Snickers |
|---|---|---|---|
| Mars and Galaxy | Mars and Yorkie | Mars and Snickers | |
| Galaxy and Yorkie | Galaxy and Snickers | | |
| Yorkie and Snickers | | | |

There are two methods to work out the number of

combinations when we choose *r* items from *n* items. The first method is to use the numbers in Pascal's triangle:

| Row | | | | | | | | | | | | | | | | |
|---|---|---|---|---|---|---|---|---|---|---|---|---|---|---|---|---|
| 0 | | | | | | | | 1 | | | | | | | | |
| 1 | | | | | | | 1 | | 1 | | | | | | | |
| 2 | | | | | | 1 | | 2 | | 1 | | | | | | |
| 3 | | | | | 1 | | 3 | | 3 | | 1 | | | | | |
| 4 | | | | 1 | | 4 | | 6 | | 4 | | 1 | | | | |
| 5 | | | 1 | | 5 | | 10 | | 10 | | 5 | | 1 | | | |
| 6 | | 1 | | 6 | | 15 | | 20 | | 15 | | 6 | | 1 | | |
| 7 | 1 | | 7 | | 21 | | 35 | | 35 | | 21 | | 7 | | 1 | |
| 8 | 1 | 8 | | 28 | | 56 | | 70 | | 56 | | 28 | | 8 | | 1 |

The table can be written out easily when needed because each number is the sum of the two numbers immediately above it in the triangle. So it's easy to add more rows to it if needed.

The **row number** represents the number of items in the group we choose from. The place in that row is the number of items we choose from that group. We start the count on the left of the row at $r = 0$.

For example, the number of ways of choosing 2 items from a list of 7 is the third item in the 7th row, i.e.:

| 1 | 7 | 21 | 35 | 35 | 21 | 7 | 1 |
|---|---|---|---|---|---|---|---|
| $r=0$ | $r=1$ | $r=2$ | $r=3$ | $r=4$ | $r=5$ | $r=6$ | $r=7$ |

Note: observe how the **first** item in the 7th row is 1, where $r = 0$. The **second** item is 7 where $r = 1$ and the **third** item is 21 where $r = 2$.

The second method to work out the number of combinations when we choose *r* items from *n* items is to use the symbol $_nC_r$. This symbol means "the number of ways to choose *r* items from a list of *n* items".

The advantage of using this method is that it can be calculated on a scientific calculator. Check the answer above, on your calculator, to confirm that $_7C_2 = 21$.

## Exercise 28C

1. Evaluate the following using Pascal's triangle, Do not use your calculator.
   (a) $_6C_4$
   (b) $_8C_2$
   (c) $_5C_4$

2. Evaluate the following using a scientific calculator:
   (a) $_4C_2$

## Exercise 28C...

   (b) $_7C_5$
   (c) $_6C_3$

3. How many different groups of 5 letters can be formed from the letters of the word 'SANDYBEG'?

4. Paul makes a random playlist from an album with 8 tracks on it. How many different playlists with 3 tracks may he pick?

5. Evadne is captain of her civic grass bowls club. The senior squad has 6 members in it. In how many different ways may she select a team of 2 players?

6. Even Steven must make up a new 4-digit pin number for his bank account. True to his name, he decides to only use even numbers 2, 4, 6, 8, or 0 using each digit only once. How many different sets of 4 numbers will he have to consider?

7. Josephine aims to finish 5 of her homeworks tonight. After a stressful week, she has a list of 7 homeworks to choose from. How many different ways may she select the homeworks to complete tonight?

8. Ciaran has 7 books unopened as gifts from friends for his birthday. If he takes 3 books on holiday to read, how many different sets of 3 may he select?

9. Aoife's prize in a writing competition is to take any 3 family members with her for a week in the Azores. Not everyone will be happy. Her family has 7 members, including herself. In how many different combinations may she select the group for the trip?

10. A girl puts in a ponytail every morning. It is always tied using 2 different bobbles. She has 8 different bobbles to choose from. How many different combinations of bobbles may she select?

## 28.4 Further Problems

Many counting problems involve a combination of a number of the techniques of this chapter. For example:

3. To pass a flute exam, a pupil must pass in 4 minor tests out of 8 and pass in 5 major tests out of 6. In how many different combinations may a pupil pass the exam?

The pupil may pass the minor tests in $_8C_4 = 70$ ways

The pupil may pass the major tests in $_6C_5 = 6$ ways

Since they have to pass both major tests and minor tests, the multiplication principle then applies.

So a pass may be achieved in $70 \times 6 = 420$ ways.

## Exercise 28D

1. The head gardener in Mount Selwyn House plans the layout of the Market Garden. She will choose 4 root vegetables, 3 beans and 5 leaf vegetables from a catalogue of 8 root vegetables, 7 types of beans and 7 leaf vegetables. How many vegetable displays may she create?

2. Jake plans to paint his den. He will choose 2 colours for his roof and 2 colours for his walls from the 8 tins in the shed, not repeating the roof colours. How many colour schemes may he end up with?

3. The new Maths For All exam will require candidates to answer 5 questions out of 7 in the first section and 4 out of 8 long questions in the second section. How many different ways may a candidate complete the exam?

4. Belleek Floral Art Association plans to elect its new committee of four members. There must be a single chair together with three other committee members. All these must be chosen from the seven subscribing full members. How many committees might be formed?

5. Finn is going to borrow his usual quota of books from the school library. He will pick 2 of the 6 remaining history books he hasn't read; 1 of the 7 encyclopaedias; and 2 of the 7 maths books. How many different selections of books may he pick?

6. Caoimhe is picking her camogie team for Saturday. She is stuck with the usual 8 mid-fielders, but she must pick a keeper from the two hopefuls, three full-backs from five possibles and three full-forwards from the four usuals. How many different teams are possible?

## Exercise 28D...

7. The school prefect leaders must be chosen this week. A head girl and 3 deputy head girls mustbe chosen from 9 senior female prefects and a head boy and 3 deputy head boys must be chosen from 7 senior male prefects. How many top teams may be formed?

8. I always form my four-digit security code by picking the first two digits to be different odd digits and the third and fourth digits to be different even digits (excluding zero). How many different security codes may I invent?

# CHAPTER 29: BOOLEAN ALGEBRA

## 29.1 Introduction

The algebra of logic was invented by the Englishman George Boole (1815–1864) while he was Professor of Mathematics at University College Cork. Named **Boolean algebra** in his honour, it laid the foundation for the development of modern computing.

## 29.2 Propositions

Boolean algebra involves combinations of **propositions** whose values are either 'true' or 'false'. Examples of simple propositions are:

- It is raining today.
- Chelsea will win the Cup.
- Norway is a country in America.
- Not every sentence is a preposition.

By contrast, none of the following sentences is a proposition:

- Watch out for the elephants!
- Have a nice day.
- Where are you going?
- Friends, Romans, countrymen lend me your ears.

The way to tell whether a sentence is a proposition is to ask yourself whether the sentence can be either true or false.

### Exercise 29A: *Which of the following sentences are propositions?*

1. The rain in Spain falls mainly on the plain.
2. Lizards are 3 metres tall.
3. How lovely is the Autumn rain.
4. I voted for the Unity Party.
5. Don't forget it!
6. Please don't!
7. Cecilia said, "No I won't".
8. We know where you live.
9. Where do you live?
10. Carrots are green.
11. Roses are red.
12. Are violets blue?
13. Think pink!
14. My cousin is a yellow belly.

## 29.3 Boolean Variables And Negation

In Boolean algebra propositions are represented by Boolean variables (which we will just call **variables** for the rest of this chapter). By tradition we use the lower-case letters $p$, $q$, $r$ and $s$ for propositions. Each such variable can only have one of two possible values: 'true' or 'false'. For example:

| Variable | represents proposition | has value |
|---|---|---|
| $p$ | Cullybackey is in County Antrim | true |
| $q$ | Mexico is the capital of Brazil | false |
| $r$ | 7 is an even number | false |
| $s$ | 5 plus 3 equals 8 | true |

The opposite of the variable $p$ is 'not $p$' and this is denoted by:

$$\sim p$$

For example, if $p$ represents the statement "All the inhabitants of Clogher are left-handed" then the expression $\sim p$ would represent "Not every inhabitant of Clogher is left-handed." Be careful: $\sim p$ does **not** mean "All the inhabitants of Clogher are right-handed". Even if only one person in Clogher was right-handed then $p$ would be false.

## 29.4 Boolean Connectives

Of course, language is more complicated than the simple statements above. We need the ability to make compound statements which join simple propositions together. In Boolean algebra the connectives **AND** and **OR** are used.

For example, if $p$ represents "Fiona speaks French" and $q$ represents "Eimear can swim" then:

$p$ AND $q$

stands for

"Fiona speaks French and Eimear can swim"

and

$p$ OR $\sim q$

stands for

"Fiona speaks French or Eimear can't swim"

The symbols ∧ or ∨ are sometimes used for AND and OR, but we will just use the words AND and OR.

## Exercise 29B

A series of propositions represent the following sentences:

*p* represents "Michael can play football well".
*q* represents "Brussels sprouts are good to eat".
*r* represents "Sian is clever".
*s* represents "Tuesday is violet day".

Write out sentences which mean the same as:

1. *p* AND *r*

2. ~*s*

3. *q* OR *r*

4. *p* AND (*q* OR *s*)

5. ~*r* AND ~*p*

6. ~*q*

7. *r* OR ~*p*

8. (*p* AND *r*) OR (*p* AND *s*)

9. *p* AND (*r* OR *s*)

10. ~(*q* OR *s*)

The truth of a compound statement can then be worked out by using the following rules:

### AND
true AND true = true
true AND false = false
false AND false = false

### OR
true OR true = true
true OR false = true
false OR false = false

For example:

1. Given the following propositions:

   "The river Bann flows into Lough Neagh" = true
   "Belfast is the capital of Northern Ireland" = true
   "Ireland is in Asia" = false

   work out the truth of the compound propositions:
   (a)  "Belfast is the capital of Northern Ireland" OR "Ireland is in Asia",
   (b)  "The river Bann flows into Lough Neagh" OR ("Belfast is the capital of Northern Ireland" AND "Ireland is in Asia").

(a)  From the given propositions, this can be rewritten as:
    true OR false

From the rules above, the truth of the compound statement is:
    true

(b)  From the given propositions, this can be rewritten as:
    true OR (true AND false)

which equals:
    true OR false

which equals:
    true

## Exercise 29C

Evaluate the truthfulness of the following compound statements:

1. "All dogs are cats" OR "5 times 7 equals thirty-five".

2. "Yellow is a colour in the rainbow" AND "There are five vowels in the alphabet".

3. "All dogs are cats" AND "5 times 7 equals thirty-five".

4. "Yellow is a colour in the rainbow" OR "There are five vowels in the alphabet".

5. "5 is less than 6" OR "–5 is less than –6".

6. "5 is less than 6" OR "–5 is more than –6".

7. "5 is less than 6" AND "–5 is less than –6".

8. "5 is less than 6" AND "–5 is more than –6".

9. "Pigs are reptiles" AND ("Every month has more than 29 days" OR "The number 7 is prime").

10. "Pigs are reptiles" OR ("Every month has more than 29 days" AND "The number 7 is prime").

11. ("Pigs are reptiles" AND "Every month has more than 29 days") OR "The number 7 is prime".

12. ("Pigs are reptiles" OR "Every month has more than 29 days") AND "The number 7 is prime".

## Exercise 29C...

A series of propositions represent the following sentences:

$p$ represents "Every four-wheeled vehicle is a car".
$q$ represents "Slieve Donard is smaller than Mount Everest".
$r$ represents "Every even number is a multiple of two".
$s$ represents "Soccer teams have 40 players on the field at any one time".

Evaluate the truthfulness of the following compound statements:

**13.** $p$ OR ($q$ AND $s$)

**14.** ~$p$ AND ($s$ OR ~$q$)

**15.** ($q$ OR ~$s$) AND ($p$ OR $r$)

**16.** (~$q$ AND $s$) OR ($q$ AND ~$s$)

**17.** (~$r$ AND $p$) OR ($r$ AND ~$p$)

**18.** ~$s$ AND (~$q$ or ~$r$)

**19.** $s$ OR ($r$ AND ~$p$)

**20.** (~$p$ OR ~$q$) AND (~$r$ OR ~$s$)

## 29.5 Truth Tables

To prove whether two Boolean expressions are equal, we need to consider every possibility for the truth values of the variables in the expression.

As we have seen, every Boolean variable can take on only one of two values – 'true' or 'false'. Thus, an expression involving 2 variables, $p$ and $q$, must consider all four possibilities, namely:

- $p$ is true and $q$ is true
- $p$ is true and $q$ is false
- $p$ is false and $q$ is true
- $p$ is false and $q$ is false

These possibilities are usually summarised in a **truth table** as shown below (T = true and F = false):

| $p$ | $q$ |
|-----|-----|
| T | T |
| T | F |
| F | T |
| F | F |

When three variables $p$, $q$ and $r$ are involved, we must consider $2 \times 2 \times 2 = 8$ possibilities, namely:

| $p$ | $q$ | $r$ |
|-----|-----|-----|
| T | T | T |
| T | T | F |
| T | F | T |
| T | F | F |
| F | T | T |
| F | T | F |
| F | F | T |
| F | F | F |

And so on for 4 or more variables.

For example:

**2.** Write down the truth table for:
(a) $p$ AND $q$
(b) $p$ OR $q$
(c) ~$p$ AND ~$q$
(d) ($p$ AND ~$q$) OR $r$

(a)

| $p$ | $q$ | $p$ AND $q$ |
|-----|-----|-------------|
| T | T | T |
| T | F | F |
| F | T | F |
| F | F | F |

(b)

| $p$ | $q$ | $p$ OR $q$ |
|-----|-----|------------|
| T | T | T |
| T | F | T |
| F | T | T |
| F | F | F |

(c)

| $p$ | $q$ | ~$p$ | ~$q$ | ~$p$ AND ~$q$ |
|-----|-----|------|------|---------------|
| T | T | F | F | F |
| T | F | F | T | F |
| F | T | T | F | F |
| F | F | T | T | T |

(d)

| $p$ | $q$ | $r$ | ~$q$ | $p$ AND ~$q$ | ($p$ AND ~$q$) OR $r$ |
|-----|-----|-----|------|--------------|------------------------|
| T | T | T | F | F | T |
| T | T | F | F | F | F |
| T | F | T | T | T | T |
| T | F | F | T | T | T |
| F | T | T | F | F | T |
| F | T | F | F | F | F |
| F | F | T | T | F | T |
| F | F | F | T | F | F |

## Exercise 29D: *Construct truth tables for the following expressions.*

1. $p$ OR $\sim q$
2. $\sim(p$ OR $q)$
3. $\sim p$ OR $\sim q$
4. $p$ OR $(q$ AND $r)$
5. $p$ AND $(q$ OR $r)$
6. $\sim p$ AND $(q$ OR $r)$
7. $p$ OR $(q$ OR $r)$
8. $(p$ AND $\sim q)$ OR $(\sim p$ AND $q)$

## 29.6 Proving Two Boolean Expressions To Be Equivalent

As we have seen in the previous section, two Boolean variables can only have four different possible alternative arrangements of truth and falsehood. These possibilities may be completely listed in the rows of a truth table. So, to demonstrate that different expressions formed from these two variables are equivalent, all we must do is to show that their truth tables are identical. For example:

3. Show that $\sim(p$ AND $q)$ is equivalent to $\sim p$ OR $\sim q$

We draw out their truth tables:

| $p$ | $q$ | $p$ AND $q$ | $\sim(p$ AND $q)$ |
|---|---|---|---|
| T | T | T | F |
| T | F | F | T |
| F | T | F | T |
| F | F | F | T |

| $p$ | $q$ | $\sim p$ | $\sim q$ | $\sim p$ OR $\sim q$ |
|---|---|---|---|---|
| T | T | F | F | F |
| T | F | F | T | T |
| F | T | T | F | T |
| F | F | T | T | T |

As we have listed the truth values of $p$ and $q$ in the same order in the first two columns of each table and as the final columns in these two truth tables are the same, we see that $\sim(p$ AND $q)$ is equivalent to $\sim p$ OR $\sim q$.

## Exercise 29E: *Investigate whether or not the following pairs of Boolean expressions are equivalent.*

1. $\sim r$ OR $q$       $r$ OR $\sim q$
2. $\sim(p$ OR $\sim q)$       $\sim p$ AND $q$
3. $p$ AND $q$       $\sim p$ OR $\sim q$
4. $(p$ OR $q)$ AND $r$       $(p$ OR $r)$ AND $(q$ OR $r)$
5. $p$ AND $(p$ OR $q)$       $p$
6. $(p$ AND $q)$ OR $r$       $(p$ OR $r)$ AND $(q$ OR $r)$

## 29.7 Additional Activities

In this section we consider two more Boolean connectives, and two rules known as De Morgan's Laws.

### Exclusive OR

The OR connector, that we have already met, is true when either of the propositions is true or when both are true. The **Exclusive OR** connective is **only** true when one of the propositions is true and the other is false. It is false when both propositions are true. The Exclusive OR is usually denoted by the operator **XOR**. Its truth table is given below:

| $p$ | $q$ | $p$ XOR $q$ |
|---|---|---|
| T | T | F |
| T | F | T |
| F | T | T |
| F | F | F |

### Implication

The meaning of the connective '$p$ implies $q$' is that 'when $p$ is true $q$ is true'. When $p$ is false we define '$p$ implies $q$' to be true irrespective of the value of $q$. Its truth table is given below:

| $p$ | $q$ | $p$ implies $q$ |
|---|---|---|
| T | T | T |
| T | F | F |
| F | T | T |
| F | F | T |

## Exercise 29F

1. Find a logical expression which is equivalent to $p$ XOR $q$ as a combination of AND, OR and ~.

2. Are the expressions '$p$ implies $q$' and '$\sim q$ implies $\sim p$' logically equivalent?

3. Find another logical expression which is equivalent to '$p$ implies $q$' as a combination of AND, OR and ~.

4. Prove that the expressions $\sim(p$ AND $q)$ and $\sim p$ OR $\sim q$ are logically equivalent.

5. Find a logical expression that is equivalent to $\sim(p$ OR $q)$. Prove the equivalence.

### De Morgan's Laws

The equivalences in questions 4 and 5 in Exercise 29F illustrate two laws that are known as De Morgan's Laws. They are very useful in Boolean algebra. Thus:

$\sim(p$ AND $q) = \sim p$ OR $\sim q$

and

$\sim(p$ OR $q) = \sim p$ AND $\sim q$

# CHAPTER 30: LINEAR PROGRAMMING

## 30.1 Introduction

In life we are surrounded by opportunities to pick the best, the cheapest, the fastest, the most compact… etc. Think about these scenarios:

- Dad has given you a budget to spend on your new phone, but there are so many different contracts. Mixtures of data, minutes, texts, all at varying prices are presented – yet none seem to give the best value outright!
- A teacher has some money to spend on resources for her class. Her pupils need textbooks to learn from, yet she also needs the latest presentational media to display the ideas from her course. In addition, the added value of a school trip to see the subject in the real world would be very enlightening and motivating. Plug-in apps make revising topics more efficient. But there isn't enough cash to buy everything.
- A technologist is designing a printed circuit board to control some new medical apparatus. It has to fit into a very limited space, yet it still needs to include communication ports, memory, the fastest processor available and control software.
- A family wishes to book a summer holiday. Everyone loves to travel as far away from home as possible to the most exciting activities. How can the limited finances best stretch to include shark diving, river rafting, bungee jumping or adventure camping, all at the farthest side of the world?

## 30.2 Linear Programming

Problems like these can be tackled using **linear programming**. For example:

.................................................................

1. A bakery makes ultimate flapjacks and diet flapjacks. The ingredients for these are:

| Flapjack type | Butter | Sugar | Oats |
|---|---|---|---|
| Ultimate | 40g | 60g | 100g |
| Diet | 60g | 15g | 100g |

The manager wants to (a) make as many as possible and (b) maximise their profit. While the bakery has more than enough oats for today's bake, they only have 7.2 kg of butter and 3.6 kg of sugar. The manager wishes to decide how many of each type of flapjack to make. Use linear programming to model the situation.

The items which will vary in the study are the numbers of ultimate flapjacks and diet flapjacks, so for the decision variables, we choose:

$x$ = number of ultimate flapjacks to make

and

$y$ = number of diet flapjacks to make

Considering that the bakery only has 7.2 kg of butter, we can say that the total used to make $x$ ultimate flapjacks and $y$ diet flapjacks must be less than or equal to 7.2 kg. Thus, measuring in grams:
$$40 \times x + 60 \times y \leq 7200$$

which becomes, on dividing by 20:
$$2x + 3y \leq 360$$

Next, considering the amount of sugar, the total used to make $x$ ultimate flapjacks and $y$ diet flapjacks must be less than or equal to 3.6 kg. Thus, measuring in grams:
$$60 \times x + 15 \times y \leq 3600$$

which becomes, on dividing by 15:
$$4x + y \leq 240$$

Finally, the bakery obviously cannot make negative numbers of flapjacks so we can say:
$$x \geq 0$$
and
$$y \geq 0$$

So the solution region is defined by the 4 inequalities:
$$2x + 3y \leq 360 \quad 4x + y \leq 240 \quad x \geq 0 \quad y \geq 0$$

So we can draw the solution region, **R**:

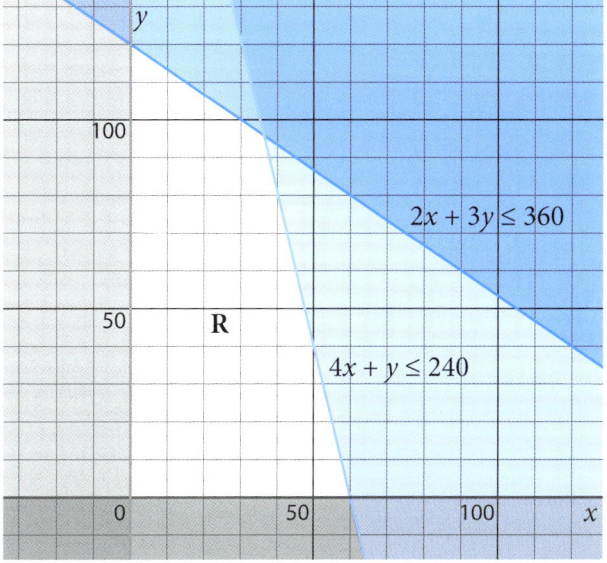

Any $(x, y)$ pair within the region **R** represents a valid solution to the set of inequalities.

# 30.3 Solving Systems Of Inequalities

Note: This section is a revision of prior material which is essential to the linear programming method. If you are familiar with this material, you may wish to move to the next section.

## The graphical solution of an inequality in a single variable

A single inequality, in one variable, is usually represented on a single dimensional number line. For example, the solution to $3 < 2x + 5 \leq 13$ is:

$$3 < 2x + 5 \leq 13$$
$$-2 < 2x \leq 8$$
$$-1 < x \leq 4$$

This is represented on the real number line as:

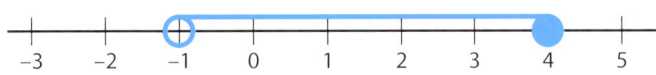

Note that the solution region is a segment of a line. Conventionally, when the end point is **excluded** from the solution region, the circle is **open** (the value $-1$ above). When the end point is **included** in the solution region, the circle is **shaded in** (the value 4 above).

This same inequality can be represented in a two dimensional inequality as:

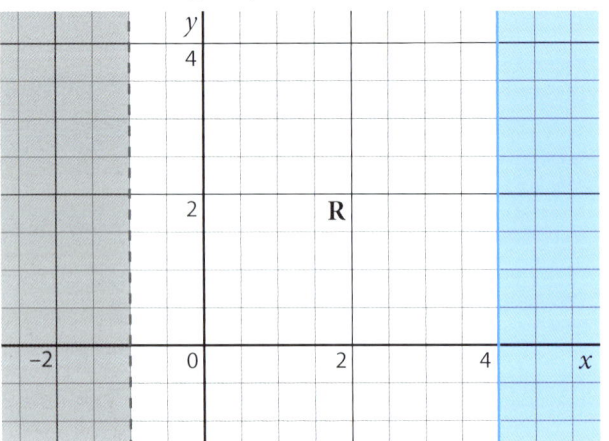

Note that to mark the solution region, it is only necessary to place a capital **R** in the area where all the inequalities are simultaneously true. Some textbooks also shade the sides of the lines where the inequality is false (as in the diagram above). In this case, the solution region is left unshaded.

In this 2D diagram, the solution region is a strip bounded by two vertical lines $x = -1$ and $x = 4$. Every point to the left of this region has an $x$-coordinate less than $-1$. Every point to the right of this region has an $x$-coordinate greater than 4.

Also note that when the values of $x$ on the line are **excluded** from the solution region, the line is **dashed**, as for $x = -1$ above. When the values of $x$ on the line are to be **included** in the solution region the line is **solid**, as for $x = 4$ above.

## The graphical solution of an inequality in two variables

When an inequality involves both $x$ and $y$-coordinates, the same principles are followed. For example, to illustrate the inequality:

$$x + y \leq 4$$

on a graph, we first draw the line:

$$x + y = 4$$

Then, indicate on which side of the line the inequality is true by:

• placing a capital R on that side, or
• shading the opposite side of the line, i.e. the region where the inequality is false, or
• both of the above.

For example:

2. Draw the solution region of the inequality $x + y > 4$.

Using the above method, the solution is:

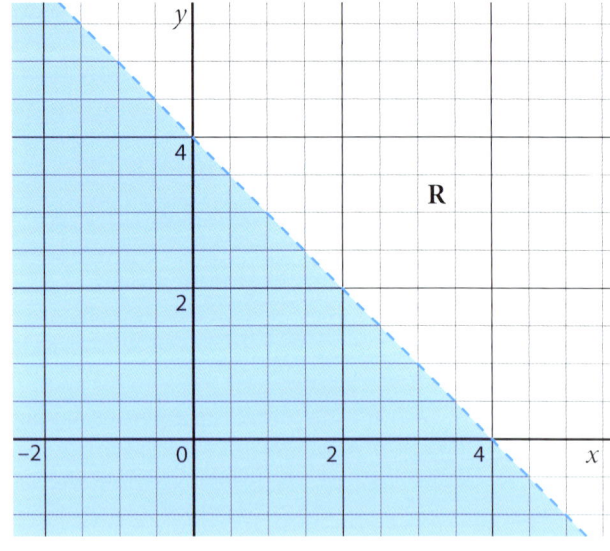

## The graphical solution of multiple inequalities

Multiple inequalities are handled in the same way. For example, the solution set for the inequalities:

$$2x + y \leq 6$$
$$x + 2y \leq 6$$
$$-2 \leq x$$
$$-1 \leq y$$

is shown by the following diagram:

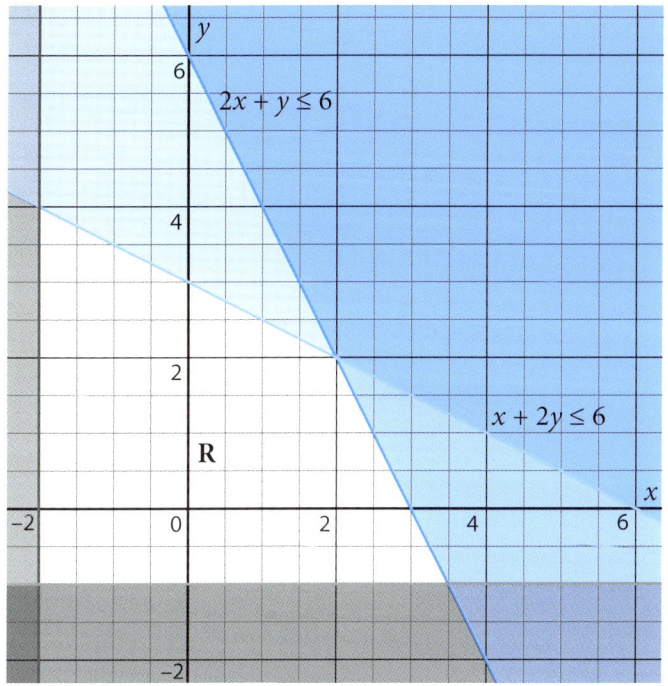

Note that every point **within** the solution region satisfies every inequality. For example, (1, 1) is in the middle of the region and, substituting $x = 1$ and $y = 1$ we can see that:

- for inequality $2x + y \leq 6$: $2 \times 1 + 1 = 3 \leq 6$
- for inequality $x + 2y \leq 6$: $1 + 2 \times 1 = 3 \leq 6$
- for inequality $-2 \leq x$, clearly $-2 \leq 1$, and
- for inequality $-1 \leq y$, clearly $-1 \leq 1$.

However, every point **outside** the solution region violates at least one of the inequalities. For example, (3, 1) is outside the region and we can see that:

- for inequality $x + 2y \leq 6$: $3 + 2 \times 1 = 5 \leq 6$
- for inequality $-2 \leq x$, clearly $-2 \leq 3$, and
- for inequality $-1 \leq y$, clearly $1 \leq 3$, and

but:

- for inequality $2x + y \leq 6$: $2 \times 3 + 1 = 7$
  and 7 is definitely not less than 6.

Note also that if an inequality includes an equals sign, then points on the **boundary** are **within** the solution region. For example, (2, 2) is on the intersection of $2x + y \leq 6$ and $x + 2y \leq 6$ and satisfies both inequalities. Therefore it is within the solution region.

**Exercise 30A**: *Draw the solution regions of the following systems of equations:*

1. $x \geq 0$, $y \geq 0$, $2x + 3y \leq 24$, $x + y \leq 10$
2. $x \geq 0$, $y \geq 0$, $x \leq 8$, $3x + 2y \leq 30$, $y \leq 12$
3. $x \leq 8$, $y \leq 6$, $x + 4y \geq 8$, $2x + y > 8$
4. $x \leq 16$, $y \leq 14$, $2x + 5y > 5$, $4x + 3y \geq 6$
5. $x \leq 8$, $y \leq 10$, $x + y > 3$
6. $x \leq 15$, $y \leq 18$, $6x + y > 3$, $3x + 4y > 24$, $x + 5y > 15$
7. $x \geq 2$, $y \geq 3$, $x \leq 8$, $y \leq 6$
8. $x \leq 20$, $x \geq 2y - 1$, $x + 2y \geq 12$
9. $x \leq 12$, $y \leq 6$, $3x + 2y \geq 12$, $2x + 7y \geq 14$
10. $x \leq 4$, $y \leq 5$, $3x + y \geq 3$, $x + 2y > 4$

## 30.4 Optimising Using The Linear Programming Method

Linear programming can be used to **optimise** decisions, for example to find the best way to maximise profit. In the flapjack bakery in example 1 we modelled the requirements for the days' baking as a set of inequalities and plotted these on a pair of axes to show the solution region, **R**. Now let us examine two optimisations for the bakery:

.............................................................................

3. (a) How many ultimate flapjacks and how many diet flapjacks should the bakery make so that the biggest number of flapjacks is baked?

(b) How many of each type of flapjack should the bakery make to maximise their total profit?

(a) First, let us define a function $N$ – called the objective function – which is the total number of flapjacks made:

$N = x + y$
where:

   $x$ = number of ultimate flapjacks to make
and

   $y$ = number of diet flapjacks to make

This formula can be plotted on the graph if we try various values for $N$. The following graph shows three lines representing $x + y = 50$, $x + y = 100$ and $x + y = 120$.

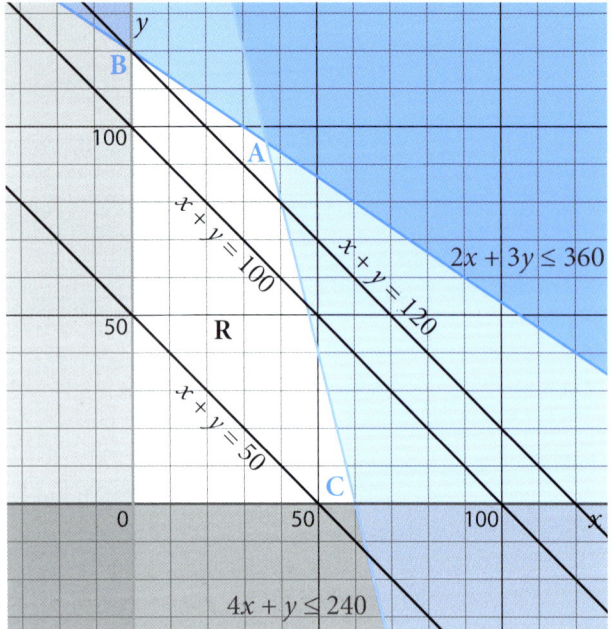

The different lines plotted are all parallel to each other and by continuing the pattern it can be seen that the vertex in the solution region which will permit $N$ to be a maximum will be vertex **A**.

This may be read off the graph if the scale is sufficiently large. As this is not the case here, we can find the coordinates of A by solving the equations of the two lines that intersect at A simultaneously:

$$4x + y = 240 \qquad (1)$$
$$2x + 3y = 360 \qquad (2)$$

Multiplying (2) by 2 gives:
$$4x + 6y = 720$$
$$4x = 720 - 6y \qquad (3)$$

Substituting (3) into (1):
$$4x + y = 240$$
$$720 - 6y + y = 240$$
$$5y = 480$$
$$y = 96$$

Substituting this value of $y$ into (1):
$$4x + 96 = 240$$
$$4x = 144$$
$$x = 36$$

So the maximum number of flapjacks:
$N = 36 + 96 = \mathbf{132}$

This happens when 36 ultimate flapjacks and 96 diet flapjacks are made.

Note that this method involves using a search line or **objective function**. This is, in this case, a line with gradient of –1. We plotted three such lines above with $y$-intercepts at 50, 100 and 120.

The general equation for the objective function is:
$$N = x + y$$
$$\text{or} \quad y = -x + N$$

**(b)** Let us use this same model for the second optimisation, to maximise the profit. The selling price for the flapjacks is:

| Flapjack type | Selling price |
|---|---|
| Ultimate | 45p |
| Diet | 70p |

So the profit can be calculated by the formula:

$P = 0.45x + 0.7y$

where the profit, $P$, is in pounds (hence the flapjacks are priced using 0.45 and 0.7 instead of 45p and 70p).

From the solution to part (a), we can use a quicker method to find the answer by observing that the maximum or minimum for any expression usually occurs at or near one of the vertices of the solution region (A, B, or C in the previous diagram). So we evaluate the objective function, $P = 0.45x + 0.7y$, at the 3 vertices where $x$ and $y$ tend to be greatest. The solutions are:

| | $x$ | $y$ | $P$ |
|---|---|---|---|
| A | 36 | 96 | £83.40 |
| B | 0 | 120 | £84 |
| C | 60 | 0 | £27 |

Thus we see that the maximum profit is £84 and this happens if we just make 120 diet flapjacks and no ultimate flapjacks.

## 30.5 Summary of Linear Programming

Linear programming provides a way of optimising amongst the varying solutions to a real-world problem.

We start by picking the items which we intend to vary as we consider different solutions. These are called the **decision variables**. In CCEA GCSE Further Maths there will always be two decision variables, $x$ and $y$.

Then for each resource which is limited, we design an inequality that describes that resource constraint in terms of these decision variables. The full list of these mathematical constraints is called the **set of inequalities**.

Then we graph the solution region of these inequalities.

The quantity which we are trying to optimise (the shortest time or the least cost etc) is written as an expression involving the decision variables. This expression is known as the **objective function**.

By this stage, we have produced a mathematical model of the real-world problem. This model may only be a limited description – the real world is very complex – but we will satisfy ourselves with the restricted solution which our model produces.

By using one of the methods described in example 3, we **optimise** this objective function, picking the best value we can obtain at all the points in the solution region. This will result not only in the shortest time or the least cost, but also will tell us at which values of $x$ and $y$ it occurs.

The final step in any linear programming solution is to translate the values of these decision variables from mathematical equations into statements that apply to the real world. These statements will be sentences like "Buy 6 hours of river rafting" or "Make the microchip to have dimensions 7.5 mm by 13 mm".

In summary, the linear programming process is:
a. Identify a real world problem;
b. Model using variables;
c. Solve using linear programming;
d. Translate the solution back into the real-world.

### Exercise 30B: *linear programming scenarios*

When drawing the solution region R in each of these scenarios, don't forget to include the condition that $x$ and $y$ must be positive, as the two inequalities $x \geq 0$ and $y \geq 0$.

1. Andrew is planning a caravan holiday incorporating visits to both Seaview caravan park and Mountain Ridge caravan park. A site at Seaview costs £14 per night and a site at Mountain Ridge costs £10 per night. Andrew has £180 to spend and can stay no longer than 14 nights. As he plans to meet a camping friend at Seaview, he wants to stay longer there than at Mountain Ridge. Let $x$ be the number of nights spent at Seaview and $y$ the number of nights spent at Mountain Ridge.
   (a) By considering cost, show that $x$ and $y$ must satisfy the inequality $7x + 5y \leq 90$.
   (b) Write down an inequality satisfying the maximum length of the stay.
   (c) Write down an inequality describing a

### Exercise 30B...

longer stay in Seaview than in Mountain Ridge.
   (d) Illustrate the three inequalities by a suitable diagram on graph paper. Write the letter R in the solution region.
   (e) Find the longest stay in Seaview which permits a 14 night holiday.
   (f) Find the number of nights that Andrew must spend at each site for a 14 night holiday at the lowest cost.

2. Clodagh, the chef in a home bakery, plans to ice up birthday cakes and wedding cakes. She is planning her day's work. A birthday cake takes 15 minutes to finish and a wedding cake takes 27 minutes. She has a four-and-a-half hour shift in which to work (excluding time for breaks). Let $x$ be the number of birthday cakes and $y$ the number of wedding cakes iced.
   (a) Show that the inequality describing the time taken is $5x + 9y \leq 90$.

Each birthday cake uses 800 g of icing sugar and each wedding cake uses 1 kg of icing sugar. A total of 12 kg of icing sugar is available.
   (b) Write down an inequality in terms of $x$ and $y$ satisfying the amount of icing sugar available.

The batch must include at least 3 wedding cakes.
   (c) Write down an inequality for this restriction.
   (d) Illustrate the three inequalities by a suitable diagram on graph paper. Write the letter R in the solution region.

The profit from each birthday cake is £9 and the profit from each wedding cake is £12.
   (e) Find the number of birthday cakes and wedding cakes that Clodagh should make to give the maximum profit.

3. A food depot for supply of food to those in famine areas is distributing sacks of rice and beans. A sack of rice weighs 10 kg and takes up 50 litres of space. There are 35 sacks of rice. A sack of beans weighs 25 kg and also takes up 50 litres of space. There are 20 sacks of beans. A particular delivery truck can carry up to 600 kg and has space for 2000 litres of payload. If that truck carries $x$ sacks of rice and $y$ sacks of beans:

## Exercise 30B...

(a) Show that one inequality satisfied by $x$ and $y$ is: $x \leq 35$.

(b) Find a similar inequality for $y$.

(c) By considering weight, show that $2x + 5y \leq 120$.

(d) Find a similar inequality in $x$ and $y$.

(e) Plot this system of inequalities on 2 cm graph paper, taking 2 cm to represent 10 units. Note that both $x$ and $y$ must be positive. Indicate the solution region with by a capital R.

One sack of rice will provide for 160 meals. One sack of beans will provide for 800 meals.

(f) Write down the objective function if it is desired to maximize the number of meals.

(g) Find the maximum number of meals possible and the number of sacks of each type required to achieve this.

4. A small manufacturer in Enniskillen needs to install two new types of machines. The A-type costs £2500 and covers a floor area of 12 m². The B-type costs £6000 and covers a floor area of 6 m². The total money available for spending is £30,000 and the total floor space available is 72 m². Let $x$ be the number of A-type machines installed, and $y$ the number of B-type machines installed.

(a) Show that $x$ and $y$ satisfy the inequality $5x + 12y \leq 60$.

(b) Show that $x$ and $y$ satisfy the inequality $2x + y \leq 12$.

(c) There must be at least two of each machine. Write down a further two inequalities.

(d) Illustrate the four inequalities by a suitable diagram on graph paper. Write the letter R in the solution region.

(e) If the maximum number of B-type machines are installed, how many A-type machines may be installed?

(f) What is the largest number of machines that can be installed?

(g) Assuming the largest number of machines is installed, what is the least floor area that needs to be used?

## Exercise 30B...

5. A developer plans to construct two types of house in a new development on 27,000 m² of land in Lurgan. A detached house requires 1350 m² of land while a town-house requires 1080 m². Let $x$ be the number of detached houses and $y$ the number of town-houses to be built.

(a) Show that $5x + 4y \leq 100$.

The number of detached houses must be at least one quarter of the total number of dwellings.

(b) Show that $y \leq 3x$.

At least 4 town-houses must be built.

(c) Write down an inequality which satisfies this condition.

(d) Illustrate the three inequalities by a suitable diagram on graph paper. Write the letter R in the solution region.

(e) What is the maximum number of detached houses that may be built?

(f) Various combinations of detached houses and town-houses give the maximum number of dwellings. Which of these solutions gives the greatest ratio of town-houses to detached houses?

6. A kitchen showroom is designed to display two types of cupboards. The Berry costs £800 and covers an area of 3 m². The Hollywood costs £500 and covers an area of 1.5 m². Let $x$ be the number of Berry and $y$ be the number of Hollywood cupboards displayed. The total cost of cupboards must be less than or equal to £8000.

(a) Write down an inequality which satisfies this condition.

The total area to be used must not be more than 27 m².

(b) Write down an inequality which satisfies this condition.

Both $x$ and $y$ must be positive.

(c) Illustrate the four inequalities by a suitable diagram on graph paper. Write the letter R in the solution region.

(d) Write down an expression for the total number of cupboards.

(e) Find the maximum total number of cupboards satisfying all the above restrictions.

## Exercise 30B...

7. A collection of rectangular garden plots each of length $x$ m and width $y$ m is to be created. The length of each garden plot must be no more than 35 m. The width must not be less than 8 m.

   (a) Express these two conditions as inequalities.

   Each garden plot must satisfy the inequality $x + 20 \geq 2y$. In addition, the perimeter of each plot must not be less than 34 m.

   (b) Express this condition as an inequality.

   (c) Illustrate the four inequalities by a suitable diagram on graph paper. Write the letter R in the solution region.

   (d) What is the maximum perimeter of any garden plot?

   (e) If a garden plot is a square, what is the largest possible side length?

   (f) What is the minimum area of all the possible plots?

8. The Flambeaus are planning to pave a patio in their garden. Two colours of tile will be used: yellow tiles with an area of 0.2 m$^2$ and green tiles with an area of 0.04 m$^2$. The maximum area to be tiled is 28.8 m$^2$. Let $x$ be the number of yellow tiles and $y$ be the number of green tiles used.

   (a) Express the restriction on areas as an inequality.

   Mme Flambeau wants to pave at least 14.4 m$^2$ with yellow tiles only.

   (b) Express this as an inequality.

   M. Flambeau wants to pave at least 8 m$^2$ with green tiles.

   (c) Express this as an inequality.

   (d) Illustrate the three inequalities by a suitable diagram on graph paper. Write the letter R in the solution region.

   The cost of laying one yellow tile is £2 and the cost of laying one green tile is 70p.

   (e) Write an expression in terms of $x$ and $y$ for the total cost of laying out the patio.

   (f) The Flambeau family want to pave the maximum area of 28.8 m$^2$. M. Flambeau wants to use as many green tiles as possible. However, Mme. Flambeau wants the cheapest patio possible. What are the respective costs of the two alternatives?

**171**

# CHAPTER 31: TIME SERIES

## 31.1 Introduction

Imagine the summer sales of ice creams by a certain ice cream van in Newcastle. The total sales of ice creams by this van during the summer months for the years 2013 to 2016 are listed in the table below:

|  | June | July | August | September |
|---|---|---|---|---|
| 2013 | 169 | 284 | 262 | 155 |
| 2014 | 185 | 300 | 278 | 171 |
| 2015 | 201 | 316 | 294 | 187 |
| 2016 | 217 | 332 | 310 | 203 |

This list of values forms a **time series**. The pattern of sales is better seen in a plot of the values, as shown below:

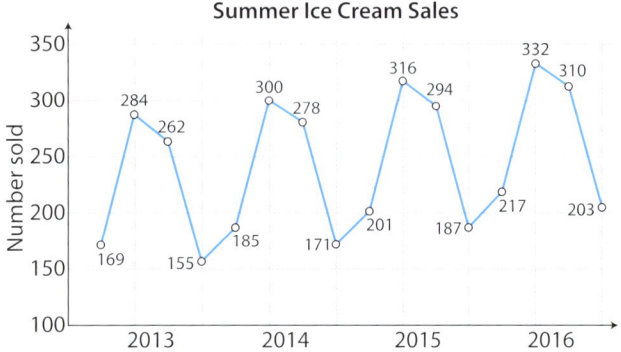

Why might sales follow such a pattern? It is easy to suggest an explanation: In June the sun shines and people want to buy ice cream. By July, everyone is off school. There are also lots of holidaymakers so sales of ice cream rise to a peak. In August the school holidays continue but many people go back to school before the end of the month, so sales drop a little. In September people continue to enjoy treats – but their opportunities are greatly reduced so sales fall off further.

(Note: This example is not suggesting that no sales of ice cream take place during the rest of the year. We are just focusing on sales during the summer months.)

There is an additional trend in the above plot. While there is a similar rise and fall in sales during each summer, there is also an increase in the level of sales year on year. This could be accounted for by the number of people in Newcastle during the summer increasing (or the usual inhabitants just eating more ice cream)!

Thus the pattern of the sales data has two components:

- Firstly, there is a repeated **cyclic** effect. Smaller sales in June rising to a peak in July. Then a slight fall-off in August with only a tail left in September.

- Secondly, the **overall** pattern is rising year after year. In this example the total sales are in fact rising by 6% each year.

Finally, it is important to note that this is a made-up example. In the real world, even if sales did tend to follow the above general pattern, there would be random day-to-day and month-to-month variations due to factors such as the weather – people are less likely to buy ice cream when it is raining.

## 31.2 Formal Definitions

Let us state some definitions. A time series is **a list of values for a variable which occur at different points in time**. Examples of time series may include:

- the price of a customer's quarterly utility bills, that is 4 times per year – a **4-cycle**;

- the number of cars on a given stretch of road during the same period each weekday, that is 5 readings at the same time each week – a **5-cycle**;

- monthly car sales by a particular showroom – a **12-cycle**.

Time series usually have three components:

- a **trend** (sometimes called a **secular variation**),

- a **repetitive** or **cyclical** element, and

- **random oscillations**.

The cyclical element often varies with days, weeks, months or seasons of the year. But this is not always the case. An example would be the performance of a sports car in tests if the tyres are changed every three trials. In this case, initially good performance will be followed by increasing deterioration.

Only rarely is a time series just the sum of a trend and a cyclical pattern. Nearly every real variable has random behaviour associated with it. So while the recurring pattern in the plot of the values will be clear, the peaks and troughs will not be identical to each other.

In CCEA GCSE Further Maths the study of time series has the following restrictions:

- We assume that data values occur at **discrete** time intervals.

- We assume that data values follow a pattern which repeats, with minor variation, **cyclically**. In any series the number of time periods in a cycle is a **constant** value. For example, if a variable is measured in each quarter of a year, then there will be 4 data values in that cycle.

- We only study time series in which the underlying trend is **linear**.

## 31.3 Identifying The Number Of Data Values In Each Cycle

The first task in analysing a time series is to note how many data values occur in the cycle before the pattern begins to repeat itself. There are two broad techniques we can use:

1. The first is to use common sense in interpreting the context. For example, if readings are being recorded for a utility bill quarterly throughout each year – say for spring, summer, autumn and winter – then each cycle will have 4 data items in it.

2. Secondly, the cycle is often implied by how the data is presented. In the ice cream example above the table has four columns which implies four data values in each cycle.

In either case, the pattern of the time series should be confirmed by plotting the data values in a graph with time on the horizontal axis. In the ice cream example, the cycle can clearly be seen to include four data values before repeating:

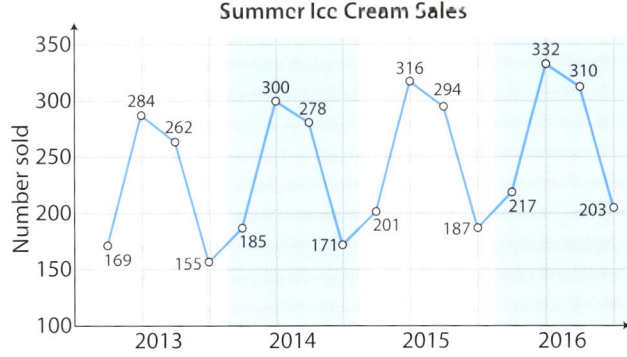

Summer Ice Cream Sales

From the table these can be seen to be the June, July, August and September values in any year.

## Exercise 31A

For each of the sets of data below:
(a) plot the data on a graph and demonstrate that it follows a repetitive cyclical pattern;
(b) state the number of data values in each cycle.

1.

|      | Q1  | Q2  | Q3  | Q4  |
|------|-----|-----|-----|-----|
| 2013 | 204 | 319 | 365 | 266 |
| 2014 | 236 | 351 | 397 | 298 |
| 2015 | 268 | 383 | 429 | 330 |
| 2016 | 300 | 415 | 461 | 362 |
| 2017 | 332 | 447 | 493 | 394 |

2.

|        | Mon | Tue | Wed | Thu | Fri |
|--------|-----|-----|-----|-----|-----|
| Week 1 | 17  | 40  | 126 | 167 | 120 |
| Week 2 | 61  | 83  | 170 | 213 | 165 |
| Week 3 | 105 | 130 | 215 | 258 | 210 |
| Week 4 | 150 | 175 | 261 | 302 | 256 |

3.

|      | Q1  | Q2  | Q3  | Q4  |
|------|-----|-----|-----|-----|
| 2013 | 214 | 180 | 83  | 133 |
| 2014 | 246 | 212 | 115 | 165 |
| 2015 | 278 | 244 | 147 | 197 |
| 2016 | 310 | 276 | 179 | 229 |
| 2017 | 342 | 308 | 211 | 261 |

4.

|        | Mon | Tue | Wed | Thu | Fri |
|--------|-----|-----|-----|-----|-----|
| Week 1 | 152 | 190 | 433 | 531 | 337 |
| Week 2 | 106 | 145 | 388 | 486 | 291 |
| Week 3 | 62  | 101 | 342 | 441 | 247 |
| Week 4 | 16  | 55  | 296 | 396 | 202 |

5.

|      | Q1  | Q2  | Q3  | Q4  |
|------|-----|-----|-----|-----|
| 2013 | 185 | 208 | 278 | 236 |
| 2014 | 150 | 171 | 242 | 200 |
| 2015 | 113 | 137 | 206 | 165 |
| 2016 | 77  | 101 | 170 | 130 |
| 2017 | 41  | 64  | 133 | 92  |

6.

| 38 | 117 | 62 | 74 | 153 | 98 | 110 | 189 | 134 | 146 | 225 | 170 |
|----|-----|----|----|-----|----|-----|-----|-----|-----|-----|-----|

7.

|      | Q1  | Q2  | Q3  | Q4  |
|------|-----|-----|-----|-----|
| 2013 | 71  | 74  | 62  | 81  |
| 2014 | 109 | 110 | 100 | 116 |
| 2015 | 144 | 145 | 136 | 152 |
| 2016 | 180 | 181 | 170 | 187 |
| 2017 | 217 | 217 | 207 | 224 |

## Exercise 31A...

**8.**

|  | Mon | Tue | Wed | Thu | Fri |
|---|---|---|---|---|---|
| Week 1 | 270 | 182 | 52 | 67 | 211 |
| Week 2 | 290 | 202 | 72 | 87 | 231 |
| Week 3 | 310 | 221 | 93 | 108 | 252 |
| Week 4 | 330 | 241 | 112 | 127 | 272 |

**9.**

|  | Q1 | Q2 | Q3 | Q4 |
|---|---|---|---|---|
| 2013 | 343 | 439 | 247 | 197 |
| 2014 | 434 | 532 | 341 | 289 |
| 2015 | 528 | 623 | 432 | 382 |
| 2016 | 618 | 715 | 524 | 474 |
| 2017 | 711 | 806 | 616 | 565 |

**10.**

|  | Q1 | Q2 | Q3 | Q4 |
|---|---|---|---|---|
| 2013 | 89 | 146 | 172 | 107 |
| 2014 | 74 | 130 | 155 | 91 |
| 2015 | 58 | 116 | 139 | 75 |
| 2016 | 41 | 99 | 124 | 59 |
| 2017 | 25 | 82 | 108 | 42 |

## 31.4 Calculating Moving Averages

Suppose we want to see the underlying trend in a time series. This requires us to remove the cyclical effects which cause variations about this trend. This is accomplished by calculating **moving averages**. For example:

1. Draw a graph of moving averages for the ice cream sales example in section 31.1.

This can be achieved by first calculating the average of the four data values in the first year:

Average value 1
= ¼(Jun13 + Jul13 + Aug13 + Sep13) = 217.5

Since the pattern repeats every four data values, we can then calculate the average of the next four successive data values. We achieve this by removing the first data item from the list (Jun 2013) and adding the fifth data item (Jun 2014). Then we calculate the average of the new set of four values:

Average value 2
= ¼(Jul13 + Aug13 + Sep13 + Jun14) = 221.5

Note that this still smooths out the cyclic pattern because it uses 4 adjacent data values, one from each month in

the cycle: July, August, September and the following June. Continuing in this manner:

Average value 3
= ¼(Aug13 + Sep13 + Jun14 + Jul14) = 225.5

Average value 4
= ¼(Sep13 + Jun14 + Jul14 + Aug14) = 229.5

Until finally:

Average value 13
= ¼(Jun16 + Jul16 + Aug16 + Sep16) = 265.5

The resulting list of **moving averages** displays the underlying trend in the time series. As each cycle contains one value for each set of 4 successive months, the average of these values will cancel out the peaks and troughs in the series.

These moving averages can then be plotted on a graph with the value against the middle of the 4 times averaged. Thus "Average value 1" is plotted over the middle of July 2013 and August 2013 and so on.

The graph is then plotted:

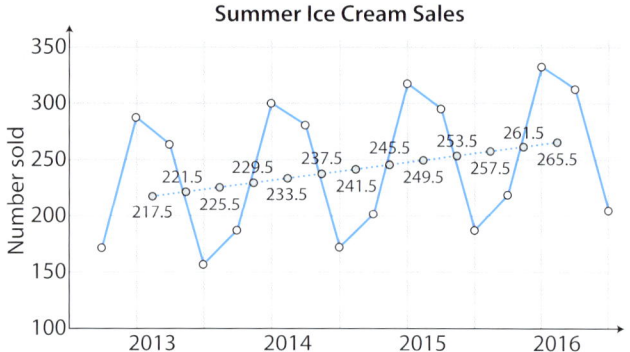

## 31.5 Making Predictions

Finally, time series may be used to make predictions of future (or past) performance by assuming that the trend identified by the moving averages continues outside the range of time values given. For example:

2. In the ice cream sales example, predict the value of the June 2017 sales.

We first use the trend line of the moving averages to estimate the next moving average. From the graph, we estimate that this value is 269.5:

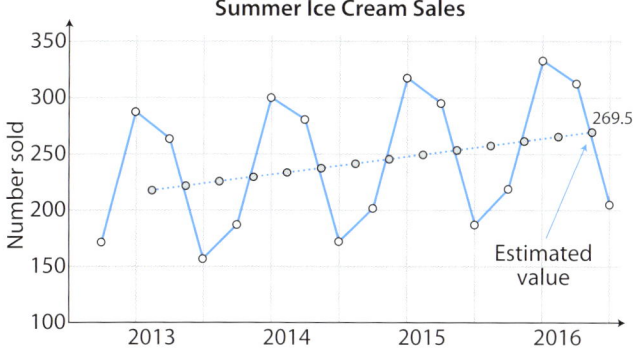

**Summary Ice Cream Sales**

Use this as the next moving average and substitute this into the usual calculation:

¼(Jul16 + Aug16 + Sep16 + Jun17) = 262

Then, filling in the values for July 16, August 16 and September 16 we can predict:

¼(332 + 310 + 203 + Jun17) = 269.5
845 + Jun17 = 4 × 269.5
Jun17 = 1078 – 845
= 233 ice creams sold.

## Exercise 31B

1. The table below shows the attendances at the matches of a local football team (in thousands) over a three-year period:

| Year | Jan-Mar | Apr-Jun | Jul-Sep | Oct-Dec |
|---|---|---|---|---|
| Year 1 | 180 | 165 | 172 | 155 |
| Year 2 | 164 | 145 | 160 | 141 |
| Year 3 | 153 | 132 | 148 | 127 |

(a) Plot these data on graph paper using suitable scales and axes.
(b) Calculate the four-point moving averages to smooth the data.
(c) Plot these moving averages.
(d) Draw the trend line and use it to estimate attendance in the first quarter of Year 4.

2. The table below shows the variation in annual share price in a commodity on the open market for the years 2000–2010.

| Year | 2000 | 2001 | 2002 | 2003 | 2004 |
|---|---|---|---|---|---|
| Price | £4.60 | £4.20 | £4.00 | £4.80 | £4.40 |

| 2005 | 2006 | 2007 | 2008 | 2009 | 2010 |
|---|---|---|---|---|---|
| £4.30 | £5.00 | £4.60 | £4.50 | £5.20 | £4.80 |

## Exercise 31B

(a) Plot these data on graph paper using suitable scales and axes.
(b) Calculate the three-point moving averages to smooth the data.
(c) Plot these moving averages.
(d) Draw the trend line and use it to estimate the share price in 2011.

3. As part of a family budget, Louise recorded the amount spent every week on shopping. The amounts are recorded in the following table:

| Week | 1 | 2 | 3 | 4 | 5 | 6 |
|---|---|---|---|---|---|---|
| Amount | £144 | £99 | £113 | £164 | £156 | £111 |

| 7 | 8 | 9 | 10 | 11 | 12 |
|---|---|---|---|---|---|
| £125 | £176 | £168 | £123 | £137 | £188 |

(a) Plot these data on graph paper using suitable scales and axes.
(b) Calculate the four-point moving averages to smooth the data.
(c) Plot these moving averages.
(d) Draw the trend line and use it to estimate the expenditure in Week 13.

4. The number of people requesting foreign currency from a bank over a three-week period is shown in the table below.

| | Week 1 | | | | |
|---|---|---|---|---|---|
| | Mon | Tue | Wed | Thu | Fri |
| Day | 1 | 2 | 3 | 4 | 5 |
| Amount | 49 | 61 | 63 | 55 | 52 |

| | Week 2 | | | | |
|---|---|---|---|---|---|
| | Mon | Tue | Wed | Thu | Fri |
| Day | 6 | 7 | 8 | 9 | 10 |
| Amount | 60 | 71 | 72 | 65 | 62 |

| | Week 3 | | | | |
|---|---|---|---|---|---|
| | Mon | Tue | Wed | Thu | Fri |
| Day | 11 | 12 | 13 | 14 | 15 |
| Amount | 69 | 80 | 82 | 75 | 72 |

(a) Plot these data on graph paper using suitable scales and axes.
(b) Calculate the five-point moving averages to smooth the data.
(c) Plot these moving averages.
(d) Draw the trend line and use it to estimate the number of people on day 16.

5. The following table shows the amounts of the quarterly electricity bills for a household in Northern Ireland:

| Quarter | Q1-2016 | Q2-2016 | Q3-2016 | Q4-2016 | Q1-2017 | Q2-2017 |
|---------|---------|---------|---------|---------|---------|---------|
| Amount | £108 | £48 | £67 | £135 | £124 | £64 |

| Q3-2017 | Q4-2017 | Q1-2018 | Q2-2018 | Q3-2018 | Q4-2018 |
|---------|---------|---------|---------|---------|---------|
| £83 | £151 | £140 | £80 | £99 | £167 |

(a) Plot these data on graph paper using suitable scales and axes.
(b) Calculate the four-point moving averages to smooth the data.
(c) Plot these moving averages.
(d) Draw the trend line and use it to estimate the quarterly electricity bill for the first quarter 2019.

6. An electrical store sold the following numbers of electrical items over 15 consecutive weekdays in December.

| Week 1 | | | | | |
|--------|-----|-----|-----|-----|-----|
| | Mon | Tue | Wed | Thu | Fri |
| Day | 1 | 2 | 3 | 4 | 5 |
| Number | 36 | 48 | 51 | 45 | 43 |

| Week 2 | | | | | |
|--------|-----|-----|-----|-----|-----|
| | Mon | Tue | Wed | Thu | Fri |
| Day | 6 | 7 | 8 | 9 | 10 |
| Number | 51 | 63 | 66 | 60 | 58 |

| Week 3 | | | | | |
|--------|-----|-----|-----|-----|-----|
| | Mon | Tue | Wed | Thu | Fri |
| Day | 11 | 12 | 13 | 14 | 15 |
| Number | 66 | 78 | 81 | 75 | 73 |

(a) Plot these data on graph paper using suitable scales and axes.
(b) Calculate the five-point moving averages to smooth the data.
(c) Plot these moving averages.
(d) Draw the trend line and use it to estimate the number of items sold in day 16.

7. A small music shop has recorded the numbers of sales of chart singles over the past 12 weeks. These are listed in the table below.

| Week | 1 | 2 | 3 | 4 | 5 | 6 |
|------|-----|-----|-----|-----|-----|-----|
| Amount | 103 | 34 | 48 | 113 | 95 | 26 |

| 7 | 8 | 9 | 10 | 11 | 12 |
|-----|-----|-----|-----|-----|-----|
| 40 | 105 | 87 | 18 | 32 | 97 |

(a) Plot these data on graph paper using suitable scales and axes.
(b) Calculate the four-point moving averages to smooth the data.
(c) Plot these moving averages.
(d) Draw the trend line and use it to estimate the number of singles that will be sold in week 13.

8. The numbers of patients who missed physiotherapy appointments over four years are listed in the table below.

| | Term 1 | Term 2 | Term 3 |
|------|--------|--------|--------|
| 2013 | 213 | 238 | 151 |
| 2014 | 207 | 232 | 145 |
| 2015 | 201 | 226 | 139 |
| 2016 | 195 | 220 | 133 |

(a) Plot these data on graph paper using suitable scales and axes.
(b) Calculate the three-point moving averages to smooth the data.
(c) Plot these moving averages.
(d) Draw the trend line and use it to estimate the number of patients who missed appointments in 2017 Term 1.

## 32.1 Introduction

Suppose the editor of a magazine wants to analyse the process of creating an article for the next issue. She decides on the list of **tasks**, or activities, and how long each will take to complete: Then the editor adds a column listing any tasks which need to be completed before starting the task of that column (**prerequisite** tasks):

| Task | Description | Length (minutes) | After task |
|------|-------------|------------------|------------|
| A | Write text of article | 35 | - |
| B | Search for relevant images | 30 | - |
| C | Cut and prepare images | 10 | B |
| D | Create style for article including any border | 5 | A, C |
| E | Insert text, choosing font, size and justification | 5 | D |
| F | Insert images, cropping and wrapping | 8 | E |
| G | Write a summary of the article | 10 | A, C |
| H | Email summary to editor and sub-editor | 3 | G |

This table is called a **precedence table**.

Using either common sense or an algorithm the editor next creates an **activity network** for this process, filling in the earliest and latest start times for each task. This is shown in the diagram below.

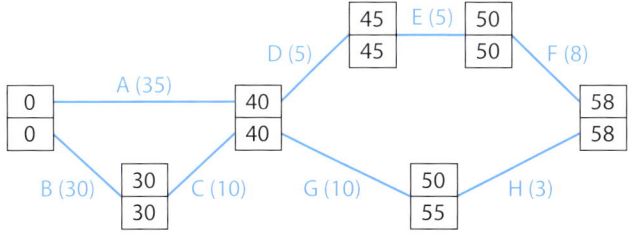

Time progresses from left to right across the diagram. Note that the tasks are represented by the **edges** or **arcs** on this network, with their lengths given in brackets. The **earliest start time (EST)** and **latest start time (LST)** for any task are given in the box **before** that task in the diagram (top and bottom, respectively).

Having constructed this activity network, the editor reads off the **critical path** – that is, the list of tasks which follow each other without a break. This path may be read easily because it passes through all the boxes where EST = LST. The critical path here is the task list:

B → C → D → E → F

Finally, the editor schedules the writing of the article to two workers in a **Gantt chart**. In this schedule, different tasks may be carried out by different people provided they only start after any prerequisite tasks (necessary prior tasks) have finished. In all cases the tasks in the critical path may be performed by the same worker(s). The editor's completed Gantt chart is shown below.

| Time | 1 | 2 | 3 | 4 | 5 | 6 | 7 | 8 | 9 | 10 | 11 | 12 | 13 | 14 | 15 | 16 | 17 | 18 | 19 | 20 |
|------|---|---|---|---|---|---|---|---|---|----|----|----|----|----|----|----|----|----|----|----|
| Wkr 1 | B | B | B | B | B | B | B | B | B | B | B | B | B | B | B | B | B | B | B | B |
| Wkr 2 | A | A | A | A | A | A | A | A | A | A | A | A | A | A | A | A | A | A | A | A |

| Time | 21 | 22 | 23 | 24 | 25 | 26 | 27 | 28 | 29 | 30 | 31 | 32 | 33 | 34 | 35 | 36 | 37 | 38 | 39 | 40 |
|------|----|----|----|----|----|----|----|----|----|----|----|----|----|----|----|----|----|----|----|----|
| Wkr 1 | B | B | B | B | B | B | B | B | B | B | C | C | C | C | C | C | C | C | C | C |
| Wkr 2 | A | A | A | A | A | A | A | A | A | A | A | A | A | A | | | | | | |

| Time | 41 | 42 | 43 | 44 | 45 | 46 | 47 | 48 | 49 | 50 | 51 | 52 | 53 | 54 | 55 | 56 | 57 | 58 |
|------|----|----|----|----|----|----|----|----|----|----|----|----|----|----|----|----|----|----|
| Wkr 1 | D | D | D | D | D | E | E | E | E | E | F | F | F | F | F | F | F | F |
| Wkr 2 | G | G | G | G | G | G | G | G | G | G | H | H | H | | | | | |

This Gantt chart shows just one possible division of work. One worker completes tasks B, C, D, E and F with no slack time. This person manages all the technical aspects of image and styles. The second worker completes tasks A, G and H, composing the text of the article and writing the summary. This second worker has 5 minutes of slack time for tasks G and H. So for example, task G could start at any point between times 41 and 46. Tasks D and G, however, must wait until tasks A and C have been completed before starting.

In the remainder of this chapter we shall consider how to:

- create an activity network from a precedence table;

- analyse an activity network to determine the earliest start times, latest start times, critical path and float times;

- produce a schedule from an activity network in the form of a Gantt chart.

## 32.2 Creating An Activity Network From A Precedence Table

First we shall consider how to construct an activity network. The starting point is the list of tasks (or activities) with their prerequisites. The lengths of the tasks need not be included at this stage.

Let us return to the example of the process of writing an article. The table below is the editor's original precedence table but omitting the descriptions and lengths:

| Task | Prerequisites |
|------|---------------|
| A | - |
| B | - |
| C | B |
| D | A, C |
| E | D |
| F | E |
| G | A, C |
| H | G |

Because this list of tasks is relatively simple, the activity network may be constructed by inspection. However another method, which is useful for more complex lists of tasks, is to use the following algorithm:

*Write out two vertical lists of the tasks.*

*Join a task in the left-hand list to a task in the right-hand list if the task in the left-hand list must follow the task in the right-hand list.*

*Repeat*

> *Make a new left-hand list by deleting those tasks in the left-hand list which are not joined to a task in the right-hand list.*

> *Also delete from the right-hand list the copies of those deleted tasks and any arrows joined to these copies in the right-hand list.*

*Until: there are no more tasks left in the left-hand list.*

*Add the deleted tasks to the activity network in order of their deletion from left to right.*

By following the first two steps of the algorithm we produce these lists:

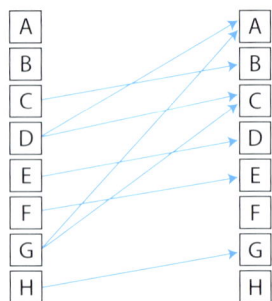

By continuing to apply the algorithm, we begin by deleting A and B and the arrows pointing to them:

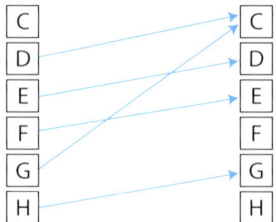

Add the deleted tasks to the activity network:

A

B

Continuing with the algorithm, we next delete C and any arrows pointing to it:

As before, add the deleted tasks to the activity network, keeping them in the order in which they were deleted:

A

B    C

Next delete D and G and the arrows pointing to them:

Again, add the deleted tasks to the activity network:

A          D

B    C    G

Next delete E and H, and the remaining arrow, and add them to the activity network. Finally, delete F and add it to the activity network. This creates the pattern:

A          D     E     F

B    C    G    H

as a basis for the activity network.

Next we draw arcs (lines) to represent each task and insert nodes (boxes) between them. Each node has two spaces: one for the earliest and one for the latest times at which the following task may start (the EST and LST). We also write the length of each task on the relevant arc. This results in the following activity network:

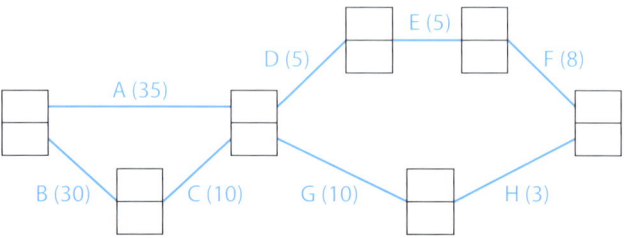

## Exercise 32A

Use the algorithm of the previous section to decide the order of the tasks from the precedence table given, and to draw an activity network.

1.

| Task | Prerequisites |
|------|---------------|
| A | – |
| B | – |
| C | A |
| D | B |
| E | C |
| F | D |
| G | E, F |

2.

| Task | Prerequisites |
|------|---------------|
| A | – |
| B | A |
| C | A |
| D | B |
| E | C |
| F | D |
| G | E |

3.

| Task | Prerequisites |
|------|---------------|
| A | – |
| B | – |
| C | A |
| D | B |
| E | C, D |
| F | C, D |
| G | E |
| H | F |

4.

| Task | Prerequisites |
|------|---------------|
| A | - |
| B | - |
| C | - |
| D | A |
| E | B |
| F | C |
| G | D, E |
| H | F |

5.

| Task | Prerequisites |
|------|---------------|
| A | - |
| B | - |
| C | A |
| D | A |
| E | B |
| F | B |
| G | C, E |
| H | D, F |

6.

| Task | Prerequisites |
|------|---------------|
| A | – |
| B | – |
| C | – |
| D | A |
| E | B |
| F | B |
| G | C |
| H | C |
| I | D, E |
| J | D, E |
| K | F, G |
| L | F, G |
| M | H |
| N | I |
| O | J, K |
| P | L, M |

7.

| Task | Prerequisites |
|------|---------------|
| A | – |
| B | – |
| C | A |
| D | A |
| E | B |
| F | C |
| G | D |
| H | E |
| I | F |
| J | G, H |

## Exercise 32A...

**8.**

| Task | Prerequisites |
|------|---------------|
| A | – |
| B | – |
| C | – |
| D | A |
| E | A |
| F | C |
| G | C |
| H | D |
| I | B, E, F |
| J | B, E, F |
| K | G |
| L | H, I |
| M | J, K |
| N | L, M |

## 32.3 Analysing An Activity Network

The next step in constructing an activity network is to fill in the earliest and latest start times for each task. We will return to the example of the editor's activity network.

The **earliest times** are written in the **top** space of every double box in the diagram. We begin by placing a zero in the top of the first box, since it can begin immediately.

We complete the forward pass through the network by using the following rule:

........................................................

*Earliest Start Times (ESTs)*

*Pass forwards through the network, from left to right – filling in at the top of each box the **earliest** time that this point could be reached after completing **every** task feeding into it (ie choose the latest of these times).*

........................................................

We can place 30 in the top of the box after task B since task B takes 30 minutes. However, we now face the question of what number to place in the single box that comes after **both** tasks A and C. Clearly the next tasks can't start until both A and C have been completed. So, we choose whichever is the longer of task A (35 minutes) and tasks B + C (30 + 10 minutes = 40 minutes). Therefore we place 40 in the box. At this point our activity network looks like this:

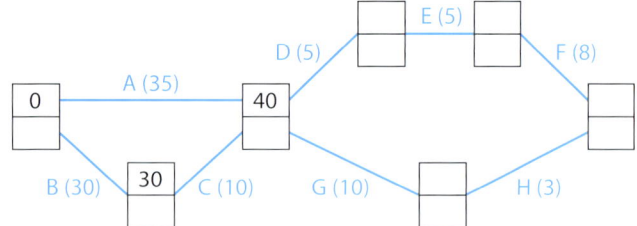

Continue to pass from left to right using the EST rule, until we reach the end of the activity network. We are done when the earliest completion time of the whole process (in this case 58 minutes) is filled in at the top of the last box. Our activity network now looks like this:

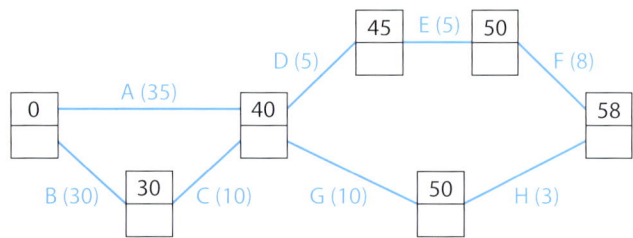

Next, we fill in the **latest start times** in the bottom space of each box. We start by filling 58 minutes into the bottom space of the final box, since we now know that that is how long the whole process takes.

We complete the backward pass through the network by using the following rule:

........................................................

*Latest Start Times (LSTs)*

*Pass backwards through the network – from right to left. Fill in at the bottom of each box the **latest** time that this point could be reached while still leaving enough time to complete **all** the following tasks (ie, choose the earliest of the following times).*

........................................................

Working from right to left, the next three spaces are easily calculated: the latest time that task H can commence is calculated by subtracting the length of H from the 58 minutes, and similarly for tasks E and F. The activity network now looks like this:

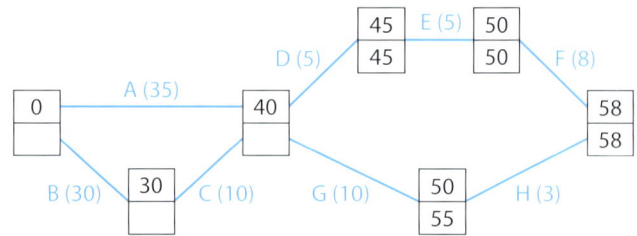

However, we now face the question of what to do when **two** tasks flow from the same box. The latest time that task D can start is after 45 – 5 = 40 minutes. The latest time that task G can start is after 55 – 10 = 45 minutes. Since both of the subsequent tasks must start we must pick the smallest of these times, i.e. 40 minutes. Therefore we place 40 in this box.

Continue to pass from right to left using the rule, until we reach the end of the activity network. Our finished activity network therefore looks like this:

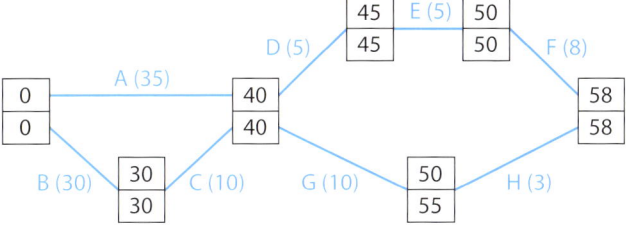

## 32.4 Critical Path

There will be at least one path through the network which has no **slack time** (i.e., there are no tasks on that path that can be delayed without impacting the overall duration of the project). This path, called the **critical path**, therefore represents the shortest possible time to complete the project. If any of the tasks on this route are extended by an amount of time, then the overall project time will be extended by an equal amount if time.

This means that the earliest start time, EST, will equal the latest start time, LST, at every node on the critical path. Therefore we can define the critical path as the list of tasks which pass through the boxes where:

**earliest start time (EST) = latest start time (LST)**

In our example, the editor finds that the critical path for the writing of the article is:

B → C → D → E → F

This means that the process of writing the article will take no less than 58 minutes to complete.

## 32.5 Float Time (Or Slack Time)

At any point in the activity network the **float time** is the amount of slack time by which the work at that point may be delayed without affecting the time to finish the project.

For any given task in an activity network, the float time is calculated by the relationship:

**float time (or slack time) for a task**
= **latest start time in the node at the right end**
 – **earliest start time in the node at the left end**
 – **length of the task**

So in our example, the editor calculates the float time for task G as follows:

Float time for G = 55 – 40 – 10 = 5 minutes

This means that writing the article summary can be delayed by up to 5 minutes after it is first possible to start the task, without affecting the overall duration of the project.

## 32.6 Scheduling And Gantt Charts

**Scheduling** is the name given to the process of turning the activity network into a plan of work, known as a Gantt chart, which involves assigning tasks to particular workers.

We begin by designing a grid listing the number of workers (rows in the grid) against a time axis (across the top of the grid). Each task is then entered into the grid, taking care that each task only begins after its prerequisites have been completed.

Since the critical path represents the minimum necessary length of the project, and all its tasks follow on in time order, so the critical path may be assigned to one worker. Doing this for our editor's example gives:

| Time | 1 | 2 | 3 | 4 | 5 | 6 | 7 | 8 | 9 | 10 | 11 | 12 | 13 | 14 | 15 | 16 | 17 | 18 | 19 | 20 |
|------|---|---|---|---|---|---|---|---|---|----|----|----|----|----|----|----|----|----|----|----|
| Wkr 1 | B | B | B | B | B | B | B | B | B | B | B | B | B | B | B | B | B | B | B | B |
| Wkr 2 | | | | | | | | | | | | | | | | | | | | |

| Time | 21 | 22 | 23 | 24 | 25 | 26 | 27 | 28 | 29 | 30 | 31 | 32 | 33 | 34 | 35 | 36 | 37 | 38 | 39 | 40 |
|------|----|----|----|----|----|----|----|----|----|----|----|----|----|----|----|----|----|----|----|----|
| Wkr 1 | B | B | B | B | B | B | B | B | B | B | C | C | C | C | C | C | C | C | C | C |
| Wkr 2 | | | | | | | | | | | | | | | | | | | | |

| Time | 41 | 42 | 43 | 44 | 45 | 46 | 47 | 48 | 49 | 50 | 51 | 52 | 53 | 54 | 55 | 56 | 57 | 58 |
|------|----|----|----|----|----|----|----|----|----|----|----|----|----|----|----|----|----|----|
| Wkr 1 | D | D | D | D | D | E | E | E | E | E | F | F | F | F | F | F | F | F |
| Wkr 2 | | | | | | | | | | | | | | | | | | |

Once the critical path tasks have been entered, the remaining tasks are entered into the grid for the other workers.

Because tasks A and C are prerequisites for task G in our example, task G can only start after A and C have been finished. That means that G can only start in the 41st minute. This means that the second worker has no task for minutes 35 to 40. There are 5 minutes unassigned for the second worker at the end of the project, showing that the slack time for tasks G and H is 5 minutes. Once all the remaining tasks have been entered into the grid, the result – called a Gantt chart – is as follows:

| Time | 1 | 2 | 3 | 4 | 5 | 6 | 7 | 8 | 9 | 10 | 11 | 12 | 13 | 14 | 15 | 16 | 17 | 18 | 19 | 20 |
|---|---|---|---|---|---|---|---|---|---|---|---|---|---|---|---|---|---|---|---|---|
| Wkr 1 | B | B | B | B | B | B | B | B | B | B | B | B | B | B | B | B | B | B | B | B |
| Wkr 2 | A | A | A | A | A | A | A | A | A | A | A | A | A | A | A | A | A | A | A | A |

| Time | 21 | 22 | 23 | 24 | 25 | 26 | 27 | 28 | 29 | 30 | 31 | 32 | 33 | 34 | 35 | 36 | 37 | 38 | 39 | 40 |
|---|---|---|---|---|---|---|---|---|---|---|---|---|---|---|---|---|---|---|---|---|
| Wkr 1 | B | B | B | B | B | B | B | B | B | B | C | C | C | C | C | C | C | C | C | C |
| Wkr 2 | A | A | A | A | A | A | A | A | A | A | A | A | A | | | | | | | |

| Time | 41 | 42 | 43 | 44 | 45 | 46 | 47 | 48 | 49 | 50 | 51 | 52 | 53 | 54 | 55 | 56 | 57 | 58 |
|---|---|---|---|---|---|---|---|---|---|---|---|---|---|---|---|---|---|---|
| Wkr 1 | D | D | D | D | D | E | E | E | E | F | F | F | F | F | F | F | F | F |
| Wkr 2 | G | G | G | G | G | G | G | G | G | G | G | H | H | H | | | | |

## 32.7 Further Scheduling

There is no algorithm which will always produce the best Gantt chart for an activity network.

However, although not on the specification, for those who find algorithms useful, one possible method is the First Scheduling Method. This may be stated as:

........................................................................

*Repeat for each worker who is free:*

    *For all tasks which have not yet started:*

        *For all tasks which may be started (ie, all their prerequisites are completed):*

            *Choose a task with the least latest start time (LST) at the left-hand (prior) node.*

*Increment time.*

........................................................................

## Exercise 32B

In each of the following activity networks, the number in brackets on each edge represents the time in days which it will take one person to complete that task.

1.

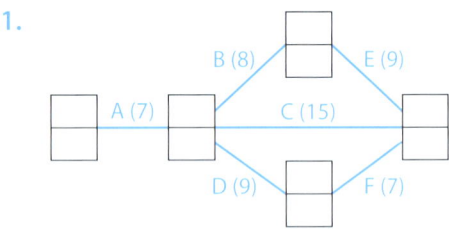

(a) Complete the earliest start times (ESTs) and latest start times (LSTs) and write down the critical path.

(b) Design a Gantt chart to schedule this activity

network using 3 persons in the shortest possible time.

2.

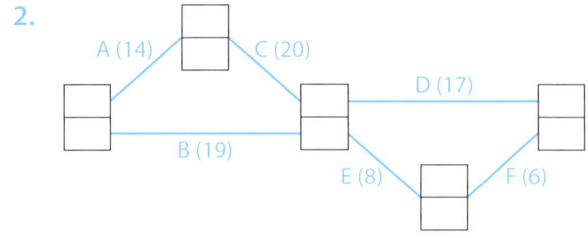

(a) Complete the earliest start times (ESTs) and latest start times (LSTs) and write down the critical path.

(b) Design a Gantt chart to schedule this activity network using 2 persons in the shortest possible time.

3.

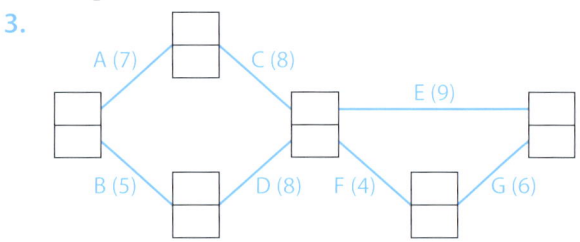

(a) Complete the earliest start times (ESTs) and latest start times (LSTs) and write down the critical path.

(b) Design a Gantt chart to schedule this activity network using 2 persons in the shortest possible time.

4.

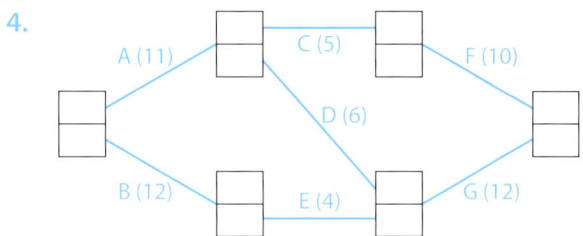

(a) Complete the earliest start times (ESTs) and latest start times (LSTs) and write down the critical path.

(b) Design a Gantt chart to schedule this activity network using 2 persons in the shortest possible time.

5.

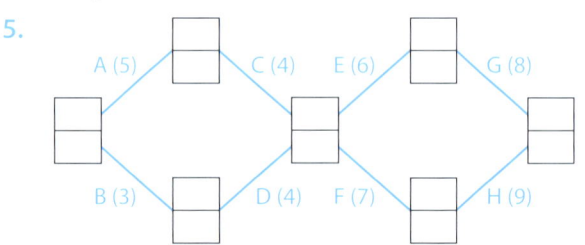

## Exercise 32B...

(a) Complete the earliest start times (ESTs) and latest start times (LSTs) and write down the critical path.

(b) Design a Gantt chart to schedule this activity network using 2 persons in the shortest possible time.

6.

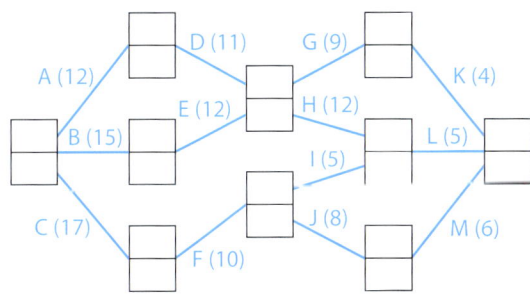

(a) Complete the earliest start times (ESTs) and latest start times (LSTs) and write down the critical path.

(b) Design a Gantt chart to schedule this activity network using 3 persons in 30 days.

7. For the activity network below, complete the earliest start times (ESTs) and latest start times (LSTs) and write down the critical path.

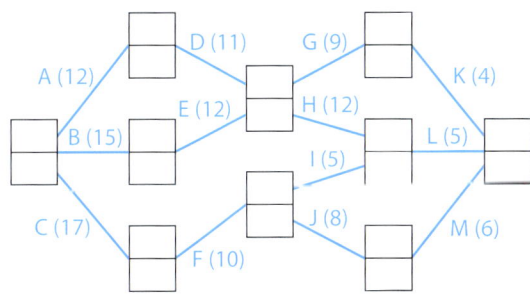

8. For the activity network below, complete the earliest start times (ESTs) and latest start times (LSTs) and write down the critical path.

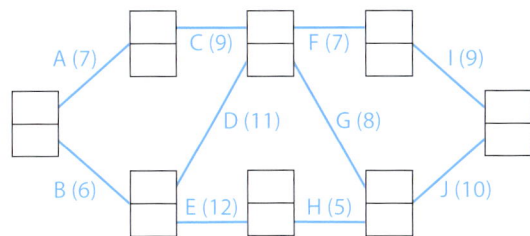

## Exercise 32B...

9. For the activity network below, complete the earliest start times (ESTs) and latest start times (LSTs) and write down the critical path.

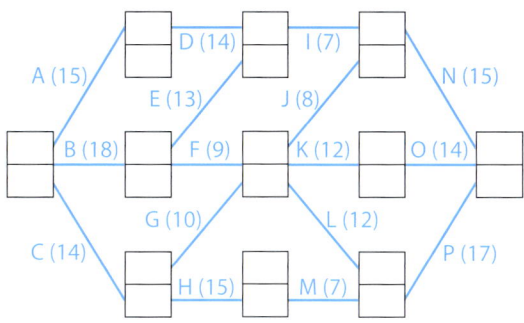

10. For the activity network below, complete the earliest start times (ESTs) and latest start times (LSTs) and write down the critical path.

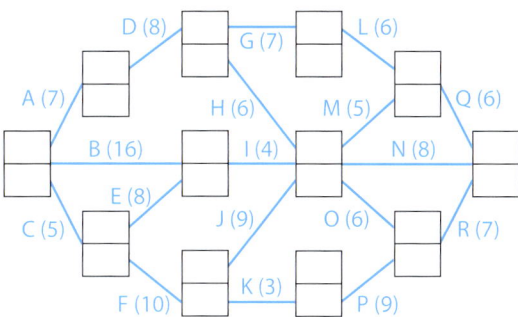

# Answers

## Exercise 1A

1. $\dfrac{11x + 17}{12}$

2. $\dfrac{3x - 16}{10}$

3. $\dfrac{-1}{12}$

4. $\dfrac{5x - 12}{8}$

5. $\dfrac{11x - 8}{20}$

6. $\dfrac{-2x + 24}{(3x - 2)(x + 5)}$

7. $\dfrac{3x + 24}{(2 - x)(x + 4)}$

8. $\dfrac{8x - 18}{(3 - 2x)(x - 3)}$

9. $\dfrac{11x - 23}{(2x - 1)(x - 4)}$

10. $\dfrac{12x - 1}{(x - 3)(2x + 1)}$

## Exercise 1B

1. $\dfrac{11x + 8}{x(x - 3)(x + 2)}$

2. $\dfrac{9x + 10}{2x(x - 3)(x + 2)}$

3. $\dfrac{7x + 5}{(x + 3)(x - 1)(x + 5)}$

4. $\dfrac{7x + 21}{(x + 4)(x - 2)(2x + 1)}$

5. $\dfrac{5x - 2}{x(x - 4)(x + 2)}$

6. $\dfrac{x + 26}{(x + 1)(x + 5)(x - 2)}$

7. $\dfrac{x + 20}{2x(x - 3)(x + 4)}$

8. $\dfrac{-x - 2}{(x + 4)(x - 1)(x - 2)}$

9. $\dfrac{-x + 10}{(x + 5)(x - 2)(x + 2)}$

10. $\dfrac{x - 16}{(x + 2)(x - 4)(2x - 1)}$

## Exercise 1C

1. $\dfrac{13x + 4}{3x(x + 1)(x + 2)}$

2. $\dfrac{7x + 18}{(x + 2)(x - 2)(x + 4)}$

3. $\dfrac{13x - 14}{(x + 4)(x - 3)(2x - 1)}$

4. $\dfrac{10x - 3}{2x(x - 5)(2x - 1)}$

5. $\dfrac{7x - 5}{(x - 2)(x - 5)(x + 5)}$

6. $\dfrac{6}{x(x + 1)(2x - 1)}$

7. $\dfrac{x + 8}{(x + 2)(x - 4)(x + 4)}$

8. $\dfrac{-4x - 9}{x(x - 2)(2x + 3)}$

9. $\dfrac{3x + 35}{(x + 4)(x - 3)(2x + 5)}$

10. $\dfrac{-5x - 7}{(x + 2)(x - 3)(4x - 1)}$

## Exercise 1D

1. $\dfrac{10xy}{v^2}$

2. $\dfrac{t}{nv}$

3. $\dfrac{4q^2}{rn}$

4. $\dfrac{9wt}{v^2}$

5. $\dfrac{10rw}{vq}$

6. $\dfrac{6a^3b^2}{5c}$

7. $\dfrac{8qn}{5}$

8. $\dfrac{2vt}{3wn}$

9. $\dfrac{18c}{7ab}$

10. $\dfrac{10qv^3}{3r}$

## Exercise 1E

1. $\dfrac{2x - 1}{x - 2}$

2. $\dfrac{3x}{2x - 1}$

3. $\dfrac{x + 5}{x + 4}$

4. $\dfrac{4x - 3}{x - 3}$

5. $\dfrac{x + 5}{x + 2}$

6. $\dfrac{4x}{x + 2}$

7. $\dfrac{2x - 1}{x - 2}$

8. $\dfrac{x + 5}{2x + 3}$

9. $\dfrac{4x}{2x + 1}$

10. $\dfrac{5x - 2}{x - 5}$

## Exercise 1F

1. $\dfrac{2x}{x + 4}$

2. $\dfrac{5(x - 3)}{2(3x - 2)}$

3. $\dfrac{3(x + 5)}{4(x - 2)}$

4. $\dfrac{3(3x + 2)}{2(x - 2)}$

5. $\dfrac{8(2x - 5)}{15(x + 4)}$

6. $\dfrac{8(x + 2)}{3x - 1}$

7. $\dfrac{x - 7}{2(x + 5)}$

8. $\dfrac{3(x + 5)}{4(4x + 3)}$

9. $\dfrac{4(x + 6)}{3(x - 2)}$

10. $\dfrac{3(4x - 1)}{2(x - 2)}$

## Exercise 1G

1. $x^3 + 8x^2 + 17x + 10$
2. $x^3 + 3x^2 - 10x - 24$
3. $x^3 + 8x^2 + 11x - 20$
4. $x^3 - 5x^2 - 2x + 24$
5. $3x^3 + 13x^2 + 2x - 8$
6. $6x^3 + 23x^2 - 33x + 10$
7. $24x^3 - 2x^2 - 31x - 12$
8. $x^3 + 12x^2 + 48x + 64$
9. $x^3 - 9x^2 + 27x - 27$
10. $8x^3 + 60x^2 + 150x + 125$
11. $x^3 + 6x^2y + 12xy^2 + 8y^2$
12. $x^3 + 3x^2y - 13xy^2 - 15y^2$
13. $a = 10, b = -59, c = -8, d = 12$
14. $a = 3, b = -1, c = -22, d = 24$
15. $a = 42, b = -115, c = -4, d = 32$

## Exercise 1H

1. $(3x^3 + 13x^2 - 18x - 40)$ cm$^3$
2. $(8x^3 - 12x^2 + 6x - 1)$ cm$^3$
3. $(x^3 - 5x^2 - 8x + 48)\pi$ cm$^3$
4. £$(2x^3 + 3x^2 - 18x + 8)$
5. $(2x^3 - 3x^2 - 29x - 30)$ cm$^3$

## Exercise 1J

1. $x + 1$

2. $\dfrac{-8}{x - 4}$

3. $2(x + 4)$

4. $\dfrac{x}{x + 3}$

## Exercise 2A

1. ⁴⁄₃ or −⁴⁄₃
2. −²⁄₃ or 1
3. 0 or −⁷⁄₂
4. 5 or −³⁄₂
5. −½ or ⅔
6. −⅔ or 4
7. −5 or ¾
8. 0 or ⁷⁄₃
9. ⅔ or −⁹⁄₂
10. 7 or ³⁄₂
11. −½ or −⅔
12. ⅖ or −⅖

## Exercise 2B

1. 5.45 or 0.55
2. 1.64 or −2.14
3. 2.10 or −1.43
4. −0.23 or −8.77
5. 2.14 or −1.64
6. 0.55 or −1.22
7. 1.37 or −1.17
8. −0.27 or −3.73
9. 0.44 or −1.69
10. 4.16 or −2.16

## Exercise 2C

1. 9 cm, 12 cm
2. 8 cm, 6 cm
3. 35p
4. 20 cm, 15 cm

## Exercise 2D

1. 4 or ⁷⁄₃
2. 2 or ⅔
3. 1 or –6
4. 3 or ⁵⁄₃
5. 2 or –½
6. 5 or ⁵⁄₃
7. 3 or ⅝
8. 2 or –½
9. 3 or ³⁄₂
10. 5 or ⁵⁄₂

## Exercise 2E

1. 3 or –⁵⁄₂
2. –3
3. 5 or ³⁄₂
4. 4 or ⁵⁄₄
5. –2 or 0
6. 3 or ½
7. –4 or 5
8. 3 or ⅔
9. 6 or ¹⁰⁄₃

## Exercise 2F

1. $-3 \pm\sqrt{12}$
2. $1 \pm\sqrt{6}$
3. $\dfrac{-1 \pm\sqrt{17}}{2}$
4. $\dfrac{3 \pm\sqrt{29}}{2}$
5. $-4 \pm\sqrt{11}$
6. $5 \pm\sqrt{27}$
7. $\dfrac{-5 \pm\sqrt{41}}{2}$
8. $\dfrac{7 \pm\sqrt{69}}{2}$
9. $-2 \pm\sqrt{13}$
10. $5 \pm\sqrt{28}$
11. (a) $x^2 - 4x - 10 = 0$ (b) $x = 2 + \sqrt{14}$

## Exercise 2G

1. (a) –12 (b) –3
2. (a) –3 (b) 2
3. (a) –11 (b) –4
4. (a) –9 (b) 1
5. (a) –3 ¼ (b) ½
6. (a) 5 ¾ (b) –1 ½
7. (a) 2 (b) 3
8. (a) 10 (b) –5

## Exercise 3A

1. 5, 1, 4
2. 3, 2, 5
3. 4, 2, 3
4. 2, –5, 3
5. 4, –1, –2
6. –2, 3, 4
7. 5, 2, 4
8. 7, –3, 5
9. 2, 4, –5
10. 5, 3, 6

## Exercise 3B

1. (d) 60p, 35p, 20p (e) £39.10
2. (d) 8, 5, 3 (e) 112
3. (d) £160, £120, £85 (e) £170
4. (d) £20, £30, £90 (e) 35%
5. (d) £6.50, £4.75, £5.50 (e) 12

6. (d) 600g, 950g, 870g
   (e) 21, 24, 15
7. 66
8. Form 3 simultaneous equations based on the points provided, solve, and then show that the value for $y = -296$ when $x = -5$.

## Exercise 4A

1.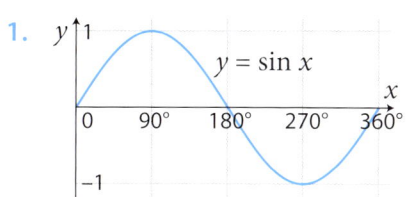

2.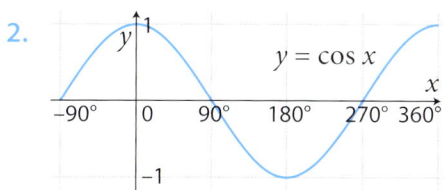

3.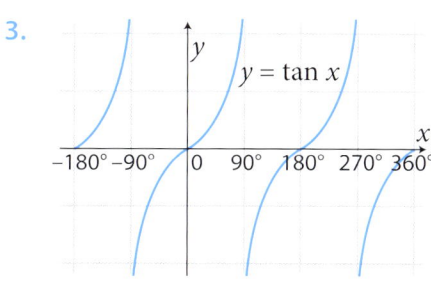

4.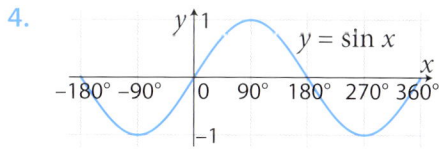

5.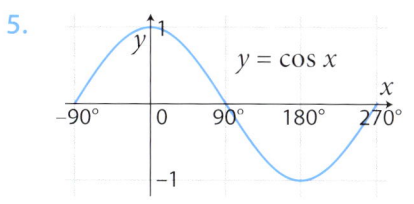

6.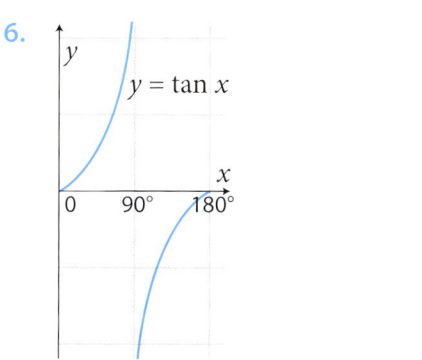

## Exercise 4B

1. 62.48° or 297.52°

2. 229.64° or 310.36°
3. 71.57° or 251.57°
4. 11.54° or 168.46°
5. 138.59° or 221.46°
6. 149.04° or 329.04°

## Exercise 4C

1. 53.13° or –53.13°
2. –19.88° or –160.12°
3. 116.57° or –63.43°
4. 47.65° or 132.35°
5. 110.43° or –110.43°
6. 123.69° or –56.31°

## Exercise 4D

1. 9.28° or 50.72°
2. 49.60° or 130.40°
3. 13.11° or 58.11°
4. 213.74° or 246.26°
5. 108.11° or 301.89°
6. –16.57° or 163.44°
7. –108.32° or 390.32°
8. 88.44° or –91.57°
9. 27.84° or –8.16°
10. 350.04° or 669.96°

## Exercise 5A

1. $-5 \le x \le -3$
2. $x < 0$ and $x > 2$
3. $-4 < x < 4$
4. $x \le -5$ and $x \ge -2$
5. $4 < x < 5$
6. $x \le 0$ and $x \ge 8$
7. $-3 \le x \le 2$
8. $x < -2$ and $x > 2$
9. $-7 < x < -2$
10. $x \le -1$ and $x \ge 0$
11. $-2 \le x \le 7$
12. $x \le -9$ and $x \ge 9$
13. $x \le 2$ and $x \ge 4$
14. $-6 < x < 3$
15. $x < 0$ and $x > 9$
16. $-6 \le x \le 6$
17. ⅔ $< x < 4$
18. $x < -3$ or $x > -½$
19. $-¼ \le x \le ¼$
20. $x \le -⅔$ or $x \ge ³⁄₂$
21. $-¾ < x < 2$
22. $x < -⅗$ or $x > ⅗$
23. ⅓ $< x < 4$
24. $x \le -2$ or $x \ge ⅕$

## Exercise 5B

1. £9000
2. $0 \le x \le 5$
3. $T \le -7$ or $T \ge 7$
4. $a < 0$ or $a > 2$
5. 11
6. $A < 12$
7. $2 < x < 7$
8. $5 \le h \le 40$

## Exercise 6A

1. 6
2. $4x - 3$
3. $6x + 1$
4. $6x^2 + 6x - 5$
5. $12x^2 - 12x + 1$
6. $3 - 2x + 21x^2$
7. $-3 + 4x - 3x^2$
8. $4x^3 - 4x$
9. $18x^2 - 3$
10. $8x - 3x^2 + 8x^3$
11. $10x^4 - 12x^3 + 6x^2 - 12x + 1$
12. $12x^2 - 14x$
13. $24x^3 - 4x + 1$
14. $3 - 3x^2$
15. $6x^2 - 8x - 7$
16. $-2 + 6x - 3x^2$
17. $6x^2 - 2x + 4$
18. $8x - 5$
19. $2ax + b$
20. $24x^2 - v$
21. $18x + t$

## Exercise 6B

1. $\frac{3}{4}x^2 - \frac{4}{5}x + 1$
2. $6x^2 - \frac{2}{5}x + \frac{3}{4}$
3. $12x^2 - \frac{4}{7}x + \frac{1}{3}$
4. $\frac{3}{5}x^2 - 3x + 4$
5. $\frac{2}{3}x^2 + \frac{1}{2}x$
6. $\frac{3}{2}x + \frac{1}{5}$
7. $9x^2 - \frac{3}{2}x + 1$
8. $-\frac{1}{5} + 5x$
9. $7x^2 - \frac{4}{5}x + \frac{1}{4}$
10. $\frac{1}{2} - \frac{5}{3}x + 7x^2$

## Exercise 6C

1. $\dfrac{-12}{x^3}$
2. $\dfrac{-12}{x^4}$
3. $\dfrac{-20}{x^5}$
4. $\dfrac{-21}{2x^8}$
5. $\dfrac{-5}{2x^3}$
6. $\dfrac{-6}{7x^4}$
7. $\dfrac{-12}{x^4}$
8. $\dfrac{-15}{x^6}$
9. $\dfrac{-3}{2x^4}$
10. $\dfrac{-1}{x^3}$

## Exercise 6D

1. $18x^2 - \dfrac{8}{x^5}$
2. $2 - \dfrac{15}{x^6}$
3. $10x^4 + 3 + \dfrac{8}{x^3}$
4. $4x^5 + \dfrac{4x}{3}$

5. $3x^3 + 1 + \dfrac{9}{4x^4}$
6. $7x + \dfrac{4}{7x^3}$
7. $12x^2 + 2x + \dfrac{4}{x^5}$
8. $4x - \dfrac{2}{3x^3}$
9. $8x - 7 - \dfrac{4}{x^3}$
10. $5 - \dfrac{8}{3x^5}$
11. $14x - \dfrac{12}{x^7}$
12. $12x^3 - \dfrac{10}{x^6} - 3$
13. $8x^5 + \dfrac{9}{2x^7}$
14. $8x^3 + 5 + \dfrac{10}{3x^6}$
15. $15x^4 + 2x^2 + \dfrac{3}{x^3}$

## Exercise 6E

1. $12x^3 - 21x^2 + 4x$ , $36x^2 - 42x + 4$
2. $6 + 4x$ , $4$
3. $6x^2 + 14x - 5$ , $12x + 14$
4. $3 - \dfrac{4}{x^3}$ , $\dfrac{12}{x^4}$
5. $-1 - 2x$ , $-2$
6. $4 - 4x$ , $-4$
7. $12x - \dfrac{2}{x^3}$ , $12 + \dfrac{6}{x^4}$
8. $2x^2 - 4$ , $4x$
9. $6x^9 - \dfrac{2}{5x^3}$ , $54x^8 + \dfrac{6}{5x^4}$
10. $3x - \dfrac{4}{3x^3}$ , $3 + \dfrac{4}{x^4}$
11. $12x^2 + \dfrac{6}{x^4}$ , $24x - \dfrac{24}{x^5}$
12. $12x + \dfrac{1}{2x^4}$ , $12 - \dfrac{2}{x^5}$
13. $6x - 1 + \dfrac{2}{x^3}$ , $6 - \dfrac{6}{x^4}$
14. $2 + 6x + \dfrac{12}{x^4}$ , $6 - \dfrac{48}{x^5}$
15. $6 - \dfrac{8}{5x^5}$ , $\dfrac{8}{x^6}$

## Exercise 7A

1. 1
2. 27
3. $-5$
4. 10
5. $3\frac{8}{15}$
6. 2
7. 16
8. $-1$
9. $-\frac{3}{16}$
10. $6\frac{1}{4}$
11. $-1\frac{1}{4}$
12. 17
13. $-20$
14. $25\frac{1}{32}$
15. $\frac{3}{8}$

## Exercise 7B

1. $(3, 6)$
2. $(-2, -2)$
3. $(4, 47)$
4. $(-1, 13)$
5. $(2, 1)$
6. $(-2, -2)$
7. $(-3, -7)$
8. $(3, 16)$
9. $(-4, 64)$
10. $(2, 6)$
11. $(\frac{5}{8}, 5\frac{7}{16})$
12. $(-\frac{2}{5}, -1\frac{2}{5})$
13. $(-\frac{1}{3}, 7\frac{1}{3})$

## Exercise 7C

1. $(1, 1)$ and $(0, -2)$
2. $(2, 37)$ and $(-1\frac{1}{6}, -26\frac{73}{108})$
3. $(-1, -9)$ and $(1\frac{3}{9}, 10\frac{157}{243})$
4. $(-2, 11)$ and $(\frac{5}{3}, -5\frac{19}{27})$
5. $(2, 8)$ and $(-\frac{2}{3}, -6\frac{14}{27})$
6. $(1, -\frac{1}{6})$ and $(-4, 15\frac{2}{3})$
7. $(-1, -9)$ and $(\frac{5}{3}, 5\frac{14}{27})$
8. $(2, -2\frac{2}{3})$ and $(-\frac{1}{2}, -4\frac{23}{24})$
9. $(-1, -10)$ and $(\frac{4}{3}, 13\frac{16}{27})$
10. $(2, 7)$ and $(0, 7)$
11. $(\frac{1}{2}, -2\frac{3}{4})$ and $(-3, 83)$
12. $(-\frac{2}{3}, -\frac{5}{27})$ and $(4, -51)$
13. $(4, -75)$ and $(-2, 33)$

## Exercise 7D

1. $y = 7x - 14$
2. $y = 12x - 8$
3. $y = -11x + 31$
4. $y = 23x + 30$
5. $y = 19x + 9$
6. $y = 25x + 20$
7. $y = 4x + 6$
8. $y = 4x - 5\frac{1}{2}$
9. $y = -\frac{1}{4}x + 2$
10. $y = \frac{3}{2}x + 1$

## Exercise 7E

1. $y = -\frac{1}{17}x + 14\frac{2}{17}$
2. $y = -\frac{1}{7}x + \frac{1}{7}$
3. $y = -\frac{1}{21}x - 23\frac{2}{21}$
4. $y = -\frac{1}{19}x - 11\frac{1}{19}$
5. $y = \frac{1}{2}x + 6$
6. $y = \frac{1}{11}x + 7\frac{10}{11}$
7. $y = \frac{4}{3}x - 23\frac{23}{12}$
8. $y = -\frac{1}{6}x - 5$
9. $y = 2x + 3$
10. $y = \frac{4}{31}x + 4\frac{47}{124}$

## Exercise 7F

1. (a) $y = 13x - 11$
   (b) (i) $(0, -11)$ (ii) $(\frac{11}{13}, 0)$
2. (a) $y = \frac{1}{9}x + 13\frac{1}{3}$
   (b) (i) $(0, 13\frac{1}{3})$ (ii) $(-120, 0)$
3. (a) $y = -6x + 3$ (b) $(-3, 21)$
4. (a) $y = \frac{1}{9}x + \frac{7}{9}$ (b) $(5, \frac{4}{3})$
5. (a) $y = 4x + \frac{11}{6}$ (b) $(0, \frac{11}{6})$
6. (a) $y = \frac{1}{6}x + 1\frac{1}{6}$

(b) (i) (–7, 0) (ii) (2, 1 ½)
7. (a) $y = 11x + 25$
   (b) (i) ($-^{25}/_{11}$, 0) (ii) (–3, –8)
8. (a) $y = -^{1}/_{7}x - 2\,^{1}/_{7}$
   (b) (i) (0, $-2\,^{1}/_{7}$) (ii) (6, –3)
9. (a) $y = -x - 4$
   (b) (i) (0, –4) (ii) (5, –9)
10. (a) $y = -^{1}/_{5}x + 2\,^{3}/_{10}$
    (b) (i) (11 ½, 0) (ii) (4, 1 ½)

## Exercise 7G

1. (2, 4)
2. (1, 6)
3. (1, –4) (⅓, $-3\,^{23}/_{27}$)
4. (1, 5 ½) (–⅙, $7\,^{89}/_{216}$)
5. (⁴⁄₃, 3) (–⁴⁄₃, –3)
6. (4, –4)
7. (1 ½, –8 ¼)
8. (⅔, 8 ⅔) (–⅔, –8 ⅔)
9. (2, –5) (⅔, $-1\,^{4}/_{27}$)
10. (5, $-43\,^{1}/_{6}$) (–½, $1\,^{7}/_{24}$)

## Exercise 8A

1. (2, –11) Min
2. (–2, –11) Min
3. (3, 18) Max
4. (2 ½, –9 ¼) Min
5. (–2, 11) Max
6. (3 ½, 13 ¼) Max
7. (–¼, –5 ¼) Min
8. (–½, 5 ¼) Max
9. (3, –16) Min
10. (–2, 12) Max

## Exercise 8B

1. (2, –40) Min (–3, 85) Max
2. (4, –109) Min (–1, 16) Max
3. (4, 9) Min (2, 13) Max
4. (⅓, $-2\,^{14}/_{27}$) Min (–3, 16) Max
5. (½, 1) Min (–½, 3) Max
6. (2, 6) Min (⁴⁄₃, $6\,^{4}/_{27}$) Max
7. (⅚, $6\,^{37}/_{108}$) Max (3, –14) Min
8. (⅔, $-2\,^{22}/_{27}$) Min (–4, 48) Max
9. (⁵⁄₃, $-31\,^{7}/_{27}$) Min (–³⁄₂, 32 ¼) Max
10. (4, –184) Min (–6, 316) Max
11. (–5, –170) Min (3, 86) Max
12. (–1, 8) Max (–2, 7) Min
13. (½, 21 ¼) Min (2, 28) Max

## Exercise 8C

1.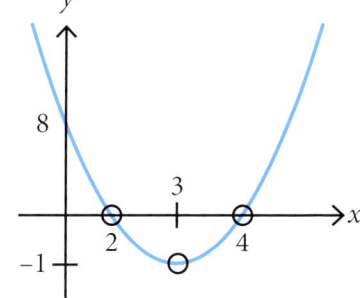

2.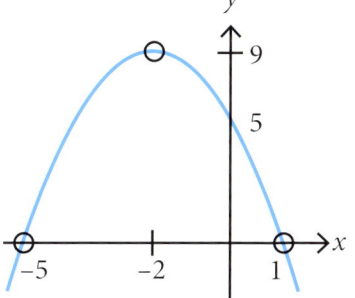

3.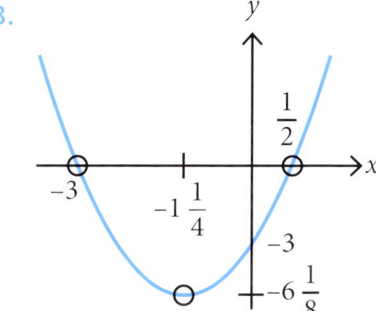

4.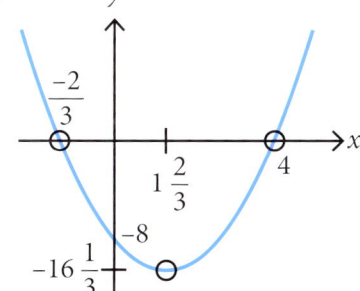

5.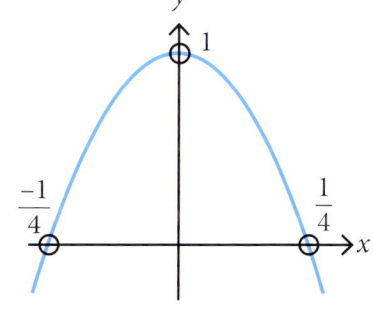

6.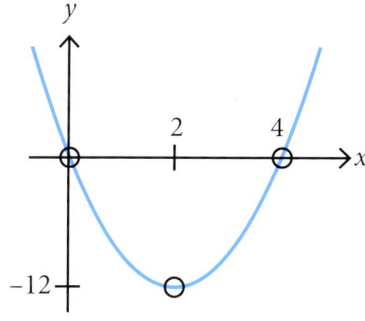

7.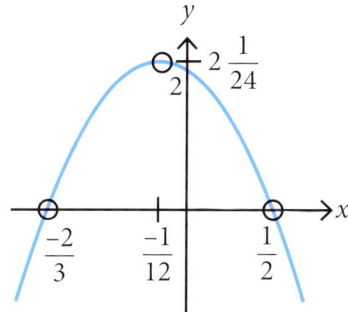

8.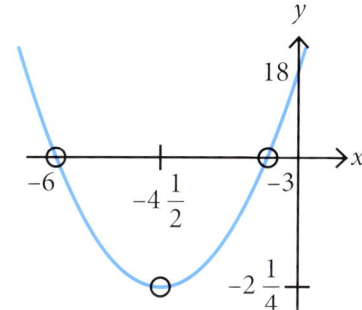

9.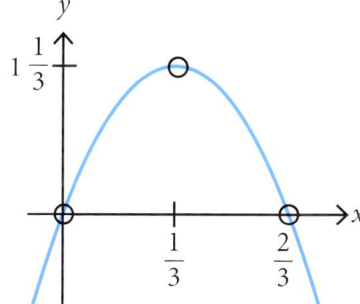

10.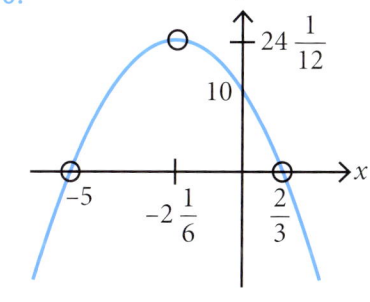

## Exercise 8D

**1.**

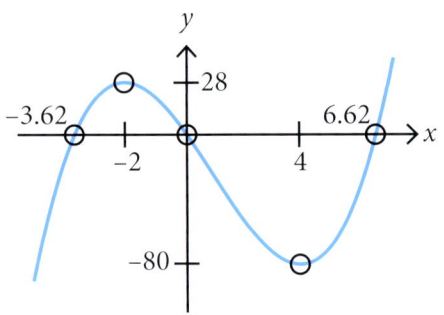

**2.**

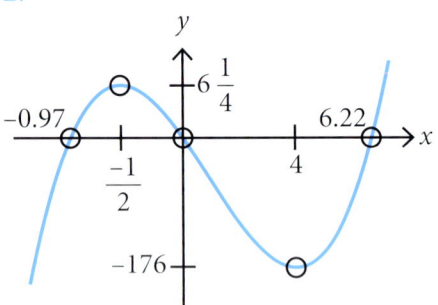

**3.**

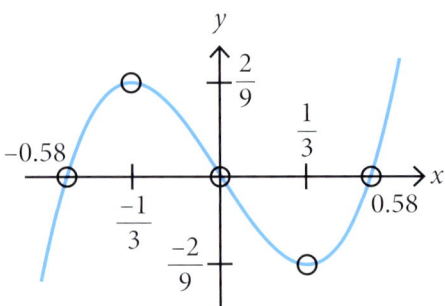

**4.**

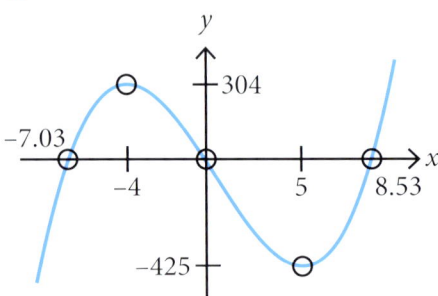

**5.**

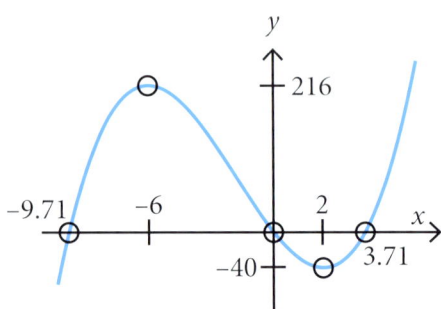

**6.**

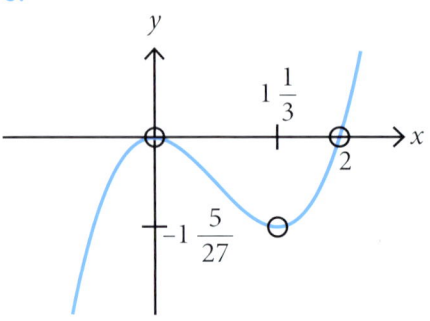

**7.**

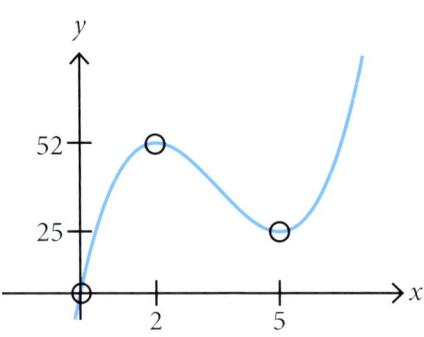

**8.**

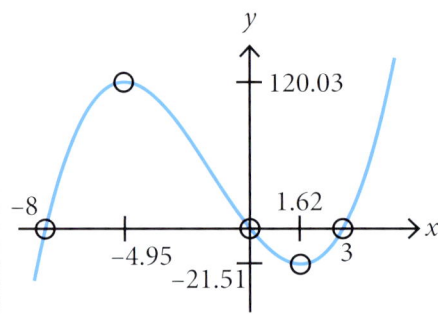

**9.**

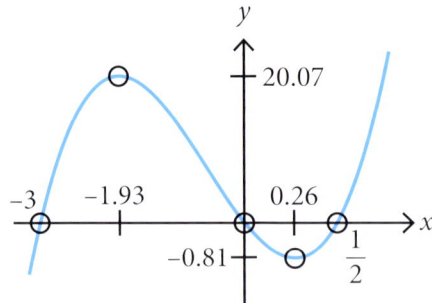

**10.**

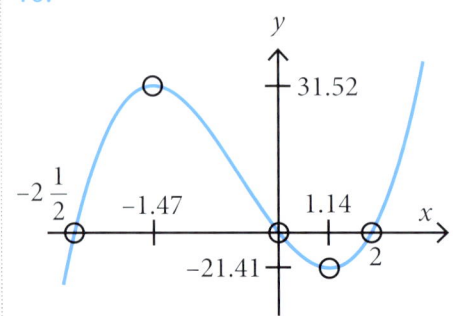

**11.**

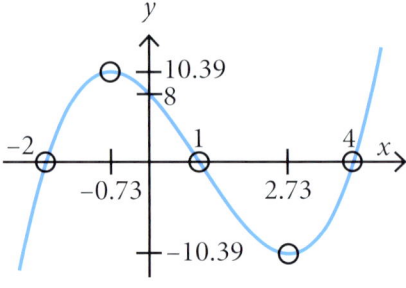

**12.**

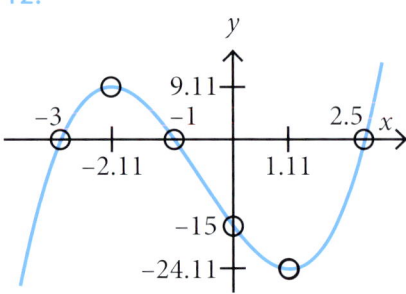

## Exercise 8E

1. −768
2. (a) $x = 30$ and $y = 15$ (b) 450 m$^2$
3. 3.2 km
4. (a) $x = 10$ and $y = 10$ (b) £3
5. (a) $x = 24$ and $y = 6$ (b) 48 m
6. (a) $x = 26$ and $y = 13$ (b) 52 m
7. (a) $x = 2$ and $y = 4$ (b) 64 cm$^2$
8. £22.75
9. 12 m
10. 3 years

## Exercise 9A

1. $3x^3 + 3x + C$
2. $4x^3 + 2x^2 − 2x + C$
3. $4x^4 − 3x^3 − 3x^2 + 3x + C$
4. $7x − x^2 + C$
5. $2x^2 + x^3 + C$
6. $\frac{3}{2}x^4 − 2x^2 − x + C$
7. $\frac{3}{5}x^5 − \frac{1}{2}x^4 + \frac{7}{3}x^3 + C$
8. $\frac{2}{25}x^5 + 3x^2 + C$
9. $\frac{1}{7}x^3 − x^2 + C$
10. $\frac{5}{32}x^4 + \frac{1}{12}x^3 + \frac{1}{2}x^2 + C$
11. $3x^2 − \frac{4}{3}x^3 + 7x + C$
12. $9x − x^2 − 2x^3 + C$
13. $5x^2 + \frac{1}{3}x^3 − 3x + C$
14. $\frac{1}{6}x^4 + \frac{2}{5}x^3 − x + C$
15. $2x^2 − \frac{2}{25}x^5 + 5x + C$
16. $2x^2 − 7x + C$
17. $x^4 − \frac{7}{3}x^3 + \frac{5}{2}x^2 − 2x + C$
18. $3x^2 − \frac{1}{9}x^6 + C$

## Exercise 9B

1. $\dfrac{-4}{x} + C$

2. $\dfrac{-4}{x^2} + C$

3. $\dfrac{-1}{2x^4} + C$

4. $\dfrac{-3}{5x} + C$

5. $\dfrac{-1}{7x^2} + C$

6. $\dfrac{-1}{5x^3} + C$

7. $2x^2 + \dfrac{4}{x} + C$

8. $\dfrac{x^3}{3} + 3x + \dfrac{1}{x^2} + C$

9. $\dfrac{x^3}{2} + \dfrac{2}{3x} + C$

10. $6x - \dfrac{1}{2x} + C$

11. $2x^2 + \dfrac{1}{8x^4} + C$

12. $\dfrac{-5}{3x} + \dfrac{x^3}{3} + C$

13. $\dfrac{x^4}{2} + \dfrac{1}{4x^2} + C$

14. $3x^2 + 2x + \dfrac{4}{x} + C$

15. $x^3 - 5x - \dfrac{2}{5x} + C$

## Exercise 9C

1. 3
2. $^{15}/_{32}$
3. $^2/_5$
4. $^7/_{40}$
5. $24\ ^{23}/_{48}$
6. $12\ ^1/_3$

## Exercise 9D

1. (a) $y = 3x^2 - 3x + 3$ (b) 39
2. (a) $y = 4x + x^2 + 5$ (b) 17
3. (a) $y = x^3 - 2x^2 - 3$ (b) −48
4. (a) $y = 3x^2 + \tfrac{1}{3}x^3 - 5\ ^2/_3$ (b) $30\ ^1/_3$
5. (a) $y = \dfrac{-4}{x} + 6$ (b) (−2, 8)
6. (a) $y = 2x^3 - x^2 + 5x - 59$ (b) (4, 73)
7. (a) $y = ^3/_2\, x^2 + 4x - 3\ ^1/_2$ (b) (−2, −5 ½)
8. (a) $y = 6x - x^2 + x^3 + 28$ (b) (6, 244)

## Exercise 10A

1. $8\ ^2/_3$
2. $12\ ^2/_3$
3. $16\ ^2/_3$
4. 42
5. $18\ ^2/_3$
6. $40\ ^2/_3$
7. $5\ ^1/_6$
8. $8\ ^2/_3$
9. 11
10. 8
11. $55\ ^1/_2$
12. $22\ ^2/_3$
13. $9\ ^1/_3$
14. $27\ ^5/_6$
15. 12

## Exercise 10B

1. (a) 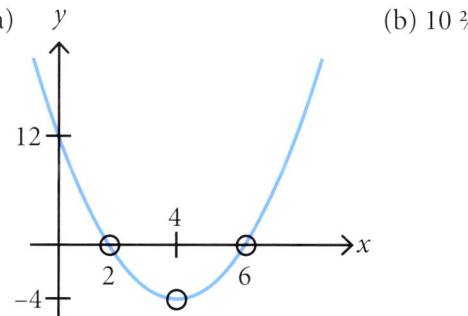 (b) $10\ ^2/_3$

2. (a) 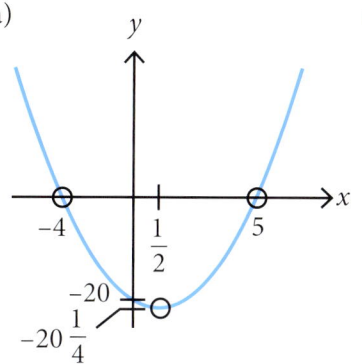 (b) 121 ½

3. (a) 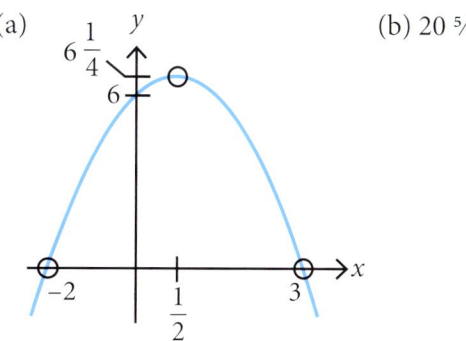 (b) 20 ⅚

4. (a) 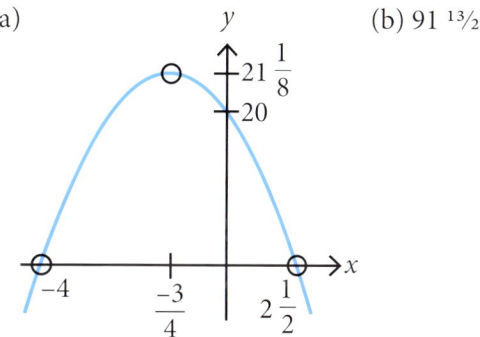 (b) 91 $^{13}/_{24}$

5. (a) 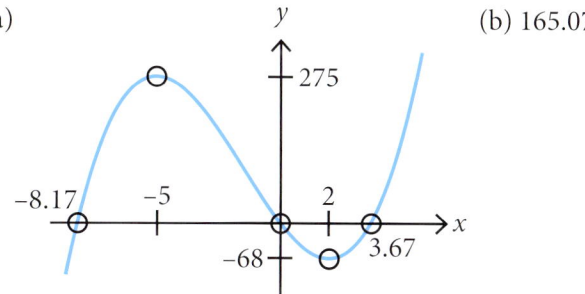 (b) 165.07

6. (a) 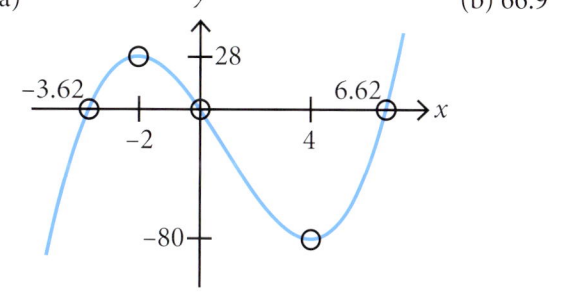 (b) 66.9

189

7. (a) 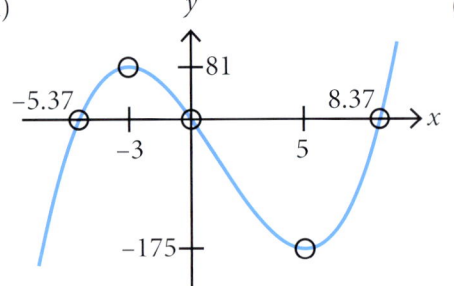 (b) 286.1

8. (a) 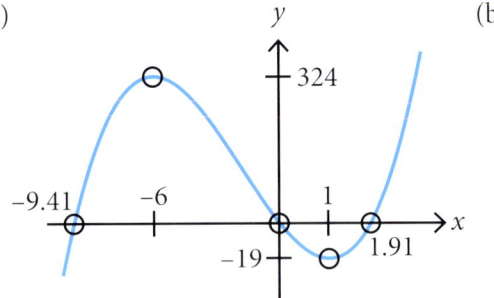 (b) 24.2

9. (a) 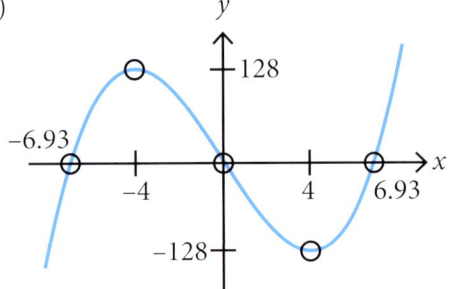 (b) 576.0

10. (a) 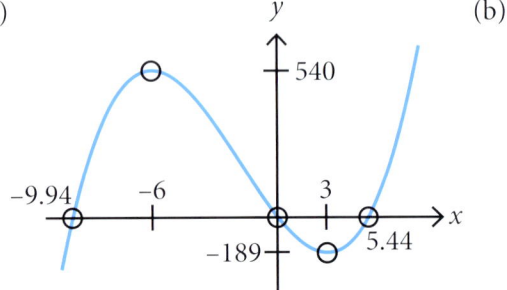 (b) 677.2

11. (a) 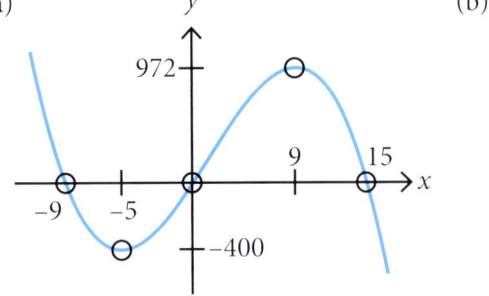 (b) 2369.25

## Exercise 11A

1. $\begin{pmatrix} -1 \\ 3 \end{pmatrix}$

2. $\begin{pmatrix} -4 \\ -4 \end{pmatrix}$

3. $\begin{pmatrix} 4 & 2 \end{pmatrix}$

4. $\begin{pmatrix} 3 & -1 \end{pmatrix}$

5. $\begin{pmatrix} -x \\ -2 \end{pmatrix}$

6. $\begin{pmatrix} 2 & -4y \end{pmatrix}$

7. $\begin{pmatrix} -x \\ -y \end{pmatrix}$

8. $\begin{pmatrix} -4x & 3y \end{pmatrix}$

9. $\begin{pmatrix} -5 & -10 \\ 14 & -2 \end{pmatrix}$

10. $\begin{pmatrix} 0 & -15 \\ -1 & 11 \end{pmatrix}$

11. $\begin{pmatrix} 4x & 3y \\ 6 & 2t \end{pmatrix}$

12. $\begin{pmatrix} -1 & 2 \\ -7 & 6 \end{pmatrix}$

13. $\begin{pmatrix} 10n & -3m \\ -14 & -3q \end{pmatrix}$

14. $\begin{pmatrix} -2.8 & 2.2 \\ -7.5 & 7.5 \end{pmatrix}$

15. $\begin{pmatrix} 4.9 & 8.9 \\ 1.7 & -11.8 \end{pmatrix}$

16. $\begin{pmatrix} -8 & -5 \\ 9 & 3 \end{pmatrix}$

17. $\begin{pmatrix} -2 & 15 \\ -5 & 10 \end{pmatrix}$

18. $\begin{pmatrix} 10 & -1 \\ 1 & 2 \end{pmatrix}$

19. $\begin{pmatrix} -8 & -1 \\ 5 & 10 \end{pmatrix}$

20. $\begin{pmatrix} 2 & 0 \\ -3 & -6 \end{pmatrix}$

21. $\begin{pmatrix} 2 & -2 \\ 6 & 12 \end{pmatrix}$

22. $\begin{pmatrix} -2 & 17 \\ -14 & -8 \end{pmatrix}$

23. $\begin{pmatrix} -10 & 16 \\ -9 & 2 \end{pmatrix}$

24. $\begin{pmatrix} -6 & -16 \\ 10 & 0 \end{pmatrix}$

## Exercise 11B

1. $\begin{pmatrix} 25 & 30 \\ -10 & 20 \end{pmatrix}$

2. $\begin{pmatrix} -9 & -6 \\ 18 & -15 \end{pmatrix}$

3. $\begin{pmatrix} -5 & 20 \\ -15 & 30 \end{pmatrix}$

4. $\begin{pmatrix} 24 & -40 \\ -40 & 24 \end{pmatrix}$

5. $\begin{pmatrix} -63 & 56 \\ 21 & -42 \end{pmatrix}$

6. $\begin{pmatrix} 2½ & 3 \\ -1 & 2 \end{pmatrix}$

7. $\begin{pmatrix} 0.3 & -0.5 \\ -0.5 & 0.3 \end{pmatrix}$

8. $\begin{pmatrix} -1½ & -1 \\ 3 & -2½ \end{pmatrix}$

9. $\begin{pmatrix} 7 & 10 \\ 2 & 3 \end{pmatrix}$

10. $\begin{pmatrix} 0 & -7 \\ 14 & -21 \end{pmatrix}$

11. $\begin{pmatrix} -14 & 0 \\ 18 & -36 \end{pmatrix}$

12. $\begin{pmatrix} -30 & -28 \\ 36 & -37 \end{pmatrix}$

13. $\begin{pmatrix} 22 & -1 \\ -12 & 17 \end{pmatrix}$

14. $\begin{pmatrix} -24 & 38 \\ 1 & -2 \end{pmatrix}$

15. $\begin{pmatrix} -2 & 13 \\ 6 & 2 \end{pmatrix}$

16. $\begin{pmatrix} -6 \\ 15 \end{pmatrix}$

17. $\begin{pmatrix} 6 & -8 \end{pmatrix}$

18. $\begin{pmatrix} 8 \\ -28 \end{pmatrix}$

19. $\begin{pmatrix} 2 & 10 \end{pmatrix}$

20. $\begin{pmatrix} -1 \\ 2½ \end{pmatrix}$

21. $\begin{pmatrix} 2¼ & -3 \end{pmatrix}$

22. $\begin{pmatrix} -12 \\ 36 \end{pmatrix}$

23. $\begin{pmatrix} 1 & -4½ \end{pmatrix}$

## Exercise 11C

1. $\begin{pmatrix} 2 & 5 \\ 10 & 12 \end{pmatrix}$

2. $\begin{pmatrix} 9 & -7 \\ 5 & -2 \end{pmatrix}$

3. $\begin{pmatrix} 16 & -6 & 1 \end{pmatrix}$

4. $\begin{pmatrix} -3 \\ -4 \end{pmatrix}$

5. $\begin{pmatrix} 5 & 1 \\ 2 & -2 \end{pmatrix}$

6. $\begin{pmatrix} 3 & -2 \\ 1 & -2 \end{pmatrix}$

7. $\begin{pmatrix} 1 & -1 \\ -1 & 3 \end{pmatrix}$

8. $\begin{pmatrix} 2 & 3 \\ -6 & 7 \end{pmatrix}$

9. $\begin{pmatrix} 2 & -1 \\ -3 & -1 \end{pmatrix}$

10. $\begin{pmatrix} 3 & 3 \\ -4 & 3 \end{pmatrix}$

## Exercise 11D

1. $(-22)$
2. $\begin{pmatrix} -8 & 16 \\ -4 & 8 \end{pmatrix}$
3. $\begin{pmatrix} 14 \\ 13 \end{pmatrix}$
4. $(-1)$
5. $\begin{pmatrix} -10 & 6 \\ 15 & -9 \end{pmatrix}$
6. $\begin{pmatrix} -14 \\ 4 \end{pmatrix}$
7. $(-16)$
8. $\begin{pmatrix} -12 & 6 \\ 20 & -10 \end{pmatrix}$
9. $\begin{pmatrix} -20 \\ 30 \end{pmatrix}$
10. $\begin{pmatrix} -17 & 29 \\ -5 & 7 \end{pmatrix}$
11. $\begin{pmatrix} 19 & -30 \\ 1 & 8 \end{pmatrix}$
12. $\begin{pmatrix} -8 & 13 \\ 21 & -35 \end{pmatrix}$
13. $\begin{pmatrix} -10 & -1 \\ 26 & 0 \end{pmatrix}$
14. $\begin{pmatrix} 24 & 5 \\ -22 & 3 \end{pmatrix}$
15. $\begin{pmatrix} -17 & 29 \\ 15 & -26 \end{pmatrix}$
16. $\begin{pmatrix} 24 & 5 \\ 4 & 29 \end{pmatrix}$
17. $\begin{pmatrix} 7 & -12 \\ -18 & 31 \end{pmatrix}$
18. $\begin{pmatrix} 19 & -30 \\ -18 & 31 \end{pmatrix}$

## Exercise 11E

1. $-18$
2. $58$
3. $-3$
4. $-44$
5. $72$
6. $-7$
7. $17$
8. $-22$
9. $18$
10. $-16$

## Exercise 11F

1. $\frac{1}{48}\begin{pmatrix} 2 & 6 \\ -7 & 3 \end{pmatrix}$
2. $\frac{-1}{2}\begin{pmatrix} -4 & 2 \\ -5 & 3 \end{pmatrix}$ or $\frac{1}{2}\begin{pmatrix} 4 & -2 \\ 5 & -3 \end{pmatrix}$
3. $\frac{-1}{24}\begin{pmatrix} 2 & -4 \\ -5 & -2 \end{pmatrix}$ or $\frac{1}{24}\begin{pmatrix} -2 & 4 \\ 5 & 2 \end{pmatrix}$
4. $\frac{-1}{14}\begin{pmatrix} -2 & -5 \\ -4 & -3 \end{pmatrix}$ or $\frac{1}{14}\begin{pmatrix} 2 & 5 \\ 4 & 3 \end{pmatrix}$
5. $\frac{-1}{7}\begin{pmatrix} -4 & -5 \\ -3 & -2 \end{pmatrix}$ or $\frac{1}{7}\begin{pmatrix} 4 & 5 \\ 3 & 2 \end{pmatrix}$
6. $\begin{pmatrix} -3 & -2 \\ -8 & -5 \end{pmatrix}$
7. $\frac{-1}{30}\begin{pmatrix} 3 & -6 \\ -4 & -2 \end{pmatrix}$ or $\frac{1}{30}\begin{pmatrix} -3 & 6 \\ 4 & 2 \end{pmatrix}$
8. $\frac{1}{19}\begin{pmatrix} 4 & 3 \\ -5 & 1 \end{pmatrix}$
9. $\frac{-1}{26}\begin{pmatrix} 2 & -4 \\ -5 & -3 \end{pmatrix}$ or $\frac{1}{26}\begin{pmatrix} -2 & 4 \\ 5 & 3 \end{pmatrix}$
10. $\begin{pmatrix} -5 & -3 \\ 3 & 2 \end{pmatrix}$
11. $\frac{-1}{2}\begin{pmatrix} -2 & -4 \\ -3 & -5 \end{pmatrix}$ or $\frac{1}{2}\begin{pmatrix} 2 & 4 \\ 3 & 5 \end{pmatrix}$
12. $\frac{1}{13}\begin{pmatrix} 3 & 2 \\ -5 & 1 \end{pmatrix}$
13. $\frac{1}{14}\begin{pmatrix} 3 & -4 \\ 5 & -2 \end{pmatrix}$
14. $\frac{-1}{33}\begin{pmatrix} -2 & -5 \\ -7 & -1 \end{pmatrix}$ or $\frac{1}{33}\begin{pmatrix} 2 & 5 \\ 7 & 1 \end{pmatrix}$
15. $\frac{1}{38}\begin{pmatrix} 4 & 2 \\ -7 & 6 \end{pmatrix}$
16. $\frac{-1}{14}\begin{pmatrix} -3 & -5 \\ -4 & -2 \end{pmatrix}$ or $\frac{1}{14}\begin{pmatrix} 3 & 5 \\ 4 & 2 \end{pmatrix}$
17. det = 0. You cannot divide 1 by 0. Therefore it has no inverse.
18. det = 0. You cannot divide 1 by 0. Therefore it has no inverse.
19. 6
20. $-\frac{20}{3}$

## Exercise 11G

1. $\frac{-1}{14}\begin{pmatrix} -41 \\ 36 \end{pmatrix}$ or $\frac{1}{14}\begin{pmatrix} 41 \\ -36 \end{pmatrix}$
2. $\frac{-1}{6}\begin{pmatrix} -10 \\ -17 \end{pmatrix}$ or $\frac{1}{6}\begin{pmatrix} 10 \\ 17 \end{pmatrix}$
3. $\begin{pmatrix} 0 \\ -1 \end{pmatrix}$
4. $\frac{-1}{14}\begin{pmatrix} 18 \\ -10 \end{pmatrix}$ or $\frac{1}{14}\begin{pmatrix} -18 \\ 10 \end{pmatrix}$
5. $\frac{-1}{14}\begin{pmatrix} -13 & 14 \\ -6 & 0 \end{pmatrix}$ or $\frac{1}{14}\begin{pmatrix} 13 & -14 \\ 6 & 0 \end{pmatrix}$
6. $\frac{-1}{13}\begin{pmatrix} -36 & -41 \\ -14 & -21 \end{pmatrix}$ or $\frac{1}{13}\begin{pmatrix} 36 & 41 \\ 14 & 21 \end{pmatrix}$
7. $\frac{-1}{6}\begin{pmatrix} 14 & -36 \\ 22 & -51 \end{pmatrix}$ or $\frac{1}{6}\begin{pmatrix} -14 & 36 \\ -22 & 51 \end{pmatrix}$
8. $\frac{-1}{14}\begin{pmatrix} -21 & 41 \\ 14 & -36 \end{pmatrix}$ or $\frac{1}{14}\begin{pmatrix} 21 & -41 \\ -14 & 36 \end{pmatrix}$
9. $\frac{-1}{13}\begin{pmatrix} -51 & 36 \\ -22 & 14 \end{pmatrix}$ or $\frac{1}{13}\begin{pmatrix} 51 & -36 \\ 22 & -14 \end{pmatrix}$
10. $\frac{-1}{6}\begin{pmatrix} 0 & -14 \\ 6 & -13 \end{pmatrix}$ or $\frac{1}{6}\begin{pmatrix} 0 & 14 \\ -6 & 13 \end{pmatrix}$
11. $\frac{-1}{14}\begin{pmatrix} -8 & 27 \\ 20 & -36 \end{pmatrix}$ or $\frac{1}{14}\begin{pmatrix} 8 & -27 \\ -20 & 36 \end{pmatrix}$
12. $\frac{-1}{6}\begin{pmatrix} 26 \\ 34 \end{pmatrix}$ or $\frac{1}{6}\begin{pmatrix} -26 \\ -34 \end{pmatrix}$
13. $\frac{-1}{13}\begin{pmatrix} -225 & 26 \\ -94 & 0 \end{pmatrix}$ or $\frac{1}{13}\begin{pmatrix} 225 & -26 \\ 94 & 0 \end{pmatrix}$
14. $\frac{-1}{14}\begin{pmatrix} 159 \\ -128 \end{pmatrix}$ or $\frac{1}{14}\begin{pmatrix} -159 \\ 128 \end{pmatrix}$

## Exercise 11H

1. $x = 4$ $y = -2$
2. $x = -2$ $y = 5$
3. $x = 3$ $y = -2$
4. $x = 1\frac{1}{2}$ $y = 4$
5. $x = -3$ $y = -4$
6. $x = 2$ $y = -4$
7. $x = -3$ $y = 4$
8. $x = -3\frac{1}{2}$ $y = 6$
9. $x = 5$ $y = -2$
10. $x = -2$ $y = -7$
11. $x = 2$ $y = 5$
12. $x = 6$ $y = 3$
13. $x = 4$ $y = -2$
14. $x = -3$ $y = 5$
15. $x = -2$ $y = -3$
16. $x = 4$ $y = -2$
17. $x = -1$ $y = 3$
18. $x = -2$ $y = -4$
19. $x = 3$ $y = -2$
20. $x = -3$ $y = -4$
21. $x = 2$ $y = -6$
22. $x = -3$ $y = 2$
23. $x = 1$ $y = -4$
24. $x = -2$ $y = -3$
25. $x = 5$ $y = -2$

## Exercise 12A

1. 2
2. 5
3. $-1$
4. 3
5. 4
6. 0
7. 2
8. 3
9. 6
10. $-3$

## Exercise 12B

1. $x + y$
2. $x - y$
3. $2x + y$
4. $y - 3z$
5. $\frac{1}{2}(x - y)$ or $\frac{1}{2}x - \frac{1}{2}y$
6. $\frac{1}{2}y - \frac{1}{2}z$
7. $3x + y - z$
8. $x + 4y - 5z$
9. $\frac{1}{2}x - \frac{3}{2}z$
10. $\frac{1}{2}x + \frac{1}{4}z - \frac{1}{4}y$

## Exercise 12C

1. 2
2. 4
3. 6
4. 3
5. 5
6. 2
7. 3
8. 5
9. 2
10. 4
11. 2
12. 6

## Exercise 12D

1. 81
2. 256
3. 25
4. 343
5. 9
6. 8
7. 16
8. 36
9. 125
10. 64
11. 0.2 or ⅕
12. 32
13. 216
14. ⅑
15. 8

## Exercise 12E

1. 2
2. 3
3. 4
4. 3
5. 5
6. 2
7. 2
8. 2 ½
9. 2
10. ⅔
11. 3

## Exercise 12F

1. (a) p + q  (b) p – q  (c) 3q
   (d) 2p + 3q
2. (a) q – p  (b) 2p + q  (c) 4p
   (d) p + 2q
3. (a) p + q  (b) 2p + q  (c) 3p  (d) 2q
4. (a) p + q  (b) 5p  (c) 4p + q
   (d) q – p
5. (a) p + q  (b) q – p  (c) 2p + 2q
   (d) 3q
6. (a) p + q  (b) q – p  (c) 6p
   (d) 2p + q
7. (a) p + q  (b) p – q  (c) p + 2q
   (d) 3p

## Exercise 12G

1. (a) p + q  (b) 2p + q  (c) p + 2q
   (d) 1 + p  (e) 2 + q  (f) q – p
2. (a) p + q  (b) 2p + q  (c) p + 2q
   (d) 3 + p  (e) 2 + q
3. (a) q – p  (b) 2p + q  (c) p + 2q
   (d) 1 + p  (e) 2 + q  (f) 1 + p + q
4. (a) p + q  (b) q – p  (c) 2p + q
   (d) 1 + p  (e) 2 + q
5. (a) p + q  (b) q – p  (c) 1 + p
   (d) 2p + q  (e) p + 2q  (f) 1 + p + q
6. (a) p + q  (b) 1 + p  (c) 1 + q
   (d) 2p + q  (e) p – q
7. (a) p + q  (b) 1 + p  (c) 1 + q
   (d) 2p + q  (e) 1 – 2p

8. (a) 1 + p  (b) 2 + q  (c) q – p
   (d) 2p + q  (e) q – 2p  (f) 1 + p + q
9. (a) p + q  (b) 2 + p  (c) 1 + q
   (d) q – p  (e) 1 + p + q

## Exercise 13A

1. 1.40
2. –0.827
3. 0.683
4. 0.631
5. –1.66
6. 1.51
7. 1.44
8. –2.11
9. 2.52
10. 5.13
11. –1.89
12. 0.648

## Exercise 13B

1. –0.290
2. 0.658
3. –0.661
4. 4.21
5. 0.295
6. –15.4
7. 0.815
8. 0.127
9. –0.0155
10. 2.89

## Exercise 13C

1. 2.83
2. –5.65
3. –1.10
4. –2.44
5. –0.287
6. 2.88
7. 2.49
8. 1.02
9. –0.154
10. –87.8

## Exercise 14A

1. (a) (i) 0.85 (ii) 3.64 (b) (i) 48.42
   (ii) 36.24
2. (a) (i) –0.42 (ii) 24.16 (b) (i) 3.03
   (ii) 62 assuming that the formula
   holds for values of $W$ greater than
   3.96.
3. (a) (i) 1.76 (ii) 3.24 (b) (i) 239.90
   (ii) 26.15
4. (a) (i) 0.46 (ii) 1.74 (b) (i) 13.21
   assuming that the formula holds
   for values of $f$ greater than 78.
   (ii) 32
5. (a) (i) –0.72 (ii) 18.24 (b) (i) 3.25
   (ii) 16.5
6. (a) (i) –0.25 (ii) 174 (b) (i) 73.74
   (ii) 7 assuming that the formula
   holds for values of $D$ greater than
   100.46.

## Exercise 14B

1. (b) (i) 1.15 (ii) 1.68 (c) 46.65
   (d) 14
2. (b) (i) –0.82 (ii) 2200 (c) 157
   (d) £32.65
3. (b) (i) –0.92 (ii) 2740 (c) £242000
   (d) 34, assuming that the
   relationship holds for values of $C$
   less than £113000.
4. (b) (i) –0.86 (ii) 240 (c) 57

(d) £4.20
5. (b) (i) 0.92 (ii) 0.15 (c) 15.99 litres
   (d) 400 km assuming that the
   relationship holds for values of $D$
   greater than 361.6 km.

## Exercise 15A

1. (a) 3 m/s (b) 0 m/s (c) 3 m/s in
   the opposite direction
2. (a) 6 m/s (b) 0 m/s (c) 4 m/s in
   the opposite direction
3. (a) 1.6 m/s (b) 0 m/s (c) 2 m/s in
   the opposite direction
4. (a) 11 m/s (b) 0 m/s (c) 6.25 m/s
   in the opposite direction
5. (a) 6.8 m/s (b) 2 m/s in the
   opposite direction (c) 7 m/s in the
   opposite direction
6. (a) 2.4 m/s (b) 2⅓ m/s in the
   opposite direction (c) 3.5 m/s in
   the opposite direction

## Exercise 15B

1. (a) 1.5 m/s², 0 m/s², –4 m/s²
   (b) 138 m
2. (a) 1.6 m/s², 0 m/s², –2 m/s²
   (b) 92 m
3. (a) 2 m/s², 0 m/s², –2.5 m/s²
   (b) 111 m
4. (a) 1.6 m/s², 0 m/s², –3.8 m/s²
   (b) 423.5 m
5. (a) 2.4 m/s², –2 m/s² (b) 264 m
6. (a) 0.8 m/s², –0.9 m/s² (b) 80 m
7. (a) 1.6 m/s², 0 m/s², –2 m/s²
   (b) 140 m
8. (a) 2.5 m/s², 0 m/s², –9 m/s²
   (b) 371.25 m
9. (a) 1 ⅔ m/s², 0 m/s², –5 m/s²
   (b) 540 m
10. (a) ⅔ m/s², 0 m/s², –2.6 m/s²
    (b) 348.5 m
11. (a)

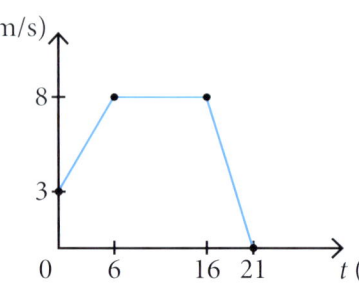

(b) (i) ⅚ m/s² (ii) 1.6 m/s² (iii)
133 m

12. (a)

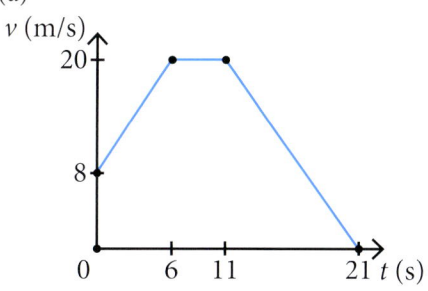

(b) (i) 2 m/s² (ii) 2 m/s² (iii) 284 m

13. (a)

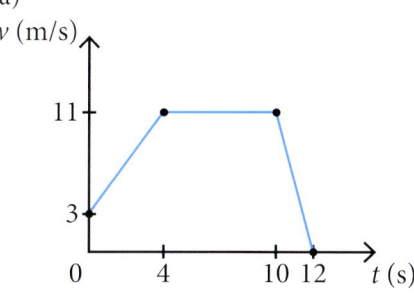

(b) (i) 2 m/s² (ii) 5.5 m/s² (iii) 105 m

14. (a)

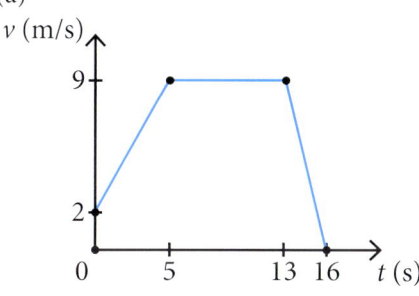

(b) (i) 1.4 m/s² (ii) 3 m/s² (iii) 113 m

15. (a)

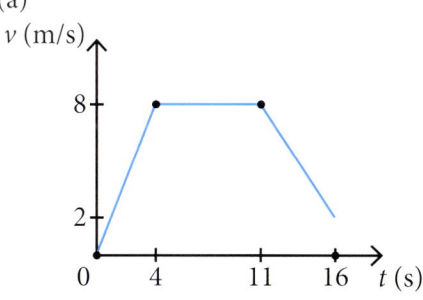

(b) (i) 2 m/s² (ii) 1.2 m/s² (iii) 97 m

16. (a)

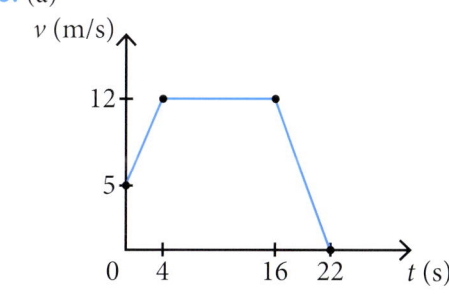

(b) (i) 1.75 m/s² (ii) 2 m/s² (iii) 214 m

17. (a)

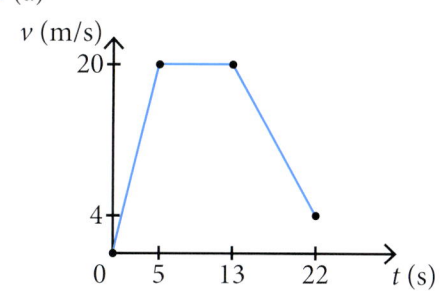

(b) (i) 4 m/s² (ii) 1 ⁷⁄₉ m/s² (iii) 318 m

## Exercise 15C

1. (a)

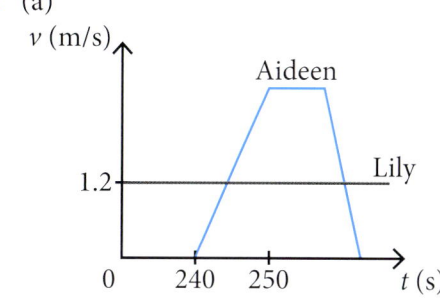

(b) (i) 8 m/s (ii) 345.9 m (iii) 0.4 m/s² (iv) 56 m

2. (a)

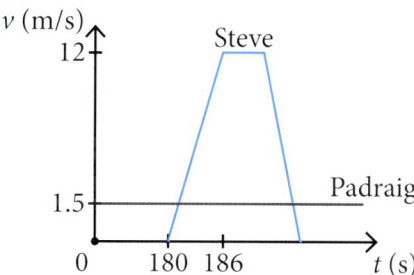

(b) (i) 209 s (ii) 313.7 m (iii) 45 m

## Exercise 16A

1. (a) 1.5 m/s² (b) 24m
2. (a) ⅔ m/s² (b) 24m
3. (a) 14 m/s (b) 44 m
4. (a) 15 m/s
   (b) 0.625 m/s²
5. (a) 4 s (b) 2.25 m/s²
6. (a) 80 m (b) 10 s
7. (a) 2 m/s (b) ⅙ m/s²

8. (a) 22 m/s (b) 78 m
9. (a) 3 m/s (b) 8 s
10. (a) 6 m/s² (b) 32 m/s
11. (a) 33.5 m/s (b) 9 s
12. (a) 7 m/s (b) 17 m
13. (a) 3 m/s² (b) 7 s
14. (a) 3.55 m/s²
    (b) 139.425 m

## Exercise 16B

1. (a) 6 m/s (b) 18m
2. (a) 17 m/s (b) 4 s
3. (a) 3 m/s² (b) 4 s
4. (a) 1.5 s (b) 12.75 m

5. (a) 1.5 m/s² (b) 3 m
6. (a) 8 m/s (b) 3 s
7. (a) 8 m/s (b) 7.5 m
8. (a) 24 m/s (b) 12 m/s²

## Exercise 16C

1. (a) 25 m/s (b) 31.25 m

ANSWERS

2. (a) 9.8 m (b) 1.4 s
3. (a) 6.07 m/s (b) 0.607 s
4. (a) 3.44 m (b) 1.66 s
5. (a) 26.3 m (b) 131.5 m
   (c) 51.3 m/s
6. (a) 0.722 m (b) 0.169 s and 0.591 s
7. (a) 0.736 s (b) 35.5 m
8. (a) 0.44 m/s going down
   (b) 0.156 s (c) 0.122 m
   (d) 0.0647 s and 0.247 s

## Exercise 16D

1. (a) 0.264 s (b) 1.05 m (c) 0.605 m
2. (a) 0.867 s (b) 3.76 m (c) 8.67 m/s
   and 8.97 m/s
3. (a) 4.05 m (b) 1.4 s (c) 9 m/s
   (d) 0.168 s and 0.832 s
4. (a) 8.912 m (b) 1.66 s (c) 13.4 m/s
   (d) 0.07 s to 0.57 s
5. (a) 0.523 s (b) 0.932 m (c) 0.422 s
6. (a) 0.625 s (b) 3.05 m (c) 1.8 m

## Exercise 17A

1. 20 N          5. 8 kg
2. 6 kg          6. 1.5 m/s$^2$
3. 5 m/s$^2$     7. 22.4 N
4. 24 N          8. 30 kg

## Exercise 17B

1. (a) 6 N (b) 51 m
2. (a) 27 N (b) 2 s
3. (a) 27 N (b) 7 m/s
4. (a) 56 N (b) 37 m/s
5. (a) 24 N (b) 6 s
6. (a) 22.4 N (b) 37.5 m
7. (a) 24 N (b) 39 m/s
8. (a) 37.5 N (b) 8 m/s

## Exercise 17C

1. (a) 14 N (b) 4 m/s
2. (a) 16 N (b) 1.5 s
3. (a) 36 N (b) 18 m
4. (a) 21 N (b) 7 m/s
5. (a) 10 N (b) 4 s
6. (a) 10.5 N (b) 2 s
7. (a) 12 N (b) 13.5 m
8. (a) 20 N (b) 5 m/s
9. (a) 9 N (b) 4 s
10. (a) 12.6 N (b) 17.5 m

## Exercise 18A

1. Horizontal component = 22.6 N
   Vertical component = 8.21 N

2. Horizontal component = 0.923 N
   Vertical component = 2.54 N
3. Horizontal component = 11.1 N
   Vertical component = 11.5 N
4. Horizontal component = 11.8 N
   Vertical component = 2.08 N
5. Horizontal component = 6.14 N
   Vertical component = 12.6 N
6. Horizontal component = 20.1 N
   Vertical component = 28.7 N
7. Horizontal component = 43.7 N
   Vertical component = 31.7 N
8. Horizontal component = 21.1 N
   Vertical component = 39.7 N
9. Horizontal component = 2.82 N
   Vertical component = 1.9 N
10. Horizontal component = 41.8 N
    Vertical component = 32.6 N

## Exercise 18B

1. 21.7 N at 87.6° with the horizontal
2. 3.23 N at 47.7° with the horizontal
3. 29.4 N at 42.0° with the horizontal
4. 45.8 N at 20.8° with the horizontal
5. 2.87 N at 76.1° with the horizontal
6. 240 N at 24.6° with the horizontal
7. 3.37 N at 64.1° with the horizontal
8. 50.1 N at 3.58° with the horizontal
9. 19.6 N at 12.6° with the horizontal
10. 4.06 N at 41.5° with the horizontal

## Exercise 18C

1. 13 N at 32.5° with the horizontal
2. 12.1 N at 65.6° with the horizontal
3. 3.61 N at 56.3° with the horizontal
4. 55.1 N at 4.16° with the horizontal
5. 9.22 N at 77.5° with the horizontal
6. 4.27 N at 32.6° with the horizontal
7. 26.4 N at 65.4° with the horizontal
8. 28.4 N at 27.6° with the horizontal
9. 12.5 N at 28.6° with the horizontal
10. 17.7 N at 42.7° with the horizontal

## Exercise 18D

1. 19.9 N at 21.0° with the inclined plane
2. 7.53 N at 7.7° with the inclined plane
3. 13.8 N at 24.4° with the inclined plane
4. 196 N at 6.56° with the inclined plane

5. 2.56 N at 22.8° with the inclined plane
6. 99.5 N at 11.4° with the inclined plane

## Exercise 18E

1. A = 1.38 N    B = 7.92 N
2. C = 38.1 N    D = 28.8 N
3. V = 52.6 N    W = 16.2 N
4. F = 18.7 N    G = 17.6 N
5. H = 13.9 N    I = 15.8 N
6. L = 54.3 N    M = 66.3 N
7. P = 49.7 N    Q = 12.9 N
8. R = 3.07 N    S = 4.92 N
9. U = 56.4 N    V = 77.7 N
10. X = 50.4 N   Y = 19.4 N

## Exercise 18F

1. R = 16.7 N    Q = 19.9 N
2. R = 5.91 N    Q = 4.45 N
3. R = 27.5 N    Q = 39.3 N
4. R = 1.33 N    Q = 2.51 N
5. R = 283 N     Q = 138 N
6. R = 10.2 N    Q = 33.5 N

## Exercise 18G

1. R = 26.6 N    Q = 25.6 N
2. R = 2.78 N    Q = 3.41 N
3. R = 233.8 N   Q = 294.8 N
4. R = 63.8 N    Q = 61.5 N
5. R = 7.63 N    Q = 5.91 N
6. R = 46.3 N    Q = 53.6 N

## Exercise 19A

1. 6.4 N at 51.3° with the horizontal
2. 7.28 N at 15.9° with the horizontal
3. 6.71 N at 63.4° with the horizontal
4. 17 N at 61.9° with the horizontal
5. 3.16 N at 71.6° with the horizontal
6. 5.39 N at 21.8° with the horizontal
7. 13 N at 22.6° with the horizontal
8. 4.47 N at 26.6° with the horizontal
9. 7.81 N at 50.2° with the horizontal

194

10. 7.62 N at 23.2° with the horizontal

## Exercise 19B

1. 10 m/s
2. 8.06 m/s
3. 8.25 m/s
4. 2.24 m
5. 26 m
6. 11.4 m

## Exercise 19C

1. $(6\mathbf{i} + 2\mathbf{j})$ N
2. $(-5\mathbf{i} + 2\mathbf{j})$ N
3. $(-5\mathbf{i} - \mathbf{j})$ N
4. $(\mathbf{j})$ N
5. $(3\mathbf{i})$ N
6. $(4\mathbf{i} - \mathbf{j})$ N
7. $(-2\mathbf{i} - 4\mathbf{j})$ N
8. $(-3\mathbf{i} - 2\mathbf{j})$ N
9. $(6\mathbf{i} + 3\mathbf{j})$ N
10. $(\mathbf{i} + 12\mathbf{j})$ N

## Exercise 19D

1. $(\mathbf{i} - 2\mathbf{j})$ N
2. $(-3\mathbf{i} + 4\mathbf{j})$ N
3. $(\mathbf{i} + 5\mathbf{j})$ N
4. $(-4\mathbf{i} - 2\mathbf{j})$ N
5. $(3\mathbf{i} + 8\mathbf{j})$ N
6. $(-2\mathbf{i} + 3\mathbf{j})$ N
7. $(5\mathbf{i} - \mathbf{j})$ N
8. $(-2\mathbf{j})$ N
9. $(4\mathbf{i} + 3\mathbf{j})$ N
10. $(-3\mathbf{i} - \mathbf{j})$ N

## Exercise 19E

1. $(\mathbf{i} - 3\mathbf{j})$ m/s$^2$
2. $(-\mathbf{i} + 4\mathbf{j})$ N
3. $(-\mathbf{i} - 2\mathbf{j})$ m/s$^2$
4. $(-2\mathbf{i} - 6\mathbf{j})$ N
5. $(-2\mathbf{i} + 3\mathbf{j})$ m/s$^2$
6. $(-3\mathbf{i} + 8\mathbf{j})$ N
7. $(-\mathbf{i} + 3\mathbf{j})$ m/s$^2$
8. $(-3\mathbf{i} - 5\mathbf{j})$ N
9. $(3\mathbf{i} + 2\mathbf{j})$ m/s$^2$
10. $(-2\mathbf{i} + 5\mathbf{j})$ N

## Exercise 19F

1. (a) $(4\mathbf{i} - 12\mathbf{j})$ N (b) $(6\mathbf{i} - 11\mathbf{j})$ m/s
   (c) $(13.5\mathbf{i} - 19.5\mathbf{j})$ m
2. (a) $(2\mathbf{i} + 2\mathbf{j})$ m/s$^2$ (b) $(3\mathbf{i} + 6\mathbf{j})$ m/s
   (c) $(2\mathbf{i} + 8\mathbf{j})$ m
3. (a) $(2\mathbf{i} + 6\mathbf{j})$ N (b) $(-2\mathbf{i} - 4\mathbf{j})$ m/s
   (c) $(6\mathbf{i} + 30\mathbf{j})$ m
4. (a) $-7.5\mathbf{j}$ m/s$^2$ (b) $(4\mathbf{i} - 33\mathbf{j})$ m/s
   (c) $(16\mathbf{i} - 72\mathbf{j})$ m
5. (a) $(-12\mathbf{i} - 30\mathbf{j})$ N (b) $(3\mathbf{i} + 4\mathbf{j})$ m/s
   (c) $-10.5\mathbf{j}$ m
6. (a) $(2.5\mathbf{i} + 12.5\mathbf{j})$ m/s$^2$
   (b) $(10.5\mathbf{i} + 57.5\mathbf{j})$ m/s
   (c) $(21.25\mathbf{i} + 131.25\mathbf{j})$ m
7. (a) $(-14\mathbf{i} + 7\mathbf{j})$ N (b) $(4\mathbf{i} - 3\mathbf{j})$ m/s
   (c) $(-4\mathbf{i} + \mathbf{j})$ m/s
8. (a) $(4\mathbf{i} + 2\mathbf{j})$ m/s$^2$ (b) $(7\mathbf{i} + 7\mathbf{j})$ m/s
   (c) $(6\mathbf{i} + 10\mathbf{j})$ m
9. (a) $(-8\mathbf{i} + 16\mathbf{j})$ N (b) $(5\mathbf{i} - 2\mathbf{j})$ m/s
   (c) $(\mathbf{i} + 6\mathbf{j})$ m/s

10. (a) $(-30\mathbf{i} + 18\mathbf{j})$ m/s$^2$
    (b) $(172\mathbf{i} - 96\mathbf{j})$ m/s
    (c) $(492\mathbf{i} - 252\mathbf{j})$ m

## Exercise 19G

1. $(10\mathbf{i} - 24\mathbf{j})$ m/s
2. $(-18\mathbf{i} + 24\mathbf{j})$ m/s
3. $(45\mathbf{i} + 24\mathbf{j})$ m/s
4. $(-21\mathbf{i} - 72\mathbf{j})$ m/s
5. $(36\mathbf{i} + 27\mathbf{j})$ m/s
6. $(-36\mathbf{i} + 15\mathbf{j})$ m/s

## Exercise 20A

1. (a) 25 N (b) 40 N
2. (a) 18 N (b) 28 N
3. (a) 25 N (b) 48 N

## Exercise 20B

1. (a) 27.36 N (b) 75.18 N
2. (a) 80.30 N (b) 89.18 N
3. (a) 28.3 N (b) 20.5 N
4. (a) 52.6 N (b) 32.2 N
5. (a) 17.0 N (b) 12.0 N
6. (a) 22.6 N (b) 9.5 N
7. (a) 71.3 N (b) 33.6 N
8. (a) 21.4 N (b) 11.0 N
9. (a) 12.9 N (b) 7.9 N
10. (a) 67.2 N (b) 20.1 N

## Exercise 20C

1. (a) 9.65 m/s$^2$ (b) 0.259 s
2. (a) 26.4 N (b) 112 m
3. (a) 7.2 m/s$^2$ (b) 1.22 s
4. (a) 20.4 N (b) 12 m/s
5. (a) 1.53 m/s$^2$ (b) 19.2 m
6. (a) 30.5 N (b) 10 s
7. (a) 0.508 m/s$^2$ (b) 2.89 m/s
8. (a) 44.8 N (b) 3 m/s
9. (a) 1.63 m/s$^2$ (b) 6.53 m
10. (a) 1.5 m/s$^2$ (b) 18.75 m/s
11. (a) 18.42 N (b) 77 m/s
12. 25.3 N
13. 22.5 N
14. 8 kg
15. 3.32 m/s$^2$

## Exercise 20D

1. 35.83 N
2. 8.12 N
3. 71.22 N
4. 56.4 N
5. 10.67 N
6. 7.79 N
7. 69.3 N
8. 8.47 N
9. 50.1 N
10. 20.94 N

## Exercise 21A

1. (a) 1.18 m/s$^2$ (b) 460 kg
2. (a) 1.45 m/s$^2$ (b) 1079 N
3. (a) 837 N (b) 1422 N
4. (a) 1423.75 N (b) 1056.25 N
5. (a) 3500 N (b) 254 kg
6. (a) 1440 kg (b) 277 kg
7. (a) 1.34 m/s$^2$ (b) 346.4 N
8. (a) 1505 kg (b) 785 N

## Exercise 21B

1. (a) 1.2 m/s$^2$ (b) 1094 N
2. (a) 1.32 m/s$^2$ (b) 1084 N
3. (a) 1124.68 N (b) 1.45 N per kg
4. (a) 861.12 N (b) 1.66 N per kg
5. (a) 3370.72 N (b) 442 kg
6. (a) 1165 kg (b) 429 kg
7. (a) 1.28 m/s$^2$ (b) 0.77 N per kg
8. (a) 1275 kg (b) 748.84 N

## Exercise 21C

1. (a) 2253 N (b) 378 N (c) 445.5 N
   (d) 2545.5 N (e) 0.84 m/s$^2$
2. (a) 2403 N (b) 513 N (c) 675 N
   (d) 2970 N (e) 0.95 m/s$^2$
3. (a) 4620 N (b) 2700 N (c) 3120 N
   (d) 5376 N (e) 1.8 m/s$^2$
4. (a) 4670 N (b) 2800 N (c) 7.2 m
   (d) 2 m/s (e) 1.25 m
5. (a) 1.25 m/s$^2$
   (b) 1643.5 N (c) 912.6 N
   (d) 730.9 N (e) 1380.9 N (f) 14.2 s
6. (a) 1.6 m/s$^2$ (b) 1471.52 N
   (c) 1176 N (d) 4089.12 N
   (e) 7.06 s (f) 21.18 m

## Exercise 21D

1. (a) 3.85 m/s$^2$ (b) 5.54 N
   (c) 11.68 N
2. (a) 2 m/s$^2$ (b) 9.6 N (c) 19.2 N
3. (a) 2 m/s$^2$ (b) 2.4 N (c) 4.8 N
4. (a) 1 ⅔ m/s$^2$ (b) 5.83 N (c) 11.7 N
5. (a) 2 m/s$^2$ (b) 12 N (c) 24 N
6. (a) 3.75 m/s$^2$ (b) 6.875 N
   (c) 13.75 N
7. (a) 2.5 m/s$^2$ (b) 3.75 N (c) 7.5 N
8. (a) 4 m/s$^2$ (b) 42 N (c) 84 N

## Exercise 21E

1. (a) 2 m/s$^2$ (b) 4.8 N (c) 9.6 N
   (d) 1.1 s (e) 2.19 m/s (f) 0.24 m

(g) 0.44 s
2. (a) 3 m/s² (b) 18.2 N (c) 36.4 N
   (d) 2.16 m (e) 3.6 m/s (f) 0.648 m
   (g) 0.72 s
3. (a) 4 m/s² (b) 4.2 N (c) 8.4 N
   (d) 4.5 m (e) 6 m/s (f) 1.8 m
   (g) 1.2 s
4. (a) 4.4 m/s² (b) 20.16 N
   (c) 40.32 N (d) 0.58 s (e) 2.57 m/s
   (f) 0.33 m (g) 0.514 s
5. (a) 3 m/s² (b) 9.1 N (c) 18.2 N
   (d) 0.96 m (e) 2.4 m/s (f) 0.288 m
   (g) 0.48 s
6. (a) 4.8 m/s² (b) 19.24 N
   (c) 38.48 N (d) 0.384 m
   (e) 1.92 m/s (f) 0.384 s
7. (a) 5 m/s² (b) 7.5 N (c) 15 N
   (d) 1.2 s (e) 3.6 m (f) 1.2 s
8. (a) 6 m/s² (b) 9.6 N (c) 19.2 N
   (d) 0.5 s (e) 0.75 m (f) 0.6 s

## Exercise 21F

1. (a) 5.33 m/s² (b) 37.3 N (c) 52.8 N
2. (a) 7.14 m/s² (b) 14.3 N (c) 20.2 N
3. (a) 7.27 m/s² (b) 21.8 N (c) 30.9 N
4. (a) 6.36 m/s² (b) 2.55 N (c) 3.60 N
5. (a) 5.71 m/s² (b) 13.7 N (c) 19.4 N
6. (a) 5.79 m/s² (b) 92.6 N (c) 131 N
7. (a) 5.71 m/s² (b) 25.7 N (c) 36.4 N
8. (a) 6 m/s² (b) 4.8 N (c) 6.79 N
9. (a) 5.625 m/s² (b) 39.375 N
   (c) 55.7 N
10. (a) 5.56 m/s² (b) 267 N (c) 377 N

## Exercise 21G

1. (a) 4.86 m/s² (b) 25.7 N
   (c) 2.33 m/s (d) 0.291 s
   (e) 0.340 m
2. (a) 5 m/s² (b) 3.5 N (c) 2.53 m/s
   (d) 0.675 s (e) 0.853 m
3. (a) 3.6 m/s² (b) 153.6 N
   (c) 1.51 m/s (d) 0.252 s (e) 0.19 m
4. (a) 4.13 m/s² (b) 10.6 N
   (c) 3.15 m/s (d) 0.787 s (e) 1.24 m
5. (a) 4.43 m/s² (b) 334 N
   (c) 1.06 m/s (d) 0.353 s
   (e) 0.188 m
6. (a) 4 m/s² (b) 126 N (c) 1.90 m/s
   (d) 0.632 s (e) 0.6 m
7. (a) 3.32 m/s² (b) 4.81 N
   (c) 2.52 m/s (d) 0.6 s (e) 0.757 m

8. (a) 4.17 m/s² (b) 69.9 N
   (c) 2.66 m/s (d) 0.74 s (e) 0.983 m
9. (a) 3.41 m/s² (b) 276.9 N
   (c) 2.59 m/s (d) 0.604 s
   (e) 0.782 m
10. (a) 2.21 m/s² (b) 22.6 N
    (c) 2.26 m/s (d) 0.315 s
    (e) 0.356 m

## Exercise 22A

1. 32 N and 48 N
2. 22.7 N and 27.3 N
3. 33.75 N and 26.25 N
4. 45 N and 75 N
5. 20.16 N and 35.84 N
6. 10.3 N and 15.7 N
7. 3.48 N and 4.52 N
8. 15.2 N and 20.8 N

## Exercise 22B

1. 21.4 N and 28.6 N
2. 23.5 N and 56.5 N
3. 15 N and 9 N
4. 22.4 N and 33.6 N
5. 2.57 N and 6.43 N
6. 9.85 N and 6.15 N
7. 5.2 N and 24.8 N
8. 127.1 N and 112.9 N
9. 9.41 N and 30.59 N
10. 23.5 N and 12.5 N

## Exercise 22C

1. 6.13 m          4. 8.93 m
2. 7.83 m          5. 4.59 m
3. 4.71 m          6. 2.37 m

## Exercise 22D

1. 16.8 kg
2. 0.5 m
3. 12.65 kg
4. 5.31 m
5. 1.91 kg
6. 6.27 m
7. (a) 8 N and 12 N (b) 10 kg

## Exercise 23A

1. (a) 0.607 (b) Positive
2. (a) 0.893 (b) Positive
3. (a) –0.557 (b) Negative
4. (a) 0.768 (b) Positive
5. (a) –0.583 (b) Negative
6. (a) –0.857 (b) Negative
7. (a) 0.571 (b) Positive

8. (a) –0.720 (b) Negative
9. (a) 0.720 (b) Positive
10. (a) –0.696 (b) Negative

## Exercise 23B

*Please note that in these answers the equations of the lines of best fit are approximate and depend upon the lines drawn by the student.*

1. (a) (b)

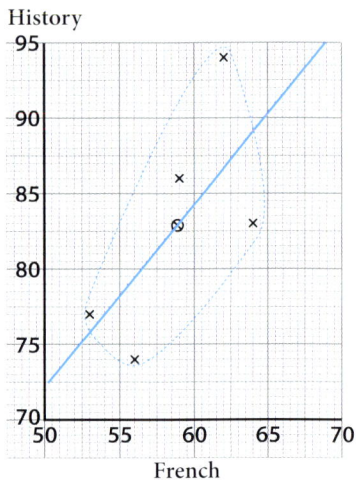

French

Mean (58.8, 82.8)
(c) $y = 1.22x + 11.32$
(d) 0.6
(e) Positive correlation

2. (a) (b)

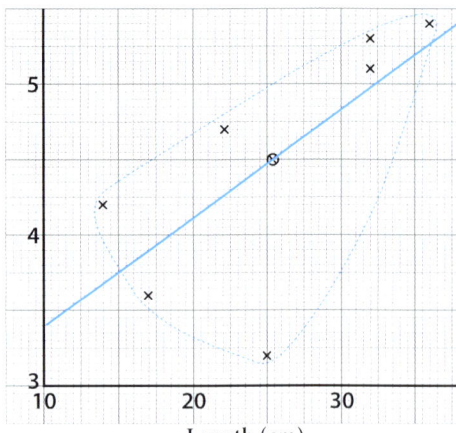

Length (cm)

Mean (25.4, 4.5)
(c) $y = 0.07x + 2.67$ (d) 0.74
(e) Positive correlation

**3.** (a) (b)

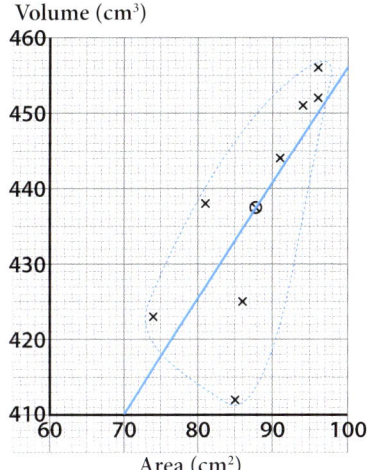

Mean (87.875, 437.625)

(c) $y = 1.55x + 301.87$ (d) 0.875 (e) Positive correlation

**4.** (a) (b)

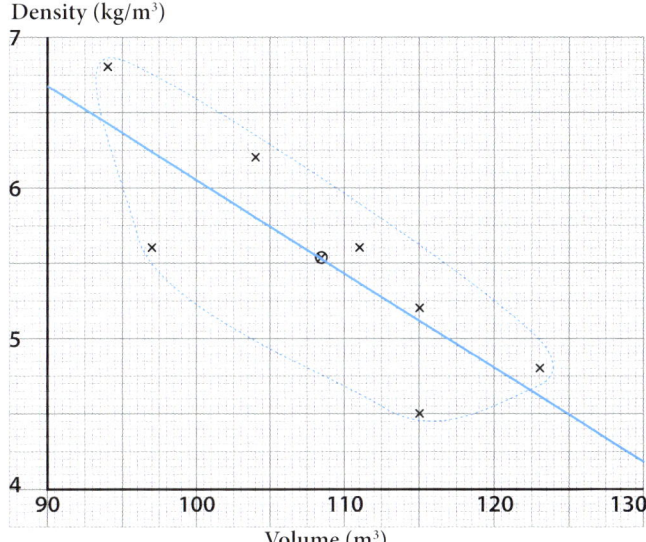

Mean (108.4, 5.53)

(c) $y = -0.063x + 12.31$ (d) $-0.839$

(e) Negative correlation

**5.** (a) (b)

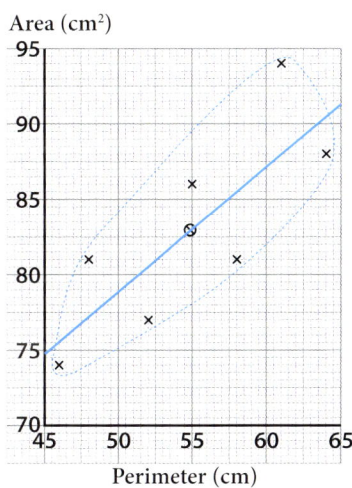

Mean (54.9, 83)

(c) $y = 0.82x + 37.85$

(d) 0.848

(e) Positive correlation

**6.** (a) (b)

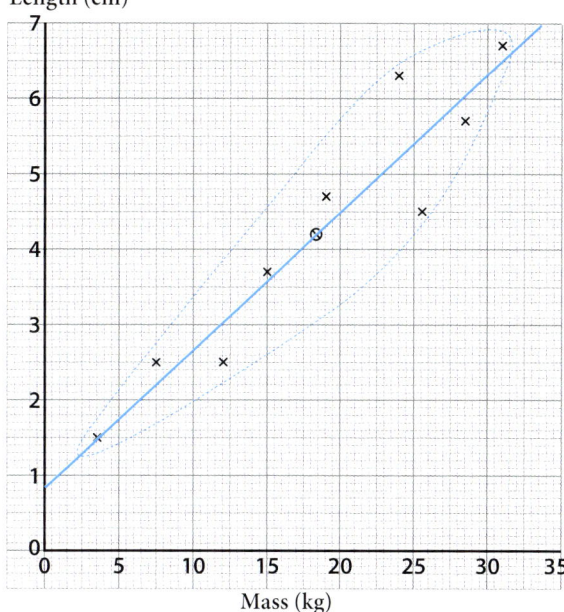

Mean (18.4, 4.2)

(c) $y = 0.18x + 0.92$

(d) 0.9125

(e) Positive correlation

**7.** (a) (b)

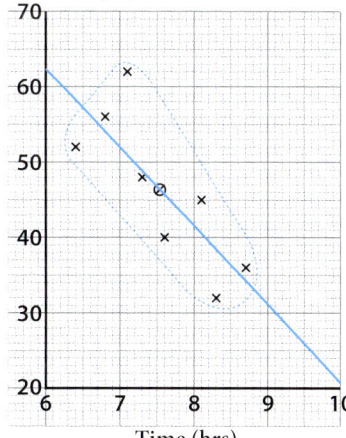

Mean (7.5375, 46.375)

(c) $y = -10.35x + 124.40$

(d) $-0.857$

(e) Negative correlation

8. (a) (b)

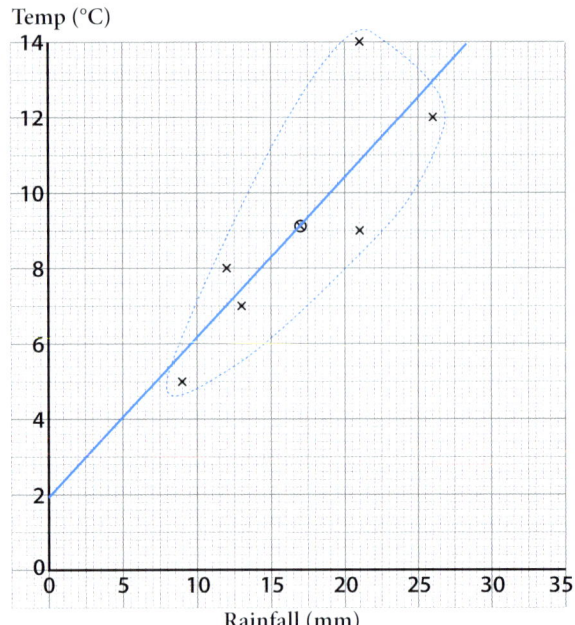

Mean (17, 9.17)
(c) $y = 0.42x + 1.99$
(d) 0.843
(e) Positive correlation

9. (a) (b)

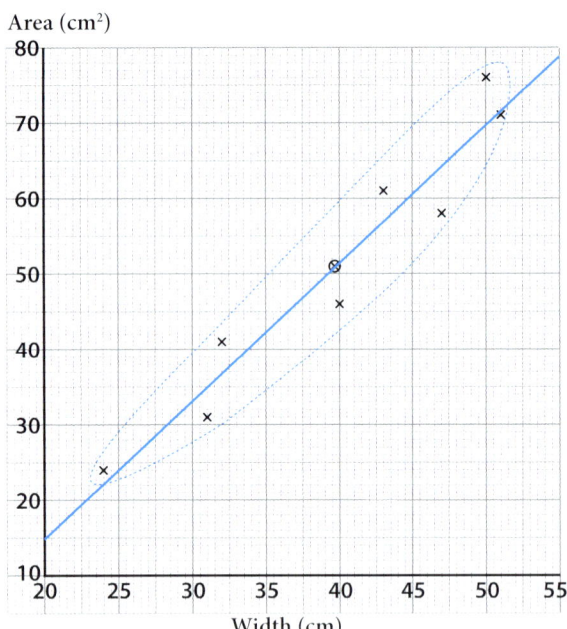

Mean (39.75, 51)
(c) $y = 1.83x - 21.60$
(d) 0.952
(e) Positive correlation

10. (a) (b)

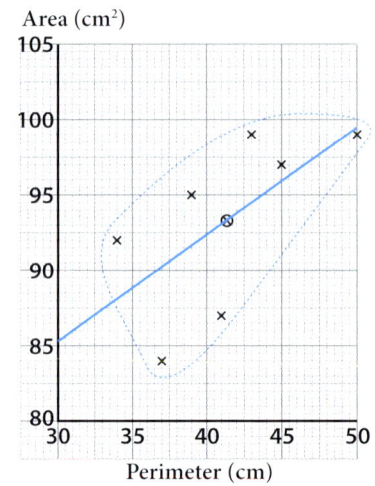

Mean (41.3, 93.3)
(c) $y = 0.71x + 63.94$
(d) 0.759
(e) Positive correlation

## Exercise 24A

1. Mean = 13.5 and standard deviation = 1.8
2. Mean = 6.72 and standard deviation = 1.62
3. Mean = 126.8 and standard deviation = 8.66
4. Mean = £5.67 and standard deviation = £2.14
5. Mean = 11.375 and standard deviation = 2.23
6. Mean = 8.25 and standard deviation = 2.49
7. Mean = 24.75 and standard deviation = 3.38
8. Mean = 20.3 and standard deviation = 3.74

## Exercise 24B

1. Mean = 2 and standard deviation = 0.837
2. Mean = 4.47 and standard deviation = 1.77
3. Mean = 3.72 and standard deviation = 2.72
4. Mean = 2.02 and standard deviation = 0.927
5. Mean = 2.625 and standard deviation = 1.84
6. Mean = 5.64 and standard deviation = 2.41
7. Mean = 26.1875 and standard deviation = 2.02
8. Mean = 8.35 and standard deviation = 2.31
9. Mean = 6.84 and standard deviation = 1.39
10. Mean = 14.25 and standard deviation = 1.87

## Exercise 24C

1. Mean = 9.9 and standard deviation = 5.39
2. Mean = 12.28 and standard deviation = 6.08
3. Mean = 6.1 and standard deviation = 2.05
4. Mean = 31.1 and standard deviation = 12.83
5. Mean = 13.3 and standard deviation = 6.78
6. Mean = 9.25 and standard deviation = 5.93
7. Mean = 12.94 and standard deviation = 6.21
8. Mean = 14.45 and standard deviation = 5.78
9. Mean = 8.18 and standard deviation = 3.89

10. Mean = 14.8 and standard deviation = 6.31
11. Mean = 21.1 and standard deviation = 7.27
12. Mean = 17.47 and standard deviation = 5.24
13. Mean = 18.84 and standard deviation = 9.03
14. Mean = 20.6 and standard deviation = 9.95

## Exercise 24D

1. (a) 11 (b) 8.73 cm
2. (a) 14 (b) £11.74
3. (a) 12 (b) £1.92
4. (a) 4 (b) 5.80 cm
5. (a) 25 (b) 12.79 km
6. (a) 5 (b) 4.23 kg
7. (a) 4 (b) 9.83 m
8. (a) 3 (b) 10.48 cm
9. (a) 6 (b) 72.21 ml

## Exercise 24E

1. Mean = 45.3 kg and standard deviation = 4.22 kg
2. Mean = 53.2 and standard deviation = 7.73
3. Mean = 43.1 and standard deviation = 7.32
4. Mean = £187.56 and standard deviation = £14.09
5. Mean = 5.2 cm and standard deviation = 0.395 cm
6. Mean = 65.6 and standard deviation = 6.576
7. Mean = 54.24 and standard deviation = 5.96
8. Mean = 50 cm and standard deviation = 7.29 cm

## Exercise 24F

1. (a) 52 and 4.7 (b) 92 and 9.4 (c) 20 and 2.35
2. (a) 60.8 cm and 11.2 cm (b) 10.2 cm and 2.8 cm (c) 14.6 cm and 1.4 cm
3. (a) 13.5 and 0.725 (b) 64 and 2.9 (c) 268 and 14.5
4. (a) 0.9 mins and 0.24 mins (b) 4.2 mins and 0.72 mins (c) 0.95 mins and 0.12 mins
5. (a) 5.8 m and 1.2 m (b) 2.6 m and

0.6 m (c) 15.4 m and 3.6 m
6. (a) 5.9 cm and 2.31 cm (b) 33.6 cm and 9.24 cm (c) 4.2 cm and 0.77 cm
7. (a) 137 and 18 (b) 38 and 6 (c) 213 and 36
8. (a) 2.2 km and 0.3 km (b) 5.6 km and 0.6 km (c) 0.9 km and 0.075 km
9. (a) 7.43 and 0.27 (b) 0.27 and 0.03 (c) 3.29 and 0.81
10. (a) 2.6 l and 0.8 l (b) 6.8 l and 1.6 l (c) 0.83 l and 0.16 l

## Exercise 25A

1. (a)

[tree diagram: red 0.5 → red 0.5, amber 0.2, green 0.3; amber 0.2 → red 0.5, amber 0.2, green 0.3; green 0.3 → red 0.5, amber 0.2, green 0.3]

(b) (i) 0.3 (ii) 0.62 (iii) 0.51

2. (a)

[tree diagram: green $\frac{12}{30}$ → green $\frac{12}{30}$, yellow $\frac{18}{30}$; yellow $\frac{18}{30}$ → green $\frac{12}{30}$, yellow $\frac{18}{30}$]

(b) (i) $^6/_{25}$ (ii) $^4/_{25}$ (iii) $^{12}/_{25}$

3. (a)

[tree diagram: chips 0.76 → burger 0.6, not 0.4; not 0.24 → burger 0.48, not 0.52]

(b) (i) 0.456 (ii) 0.5712

4. (a)

[tree diagram: French 0.7 → German 0.28, not 0.72; not 0.3 → German 0.62, not 0.38]

(b) (i) 0.196 (ii) 0.382

5. (a)

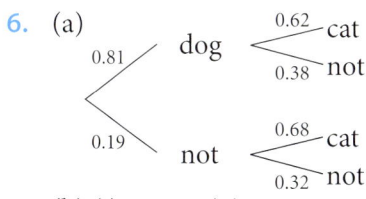

(b) (i) $^{22}/_{195}$ (ii) $^{541}/_{585}$ (iii) $^{242}/_{585}$

6. (a)

[tree diagram: dog 0.81 → cat 0.62, not 0.38; not 0.19 → cat 0.68, not 0.32]

(b) (i) 0.1292 (ii) 0.6314

7. (a)        A        B

[tree diagram: 20p $\frac{6}{10}$ → 20p $\frac{4}{11}$, 50p $\frac{7}{11}$; 50p $\frac{4}{10}$ → 20p $\frac{3}{11}$, 50p $\frac{8}{11}$]

(b) (i) $^{18}/_{55}$ (ii) $^{28}/_{55}$

8. (a)

[tree diagram: Train 0.44 → Titanic 0.35, not 0.65; not 0.56 → Titanic 0.42, not 0.58]

(b) (i) 0.154 (ii) 0.3892

## Exercise 25B

1. (a)

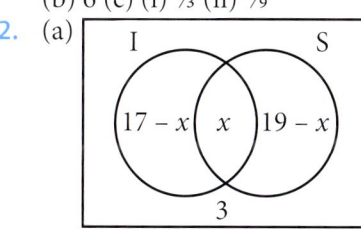

(b) 6 (c) (i) ⅓ (ii) ⅑

2. (a)

[Venn diagram: I and S circles, $17 - x$, $x$, $19 - x$, outside 3]

(b) 8 (c) (i) $^9/_{31}$ (ii) $^{12}/_{31}$

3. (a)

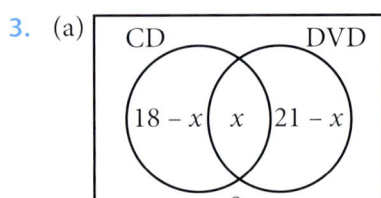

(b) 14 (c) (i) $^8/_{33}$ (ii) $^{14}/_{33}$

4. (a)

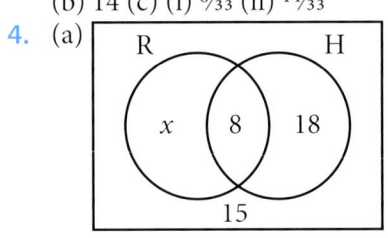

(b) (i) 14 (ii) 22 (c) (i) $^{26}/_{55}$ (ii) $^3/_{11}$

5. (a)

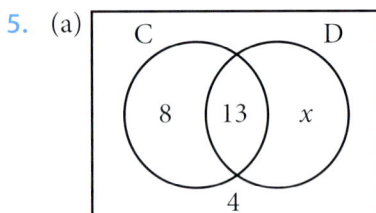

(b) 6 (c) (i) $^{13}/_{31}$ (ii) $^6/_{31}$

6. (a)

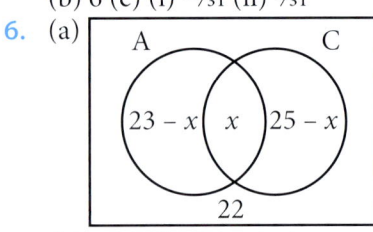

(b) 9 (c) (i) $^{14}/_{61}$ (ii) $^9/_{61}$

7. (a)

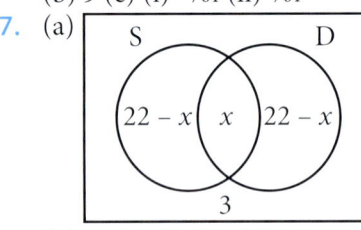

(b) 11 (c) (i) $^{22}/_{36}$ (ii) $^{11}/_{36}$

8. (a)

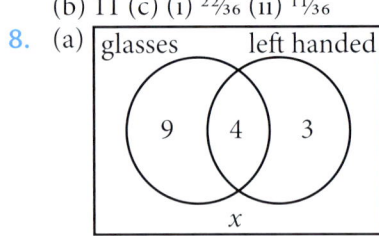

(b) 11 (c) (i) $^4/_{27}$ (ii) $^1/_3$ (iii) $^1/_9$

9. (a)

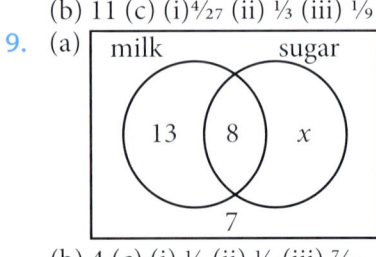

(b) 4 (c) (i) $^1/_4$ (ii) $^1/_8$ (iii) $^7/_{32}$

10. (a)

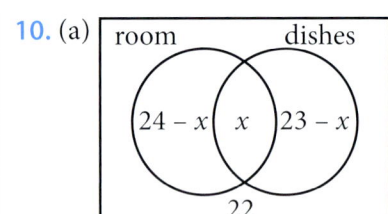

(b) 9 (c) (i) $^3/_{20}$ (ii) $^7/_{30}$ (iii) $^1/_4$

11. (a)

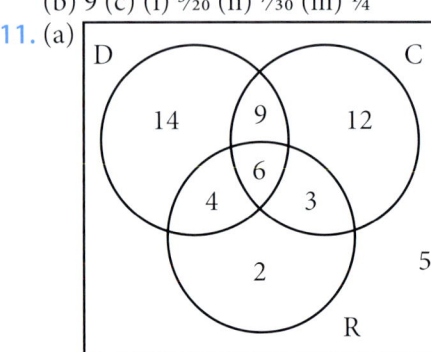

(b) (i) $^6/_{55}$ (ii) $^5/_{55}$ or $^1/_{11}$

12. (a)

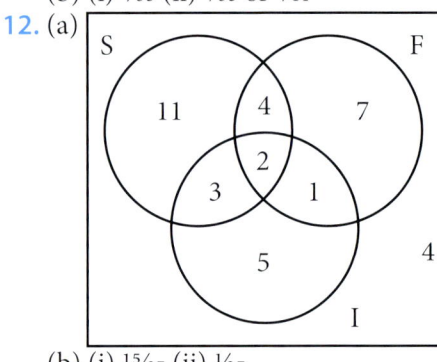

(b) (i) $^{15}/_{37}$ (ii) $^1/_{37}$

## Exercise 25C

1. (a)

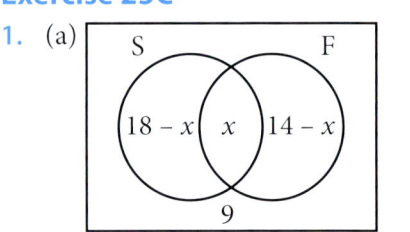

8 do both (b) (i) $^{10}/_{33}$ (ii) $^4/_7$ (iii) $^4/_9$

2. (a)

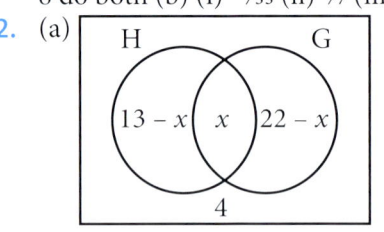

5 study both (b) (i) $^1/_2$ (ii) $^5/_{22}$ (iii) $^5/_{13}$

3. (a)

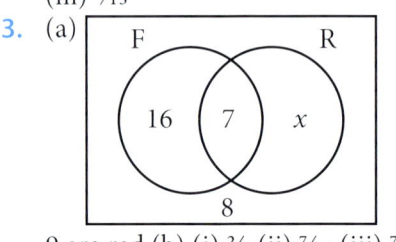

9 are red (b) (i) $^2/_5$ (ii) $^7/_{23}$ (iii) $^7/_{16}$

4. (a)

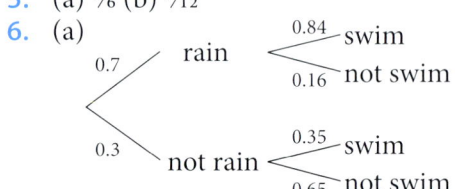

7 order both (b) (i) $^{35}/_{39}$ (ii) $^7/_{20}$ (iii) $^7/_{22}$

5. (a) $^5/_6$ (b) $^7/_{12}$

6. (a)

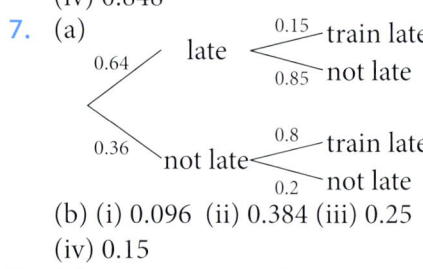

(b) (i) 0.588 (ii) 0.693 (iii) 0.84 (iv) 0.848

7. (a)

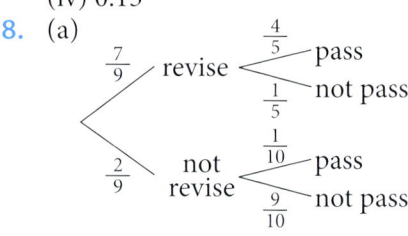

(b) (i) 0.096 (ii) 0.384 (iii) 0.25 (iv) 0.15

8. (a)

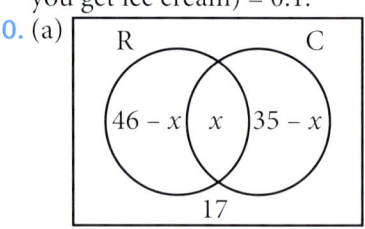

(b) (i) $^{28}/_{45}$ (ii) $^{29}/_{45}$ (iii) $^4/_5$

9. P(ice cream given that you get chips) = 0.15. P(chips given that you get ice cream) = 0.1.

10. (a)

Went to both = 7 (b) (i) $^1/_{13}$ (ii) $^1/_5$

11. (a) 0.875 (b) 0.625

12. (a) 0.778 (b) 0.583

13. (a) $^7/_{11}$ (b) $^{20}/_{33}$

## Exercise 25D

1. (a) 0.8 (b) 0.5
2. (a) 0.22 (b) 0.55
3. (a) 0.5 (b) 0.8
4. (a) 0.5 (b) 0.2
5. (a) 0.6 (b) 0.525

6. (a) $^8\!/_{35}$ (b) $^4\!/_7$
7. (a) 0.196 (b) 0.35
8. (a) 0.0384 (b) 0.16
9. (a) 0.3 (b) 0.32
10. (a) 0.76 (b) 0.6
11. (a) $^3\!/_8$ (b) $^{15}\!/_{56}$
12. (a) $^{35}\!/_{72}$ (b) $^{35}\!/_{66}$
13. (a) $^8\!/_{13}$ (b) $^2\!/_7$

## Exerise 25E

1. $^{27}\!/_{40}$   3. $^{175}\!/_{200}$   5. $^{50}\!/_{68}$
2. $^9\!/_{28}$   4. $^{14}\!/_{56}$   6. $^{22}\!/_{30}$

## Exerise 26A

1. 0.19   4. 0.034   7. 0.014
2. 0.2304   5. 0.275
3. 0.21   6. 0.076

## Exercise 26B

1. (a) 0.00041 (b) 0.894 (c) 0.503
2. (a) 0.249 (b) 0.972 (c) 0.197
3. (a) 0.230 (b) 0.337 (c) 0.683
4. (a) 0.6 (b) 0.0061 (c) 0.994
5. (a) 0.0000678 (b) 0.926 (c) 0.0617

## Exercise 27A

1. (a) 0.7852 (b) 0.2148
2. (a) 0t.0162 (b) 0.9838
3. (a) 0.9943 (b) 0.0057
4. (a) 0.1587 (b) 0.8413
5. (a) 0.9495 (b) 0.0505
6. (a) 0.7389 (b) 0.2611

## Exercise 27B

1. 0.0548   7. 0.8944
2. 0.1020   8. 0.0054
3. 0.0125   9. 0.2236
4. 0.0030   10. 0.9965
5. 0.8925   11. 0.9918
6. 0.9192   12. 0.9066

## Exercise 27C

1. 0.1056
2. 0.0329
3. 0.9599
4. (a) 0.0082 (b) 0.9641
5. (a) 0.9608 (b) 0.8315
   (c) 0.1075 (d) 0.0392
6. (a) 22.66% (b) 23202

## Exercise 28A

1. 84   4. 42
2. 24   5. 35
3. 30   6. 2

7. $30 + 8 = 38$
8. $(7 + 4) \times 15 \times 23 = 3795$

## Exercise 28B

1. 120   6. 2184
2. 5040   7. 2730
3. 5040   8. 720
4. 120   9. 212,520
5. 151,200   10. 479,001,600

## Exercise 28C

1. (a) 15 (b) 28 (c) 5
2. (a) 6 (b) 21 (c) 20
3. 56   7. 21
4. 56   8. 35
5. 15   9. 20
6. 5   10. 28

## Exercise 28D

1. $70 \times 35 \times 21 = 51,450$
2. $28 \times 15 = 420$
3. $21 \times 70 = 1470$
4. $7 \times 20 = 140$
5. $15 \times 7 \times 21 = 2,205$
6. $2 \times 10 \times 4 = 80$
7. $9 \times 56 \times 7 \times 20 = 70,560$
8. $_5P_2 \times _4P_2 = 20 \times 12 = 240$

## Exercise 29A

1. A proposition
2. A proposition
3. Not a proposition
4. A proposition
5. Not a proposition
6. Not a proposition
7. A proposition
8. A proposition
9. Not a proposition
10. A proposition
11. A proposition
12. Not a proposition
13. Not a proposition
14. A proposition

## Exercise 29B

1. Michael can play football well and Sian is clever.
2. Tuesday is not violet day.
3. Brussels sprouts are good to eat, or Sian is clever.
4. Michael can play football well and either Brussels sprouts are good to eat, or Tuesday is violet day.

5. Sian is not clever, and Michael can't play football well.
6. Brussels sprouts are not good to eat.
7. Sian is clever, or Michael can't play football well.
8. Michael can play football well and Sian is clever, or Michael can play football well and Tuesday is violet day.
9. Michael can play football well and either Sian is clever, or Tuesday is violet day.
10. It is not the case that either Brussels sprouts are good to eat, or Tuesday is violet day.

## Exercise 29C

1. true   11. true
2. true   12. false
3. false   13. false
4. true   14. false
5. true   15. true
6. true   16. true
7. false   17. true
8. true   18. false
9. false   19. true
10. false   20. true

## Exercise 29D

1. $p$ OR $\sim q$

| $p$ | $q$ | $\sim q$ | $p$ OR $\sim q$ |
|---|---|---|---|
| T | T | F | T |
| T | F | T | T |
| F | T | F | F |
| F | F | T | T |

2. $\sim(p$ OR $q)$

| $p$ | $q$ | $p$ OR $q$ | $\sim(p$ OR $q)$ |
|---|---|---|---|
| T | T | T | F |
| T | F | T | F |
| F | T | T | F |
| F | F | F | T |

3. $\sim p$ OR $\sim q$

| $p$ | $q$ | $\sim p$ | $\sim q$ | $\sim p$ OR $\sim q$ |
|---|---|---|---|---|
| T | T | F | F | F |
| T | F | F | T | T |
| F | T | T | F | T |
| F | F | T | T | T |

4. p OR (q AND r)

| p | q | r | q AND r | p OR (q AND r) |
|---|---|---|---|---|
| T | T | T | T | T |
| T | T | F | F | T |
| T | F | T | F | T |
| T | F | F | F | T |
| F | T | T | T | T |
| F | T | F | F | F |
| F | F | T | F | F |
| F | F | F | F | F |

5. p AND (q OR r)

| p | q | r | q OR r | p AND (q OR r) |
|---|---|---|---|---|
| T | T | T | T | T |
| T | T | F | T | T |
| T | F | T | T | T |
| T | F | F | F | F |
| F | T | T | T | F |
| F | T | F | T | F |
| F | F | T | T | F |
| F | F | F | F | F |

6. ~p AND (q OR r)

| p | q | r | ~p | q OR r | ~p AND (q OR r) |
|---|---|---|---|---|---|
| T | T | T | F | T | F |
| T | T | F | F | T | F |
| T | F | T | F | T | F |
| T | F | F | F | F | F |
| F | T | T | T | T | T |
| F | T | F | T | T | T |
| F | F | T | T | T | T |
| F | F | F | T | F | F |

7. p OR (q OR r)

| p | q | r | q OR r | p OR (q OR r) |
|---|---|---|---|---|
| T | T | T | T | T |
| T | T | F | T | T |
| T | F | T | T | T |
| T | F | F | F | T |
| F | T | T | T | T |
| F | T | F | T | T |
| F | F | T | T | T |
| F | F | F | F | F |

8. (p AND ~q) OR (~p AND q)

| p | q | ~p | ~q | p AND ~q | ~p AND q | (p AND ~q) OR (~p AND q) |
|---|---|---|---|---|---|---|
| T | T | F | F | F | F | F |
| T | F | F | T | T | F | T |
| F | T | T | F | F | T | T |
| F | F | T | T | F | F | F |

## Exercise 29E

1. ~r OR q          r OR ~q

| r | q | ~r | ~q | ~r OR q | r OR ~q |
|---|---|---|---|---|---|
| T | T | F | F | T | T |
| T | F | F | T | F | T |
| F | T | T | F | T | F |
| F | F | T | T | T | T |

Expressions are not equivalent as the last two columns differ.

2. ~(p OR ~q)          ~p AND q

| p | q | ~p | ~q | p OR ~q | ~(p OR ~q) | ~p AND q |
|---|---|---|---|---|---|---|
| T | T | F | F | T | F | F |
| T | F | F | T | T | F | F |
| F | T | T | F | F | T | T |
| F | F | T | T | T | F | F |

Expressions are equivalent as the last two columns are identical.

3. p AND q          ~p OR ~q

| p | q | ~p | ~q | ~p OR ~q | p AND q |
|---|---|---|---|---|---|
| T | T | F | F | F | T |
| T | F | F | T | T | F |
| F | T | T | F | T | F |
| F | F | T | T | T | F |

Expressions are not equivalent as the last two columns differ.

4. (p OR q) AND r          (p OR r) AND (q OR r)

| p | q | r | p OR r | q OR r | (p OR r) AND (q OR r) | p OR q | (p OR q) AND r |
|---|---|---|---|---|---|---|---|
| T | T | T | T | T | T | T | T |
| T | T | F | T | T | T | T | F |
| T | F | T | T | T | T | T | T |
| T | F | F | F | F | F | T | F |
| F | T | T | T | T | T | T | T |
| F | T | F | F | F | F | T | F |
| F | F | T | T | T | T | F | F |
| F | F | F | F | F | F | F | F |

Expressions are not equivalent as the sixth and eighth columns differ.

5. p AND (p OR q)          p

| p | q | p OR q | p AND (p OR q) |
|---|---|---|---|
| T | T | T | T |
| T | F | T | T |
| F | T | T | F |
| F | F | F | F |

Expressions are equivalent as the first and last columns are identical.

**6.** (*p* AND *q*) OR *r*        (*p* OR *r*) AND (*q* OR *r*)

| *p* | *q* | *r* | *p* OR *r* | *q* OR *r* | (*p* OR *r*) AND (*q* OR *r*) | *p* AND *q* | (*p* AND *q*) OR *r* |
|---|---|---|---|---|---|---|---|
| T | T | T | T | T | T | T | T |
| T | T | F | T | T | T | T | T |
| T | F | T | T | T | T | F | T |
| T | F | F | T | F | F | F | F |
| F | T | T | T | T | T | F | T |
| F | T | F | F | T | F | F | F |
| F | F | T | T | T | T | F | T |
| F | F | F | F | F | F | F | F |

Expressions are equivalent as the sixth and eighth columns are identical.

## Exercise 29F

1. (*p* AND ~*q*) OR (~*p* AND *q*)
2. Yes – proven by writing out the truth tables.
3. ~*p* OR *q*
4. Prove by writing out the truth tables.
5. ~*p* AND ~*q*   Prove by writing out the truth tables.

## Exercise 30A

1.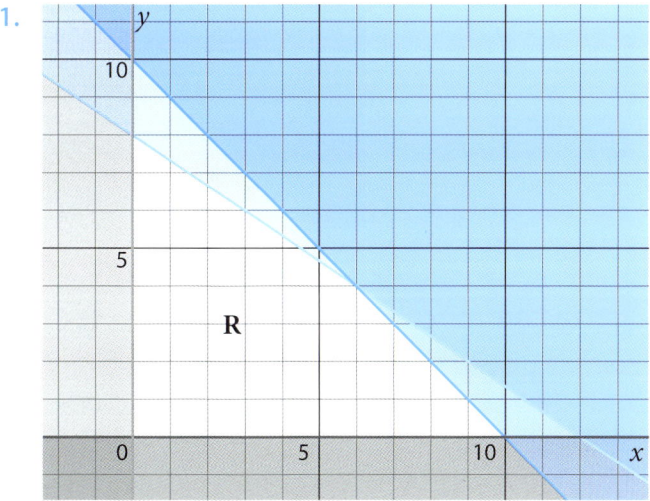

2.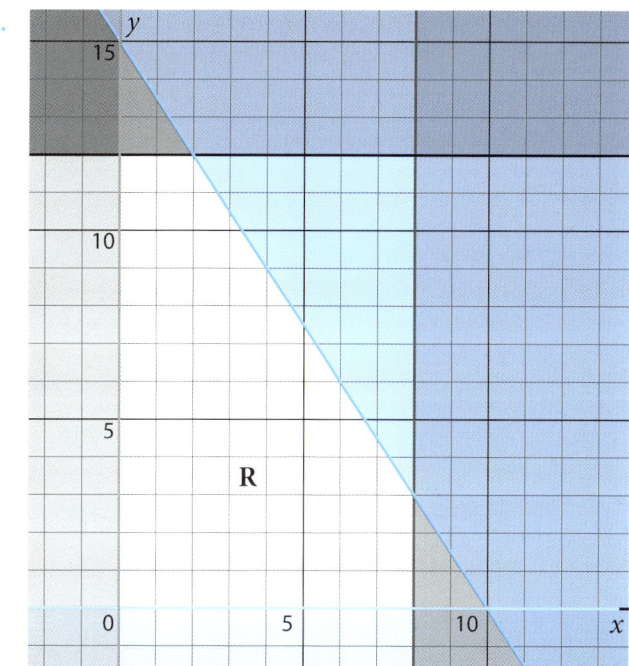

3.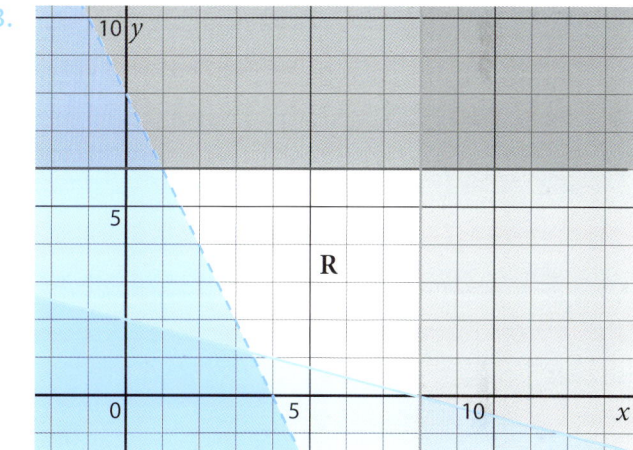

4.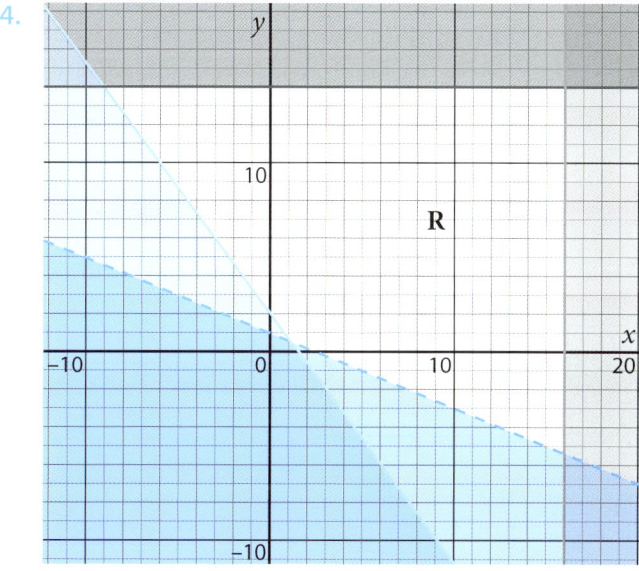

203

**5.**

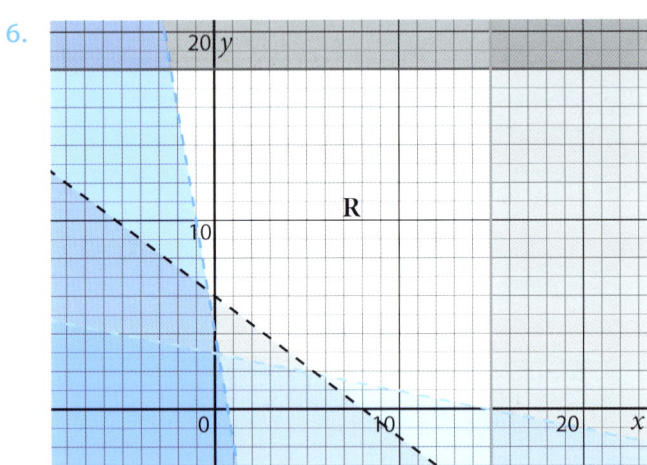

**6.**

**7.**

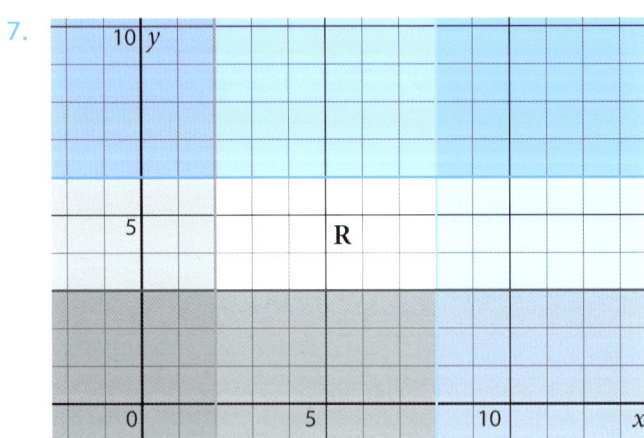

**8.**

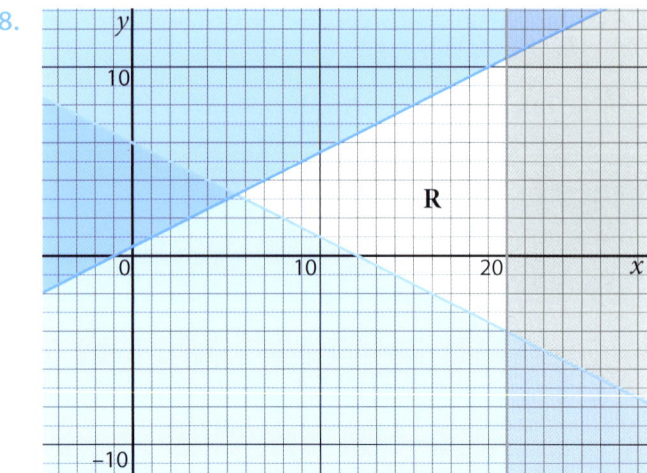

**9.**

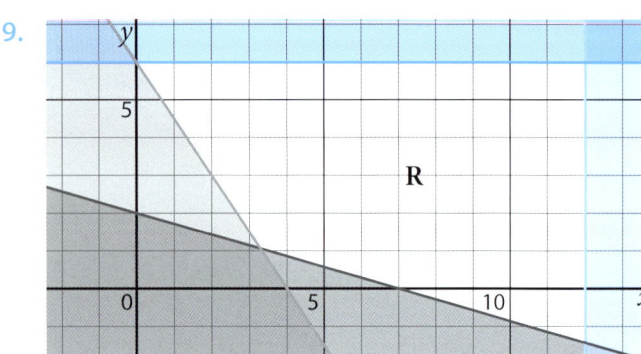

**10.**

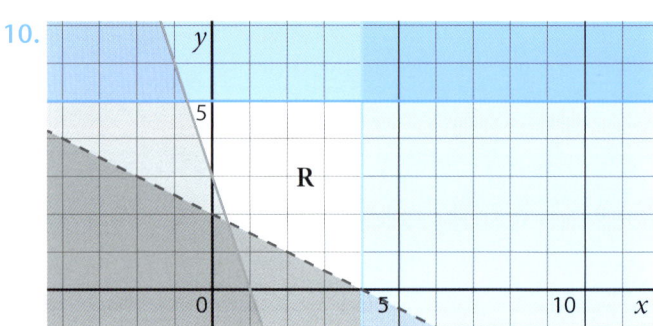

## Exercise 30B

1.  (a)    Cost $14x + 10y \leq 180$ giving $7x + 5y \leq 90$.

    (b)    Total length of stay $\leq 14$ so $x + y \leq 14$.

    (c)    Seaview stay > Mountain View stay, so $x > y$.

(d)

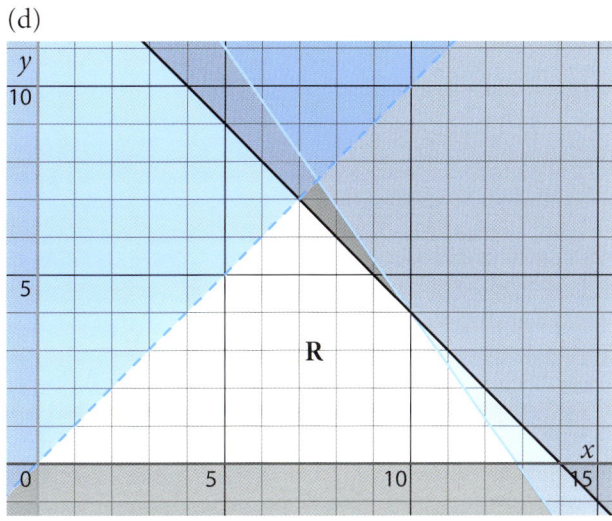

(e)  We want the largest $x$ value in R on the line $x + y \leq 14$. So answer is $x = 10$.

(f)  We want a point on $x + y = 14$ so $(8, 6)$ gives the lowest cost of £172. This means 8 nights at Seaview and 6 nights at Mountain Ridge.

2.  (a)  Time $15x + 27y \leq 4.5 \times 60$, giving $5x + 9y \leq 90$.
    (b)  Icing sugar (kg): $0.8x + y \leq 12$ so $4x + 5y \leq 60$.
    (c)  $y \geq 3$
    (d)

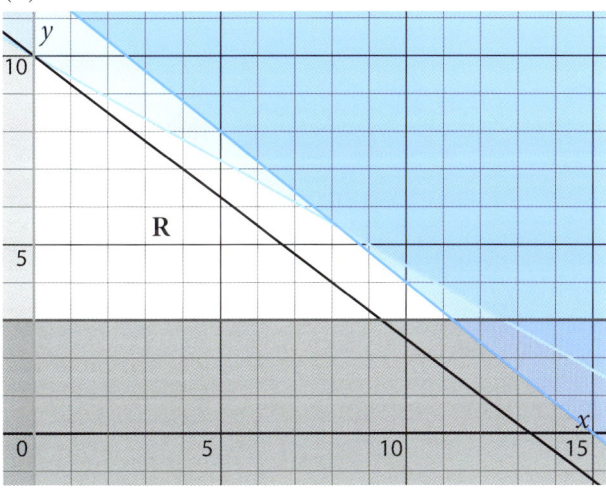

(e)  £P $= 9x + 12y$
    The search line $9x + 12y = 120$ is drawn on the diagram in part (d). This shows we must consider $(7, 6)$, $(8, 5)$ and $(10, 4)$:

| $x$ | $y$ | Profit |
|-----|-----|--------|
| 7 | 6 | £135 |
| 8 | 5 | £132 |
| 10 | 4 | £138 |

So 10 birthday cakes and 4 wedding cakes should be made for a maximum profit of £138.

3.  (a)  Rice $\leq 35$ so $x \leq 35$.
    (b)  Beans $\leq 20$ so $y \leq 20$.
    (c)  Weight $10x + 25y \leq 600$ giving $2x + 5y \leq 120$.
    (d)  Volume $50x + 50y \leq 2000$ giving $x + y \leq 40$.

(e)

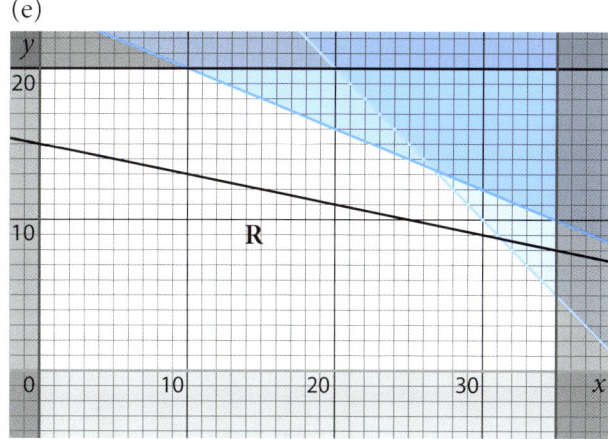

(f)  Meals $= 160x + 800y$.
(g)  The search line $160x + 800y = 12,000$ is drawn on the diagram in part (e). The maximum number of meals is 17,600 and occurs when we deliver 10 sacks of rice and 20 sacks of beans.

4.  (a)  Cost $2500x + 6000y \leq 30,000$ giving $5x + 12y \leq 60$.
    (b)  Area $12x + 6y \leq 72$ giving $2x + y \leq 12$.
    (c)  $x \geq 2$ and $y \geq 2$.
    (d)

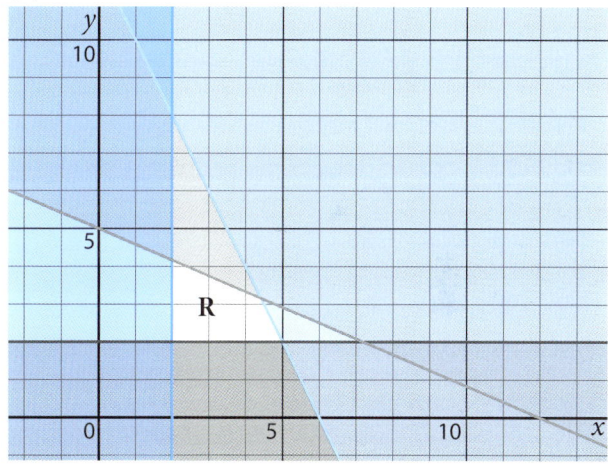

(e)  Max B-type machines $(y) = 4$. Then the number of A-type machines $(x) = 2$.
(f)  Maximum number of machines $= 7$ at $(4, 3)$ and $(5, 2)$.
(g)  Floor area for 4 A-type and 3 B-type machines 66 m² and floor area for 5 A-type and 2 B-type machines $= 72$ m², so least area is 66 m².

5.  (a)  Land $1350x + 1080y \leq 27,000$ giving $5x + 4y \leq 100$ (dividing by 270)
    (b)  Number of detached $\geq \frac{1}{4}$ of total number of houses: $x \geq \frac{1}{4}(x + y)$, giving $4x \geq x + y$, so $y \leq 3x$.
    (c)  $y \geq 4$

(d)

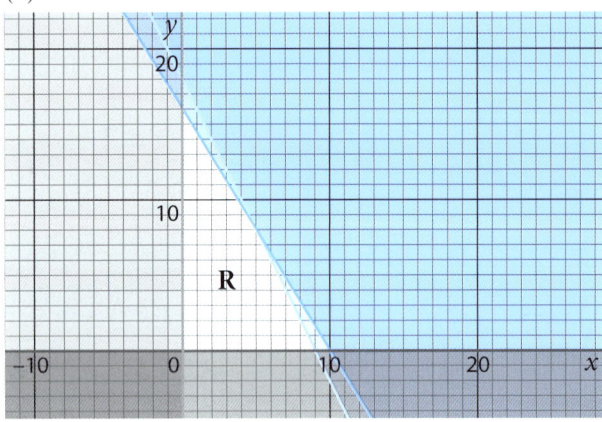

(e)    Maximum number of detached houses that may be built = maximum $x$ = 16.

(f)    Maximum number of houses is given by the solutions: (6, 17), (7, 16) or (8, 15). The maximum ratio of town houses to detached houses = max($y/x$) = 17/6, i.e. 6 detached houses to 17 town houses.

6.  (a)    Cost $800x + 500y \leq 8000$, giving $8x + 5y \leq 80$.
    (b)    Area $3x + 1.5y \leq 27$, giving $2x + y \leq 18$.
    (c)

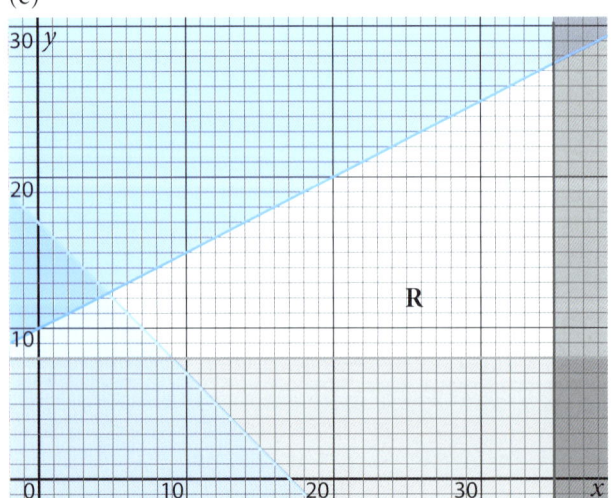

    (d)    Total number of cupboards = $x + y$.
    (e)    Maximum number of cupboards = 15.

7.  (a)    $x \leq 35$, $y \geq 8$.
    (b)    Perimeter = $2x + 2y \geq 34$, giving $x + y \geq 17$.
    (c)

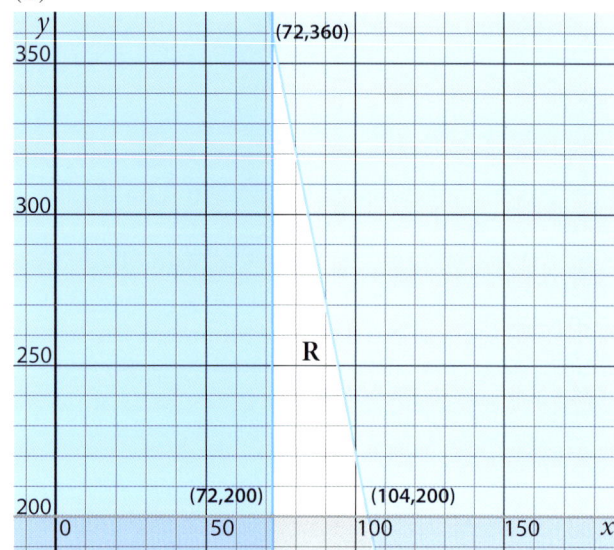

(d)    Maximum perimeter at (35, 27.5)
       = 2 × 35 + 2 × 27.5 = 125
(e)    If a square, then $x = y$. Then maximum side is at (20, 20) so maximum side = 20.
(f)    Area = $x \times y$, so minimum area is at (5, 12) and is 5 × 12 = 60 m².

8.  (a)    Area $0.2x + 0.04y \leq 28.8$, giving $5x + y \leq 720$.
    (b)    Yellow tiles $0.2x \geq 14.4$, giving $x \geq 72$.
    (c)    Green tiles $0.04y \geq 8$, giving $y \geq 200$.
    (d)

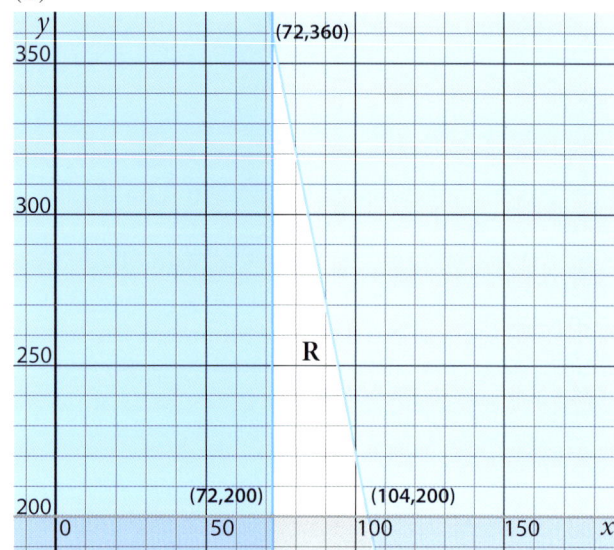

    (e)    Cost in pounds = C = $2x + 0.7y$.
    (f)    Maximum area occurs on the line $5x + y = 720$ only.
           M. Flambeau: maximum green tiles (max $y$) is at point (72, 360). Cost = 2 × 72 + 0.7 × 360 = £396.
           Mme Flambeau: minimum cost (lowest point on line) is at point (104, 200).
           Cost = 2 × 104 + 0.7 × 200 = £348.

## Exercise 31A

1.  (a)

(b)    4-cycle

206

2. (a)

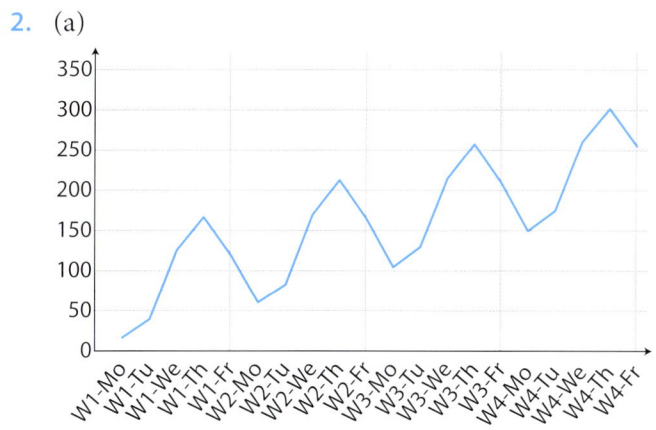

(b)    5-cycle

3. (a)

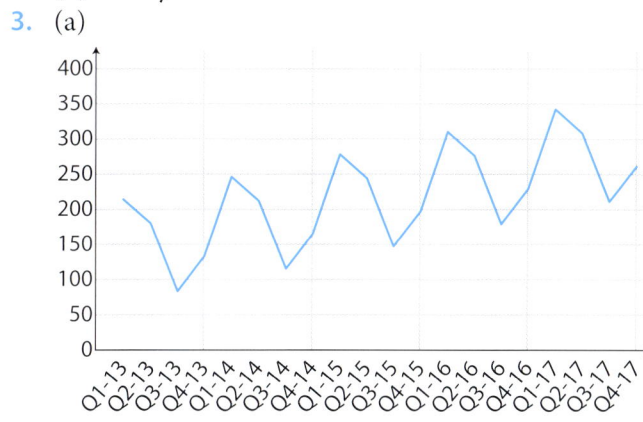

(b)    4-cycle

4. (a)

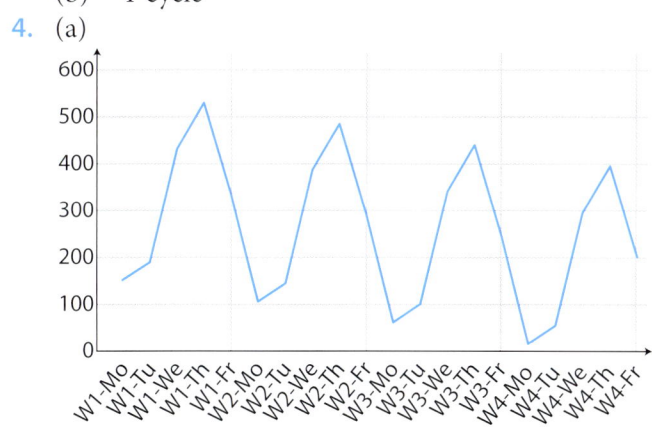

(b)    5-cycle

5. (a)

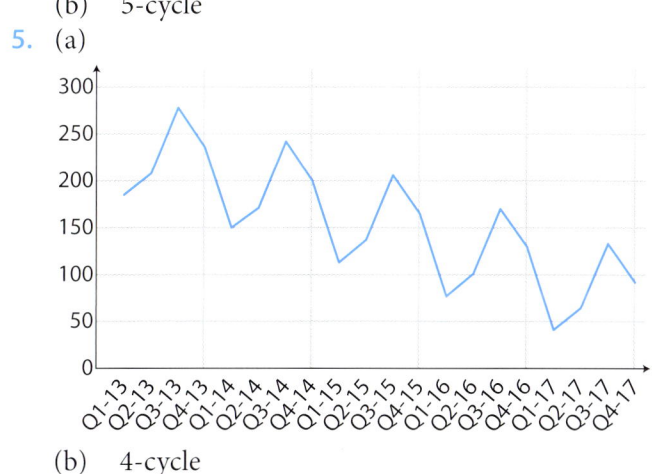

(b)    4-cycle

6. (a)

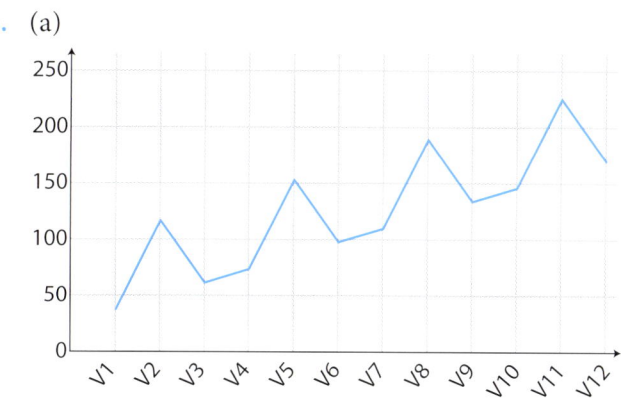

(b)    3-cycle

7. (a)

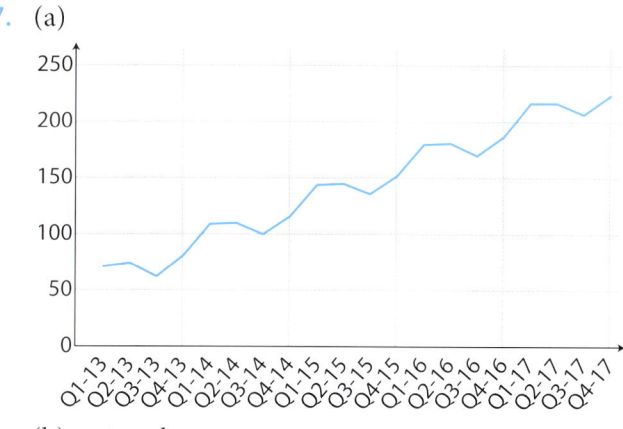

(b)    4-cycle

8. (a)

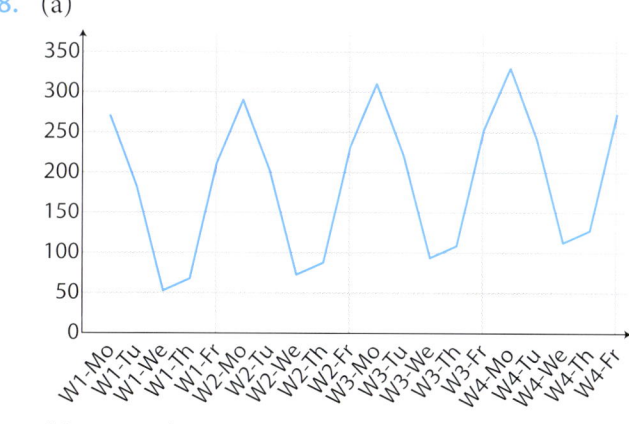

(b)    5-cycle

9. (a)

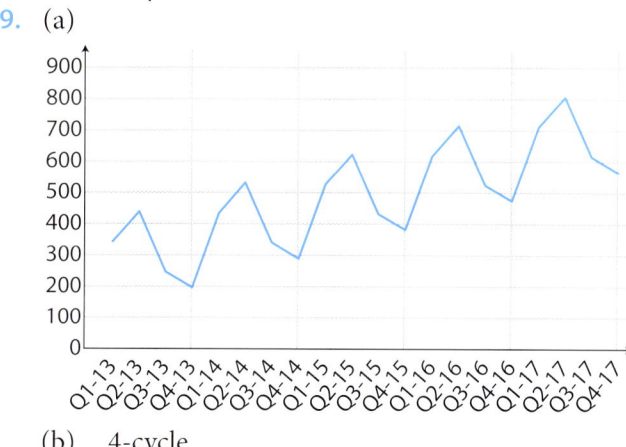

(b)    4-cycle

**10.** (a)

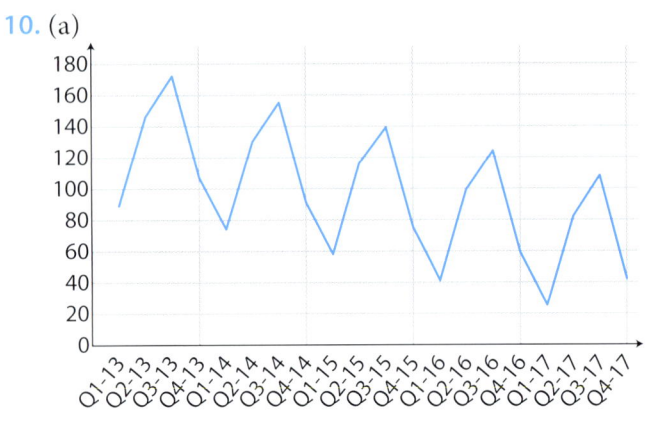

(b)     4-cycle

## Exercise 31B

**1.** (a)

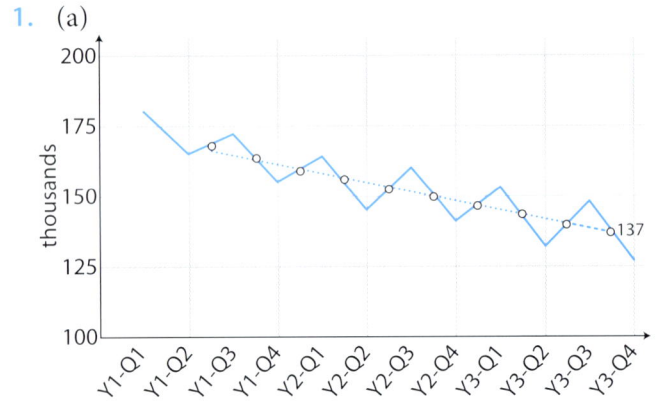

(b)

| Y1Q1–Q4 | Y1Q2–Y2Q1 | Y1Q3–Y2Q2 | Y1Q4–Y2Q3 | Y2Q1–Q4 | Y2Q2–Y3Q1 | Y2Q3–Y3Q2 | Y2Q4–Y3Q3 | Y3Q1–Q4 |
|---|---|---|---|---|---|---|---|---|
| 168 | 164 | 159 | 156 | 152.5 | 149.75 | 146.5 | 143.5 | 140 |

(c)     See part (a).

(d)     $\frac{1}{4}(132 + 148 + 127 + \{Y4Q1\ value\}) = 137$; giving Y4Q1 value = 141,000 (since values in the table are given in thousands).

**2.** (a)

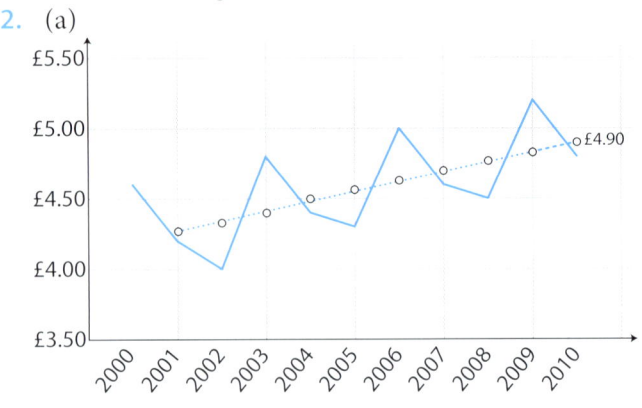

(b)

| 2001 | 2002 | 2003 | 2004 | 2005 | 2006 | 2007 | 2008 | 2009 |
|---|---|---|---|---|---|---|---|---|
| £4.27 | £4.33 | £4.40 | £4.50 | £4.57 | £4.63 | £4.70 | £4.77 | £4.83 |

(c)     See part (a).

(d)     $\frac{1}{3}(5.20 + 4.80 + \{2011\ value\}) = 4.90$; giving $\{2011\ value\} = £4.70$.

**3.** (a)

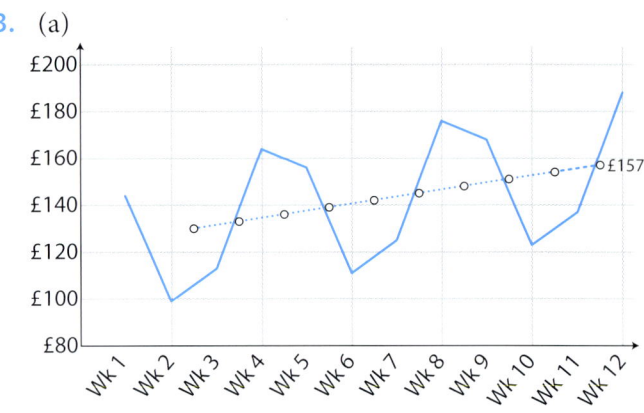

(b)

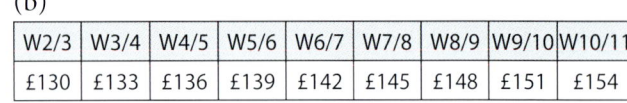

| W2/3 | W3/4 | W4/5 | W5/6 | W6/7 | W7/8 | W8/9 | W9/10 | W10/11 |
|---|---|---|---|---|---|---|---|---|
| £130 | £133 | £136 | £139 | £142 | £145 | £148 | £151 | £154 |

(c)     See part (a).

(d)     $\frac{1}{4}(123 + 137 + 188 + \{Wk\ 13\ value\}) = 157$; giving $\{Wk\ 13\ value\} = £180$.

**4.** (a)

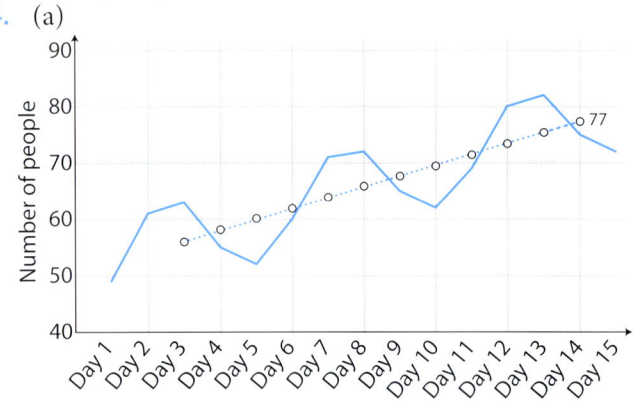

(b)

| D1–5 | D2–6 | D3–7 | D4–8 | D5–9 | D6–10 | D7–11 | D8–12 | D9–13 | D10–14 | D11–15 |
|---|---|---|---|---|---|---|---|---|---|---|
| 56 | 58.2 | 60.2 | 62 | 64 | 66 | 67.8 | 69.6 | 71.6 | 73.6 | 75.6 |

(c)     See part (a).

(d)     $\frac{1}{5}(80 + 82 + 75 + 72 + \{Day\ 16\ value\}) = 77.6$; giving $\{Day\ 16\ value\} = 79$ people.

**5.** (a)

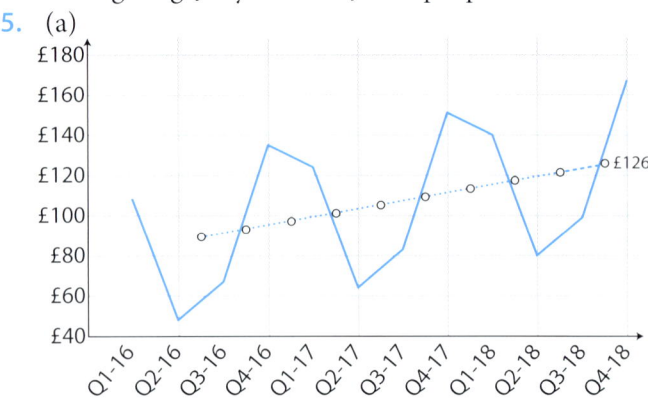

(b)

| 16-Q2/3 | 16-Q3/4 | 16-Q4/17-Q1 | 17-Q1/2 | 17-Q2/3 | 17-Q3/4 | 17-Q4/18-Q1 | 18-Q1/2 | 18-Q2/3 |
|---|---|---|---|---|---|---|---|---|
| £89.5 | £93.5 | £97.5 | £101.5 | £105.5 | £109.5 | £113.5 | £117.5 | £121.5 |

(c) See part (a).

(d) ¼(80 + 99 + 167 + {First Quarter 2019}) = 126;
giving {First Quarter 2019} = £158.

6. (a)

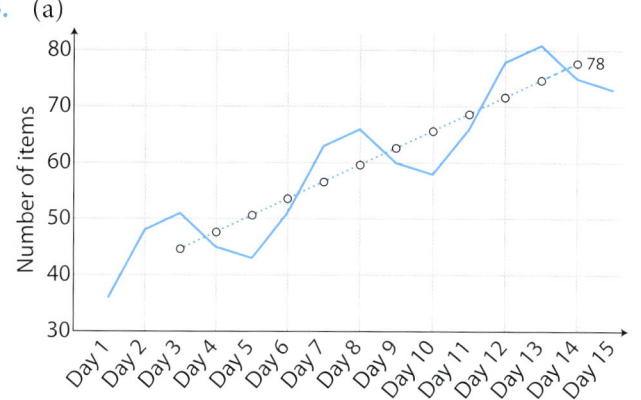

(b)

| D1-5 | D2-6 | D3-7 | D4-8 | D5-9 | D6-10 | D7-11 | D8-12 | D9-13 | D10-14 | D11-15 |
|---|---|---|---|---|---|---|---|---|---|---|
| 44.6 | 47.6 | 50.6 | 53.6 | 56.6 | 59.6 | 62.6 | 65.6 | 68.6 | 71.6 | 74.6 |

(c) See part (a).

(d) ⅕(78 + 81 + 75 + 73 + {Day 16 value}) = 78;
giving {Day 16 value} = 83.

7. (a)

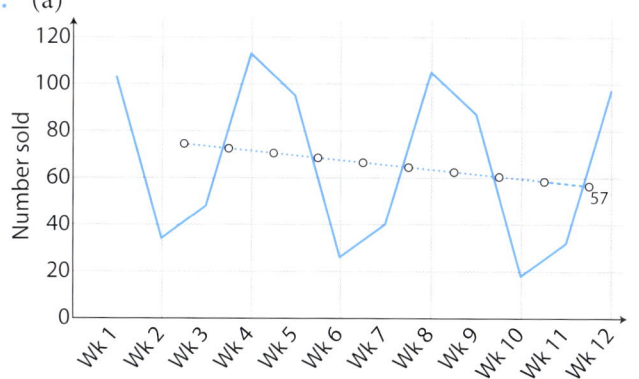

(b)

| W2/3 | W3/4 | W4/5 | W5/6 | W6/7 | W7/8 | W8/9 | W9/10 | W10/11 |
|---|---|---|---|---|---|---|---|---|
| 74.5 | 72.5 | 70.5 | 68.5 | 66.5 | 64.5 | 62.5 | 60.5 | 58.5 |

(c) See part (a).

(d) ¼(18 + 32 + 97 + {Week 13 value}) = 57;
giving {Week 13 value} = 81.

8. (a)

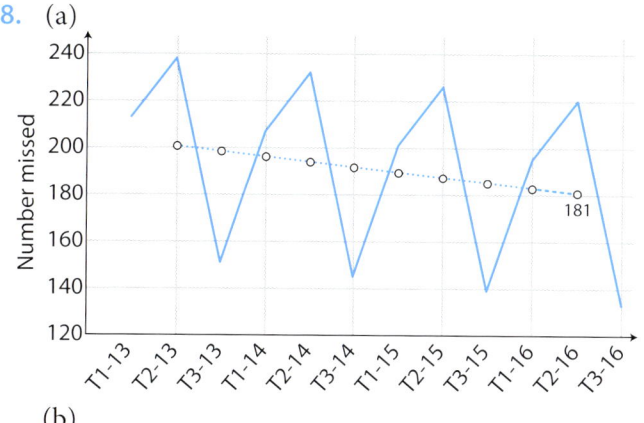

(b)

| 13T1-13T3 | 13T2-14T1 | 13T3-14T2 | 14T1-14T3 | 14T2-15T1 | 14T3-15T2 | 15T1-15T3 | 15T2-16T1 | 15T3-16T2 | 16T1-16T3 |
|---|---|---|---|---|---|---|---|---|---|
| 200.7 | 198.7 | 196.7 | 194.7 | 192.7 | 190.7 | 188.7 | 186.7 | 184.7 | 182.7 |

(c) See part (a).

(d) ⅓(220 + 133 + {2017 Term 1 value}) = 181;
giving {2017 Term 1 value} = 190.

## Exercise 32A

1.

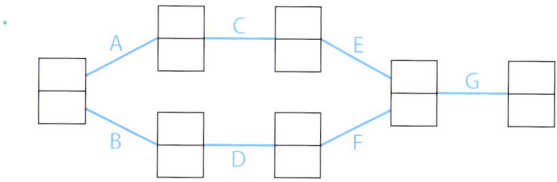

2.

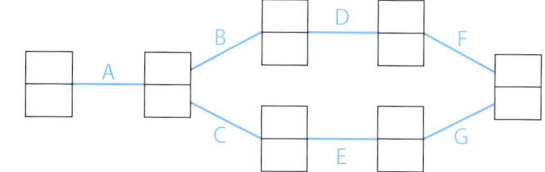

3.

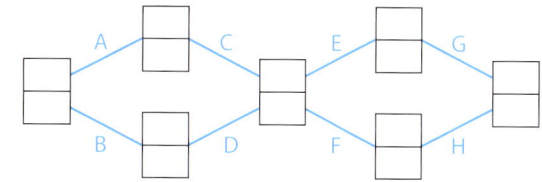

4.

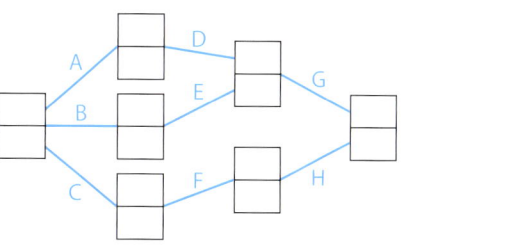

5.

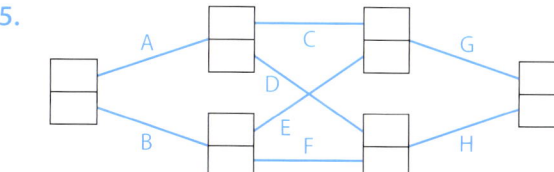

209

**6.**

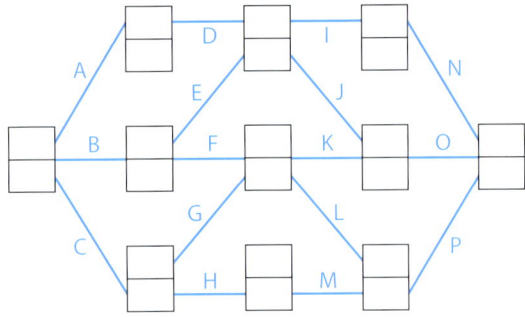

**8.**

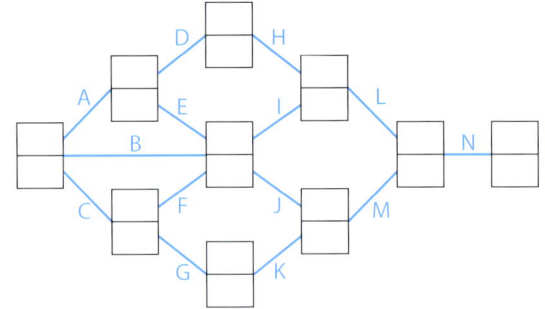

**7.**

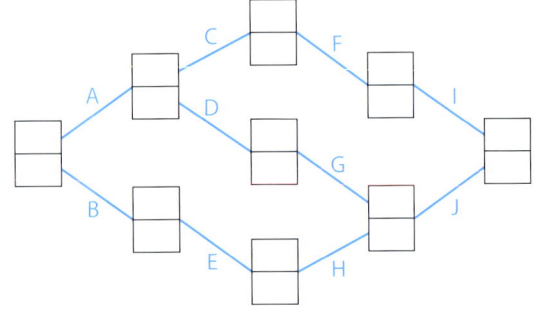

## Exercise 32B

**1.** (a)

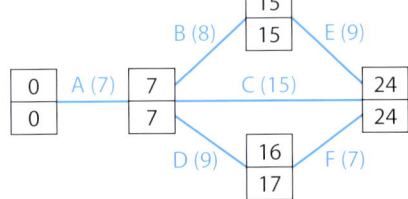

Critical path = A → B → E

(b)

| Day | 1 | 2 | 3 | 4 | 5 | 6 | 7 | 8 | 9 | 10 | 11 | 12 | 13 | 14 | 15 | 16 | 17 | 18 | 19 | 20 | 21 | 22 | 23 | 24 |
|---|---|---|---|---|---|---|---|---|---|---|---|---|---|---|---|---|---|---|---|---|---|---|---|---|
| Wkr 1 | A | A | A | A | A | A | A | B | B | B | B | B | B | B | B | B | E | E | E | E | E | E | E | E |
| Wkr 2 | | | | | | | | C | C | C | C | C | C | C | C | C | C | C | C | C | C | | | |
| Wkr 3 | | | | | | | | D | D | D | D | D | D | D | D | D | F | F | F | F | F | F | F | |

**2.** (a)

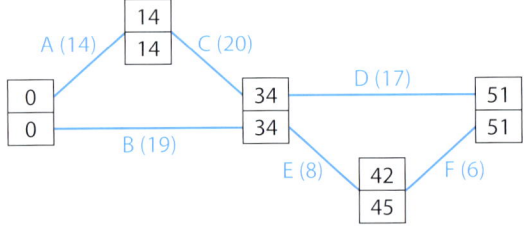

Critical path = A → C → D

(b)

| Day | 1 | 2 | 3 | 4 | 5 | 6 | 7 | 8 | 9 | 10 | 11 | 12 | 13 | 14 | 15 | 16 | 17 | 18 | 19 | 20 | 21 | 22 | 23 | 24 | 25 | 26 | 27 | 28 | 29 | 30 |
|---|---|---|---|---|---|---|---|---|---|---|---|---|---|---|---|---|---|---|---|---|---|---|---|---|---|---|---|---|---|---|
| Wkr 1 | A | A | A | A | A | A | A | A | A | A | A | A | A | A | C | C | C | C | C | C | C | C | C | C | C | C | C | C | C | C |
| Wkr 2 | B | B | B | B | B | B | B | B | B | B | B | B | B | B | B | B | B | B | B | | | | | | | | | | | |

| Day | 31 | 32 | 33 | 34 | 35 | 36 | 37 | 38 | 39 | 40 | 41 | 42 | 43 | 44 | 45 | 46 | 47 | 48 | 49 | 50 | 51 |
|---|---|---|---|---|---|---|---|---|---|---|---|---|---|---|---|---|---|---|---|---|---|
| Wkr 1 | C | C | C | C | D | D | D | D | D | D | D | D | D | D | D | D | D | D | D | D | D |
| Wkr 2 | | | | | E | E | E | E | E | E | E | E | F | F | F | F | F | F | | | |

3. (a)

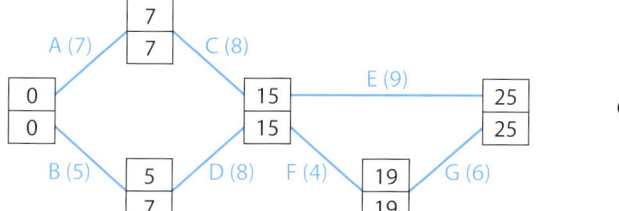

Critical path = A → C → F → G

(b)

| Day | 1 | 2 | 3 | 4 | 5 | 6 | 7 | 8 | 9 | 10 | 11 | 12 | 13 | 14 | 15 | 16 | 17 | 18 | 19 | 20 | 21 | 22 | 23 | 24 | 25 |
|---|---|---|---|---|---|---|---|---|---|---|---|---|---|---|---|---|---|---|---|---|---|---|---|---|---|
| Wkr 1 | A | A | A | A | A | A | A | C | C | C | C | C | C | C | C | F | F | F | F | G | G | G | G | G | G |
| Wkr 2 | B | B | B | B | B | B | D | D | D | D | D | D | D | D | | | E | E | E | E | E | E | E | E | |

4. (a)

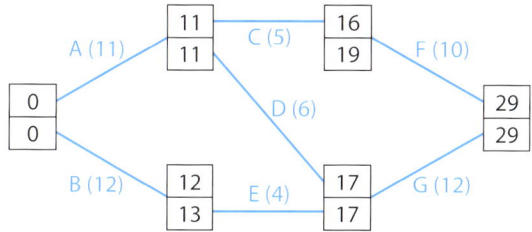

Critical path = A → D → G

(b)

| Day | 1 | 2 | 3 | 4 | 5 | 6 | 7 | 8 | 9 | 10 | 11 | 12 | 13 | 14 | 15 | 16 | 17 | 18 | 19 | 20 | 21 | 22 | 23 | 24 | 25 | 26 | 27 | 28 | 29 | 30 | 31 |
|---|---|---|---|---|---|---|---|---|---|---|---|---|---|---|---|---|---|---|---|---|---|---|---|---|---|---|---|---|---|---|---|
| Wkr 1 | A | A | A | A | A | A | A | A | A | A | A | D | D | D | D | D | D | G | G | G | G | G | G | G | G | G | G | G | G | | |
| Wkr 2 | B | B | B | B | B | B | B | B | B | B | B | B | E | E | E | E | C | C | C | C | F | F | F | F | F | F | F | F | F | F | F |

5. (a)

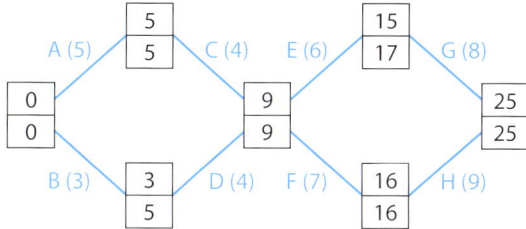

Critical path = A → C → F → H

(b)

| Day | 1 | 2 | 3 | 4 | 5 | 6 | 7 | 8 | 9 | 10 | 11 | 12 | 13 | 14 | 15 | 16 | 17 | 18 | 19 | 20 | 21 | 22 | 23 | 24 | 25 |
|---|---|---|---|---|---|---|---|---|---|---|---|---|---|---|---|---|---|---|---|---|---|---|---|---|---|
| Wkr 1 | A | A | A | A | A | C | C | C | C | F | F | F | F | F | F | F | H | H | H | H | H | H | H | H | H |
| Wkr 2 | B | B | B | D | D | D | D | | E | E | E | E | E | E | G | G | G | G | G | G | G | | | | |

6. (a)

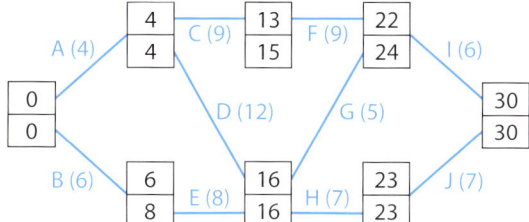

Critical path = A → D → H → J

(b)

| Day | 1 | 2 | 3 | 4 | 5 | 6 | 7 | 8 | 9 | 10 | 11 | 12 | 13 | 14 | 15 | 16 | 17 | 18 | 19 | 20 | 21 | 22 | 23 | 24 | 25 | 26 | 27 | 28 | 29 | 30 |
|---|---|---|---|---|---|---|---|---|---|---|---|---|---|---|---|---|---|---|---|---|---|---|---|---|---|---|---|---|---|---|
| Wkr 1 | A | A | A | A | D | D | D | D | D | D | D | D | D | D | D | D | H | H | H | H | H | H | H | J | J | J | J | J | J | J |
| Wkr 2 | B | B | B | B | B | B | E | E | E | E | E | E | E | | | G | G | G | G | G | | I | I | I | I | I | I | | | |
| Wkr 3 | | | | C | C | C | C | C | C | C | C | C | C | F | F | F | F | F | F | F | F | F | | | | | | | | |

**7.**

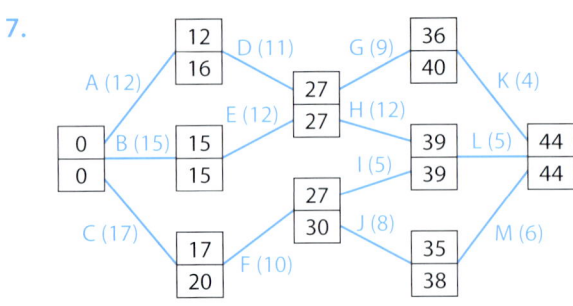

Critical path = B → E → H → L

**8.**

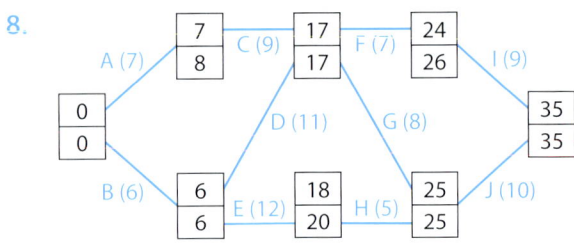

Critical path = B → D → G → J

**9.**

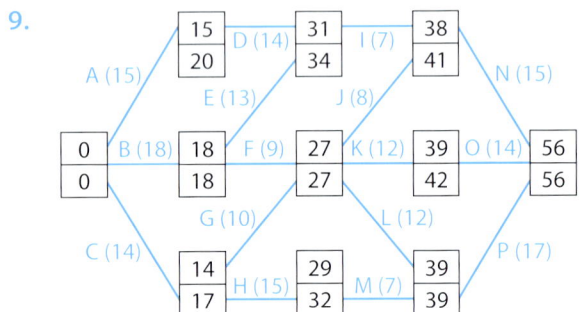

Critical path = B → F → L → P

**10.**

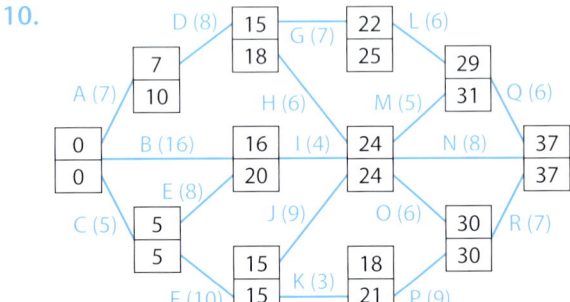

Critical path = C → F → J → O → R